The Marketing of Services

The Marketing Series is one of the most comprehensive collections of books in marketing and sales available from the UK today

Published by Butterworth-Heinemann on behalf of the Chartered Institute of Marketing, the series is divided into three distinct groups: *Student* (fulfilling the needs of those taking the Institute's certificate and diploma qualifications); *Professional Development* (for those on formal or self-study training programmes); and *Practitioner* (presented in a more informal, motivating and highly practical manner for personal use).

Formed in 1911, the Chartered Institute of Marketing is now the largest professional marketing management body in Europe with over 22,000 members and 25,000 students located worldwide. Its primary objectives are focused on the development of awareness and understanding of marketing throughout UK industry and commerce and on the raising of standards of professionalism in the education, training and practice of this key business discipline.

PROFESSIONAL DEVELOPMENT SERIES

Glossary of Marketing Terms
Norman A. Hart and John Stapleton

How to Sell a Service
Malcolm H. B. Hibbert

International Marketing Digest
Edited by Malcolm H. B. McDonald, S. Tamer

Managing Your Marketing Career
Andrew Crofts

Marketing Plans
Malcolm H. B. McDonald

Marketing to the Retail Trade
Geoffrey Randall

Professional Services Marketing
Neil Morgan

Relationship Marketing
Martin Christopher, Adrian Payne and David Ballantyne

Retail Marketing Plans
Malcolm H. B. McDonald

Solving the Management Case
Angela Hatton, Paul D. B. Roberts and Mike Worsam

The Marketing Book
Edited by Michael J. Baker

The Marketing Digest
Edited by Michael J. Thomas and Norman Waite

The Marketing of Services
D. W. Cowell

The Practice of Advertising
Edited by Norman Hart

The Practice of Public Relations
Edited by Wilfred Howard

The Principles and Practice of Export Marketing
E. P. Hibbert

The Strategy of Distribution Management
Martin Christopher

The Marketing of Services

DONALD W. COWELL

BA, MSc, PhD, FCInst M

Published on behalf of the Chartered Institute
of Marketing and the CAM Foundation

Butterworth-Heinemann Ltd
Linacre House, Jordan Hill, Oxford OX2 8DP

PART OF REED INTERNATIONAL BOOKS

OXFORD   LONDON   BOSTON
MUNICH   NEW DELHI   SINGAPORE   SYDNEY
TOKYO   TORONTO   WELLINGTON

First published 1984
Reprinted 1985, 1986, 1987, 1988, 1990, 1991 (twice), 1993

British Library Cataloguing in Publication Data
Cowell, Donald W.
The marketing of services.
1. Services industries – Management
2. Marketing
I. Title   II. Chartered Institute of Marketing
III. Cam Foundation
338.4'068'8   HD9980.5

ISBN 0 7506 0209 0

Printed and bound in Great Britain by
Redwood Press Limited, Melksham, Wiltshire

THE SERVICE ECONOMY

For a fee, there are now companies that will balance your budget, baby sit your philodendron, wake you up in the morning, drive you to work, or find you a new home, job, car, wife, clairvoyant, cat feeder, or gypsy violinist. Or perhaps you want to rent a garden tractor? A few cattle? Some original paintings? Or maybe some swingers to decorate your next cocktail party? If it is business services you need, other companies will plan your conventions and sales meetings, design your products, or supply temporary secretaries or even executives.

Source: 'Services Grow While the Quality Shrinks', *Business Week*, 30 Oct., 1971, p. 50.

CONTENTS

PREFACE

The service sector of the economy is a field of growing interest to marketing teachers, researchers and practitioners. This book is a response to this interest. It attempts to present in an introductory and structured way some of the current thinking and ideas relating to the marketing of services.

It is intended for students of business, management and marketing who are interested in organizations that market services rather than goods. Specifically it is for those who have already taken an introductory course in marketing management (at BTEC/undergraduate/postgraduate/diploma or post-experience level). Such readers will be better able to evaluate, criticize and develop further some of the ideas presented here. It is hoped that the text can form the basis for an introductory or elective course on the marketing of services which builds on marketing principles established in a basic marketing management course. Most introductory marketing management textbooks devote little attention to services. At best they include a separate chapter on the subject, at worst they ignore services completely. This book attempts to extend such insubstantial treatments of the subject. It is not intended to be a comprehensive marketing management textbook. It is intended to be used as a supplement to the current range of available textbooks. Hopefully it will add to what is available by focussing on the adaptations and adjustments that may be required when the product being marketed is intangible rather than tangible.

The sources I have used in preparing this book are varied. First I have drawn on my own full-time practical experience as a manager in industry, at one time responsible for providing a range of services, and on my part-time experience as a marketor of consultancy and marketing educational services. Secondly I have used the experience gained from running courses for undergraduates, postgraduates and post-experience managers – with interests in services from leisure and recreation to banking, from retailing to airlines, from freight forwarding to information services. Thirdly I have drawn on my research interests which have, over the years, focussed on services like advertising and promotional agency services, educational services, sport and leisure services and vending services. Fourthly I have drawn extensively on the contributions of a number of academic colleagues who have been writing and researching in the services area in recent years.

The book stems directly from my attempts, initially with colleagues, to offer a final year undergraduate option in the marketing of services. It represents a little of the material I have tried to assemble to contribute to that course.

The book is in four parts. Part 1 is an introduction to the service economy and deals with problems in defining services. Part 2 is devoted to the development of a marketing programme and chapters cover marketing research, marketing strategy and each element of the marketing mix. Part 3 deals with special aspects of service marketing – international marketing, competition policy and consumer protection and problems of productivity measurement in services. Part 4 examines the future of services in the economy.

The manuscript was read on behalf of the Chartered Institute of Marketing by an experienced marketor and I acknowledge the valuable suggestions and comments made. The book however still remains my personal responsibility.

Donald Cowell
Loughborough

PART 1

An introduction to the Service Economy and some ways and problems of defining Services

1. *THE SERVICE ECONOMY*

1.1 Introduction

Since the Second World War Britain has become a 'service economy', i.e. in terms of output and in terms of employment, services have become the largest sector of the economy. The shift towards service economies has been a feature of many economically developed countries in recent years. In 1968, Fuchs wrote:

> 'The United States is now pioneering in a new stage of economic development. During the period following World War II, this country became the world's first "service economy" – that is the first nation in which more than half of the employed population is not involved in the production of food, clothing, houses, automobiles or other tangible goods.'[1]

In 1972, Smith writing of the United Kingdom observed:

> 'If transport is included in the service sector, by 1966 the United Kingdom just about qualified for admission to the exclusive club of service economies, since services claimed, for the first time, half of the labour force. Reckoned on the basis of full-time equivalents, the proportion of the labour force in services was slightly less than half; this reflected the sectors disproportionate reliance on part-time workers.'[2]

A number of authors believe that this transformation of advanced economies has been neglected by many groups. Fuchs[1] suggests that the service sector of the economy is the stepchild of economic research. Lewis[3] argues that contemporary economic theories and statistics are biased in their treatment of services; services need to be legitimized as valid forms of wealth to dispel the myth about their non-productive character. Smith[2] identifies weaknesses in the statistical treatment of services as far as the measurement and interpretation of service output changes are concerned. Heilbroner[4] believes that the more general implications of the service economy have not been understood, in particular the increased vulnerability of the economy to labour stoppage. He argues that, to some extent the vulnerability in manufacturing is cushioned by inventories, but with services the margin of safety is reduced. In such circumstances, because of the severity of interruptions (e.g. dangers to health or security) the growth of services increases the possibility of government interference in the market mechanism towards a planned economic system in order to maintain 'essential services'. Quite apart from these economic and political dimensions the shifting of large segments of the working population into service occupations 'has also been largely neglected by sociologists' according to Gersuny and Rosengren[5]. Marketors too have written of the neglect of services in contemporary treatments of marketing. This neglect of services is surprising when the current importance of services in the economy is considered.

3

1.2 The Service Economy

The importance of services in the United Kingdom economy can be gauged by considering a number of factors. These are:

(*a*) Services and employment;
(*b*) Services and output;
(*c*) Services and consumption;
(*d*) Services and the balance of payments.

It is important to note that the statistical information which follows should be treated with care because there may be differences in the methods of collection, the statistical definitions of services used, and the sources from which such information is obtained. This qualification is significant – whether or not one subscribes to the 'service economy thesis' can depend to a large extent upon the way in which available data are presented and interpreted.

1.21 Services and Employment

The simplest and most traditional classification of economic activities is into three groups; primary, secondary and tertiary. Primary activities include agriculture, forestry and fishing; secondary activities include manufacturing and construction industries; tertiary activities include the services and distributive trades.

Table 1.1
Total employees in employment (millions) United Kingdom

	1971	1976	1979
All employees	22.1	22.5	22.8
Services	11.6	12.9	13.3
%	52	57	58

Source: Annual Abstract of Statistics, H.M.S.O. London, 1981

Table 1.1 shows the total number of employees in employment in service industries for 1971, 1976 and 1979 against all employees in employment in the same period. While numbers employed in the period increased by about 700,000, the numbers employed in services increased by about 1.7 million. Services accounted in total for over 58% of employees in employment by 1979. Of course the increase in total service employment obscures variations in the patterns of increase and decrease within the service sector. Hollander[6] quite rightly indicates that there is no generic demand for services. Rather, what detailed consideration of available data suggests, is that certain types of service employment have grown while other types of service employment have declined. Table 1.2 shows this by considering patterns of increase and decrease in the main service groups

Table 1.2

Employees in Service Industries United Kingdom (Thousands)

	Transport and Communications	Distributive Trades	Insurance, Banking, Finance	Professional & Scientific Services	Miscellaneous Services	Public Administration and Defence*	Total Service Industries
Males							
1961	1,438	1,340	377	737	819	916	5,627
1966	1,379	1,363	423	889	963	982	5,999
1971	1,307	1,180	480	1,002	893	996	5,858
1976	1,217	1,210	542	1,173	976	1,022	6,140
1979	1,203	1,240	570	1,162	1,037	1,001	6,213
Females							
1961	240	1,427	307	1,387	1,000	395	4,755
1966	243	1,558	395	1,701	1,103	442	5,442
1971	261	1,429	496	1,987	1,053	513	5,739
1976	258	1,513	561	2,483	1,323	609	6,747
1979	279	1,565	631	2,561	1,441	632	7,109

*Excluding H.M. Armed Forces

Source: *Social Trends*, H.M.S.O. London, 1981

and the composition of the workforce within each group over an extended time period 1961 to 1979.

Table 1.2 breaks down the service sector into its component industries by sex. In 1971 the service sector employed about the same number of males and females. But between 1971 and 1979, 1,370,000 women joined the service sector compared with 355,000 men. Women outnumbered men by 1979.

The growth of total employment has not been uniform throughout the service sector. In Transport and Communications numbers fell between 1961–79. In Distribution it was little changed in 1979 compared with 1961. The largest increases have been in the numbers working in Insurance, Banking and Finance and in Professional and Scientific Services. It is also important to remember when examining figures of changes in the service sector that:

'The decline in the number of employees in the industrial sector was almost two million between 1961 and 1979 but this was partly offset by an increase of half a million men working in service industries. The number of female employees increased by one and a half million between 1961 and 1979 but again there was a fall in the industrial sector of almost three quarters of a million.'[7]

Social Trends, 1981 also indicates that:

'Between 1971 and 1977 the number of part-time workers went up by one million (i.e. about 30%) and 90% of these new workers were females.'

and that:

'In 1977 just under one-fifth of all employees in employment were part-time workers. About 85% of them were women and most were married with dependent children. Male part-time workers were older, many being over retirement age. Service industries employed almost 85% of the part-time workers. In other words almost four million employees in service industries were part-time workers in 1977.'

A feature, which the data presented so far does not reveal, is the numbers of people employed in the primary or secondary activities who pursue 'service like' occupations. Table 1.3 shows that in all manufacturing

Table 1.3

Administrative, Technical and Clerical workers in Manufacturing Industry (%)

	1971	1973	1975	1977	1979
All Manufacturing Industry	27.4	26.7	27.8	27.6	28.6
Selected examples:					
Coal and Petroleum	38.3	36.5	32.1	31.7	30.9
Chemical and Allied Industries	40.8	39.9	40.9	39.3	40.7
Clothing and Footwear	12.9	13.4	14.6	14.1	14.8
Textiles	17.4	17.4	17.7	18.6	19.7
Manufacturing (all employees)	8,058	7,830	7,490	7,292	7,155

Source: *Annual Abstract of Statistics*, H.M.S.O. London, 1981

industry, for the period 1971 to 1979, the number of people employed in administrative, technical and clerical work was over 25% of those employed; although, as the selected examples indicate there is a variation between industrial groups. Nevertheless this group of workers accounts for around another two million people in manufacturing industry alone.

Finally a broad international comparison of civilian employment by economic sector, shows that the United Kingdom has a high proportion of employment in industry; a significantly lower proportion in employment in agriculture compared with some countries like Italy, Japan and Spain; while the proportion in employment in services is above the average, but is not as high as in the United States, Canada, Australia or most of the Scandinavian and Benelux countries. These comparisons are shown in Table 1.4.

Table 1.4
Civilian Employment: by Sector international comparison, 1979 (%)

	Agriculture	Industry	Services	Total
United Kingdom	3	39	58	100
Australia	7	31	62	100
Belgium*	3	37	60	100
Canada	6	29	65	100
Denmark*	9	30	61	100
Germany (Fed Republic)	6	45	49	100
Greece†	28	30	41	100
Irish Republic*	22	31	47	100
Italy	15	38	47	100
Japan	11	35	54	100
Luxembourg*	6	44	51	100
Netherlands*	6	33	61	100
Portugal*	31	35	34	100
Spain	20	36	44	100
Sweden	6	33	62	100
United States of America	4	31	65	100

*1978 figures
†1977 figures

Source: *Social Trends*, H.M.S.O. London, 1981

The conclusions that may be drawn from the data presented so far then are:

(*a*) there has been an increase proportionately and in absolute terms in the numbers employed in service industries;

(*b*) within the service sector some categories have increased and some have decreased, in proportionate and in absolute terms;

(*c*) the composition of the workforce in the service industries has changed; more women than men now work in these industries;

(*d*) the service industries employ a very high percentage of all part-time workers in employment;

(*e*)   there are large numbers of working people occupied in service like occupations within the primary and secondary occupational sectors. Official statistics do not necessarily reflect the in house growth of services.

The shift in the distribution of occupations into the tertiary sector of the economy confirm the service economy thesis as far as the United Kingdom is concerned.

1.22 Services and Output

Trends in output too confirm the shift towards a service economy. The relative importance of the primary industries has declined since the beginning of the century; by the late 1940s the tertiary sector had overtaken the secondary industries as the major contributor to the national product. This is shown in Figure 1.1. Figure 1.1 also shows, that by 1978 in the United Kingdom, the service sector share of total output had risen over the thirty year period since 1948, to reach 55% of total output and that Public Sector Services had expanded more rapidly than the rest of the service sector.

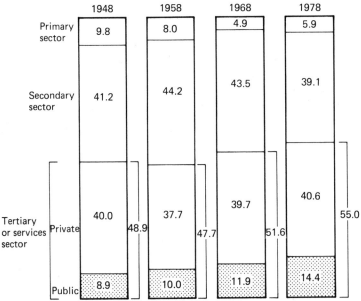

Figure 1.1 Composition of output in UK, percentage shares

Source: Whiteman, J., 'The Services Sector – a Poor Relation?', Discussion Paper No. 8, N.E.D.O., reproduced by permission of H.M.S.O., 1981

Output measures are even more suspect than measures of employment changes used in the previous section. Smith[2] looked in detail at the conceptual and practical difficulties involved in measuring quantity and quality changes in output and the unreliability of any analysis based upon them. He demonstrated how by changing the basis of output measurement, one could draw very different conclusions about inter-sectoral developments. Nevertheless service output changes do seem to be another significant indicator of the emergence of the service economy.

1.23 Services and Consumption

The service economy is characterized by changing patterns of consumption as well as of employment and output. But a most important feature as far as consumer expenditure is concerned is that while expenditures on some services have grown so too have expenditures on durable goods. Stanback's[8] United States study indicates that there is a high degree of complementarity between demand for goods and demand for services. He suggests that these complementarities stem largely from joint use and the need to distribute and maintain goods. In the producer services sector he argues:

> 'They are . . . the results of the growing complexity of the managerial task which creates new requirements for outside expertise, and the growing usefulness of producer service firms as they become increasingly specialized and add new functions. In the public sector they stem from the heavy goods content to many services (for example, health, military) and from the fact that government is to a large extent serving (and regulating) a complex industrial society.'

Certainly an examination of consumers' expenditure between 1966 and 1979 for the United Kingdom as shown in Table 1.5 does indicate fairly constant expenditure on items like food and tobacco, substantial increases on items like TV and electrical goods, (which allow consumers to produce services for themselves) and substantial increases in services like vehicle running costs and telephones. As far as consumers' expenditure on services is concerned then the service economy thesis looks less convincing. But consumer expenditure on services is only part of the equation – the figures do not include expenditure by industry, commerce and the public sector on business and professional services.

1.24 Services and the Balance of Payments

Services play an important role in Britain's export trade (*see* Chapter 14 for a fuller treatment). Service earnings from abroad are labelled 'invisible'. The contribution of invisible earnings to Britain's international transactions is shown in Table 1.6 for the decade 1969–79. In every year exports of services exceeded imports of services; whereas imports of goods exceeded exports of goods for every year shown except for 1970 and 1971. Property income from abroad too had also been in surplus for each year shown. Services alone have consistently contributed over 20% of all exports. If it had not been for this contribution the balance of payments performance would have suffered greatly over the decade illustrated.

The pattern that emerges from an interpretation of the above data is thus slightly confusing. Clearly services are important and the structure of economic activities in Britain has undergone great change in recent years. Varying definitions of the meaning of the word 'service'; differing methods

Table 1.5
Consumer Expenditure (United Kingdom)

Indices at constant 1975 prices	1966	1971	1972	1973	1974	1975	1976	1977	1978	Indices/%	1979 £ million (current prices)
Food	97	100	100	101	100	100	101	100	102	104	20,505
Housing	82	95	97	100	98	100	100	102	105	109	16,501
Fuel and Light	88	94	98	101	102	100	99	102	103	109	5,327
Alcohol											
Beer	72	89	91	97	97	100	102	102	105	106	4,838
Other	53	72	82	101	106	100	104	102	115	126	4,035
Tobacco	100	95	100	106	105	100	97	92	100	100	4,279
Clothing and footwear	79	91	96	100	99	100	101	101	111	117	8,876
Durable household goods											
Furniture, floor coverings	82	88	101	104	96	100	104	95	101	102	2,633
TV, electrical other	47	66	86	106	106	100	107	103	117	127	2,950
Transport and vehicles											
Purchase	81	130	155	147	101	100	111	103	131	141	4,728
Running	67	89	95	102	100	100	104	105	109	110	6,917
Other travel	90	92	98	104	101	100	96	96	99	108	3,795
Other goods, services and miscellaneous											
Telephone	40	70	79	91	96	100	104	109	121	134	1,293
Post	163	112	120	120	116	100	89	90	93	94	280
TV rental/relay	42	55	64	80	94	100	110	113	118	124	836
Other entertainments	82	82	85	88	94	100	107	114	121	121	1,510
Newspapers/magazines	120	109	111	110	106	100	96	95	95	96	1,177
Books	87	90	102	102	105	100	100	100	100	105	395
Other	80	91	97	102	102	100	99	101	105	107	25,215

Table 1.5
Consumer Expenditure (United Kingdom)

Indices at constant 1975 prices	1966	1971	1972	1973	1974	1975	1976	1977	1978	Indices/ %	1979 £ million (current prices)
Less expenditure by foreign tourists	45	68	72	81	89	100	123	140	133	129	3,281
Consumer expenditure abroad	113	95	103	107	94	100	89	85	106	133	1,997
Consumers' Expenditure	83	93	98	103	101	100	100	100	106	110	114,805

Source: *Social Trends*, H.M.S.O. London, 1981

Table 1.6
International Transactions (£ thousand millions) rounded

United Kingdom	1969	1970	1971	1972	1973	1974	1975	1976	1977	1978	1979
Export of goods	7.3	8.2	9.0	9.4	11.9	16.4	19.3	25.2	31.7	35.1	40.7
Export of services	2.8	3.4	3.9	4.2	5.2	6.6	7.7	10.0	11.7	12.4	14.0
Property income from abroad	1.3	1.5	1.5	1.7	2.9	3.3	2.9	4.0	4.4	5.0	7.1
Import of goods	7.5	8.2	8.9	10.2	14.5	21.7	22.7	29.1	34.0	36.7	44.1
Import of services	2.5	3.0	3.3	3.6	4.5	5.6	6.3	7.8	8.6	8.9	10.4
Property income paid abroad	0.8	0.9	1.0	1.2	1.6	1.9	2.1	2.6	3.9	4.5	6.8

Source: *Annual Abstract of Statistics*, H.M.S.O. London 1981

of measuring service employment output and consumption; concealed movements and changes underlying official data that are available; all lead to conflicting views on the precise size, scale and the growth of the service economy. It is nevertheless helpful to examine the reasons why the service economy has grown.

1.3 Reasons for the Growth of the Service Economy

A number of reasons have been put forward to explain the growth of the service economy. Three of the main explanations are examined here. They are:

(a) the lag in growth in labour productivity in services compared with the rest of the economy;
(b) the growth in intermediate demand from firms;
(c) the growth in final demand from consumers.

1.31 The Lag in Growth in Labour Productivity in Services

Part of the explanation for the growth of services is attributed to the slower growth of labour productivity, as measured by volume of output per employee. That is the amount of labour required to produce a given volume of output in other sectors of the economy like manufacturing, fell more rapidly than in services. Fuchs, in his United States study, suggested that lower output per man in services was the major explanation for the shift in employment into the service sector. He proposed a number of reasons why this was so. These included:

(a) A greater decline in hours worked per man in service than in industry.
(b) A more rapid increase in the quality of labour in industry than in service.
(c) A difference in the physical capital per worker available in industry compared with service.
(d) More rapid technological change in industry than in service; and that industry benefited more from scale economies.[1]

The weakness with these suggestions is the problem of measuring output changes in services. The statistics available, in the United Kingdom at least, are inadequate to describe accurately comparative changes in the various sectors of the economy.

1.32 The Growth in Intermediate Demand from Firms

Another part of the explanation for the growth of services is attributed to the growth of intermediate demand from firms (i.e. providing inputs to manufacturing and other sectors of the economy). Specialist firms have been set up to provide services previously carried out by existing firms (e.g. engineering services, personnel services). Alternatively specialist firms have been set up to provide new services (e.g. data processing).

Business buyers have always used an array of services like accounting, construction, banking, insurance, legal, research, advertising, public relations, training, transport, shipping and consultancy services. As advanced economies have developed so too have markets for service provision. Companies and other organizations increasingly rely on the services of specialists because of the complexity of economic organization and to obtain the economies involved in the division of labour: technological and competitive pressures require the use of services to keep up-to-date in a constantly changing environment; organizations are able to retain their flexibility by hiring in services which provide 'use' without 'ownership'; time pressures and lack of available internal resources encourage organizations to use outside services rather than having services provided internally.

1.33 The Growth in Final Demand from Consumers

Another part of the explanation for the growth of services is attributed to the growth of final demand from consumers. As society gets wealthier and as the marginal utility derived from additional increments of goods declines, then people turn to services expenditures. This argument therefore rests on the assumption of a relationship between income and spending patterns on goods and services. Consumers spend increases in income on travel, recreation, education, health care and similar services rather than on cars and clothing.

Other elements of the growth of final demand from consumers include changed lifestyles, more leisure time, longer life expectancy and the increasing complexity of life. Technological developments mean more goods – which require specialist service in fields like motor cars, stereophonic equipment, video equipment and home computers. Affluence and more discretionary income allow consumers to delegate tasks to others; this delegation of responsibility generates new types of services and service organizations. For example, part of the increase in employment in services is due to the transfer of certain kinds of household jobs (not shown in conventional employment or output measures) into the officially paid and recorded workforce (e.g. welfare services). Services formerly provided unpaid by household members are now provided by institutions recognized in official statistics.

Gersuny and Rosengren,[5] while attributing the development of the service economy to the increases in agricultural and industrial productivity which have made it possible to meet the material needs of the population, also suggest there is a linkage with final demand as far as consumer services are concerned:

> 'The need for intangibles and the capacity to purchase them reinforce each other to the extent that the economic surplus required to make their production possible occurs with industrialization and urbanization. The twin processes of industrialization and urbanization result in loss of self-sufficiency which entails a growing demand for services that individuals and families can no longer provide for themselves. Demand is also created for new types of services.'

A summary of some of the reasons for the growth of consumer service industries is given in Table 1.7.

Table 1.7
Reasons for the growth in service industries

1 Increasing affluence	Greater demand for lawn care, carpet cleaning, and other services that consumers used to provide for themselves.
2 More leisure time	Greater demand for travel agencies, travel resorts, adult education courses.
3 Higher percentage of women in the labour force	Greater demand for day care nurseries, maid service, away-from-home meals.
4 Greater life expectancy	Greater demand for nursing homes and health care services.
5 Greater complexity of products	Greater demand for skilled specialists to provide maintenance for such complex products as cars and home computers.
6 Increasing complexity of life	Greater demand for income tax preparers, marriage counsellors, legal advisers, employment services.
7 Greater concern about ecology and resource scarcity	Greater demand for purchased or leased services, such as door-to-door bus service and car rental instead of car ownership.
8 Increasing number of new products	The computer-sparked development of such service industries as programming, repair, and time sharing.

Source: Schoell, W. F. and Ivy, J. T., *Marketing: Contemporary Concepts and Practices*, Allyn and Bacon, Boston, Mass. 1981, p. 277

Exhibit 1.1

'A post-industrial society is based on services. Hence, it is a game between persons. What counts is not raw muscle power, or energy, but information. The Central person is the professional, for he is equipped, by his education and training, to provide the kinds of skill which are increasingly demanded in the post-industrial society. If an industrial society is defined by the quantity of goods as marking a standard of living, the post-industrial society is defined by the quality of life as measured by the services and amenities – health, education, recreation, and the arts – which are now deemed desirable and possible for everyone.

'The word "services" disguises different things, and in the transformation of industrial to post-industrial society there are several different stages. First, in the very development of industry there is a necessary expansion of transportation and of public utilities as auxiliary services in the movement of goods and the increasing use of energy, and an increase in the non-manufacturing but still blue-collar force.

'Second, in the mass consumption of goods and the growth of populations there is an increase in distribution (wholesale and retail), and finance, real estate, and insurance, the traditional centres of white-collar employment. Third, as national incomes rise, one finds, as in the theorem of Christian Engel, a German statistician of the latter half of the nineteenth century, that the proportion of money devoted to food at home begins to drop, and the marginal increments are used first for durables (clothing, housing, automobiles) and then for luxury items, recreation, and the like. Thus, a third sector, that of personal services, begins to grow: restaurants, hotels, auto services, travel, entertainment, sports, as people's horizons expand and new wants and tastes develop. But here a new consciousness begins to intervene. The claims to the good life which the society has promised become centred on the two areas that are fundamental to that life – health and education. The elimination of disease and the increasing numbers of people who can live out a full life, plus the efforts to expand the span of life, make health services a crucial feature of modern society; and the growth of technical requirements and professional skills makes education, and access to higher education, the condition to carry into the post-industrial society itself. So we have here the growth of a new intelligentsia, particularly of teachers. Finally, the claims for more services and the inadequacy of the market in meeting people's needs for a decent environment as well as better health and education lead to the growth of government, particularly at the state and local level, where such needs have to be met.'

Source: Bell, Daniel, *The coming of the Post-Industrial Society – a venture in social forecasting*, Heinemann, London, 1974, pp. 127–8

Daniel Bell[9] used the term 'post-industrial' to describe the services society (*see* Exhibit 1.1). While his thesis that there has been a shift into service employment appears to be true there is some evidence which suggests that the idea of a society dominated by final consumption of services may not be altogether valid.[10] First demand for some consumer services has only increased slowly or has declined (e.g. public transport, cinemas, laundries). Secondly, in some cases, the output of manufacturing has replaced that of services (e.g. cars for public transport; TV for cinemas). Indeed it has been argued that:

'Careful examination of changes in employment and consumption patterns over the last 25 years reveals, not the gradual emergence of a "service" economy but its precise opposite. . . . Instead of buying services households seem increasingly to be buying – in effect investing in – durable goods which allow final consumers to produce services for themselves.'[11]

Thirdly the proportion of marketed services in consumers' expenditure has not increased as one might expect; although consumer services like health and education, chiefly government provided, have expanded. These are not included in Table 1.8. Indeed it is the growing involvement of government – national, local, supranational (e.g. the EEC) – into producer and consumer lives, that has been an important further reason for service growth.

Table 1.8

Share of purchased services in final consumption in the UK, as a percentage of total consumers' expenditure at current price

	1952	1963	1978
Total services	17.9	17.0	17.1
Travel	4.0	3.3	3.3
Communication	0.7	0.8	1.5
Entertainment and recreation	2.1	1.7	2.0
Domestic service	0.3	0.6	0.5
Catering	5.0	5.3	4.4
Insurance	0.8	1.1	1.4
Other services	4.4	4.1	3.9

Source: Whiteman, J. 'The services sector – a poor relation?', Discussion Paper No. 8, N.E.D.O. reproduced by permission of HMSO, 1981

Of course many product manufacturers have diversified into services as Exhibit 1.2 shows (based on United States changes) and many product retailers have also entered services markets.

Exhibit 1.2

Coca-Cola introduced a multimedia learning system which eventually will be sold in the education market.

Singer (sewing machines) Corp., already possessing teaching expertise based on years of teaching women to sew, is moving into the preschool education market.

Searle & Co., pharmaceutical manufacturer, created a new service, Project Health, to market preventive medicine programs to industry.

Gerber (baby food) Products is moving into nursery schools and insurance.

Maytag introduced a plan to lease its washing machines.

Each of the above illustrates a product firm capitalizing on market opportunities presented by the manufacturing services economy.

Source: Taylor, Thayer C. 'Selling the Services Society'. *Sales Management*, 6 March, 1972, p. 23

The overall picture in the United Kingdom however does not portray a 'post industrial' society where consumer services dominate. Rather, much growth has occurred in intermediate, goods-related services and publicly-provided services. It is growth in demand for these services which seems to have caused the increase in employment in the service sector of the economy.

1.4 The Service Economy and Marketing

Coupled with the emergence of the service economy has been the growing interest of marketors in this sector. Academics and practitioners are actively exploring, applying and extending marketing ideas and practices in a wider range of services contexts, business and non-business, profit and non-profit. There has been a broadening in the range of applications to which marketors have tried to apply the marketing concept in the burgeoning service economy. Many problems exist in applying marketing ideas in such an array of contexts: not least is the practical difficulty of defining what is meant by a service anyway (*see* Chapter 2).

1.5 Summary

1 Since the Second World War many economically developed economies like the United Kingdom have become service economies.
2 In a service economy a large proportion of the working population is employed not in agriculture and manufacturing but in service jobs. In service economies too a large proportion of output is provided by the service sector. In the United Kingdom services make a significant contribution to our international trade.
3 Explanations for the growth of service economies include:

(a) A lag in the growth of labour productivity in services compared with the rest of the economy;
(b) the growth in intermediate demand from firms;
(c) the growth in final demand from consumers.

4 Marketors have begun to take more of an interest in services in recent years.

Questions for Discussion

1 What is meant by the term 'the Service Economy'?
2 What are the reasons for the growth of service economies?
3 What measures can be used to gauge how important services are in the United Kingdom economy?
4 Have all sub-sectors of the service economy experienced growth?
5 What are the two largest sub-sectors of the service economy in terms of employers?
6 Has growth in final demand from consumers been the main reason for the growth of the service economy?
7 How important is Britain's International Trade in Services?
8 What kinds of problems arise in assessing the size and scale of the service sector of the economy?
9 Identify three features associated with employment in services in recent years?
10 Identify four kinds of producer or consumer services that have developed during the past twenty years.

References and Notes

1 Fuchs, V. 'The Service Economy', National Bureau of Economic Research, New York, 1968.
2 Smith, A. D. 'The measurement and interpretation of service output changes', NEDO, London, 1972.
3 Lewis, R. *The New Service Society*, Longman, Harlow, 1973.
4 Heilbroner, R. L. *Business Civilisation in Decline*, Penguin, Harmondsworth, 1977.
5 Gersuny, C. and Rosengren, W. R. *The Service Society*, Schenkman, Cambridge, Mass. 1973.
6 Hollander, S. C. 'Is there a generic demand for services', M.S.U., Business Topics, Spring 1979, pp. 41–64.
7 *Social Trends*, 1981.
8 Stanback, T. M. *Understanding the Service Economy*, Johns Hopkins University Press, Baltimore, 1979.
9 Bell, D. *The coming of the Post Industrial Society* – a venture in social forecasting, Heinemann, London, 1974.
10 Whiteman, J. 'The Services Sector – a Poor Relation?', Discussion Paper No. 8, NEDO, London, 1981.
11 Gershuny, J. *After Industrial Society*, Macmillan, London, 1978.

2. *WHAT ARE SERVICES?*

2.1 Introduction

In the last chapter we examined the development of the service sector of the economy, its size and scale. It is now appropriate to look more closely at what is meant by the term 'services'.

On the face of it the service sector is enormously large and varied. The government is a major provider of services in the United Kingdom. They range across legal, educational, health, military, employment, credit, communications, transportation and information services. Many are provided on a non-profit basis but others may act on a commercial basis. The government is a major participant in service provision. The private non-profit sector with art and music groups, leisure facilities, charities, churches, foundations and colleges also operates in the service sector. Then of course there are the business and professional services provided by airlines, banks, insurance companies, hotels, management consultants, solicitors, architects, advertising agencies and marketing research companies. But underlying this wide range of so-called service activities there lies a major problem of defining what a service actually is.

Unfortunately there is no single, universally accepted, definition of the term. There is a good deal of debate about what services are and whether the distinctions between services and goods are of significance. To understand more fully why no concensus has emerged it is helpful to examine briefly the historical development of the use of the term, 'services'.

2.2 Historical Development

Official economic definitions give little guidance to what is the nature of a service. Definitions developed by economists do, though, throw light on how the concept has changed. Fundamentally, the economist's approaches to services have been institution based or activity based.

The emergence of the physiocrats, the group of eighteenth century French philosophers, is generally considered to herald the beginning of economics as a systematic field of study. Their belief was that the soil provided the only real form of wealth and therefore that agriculture alone was productive and all other activities than agricultural production were 'sterile'.

Adam Smith was critical of the physiocrats. He believed their 'capital error' lay in their 'representing the class of artificers, manufacturers and merchants as altogether barren and unproductive'. He asserted that material goods production was just as capable of returning a net income to producers as was agriculture and made a distinction between 'productive' and 'unproductive' labour. The criterion he used was that productiveness depended upon 'tangibility' which in turn was associated with the durability of the economic activity. Thus services he described as 'barren and unproductive because they perish generally in the very instant of their performance and do not fix or realise themselves in any vendible commodity'. He believed menial servants to be barren and unproductive as well as:

> 'The sovereign . . . with all the officers of justice and war who serve under him, the whole army and navy are unproductive labourers: also churchmen, lawyers, physicians, men of letters of all kinds: players, buffoons, musicians, opera singers. . . . Like the declaration of the actor, the harangue of the orator, or the tune of the musician, the work of them all perishes in the very instant of its production.'[1]

Jean Baptiste Say rejected Smith's notion that immaterial products are not wealth because they were not 'susceptible of conservation'. He argued that activities which have utility and give satisfaction to the consumer, like the doctor who cures a sick man, are productive, and that agriculture, manufacturing and commerce should be treated on an equal basis. Jean Baptiste Say not only argued the claims of immaterial wealth alongside material wealth, he used the term 'services' to describe them.

Alfred Marshall took the concept further when he observed that:

> 'Men cannot create material things. In the mental and moral world indeed he may produce new ideas, but when he is said to produce material things, he really only produces utilities or in other words his efforts and sacrifices result in changing the form or arrangement of matter to adapt it better for satisfaction of wants. All that he can do in the physical world is either to readjust matter so as to make it more useful, as when he makes a log of wood into a table; or to put it on the way of being made more useful by nature, as when he puts seed where the forces of nature will make it burst out into life.'[2]

He argued that there was no scientific foundation for making a distinction between the activities of the cabinet maker and the furniture dealer, the railwayman carrying coal above ground and the miner carrying it underground, the fisherman and the fishmonger; all produce utilities. All activities, in other words, are providing services to satisfy wants.

A further bridging of the divide between goods and services is reflected in more recent views which suggest that the only difference between a good and a service is that a service does not lead to a change in the form of a good.

These different views of services are summarized in Table 2.1.

The acceptance of services as legitimate activities is reflected in the current division of industry by economists into three main groups; primary, secondary and tertiary. Primary activities cover agriculture, forestry and fishing. The secondary activities refer to the manufacturing and construction industries. Tertiary activities refer to the service and distributive trades. Foote and Hatte[3] suggest a further classification of the service industries into:

Table 2.1
Historical definitions of Service

The Physiocrats (c. 1750)	All activities other than agricultural production
Adam Smith (1723–90)	All activities that do not end in tangible products
J. B. Say (1767–1832)	All non-manufacturing activities that add utility to goods
Alfred Marshall (1842–1924)	Goods (services) that pass out of existence at the moment of creation
Western Countries (1925–60)	Services do not lead to a change in the form of a good
Contemporary	An activity that does not lead to a change in the form of a good

Source: Walters, C. G. and Bergiel, B. J. *Marketing Channels*, Scott, Foresman, Glenview, Ill. 1982, p. 483

'Tertiary': including restaurants and hotels, barber and beauty shops, laundry and dry cleaning establishments, home repair and maintenance, handicrafts once performed in the home and other domestic or quasi domestic services.
'Quarternary': including transportation, commerce, communications, finance and administration; the salient characteristics being that they 'facilitate and effectuate the division of labour'.
'Quinary': including health care, education and recreation; the chief aspect of this sector being that services rendered are designed to change and 'improve' the recipient in some way. Services rendered through other sectors are intended to maintain the customer and the division of labour 'as is'.

Unfortunately the term services is still not used in a consistent way. In studies undertaken of the service economy phenomenon Fuchs,[4] for example, excluded transportation, communications and public utilities and placed them in the industry sector 'because of their dependence upon heavy capital equipment and complex technology'.

He further distinguished a service 'sub-sector' which excluded government, households and institutions and real estate; a sub-sector, it can be argued, that is somewhat restricted for a work entitled 'The Service Economy'. On the other hand Whiteman[5] in his study used services to mean:

Transport – both goods and passengers, by bus, rail, air and sea but excluding private motoring:
Communication – postal and telephone services;
Distributive trades – wholesale and retail distribution;
Insurance, banking, finance and business services;

Professional and scientific services – mainly health and education services;

Miscellaneous services – including cinemas, sports, hotels and restaurants;

Public administration and defence – the military and most of the civil service.

These two treatments of services show that in economics at least there seems to be 'no authoritative concensus on either the boundaries or the classification of the service industries'.[6]

Although services are now included in classifications of industrial activities in many western economies their provision is often regarded as secondary to the production of goods. Certainly in Britain the imposition for a period of Selective Employment Tax (SET); the discrimination of many government grants and allowances in favour of manufacturing industry over recent years; the associations of services with 'luxuries', 'inessentials' and with the satisfaction of psychological and emotional needs rather than physical needs; the treatment in the Balance of Payments figures of 'invisibles' as something separate and, by implication, of lesser importance. These and other manifestations of discrimination and second rate treatment of the service sector of the economy have served to perpetuate what Lewis calls the 'anti service myth'.[7] He believes that services in some ways are still not treated as valid forms of wealth.

2.3 Marketing Approaches to Services

In marketing there have been a number of approaches used to clarify what are services. Some of these varying approaches are now considered. They are:

(a) definitions of services;
(b) characteristics of services;
(c) functional differences;
(d) classifications of services;
(e) conceptual frameworks.

2.31 Definitions

The American Marketing Association definition of services of 1960 describes them as 'Activities, benefits or satisfactions which are offered for sale, or are provided in connection with the sale of goods'.[8] For a number of years this seems to have been the one most widely accepted and used. Its chief weakness though is that it does not discriminate sufficiently between goods and services; goods too are offered for sale because they provide 'benefits' and 'satisfactions'.

A refinement of the AMA definition is:

'Services are those separately identifiable, essentially intangible activities which provide want-satisfaction, and that are not necessarily tied to the sale of a product or another service. To produce a service may or may not require the use of tangible goods. However when such use is required, there is no transfer of title (permanent ownership) to these tangible goods.'[9]

In using this definition Stanton makes clear that activities like medical care, entertainment and repair services are included but credit, delivery and other services which exist only when there is the sale of a product or another service are excluded. He also recognizes that the consumer may take temporary possession or make temporary use of any goods that may be required in the production of a service (e.g. a hotel room.) Also by suggesting that service organizations are those which do not have as their principal aim the production of tangible products which buyers will possess permanently, he is close to the idea of Gronroos[10] that 'The service is the object of marketing, i.e. the company is selling the service as the core of its market offering'.

Another similar definition is that of Kotler 'A service is any activity or benefit that one party can offer to another that is essentially intangible and does not result in the ownership of anything. Its production may or may not be tied to a physical product'.[11]

What these and other definitional approaches share in common is their emphasis, directly or by implication, on the essentially intangible nature of a service. This quality of intangibility is central to another approach to service definition which focuses on the distinctive characteristics of services.

2.32 Characteristics of Services

A number of characteristics have been suggested to help distinguish goods and services. It is the combination of these characteristics which create the specific context in which a service organization must develop its marketing policies. The more commonly stated characteristics of services are:

(*a*) intangibility;
(*b*) inseparability;
(*c*) heterogeneity;
(*d*) perishability;
(*e*) ownership.

Intangibility

Services are essentially intangible. It is often not possible to taste, feel, see, hear or smell services before they are purchased. Opinions and attitudes may be sought beforehand, a repeat purchase may rely upon previous experience, the customer may be given something tangible to represent the service, but ultimately the purchase of a service is the purchase of something intangible. Wilson[12] suggests that the concept of tangibility may be divided further, although somewhat arbitrarily, into services providing pure intangibles (e.g. security service, museums), services providing added value to a tangible (e.g. insurance, launderettes) and services that make available a tangible (e.g. financial services, retailing). These different concepts of intangibility are illustrated in Table 2.2.

Table 2.2
Concept of Tangibility

Degree of Tangibility	*Producer Services*	*Consumer Services*
Services that are essentially intangible.	Security, communication systems, franchising, mergers and acquisitions, valuations.	Museums, auctioneering, employment agencies, entertainment, education, travel services.
Services providing added value to a tangible product.	Insurance, contract maintenance, engineering consultancy, advertising, packaging design.	Launderettes, repairs, personal care, insurance.
Services that make available a tangible product.	Wholesaling, transport, warehousing, financial services, architecture, factoring, contract R and D.	Retailing, automatic vending, mail order, hire purchase, charities, mortgages.

Source: Adapted from Wilson, Aubrey; *The Marketing of Professional Services*, (McGraw-Hill, London, 1972,) p. 8

This sub-division of services is similar to another idea which suggests there is a goods-services continuum with pure goods at one extreme and pure services at the other; but with most economic products falling between these two extremes.[13]

Bateson[14] has refined the concept of intangibility further. He suggests that intangibility is the critical characteristic distinguishing products from services and that intangibility means both 'palpable' intangibility (i.e. the service cannot be touched by the consumer) and 'mental' intangibility (i.e. the service is difficult for the consumer to grasp mentally). He suggests that these two aspects of intangibility account for some of the characteristics which separate product and service marketing:

a service cannot be touched;
precise standardization is difficult;
there is no ownership transfer;
a service cannot be patented;
production and consumption are inseparable;
there are no inventories of the service;
middlemen roles are different;
the consumer is part of the production process so the delivery system must go to the market or the customer must come to the delivery system so in market location and multi-site operations are common.

Inseparability

Services often cannot be separated from the person of the seller. A corollary of this is that creating or performing the service may occur at the same time as full or partial consumption of it. Goods are produced, sold and consumed whereas services are sold and then produced and consumed. This is illustrated in Figure 2.1 and applies particularly with some personal services, (e.g. dental treatment).

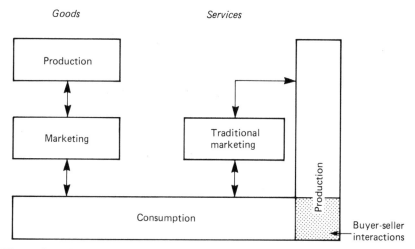

Figure 2.1 The relationship between production, marketing and consumption

Source: The illustration is developed from a figure originally in Rathmell, J. M., *Marketing in the Service Sector*, Winthrop, Cambridge, Mass. 1974, p. 7

Heterogeneity

It is often difficult to achieve standardization of output in services. Even though standard systems may be used, for example to handle a flight reservation, to book in a customer's car for service or to quote for insurance on his life. Each 'unit' of a service may differ from other 'units'. Franchise operations, like Wimpy Bars, attempt to ensure a standard of conformity, but ultimately it is difficult to ensure the same level of output in terms of quality. From the customers' viewpoint too it is difficult to judge quality in advance of purchase; although this element also applies to some product marketing.

Perishability

Services are perishable and cannot be stored. Spare seats on a package tour or an empty hotel room represent capacity lost forever. In addition, with some services, there is fluctuating demand which may aggravate the perishability feature. Key decisions have to be taken on what maximum capacity level should be available to cope with surges in demand before service levels suffer. Equally, attention has to be given in times of low levels of usage on whether spare capacity will lie idle or whether short-term policies (e.g. differential pricing, special promotions), will be adopted to even out fluctuations in demand. Some illustrations of programmes that may be adopted to compensate for fluctuating demand are shown in Table 2.3.

Table 2.3
Programmes to Compensate for Uneven Demand

Industry	Programme
Airlines	Night rates, group and tour fares, family discounts, advance purchase super savers, 24-hour round-trip discounts, and low season fares.
Hotels	Off-season and group rates, theme weekends (Valentine getaway), sports packages, family and senior citizen discounts.
Telephone	Evening, night, and weekend rates.
Barber shops	Evening appointments and family rates.
Automobile repair	Specials (tyre balancing, tuneups, and lubrication).
Dentists	Call-back reminders and family discounts.
Education	Weekend classes, adult education and military programmes.
Entertainment (Movies)	Matinee specials and midnight showtime specials.
Recreation (Bowling)	Midday specials, family night, teen night, and all-night rates.
(Parks)	Off-season specials, group and senior citizen rates, family rates, late-night rates, and advance purchase discounts.

Source: Walters, C. G. and Bergiel, B. S., *Marketing Channels*, Scott, Foresman, Glenview, Ill. 1982, p. 491

Ownership

Lack of ownership is a basic difference between a service industry and a product industry because a customer may only have access to or use of a facility (e.g. a hotel room, a credit card). Payment is for the use of, access to or hire of items. With the sale of a tangible good, barring restrictions imposed say by a hire purchase scheme, the buyer has full use of the product.

A summary of these characteristics of services with some implications is shown in Table 2.4. There is some dispute in the marketing literature as to whether some of the characteristics outlined above do help discriminate between products and services. Wyckham *et al.*[15] provide cogent counter

Table 2.4
Some constraints on the management of services and ways of overcoming them

Characteristics of service	Some implications	Some means of overcoming characteristics
Intangibility	Sampling difficult. Places strain on promotional element of marketing mix. No patents possible. Difficult to judge price and quality in advance.	Focus on benefits. Increase tangibility of service (e.g. physical representations of it). Use brand names. Use personalities to personalize service. Develop reputation.
Inseparability	Requires presence of producer. Direct sale. Limited scale of operations.	Learn to work in larger groups. Work faster. Train more competent service providers.
Heterogeneity	Standard depends upon who and when provided. Difficult to assure quality.	Careful personnel selection and training. Ensure standards are monitored. Pre-package service. Mechanize and industrialize for quality control. Emphasize bespoke features.
Perishability	Cannot be stored. Problems with demand fluctuation.	Better match between supply and demand (e.g. price reductions off peak).
Ownership	Customer has access to but not ownership of activity or facility.	Stress advantages of non-ownership (e.g. easier payment systems).

arguments for why intangibility, heterogeneity, and perishability at least are not of themselves sufficiently discriminating. They believe that there are too many exceptions to their use for services alone. They suggest that what is required is not a simple product/service scheme which differentiates on the basis of characteristics of the offer itself, but a more complex taxonomy of offerings which differentiates on the basis of product/service characteristics and market characteristics. Their criticism is valid for another approach used to define services, the functional differences approach.

2.33 Functional Differences

This approach is essentially dependent upon contrasting services marketing with goods marketing. The work of Judd[16] typifies this approach in which differentiating features between goods and services marketing are suggested. Thus:

> services cannot be stocked;
> channels of distribution for services, where they exist, are short; services lack patent protection;
> standards cannot be precise in the services sector because of the absence of mass production;
> services lack the use of packaging;
> services cannot be sampled;
> economic concepts of supply and demand and costs are difficult to apply to services because of their intangible nature;
> there appears to be limited concentration in the services sector of the economy;
> monetary values are more likely to be expressed in terms other than of 'price';
> symbolism derives from performance in the case of services rather than from possession.

The list above is similar to that shown earlier in Section 2.32 where an explanation for these functional differences lay in the service characteristic of intangibility.

The difficulty with this approach is that there are problems in defining functional features which accurately and precisely delimit the differences between goods and services. Like the 'characteristics of services' approach a number of exceptions to the general principles seem to exist.

2.34 Classifications of Services

The elusiveness of a widely accepted definition of services has not prevented the development of a variety of schemes which attempt to classify services. Some believe that classifications are not very helpful; because they can misdirect marketing thinking and often perpetuate a product orientation.[17] Others believe that classification is helpful; for it acts as a first step in obtaining an understanding of the ways in which markets operate.[18] Certainly, when undertaken from a consumer viewpoint, valuable insights can be gained into reasons for making a purchase and the ways in which products are bought. This kind of information is then useful for helping to develop marketing strategies for services and for evaluating the current strategies and tactics in use by a service marketing organization.

Many of the classification schemes suggested for services are derived from those used in marketing goods. Also it should be borne in mind that many schemes are based on assumptions about what is or not a service. An illustration of three common ways of classifying services is shown in Figure 2.2.

SELLER RELATED BASES

Nature of enterprise	*Functions performed*	*Income source*
Private, for profit Private, non-profit Public, for profit Public, non-profit	Communication Consulting Educational Financial Health Insurance	Derived from market Market plus donations Donations only Taxation

BUYER RELATED BASES

Market type	*Way in which service bought*	*Motives*
Consumer market Industrial market Government market Agricultural market	Convenience service Shopping service Speciality service Unsought service	Instrumental i.e. : means to an end Expressive i.e.: an end in itself

SERVICE RELATED BASES

Service form	*Human or machine based*	*High or low contact*
Uniform service Bespoke service	Human centred service Machine centred service	High contact service Low contact service

Figure 2.2 An illustration of some current ways of classifying services

A common method of classification is on a '*Seller Related*' basis. Thus service marketing organizations may be classified according to whether they are 'private' or 'public'; and within each grouping whether they are 'profit motivated' or 'non-profit' motivated.

The 'function performed' by the organization may too be used as a basis of classification. Thus, for example, organizations may perform educational, health, insurance or financial functions.

The 'source of income' may too be used as a basis of classification. Service marketing organizations may derive their income from taxation, from the marketplace, from donations or from a combination of sources.

'*Buyer Related*' bases include the type of market, whether consumer or industrial; the way in which the service is bought, whether as a convenience, shopping, speciality or unsought service: and the motives for purchase. Swan and Pruden[19] suggest that establishing whether the motives for purchase are 'instrumental' – that is the service is a means to an end – or 'expressive' – that is the service is an end in itself – may also provide a useful framework for classifying some services.

The last example shows classifications which are '*Service Related*'. These may be in terms of service form, (e.g. uniform or bespoke); human based or equipment based; or may involve high levels of personal contact or low levels of personal contact.

Obviously there is no one classification for a particular service. Different customers may view the same service in different ways at the same time. Thus a hotel may be chosen at random by a tired passing motorist because it is convenient. Another traveller may have studied local tourist brochures, obtained recommendations from friends and telephoned in advance to make a reservation. In addition the bases shown can be developed further to add additional dimensions to those suggested (e.g. temporal or spatial categories; rational or emotional motives; high urgency – low urgency services). Such categories may be determined by judgement or through marketing research (*see* Chapter 5). Formal research effort could uncover consumer attitudes and needs related to the service type in general and to an organization's services in particular. The research might also suggest the dimensions for determining the appropriate service class or classes; also the segmenting dimensions in the marketplace, from which appropriate marketing strategies and tactics could be developed. When this kind of information is not available from the marketplace either through ignorance or because information is not or cannot be made available (e.g. launching a totally novel kind of service) then this is where service classifications may be of particular value. They can act as a preliminary framework for looking at and thinking about markets.

2.35 Conceptual Frameworks

In recent years there have appeared a variety of conceptual approaches aimed at defining the marketing of services area. These frameworks have been put forward to help provide an understanding of the services concept. Three are outlined here: They are the ideas of:

(a) Eiglier and Langeard;
(b) Gronroos;
(c) Shostack.

Eiglier and Langeard

Eiglier and Langeard suggest that there are three fundamental characteristics of services:

intangibility;
direct organization – client relationships;
consumer participation in the production process.

They argue that these characteristics may be generalized to apply to all service marketing. In their conceptual framework they examine the problems resulting from these characteristics:

upon the enterprise;
upon the client;
from the public viewpoint.

Table 2.5 outlines their suggestions. The authors have tested this framework in an empirical study of twenty-two French companies in four types of service industries and claim legitimacy for their approach.[20]

Table 2.5
Service characteristics and their consequences

Characteristics	Organization	Client	Society
Intangibility	1 Inventory 2 Communication 3 Pricing/costing 4 Patent protection	1 Confidence 2 Search process 3 Image 4 Word-of-mouth	1 Control 2 Productivity 3 Inflation
Organization–client interface	1 Interface complexity 2 Control of the environment 3 Distribution network	1 Personalized relationship 2 Short-term captivity	1 Networks and planning 2 Elimination of dysfunctions
User's participation in production	1 Standardization 2 Innovation and behaviour change 3 Productivity and user behaviour	1 Dependence on rules and procedures 2 Identification	1 Innovation and public policy 2 Involvement

Source: Eiglier, P. and Langeard, E. in *Marketing Consumer Services: New Insights*, MSI Report 77–115, 1977, Cambridge, Mass.

Gronroos

Gronroos suggests that there are three fundamental characteristics of services:

intangibility;
a service is an activity rather than a thing;
production and consumption are to some extent simultaneous activities.

He argues that these basic characteristics of services make the marketing situation and the customer relations of service firms fundamentally different from those of consumer goods companies and that the service organization has two marketing functions, the 'traditional marketing function' and the 'interactive marketing function'. The latter is concerned with what happens in the interface between production and consumption (*see* shaded area in Figure 2.1).

He develops a further model produced by Eiglier and Langeard (Figure 2.3) which divides a service company into two parts. One part is 'invisible' to the customer; this consists of the internal organization of the firm which gives physical and management support to people working with customers. The 'visible' part of the model focusses on the three main categories of resource; the physical environment where the service is consumed; the contact personnel; and the consumer who takes part in the production process. Gronroos adds a planning dimension to the model to ensure the 'interactive marketing function' is handled in a customer-orientated way and suggests five variables which seem to be important when planning buyer/seller interactions. These are the service concept; auxiliary services; accessibility of the service; interactive personnel/customer communications; consumer influence. These variables are set within the 'traditional' marketing mix elements (*see* Figure 2.4). He then argues that the 'traditional marketing function' and the 'interactive marketing function' will play different roles at different stages of the purchasing and consumption process.[21]

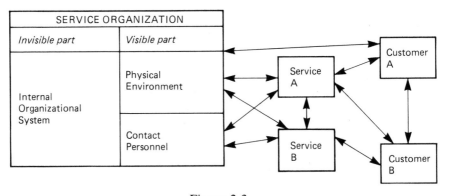

Figure 2.3

Source: Based on Eiglier, P., and Langeard, E., *Principes de politique marketing pour les enterprises de services*, L'Institut d'Administration des Enterprises, Université d'Aix-Marseille, Décembre 1976, p. 11. (Working Paper presented at Marketing of Services Workshop, France)

Shostack

Shostack too stresses the importance of intangibility as a fundamental characteristic of services. She argues that to extend marketing's conceptual

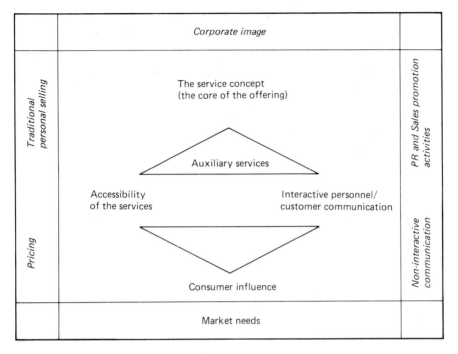

Figure 2.4

Source: Gronroos, C., 'An Applied Service Marketing Theory', Working Paper No. 57, Swedish School of Economics and Business Administration, Helsinki, 1980

boundaries a framework is required which accommodates intangibility rather than denying it.[22]

A conventional framework used in marketing is that an organization's offering to the marketplace can consist of goods, services or a combination of both. Four broad categories on offer have been distinguished and they may be seen as lying along a continuum.[11] These four categories are:

A pure tangible good

The offer consists of a pure tangible (e.g. salt, toothpaste) with no explicit services accompanying it. The objective of the sale is a tangible item.

A tangible good with accompanying services

The offer consists of a good with accompanying services (e.g. a motor car). The object of the sale is a tangible item.

A service with accompanying goods and services

The offer consists of a service with accompanying goods and/or services (e.g. passenger air transport). The object of the sale is an intangible.

A pure service

The offer consists of a service (e.g. massage). The object of the sale is an intangible item.

An extension of this goods-services or tangible-intangible dominant continuum is shown in Figure 2.5.

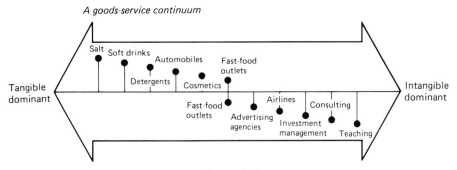

A goods-service continuum

Figure 2.5

Source: Shostack G. L., 'Breaking Free from Product Marketing', *Journal of Marketing*, Vol. 41, No. 2, April 1977, American Marketing Association, p. 77

What this continuum emphasizes is that in fact most 'products' are combinations of elements or attributes which are linked together. There are few 'pure' products and 'pure' services. Shostack suggests that marketing 'entities' are combinations of discrete elements, tangible and intangible. Her molecular model provides a way of visualizing and therefore of managing a total market entity. It can show the elements making up a product, the interrelationships between them and the dominance of goods or services, tangibles or intangibles in an offer. Figure 2.6 is a simplified example to demonstrate the notion of a product entity. Here airlines and automobiles are divided according to some of their major attributes. The two products have different 'nuclei' and they also differ in dominance. Airlines are more intangible dominant – there is no ownership of a tangible good. Airline travel cannot be physically possessed, only experienced. The inherent benefit is a service. On the other hand an automobile is more tangible dominant. A car can be physically possessed; though the benefit it yields is a service too.

2.4 Limits of Services

It is apparent from the preceding discussion that a universally acceptable definition of services has so far proved elusive. As Smith[23] observed 'No criteria are likely to provide a clear cut distinction between the two sectors (goods and service)'.

Yet for our purposes it is worth returning to Marshall who judged that both manufacturers and traders produced utilities whether they were formed from tangible or intangible components. Or as Levitt[24] put it more recently '. . . there is no such thing as service industries. There are only

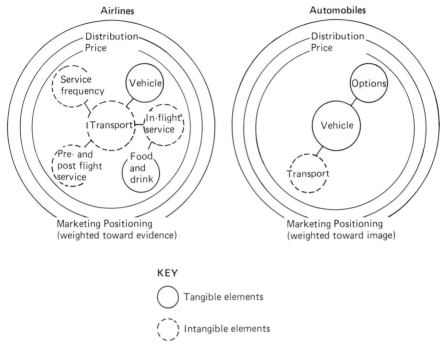

Figure 2.6 The Molecular Model

Source: Shostack G. L., 'Breaking Free from Product Marketing', *Journal of Marketing*, Vol. 41, No. 2, April 1977, American Marketing Association, p. 76

industries whose service components are greater or less than those of other industries. Everybody is in service.'

Both go back to the heart of the matter. From a marketing viewpoint both goods and services provide benefits and satisfactions; both goods and services are products.

One of the main features underlying the application of marketing is that an organization's offering goes beyond the mere physical aspects of a product. The narrow view of a product is that it is a set of tangible and intangible, physical and chemical attributes, assembled in a particular form. The broader view, the marketing view, is that a product is a set of tangible and intangible attributes which the buyer may accept as offering satisfaction of needs and wants.[9] In the broader sense then every product has intangible elements to it 'Everybody sells intangibles in the market-place no matter what is produced in the factory'.[25]

What is significant about services, where they are the objects being marketed, is the relative dominance of intangible attributes in the make-up of the 'service product'. Services are a special kind of product. They may require special understanding and special marketing efforts.

There do not appear to be fundamental differences between marketing goods and services. What differences there are, are of the sort often drawn to distinguish between 'consumer marketing' and 'industrial marketing'; that is differences of degree and of emphasis. Just as there are differences of degree and of emphasis in marketing one type of consumer product compared with another. Such differences may require distinctive marketing practices in terms of tools and techniques. But the same principles and concepts of marketing are of relevance to all fields. As Baker[26] says: '. . . the same sequence of market research, product/service planning and development, pricing, promotion, distribution, sale and after sales service would seem to be equally appropriate to all marketing situations'.

What is required in marketing is a deeper appreciation of the special problems there may be and the distinctive differences required when marketing intangibles.

The perspective adopted here is that the difference between goods and services is not fundamental, it is classificatory; and no one classification will suit all ends. The view taken here of services is wide rather than narrow: it is inclusive rather than exclusive; it 'lumps' together rather than 'splits' down.[27] The purpose in this text is to focus on the adaptations which *may* be required to general marketing principles and practices, in applying them to private and public organizations and enterprises, profit and non-profit, which provide satisfactions through the performance of activities and processes which result in products; and where the core of the product, the object of such marketing efforts, is *essentially intangible*.

The weakness with such a general approach is that the adaptations and modifications discussed do not apply in specific situations. The purpose of this book is to *suggest* possible adaptations and modifications that may be required rather than to *prescribe* adaptations and modifications that will be required. The ideas will vary in their usefulness to those interested in service marketing. It is appropriate to note the words of a distinguished writer and practitioner on the service sector:

> 'Services of all types are taking an increasing part of both organisational and personal budgets, but those engaged in service industries must of necessity lean heavily on product–marketing methods because of the lack of information on the marketing of services. This applies whether the services are professional, such as banking, consultancy, architecture, accountancy or broking: industrial, such as contract maintenance, security, transport, or design: or consumer, such as tourism, entertainment or personal care. All engaged in the sale of intangibles know, if only instinctively, that the marketing strategies and tactics for services are applied in very different ways from those for products.'[12]

For practical purposes we have drawn an arbitrary boundary around the field of our concern here. This treatment of essentially intangible products excludes fields of growing interest to marketors like:

the marketing of ideas (e.g. safer driving; religious organizations);
the marketing of people (e.g. politicians);
the marketing of charities and causes (e.g. Dr Barnardo's Homes);
the marketing of organizations (particularly those supported through the tax system (e.g. police service).

Table 2.6 shows the broad domain of our concern. Part 2 discusses the

Table 2.6
Selected Illustrative Services

Utilities
Gas
Electricity
Water supply

Transport and Communication
Railways
Road passenger
Road haulage
Sea transport
Air transport
Postal service
Telecommunications

Distributive Traders
Wholesale distribution
Retail distribution
Dealers and agents

Insurance Banking and Finance
Insurance
Banking
Finance
Property service

Business, Professional and Scientific
Advertising
Consulting
Marketing Research
Accountancy
Legal
Medical and dental
Educational services
Research services

Recreation and Leisure
Cinemas, theatres
Sport and recreation
Betting and gambling
Hotels, motels, restaurants, cafes
Public houses and clubs
Catering contractors

Miscellaneous
Repair services
Hairdressing
Private domestic
Laundries
Dry cleaning

problems of applying marketing ideas and principles in these services contexts.

2.5 Summary

1 The service sector is large and includes many different kinds of organizations.
2 Historically, economic definitions of what is a service have changed. There is still no agreement on what constitutes a service.

3 A number of approaches have been used by mark'etors to clarify what
  services are. These approaches include definitions, identifying characteristics of services, identifying functional differences, classifying services in
  various ways and conceptual frameworks for dealing with services.
4 For marketing purposes, services like goods, provide benefits and
  satisfactions. What is significant about services is the relative dominance
  of intangible attributes in the make-up of the service product.

Questions for Discussion

 1 How has the use of the term 'services' changed over the years?
 2 What is a service?
 3 What is a service product?
 4 Do 'pure' services exist?
 5 What is the difference between buying a car and hiring a car?
 6 Suggest four characteristics of services.
 7 Suggest five ways in which services may be classified.
 8 How relevant is the concept of tangibility to the definition of a service?
 9 Do shops sell goods or do they market services?
10 What difficulties arise in attempting to define a service from a
   marketing point of view?

References and Notes

 1 Smith, A. *The Wealth of Nations* (1789 ed) Modern Library, New
   York, 1937.
 2 Marshall, A. *Principles of Economics* Macmillan, 8th ed, 1947, p. 62.
 3 Foote, N. N. and Hatte, P. K. 'Social mobility and economic
   advancement', *American Economic Review*, Vol. 43, May, 1953, pp.
   364–78.
 4 Fuchs, V. 'The Service Economy', National Bureau of Economic
   Research, New York, 1968.
 5 Whiteman, J. 'The Services Sector – A Poor Relation?' Discussion
   Paper No. 8, NEDO, London, 1981.
 6 Stigler, G. 'Trends in Employment in the Service Industries', Princeton
   University Press for National Bureau of Economic Research, 1956, p.
   47.
 7 Lewis, R. *The New Service Society* Longman, Harlow, 1973.
 8 American Marketing Association: Committee on Definitions, 'Marketing Definitions: A Glossary of Marketing Terms', 1960.
 9 Stanton, W. J. *Fundamentals of Marketing* McGraw-Hill, New York,
   1981, p. 441.
10 Gronroos, C. 'A Service orientated approach to marketing of services',
   European Journal of Marketing Vol. 12, No. 8, 1978, p. 589.
11 Kotler, P. *Principles of Marketing* Prentice-Hall, Englewood Cliffs,
   1982, p. 624.
12 Wilson, A. *The Marketing of Professional Services* McGraw-Hill,
   London, 1972.

13 Rathmell, J. M. 'What is meant by Services?', *Journal of Marketing*, Oct. Vol. 30, No. 4, 1966, pp. 32–6.
14 Bateson, J. 'Do we need Service Marketing?', Marketing Consumer Services: New Insights, Report 75–115, Marketing Science Institute, Boston, 1977.
15 Wyckham, R. G., Fitzroy, P. T. and Mandry, S. D. 'Marketing of Services', *European Journal of Marketing*, Vol. 9, No. 1, 1975, pp. 59–67.
16 Judd, R. C. 'Similarities and differences in Product and Service Retailing', *Journal of Retailing*, Vol. 43, Winter 1968, pp. 1–9
17 Hughes, G. D. *Marketing Management: A Planning Approach*, Addison-Wesley, Reading, Mass. 1978, p. 410.
18 Hill, R. and Hillier, T. *Organisational Buying Behaviour* Macmillan, London 1977.
19 Swan, J. E. and Pruden, H. O. 'Marketing Insights from a classification of Services', *American Journal of Small Business*, July 1977, Vol. II, No. 1.
20 Eiglier, P. and Langeard, E. 'A New approach to Service Marketing' Marketing Consumer Services: New Insights, Report 77–115, Marketing Science Institute, Boston, 1977.
21 Gronroos, C. 'An applied service marketing theory', Working Paper No. 57, Swedish School of Economics and Business Administration, Helsinki, 1980.
22 Shostack, G. Lynn 'Breaking free from Product Marketing', *Journal of Marketing*, Vol. 41, No. 2, April 1977, pp. 73–80.
23 Smith, A. D. 'The measurement and interpretation of service output changes', NEDO, London, 1972.
24 Levitt, T. 'Production Line Approach to Service' *Harvard Business Review*, Sept.–Oct. 1972, pp. 41–52.
25 Levitt, T. 'Marketing Intangible Products and Product Intangibles', *Harvard Business Review*, May–June 1981, pp. 94–102.
26 Baker, M. J. (Editor) *Marketing: Theory and Practice* Macmillan, London, 1976.
27 Attributed to Thomas, M. J. MEG mini-conference, University of York, December 1980.

PART 2

The status of Marketing in Services. The adaptations required to Marketing Strategy Formulation, the Marketing Mix and Marketing Research

3. *MARKETING AND SERVICE ORGANIZATIONS*

3.1 Introduction

In the last chapter various approaches to defining services were considered. It was suggested that the traditional distinctions made between goods and services may not be helpful for marketing purposes. Ultimately all products are bought or used to solve problems and provide customer benefits. Also most products are composed of tangible and intangible elements. The distinction between goods and services is blurred. However organizations marketing products where the intangible elements are more dominant in the make-up of the product, may have special problems in adapting marketing ideas and practices.

Before looking at the adaptations to marketing strategies and tactics that may be required, it is useful for background purposes to outline briefly the meaning of marketing and to explore what is known of the status of marketing in the service sector. This chapter is concerned with these two matters.

3.2 What is Marketing About[1]

Marketing is described as 'the way in which an organisation matches its own human, financial and physical resources with the wants of its customers'[2] and is defined by the Institute of Marketing as 'the management process responsible for identifying, anticipating and satisfying customer requirements profitably'.

It is in fact deceptively easy to describe but extremely difficult to practice. At the heart of what marketing is about lies the so-called 'marketing concept' which managers in most types of organizations can use as a general guide to their thinking and their actions. The marketing concept may appear in different guises – some simple, some complex; but it is essentially about the following few things which contribute towards an organization's success:

(a) The purpose of an organization to create, to win, and to keep a customer. The customer is and should be central to everything the organization does.

(b) To create, to win, and to keep a customer the organization has to create, produce, and deliver goods and services that people want and value. Moreover, such products and services should be created, produced, and delivered under conditions and at prices that are relatively attractive to customers compared with those offered by competitors. Also, from the organization's point of view, the number of customers wanting such products and services must be sufficiently large to justify the conditions and prices of creation, production, and delivery.

(*c*) To continue to do these things the organization – if it is to be profitable – must generate revenue which exceeds costs and which is of sufficient size and which arises with sufficient regularity to attract, keep, and develop capital for the organization and to keep, at least abreast and, sometimes ahead of, competitive offerings. In non-profit, subsidized organizations this factor may be of less importance.

(*d*) No organization can continue to do these things by instinct or by accident. It has to clarify its purposes; it has to clarify the strategies it may employ to achieve such purposes, and it requires plans for their achievement. Usually these may be written; they need to be communicated; and they will almost certainly need to be reviewed periodically.

(*c*) Finally, there needs to be an appropriate system of rewards, audits and controls to ensure that what's meant to be done gets done and that when it doesn't something is done about it.[3]

In attempting to apply these things the fundamental features which are likely to distinguish a market-orientated organization from one which is not are that:

(*a*) Marketing is first and foremost an **attitude of mind**. The centrality of the customer to the enterprise will permeate all departments of organizations which are truly marketing-orientated. Ultimately decisions which are taken are seen to have an effect and an impact upon the customer, the basic reason for the existence of the enterprise and the source from which its lifeblood derives.

(*b*) Marketing is also a way of **organizing the enterprise**. Again the starting point for organizational design should be the customer and the attempt to ensure that the products and services produced are delivered in the most customer-effective way. All other organiza-tional-design decisions should stem from the customer and ensure that customers are created, won over, and kept by the enterprise.

(*c*) Marketing covers a **range of activities**. Once it is recognized how central the customer is to the organization then the activities necessary to ensure the serving of customer needs will emerge as a matter of course. Such activities will vary from organization to organization but will typically include:

identification of customers, their needs and wants, and the various market groups and segments that exist. In the simplest markets the customer and marketor can meet personally and information on needs and wants can be obtained directly;

the creation, production, and delivery of products and services which meet those identified needs and wants, and which are consistent with the organizations' view of the customers' need area(s) it has decided to serve and meet;

pricing the products and services, where prices are charged;

communicating with the marketplace about what products and services are available, and ensuring that the products and services are delivered in ways consistent with customer needs;

ensuring the integration of all customer-impinging activities and the monitoring of the organization's success or failure in continuing to serve customer needs and meeting changes and challenges, from competitors and from the environment in which the enterprise operates.

(*d*) In blending these activities, in designing appropriate organizational forms, in attempting to serve better the needs of customers, management will make use of an array of **techniques and tools**. Some techniques and tools will be quite distinctive and specific to the marketing area (e.g. motivation research as used in marketing research). Others will be more widely and more generally employed across the organization as a whole (e.g. linear programming, discounted cash flow). Ultimately though these techniques and tools will be used with the purpose of enabling the organization to operate as efficiently and effectively as possible in the customers' interests.

In essence then marketing is an attitude of mind; it is a way of organizing the enterprise; it is a range of activities which will employ tools and techniques in the process of identifying, anticipating, and satisfying customer requirements.

3.3 The Status of Marketing in the Service Sector

The evidence on the status of marketing in the service sector is conflicting. On the one hand it has been suggested that service dominant organizations are less market-orientated than manufacturing firms; indeed it has been suggested that growth in services has not been due to marketing developments. (Certainly many government departments and professional firms in the United Kingdom are perhaps better known for their lack of market orientation than for their zeal to meet customer needs.) In support of this argument that service organizations tend to be less market-orientated several reasons are usually offered. None of them, apart from the first, necessarily apply to all service organizations:

(*a*) The dominantly intangible nature of service products may cause more difficult marketing problems compared with physical items (e.g. display; selling service product benefits).

(*b*) Some service businesses (e.g. professional firms) are opposed to the idea of marketing. They consider it to be unprofessional to use certain marketing practices associated with goods marketing (e.g.

advertising is still restricted or forbidden by many professional services). Also they tend to think of themselves as producers of services not as marketors of services.

(c) Many service organizations are small, in direct contact with their customers and may not require the same kinds of marketing approaches as medium-size or larger organizations. Many management techniques and marketing may be considered to be irrelevant by such organizations (e.g. hairdressers, repair shops).

(d) Some service organizations have enjoyed more demand for their services than they could cope with (e.g. hospitals, universities) and have not had to try as hard to service customer needs as some other enterprises.

(e) 'Ethical' constraints may limit marketing in some service areas (e.g. private medical services).

(f) Some organizations have enjoyed monopoly powers in their service field and have failed to recognize that competition exists (e.g. between public utilities like gas and electricity).

(g) Quality of management is not as good in services organizations:

> 'top management does not yet understand (1) what marketing is or (2) its importance to a company's success. These executives seem to equate marketing with selling, and they fail to consider other parts of the marketing system. They also do not effectively co-ordinate their marketing activities. Many service firms lack an executive whose sole responsibility is marketing. . . .'[4]

(h) Even when service managers have been interested in marketing ideas they may have found little help from published work in the marketing area. Some writers in the service marketing area suggest that the available ideas are not much help to marketors of services. For example:

> Donnelly[5] suggests that the practice of considering the marketing of services using the framework developed for goods has limited thinking concerning service marketing.
>
> Eiglier[6] argues that service organizations' problems are different from the basis of his exploratory work in retail distribution, hotels, transport and banking 'service organizations nevertheless manifest some specific characteristics the consequences of which constitute problems unique to service organisations and their clients'.
>
> Gronroos[7] who has conducted research into the service sector in Sweden and Finland believes that 'traditional marketing literature has little to offer companies and organisations in the service sector'.
>
> Finally Shostack[8] argues that services' marketing requires a different approach and different concepts compared with goods' marketing.

There is no doubt that in the past marketing texts and writings confined their attention and most of their examples to goods. This is now changing and some recent texts recognize the importance of service marketing and include chapters on the subject.[9] Also some texts now specifically address themselves to the service sector in general or a specific sector of service marketing [e.g. Rathmell[10] and Wilson[11]] In the main though the discussion of how marketing may be applied to the services sector has been restricted.

On the other hand many service organizations have of course been highly market orientated. It is unreasonable and inaccurate to suggest that all are ignorant of or antipathetic towards marketing. Some extremely successful service organizations, like hire car companies, industrial cleaning service companies and hotel groups have used marketing practices. Also as competition intensifies in many parts of the service sector (e.g. financial services); as people with marketing experience from the non-service sector switch jobs to service organizations; as attempts are made in many hard-pressed service organizations to maintain quality and increase productivity in the face of competitive pressures and resource constraints (e.g. universities); as legal and ethical barriers are eroded (e.g. resistance to advertising); as these and other influences take effect they will encourage the extension of the marketing concept much more into the service sector. There are indications that the marketing concept is being increasingly accepted in the service sector particularly in industries where it was thought to be inappropriate or inapplicable.

3.31 Financial Services – an Industry in Transition

An illustration of a service industry which has adopted the marketing concept in recent years is the financial services sector.[12] It typifies an industry which has shifted towards greater customer orientation yet one where the characteristics of the services still present problems for the marketors in the industry. Firms in this industry face some interesting marketing challenges in the 1980s because of the nature of what is offered to customers, changes taking place in the industry and growing competition within it.

Individuals or corporate bodies have certain needs in relation to the money commodity. These needs which are met by those offering financial services broadly are:

advice;
deposits and savings;
loans;
leasing;
investment;
insurance;
payments and debt settlement;
factoring.

However, the institutions which offer the various services are not segregated into distinct groups, and the banks, finance companies, insurance companies, and others overlap in competing to offer financial

services. The financial services provided today are very different from what
they were ten years ago both for business and trade customers and in the
personal financial services field. In the personal sector, for example, the
market has broadened immensely from what was the situation at the end of
the Second World War. Payment methods, borrowing methods, investment methods, and insurance methods have all changed in response to
wider financial knowledge, the growth of disposable income, and cultural
changes (particularly the wider acceptance of consumer credit). Moreover,
such changes continue and have produced a need for marketing expertise
in many kinds of financial services markets. Market research, for example,
is being more extensively employed by financial services institutions as an
aid to management decision-making. This is not to suggest that marketing
is appropriate to all areas of the financial services market. There are still
some specialized areas (e.g. commodity trading) with clearly defined
groups of customers and competitors where marketing is still largely an
intuitive skill. There are other sectors too where personal and social
contacts remain of dominating importance. But in many financial services
markets there has been a shift from a technical and product orientation to a
stronger customer and profit orientation.

From the marketing point of view – and bearing in mind the problems
mentioned in Chapter 2 of generalizing too much about particular services
fields – there are some important characteristics of many financial services
which influence their marketing. Some of the more significant are:

(a) Intangibility

Financial services are intangible; they cannot be seen or touched or
smelled. The customer may be given something tangible to represent the
service like a credit card or an insurance policy, but what has been bought
is not a credit card but 'credit', not an insurance policy but 'protection' or
'security'. The tangible item given to the customer may 'say' something
about the customer or his aspirations (e.g. American Express cards or
Coutts' cheque books), but in the main financial services have little visual
appeal.

(b) Services are Performed

Products are produced whereas services are performed. Thus the quality of
a service derives not from its physical characteristics but from its
performance. A challenge facing the providers of financial services is to
ensure the consistency and quality of the service being performed even
when that service may be relatively routinized and standard; though of
course a number of financial services are of a non-routine and a non-
standard nature. Another feature of some financial services is that the
value of the service and the benefits derived are often as dependent upon
the skills, knowledge and participation of the buyer as of the seller.

(c) Need to Manage Demand

Some types of financial services organizations cannot store their product to meet fluctuations in demand, and there are no simple manufacturing changes that can be used to adapt supply of the services to demand fluctuations. Often, therefore, financial services organizations are concerned with managing demand. Indeed, where demand for the services provided is excessive, a strategy of 'demarketing' may be pursued where organizations may actively discourage customers on a permanent or a temporary basis. Other strategies may seek to synchronize supply and demand to even out irregularities in supply and demand.

(d) Essentiality versus Postponability

Some financial services are essential. For example, car drivers need to have minimal insurance cover before they can legally drive a motor vehicle. However, there may be discretion over the precise form of insurance. But equally some financial services are not essential and do not need to be bought. Their use or purchase may be inessential or, even where it becomes essential, may be delayed or postponed for some time.

There are other characteristics of some financial services too which may be important to their marketing. Some financial services (e.g. fixed term loans, mortgages and life insurance) imply some commitment where the purchaser is bound to some form of contract over time. Other financial services carry important risk factors from the purchaser's point of view (e.g. savings and investment accounts), and from the seller's point of view require emphasis upon safety, accessibility, and liquidity.

The above example illustrates the emphasis that service characteristics may have upon their purchase and therefore upon their sale. For example, where tangibility is an important characteristic then a great burden is placed upon the seller's promotional programme to describe the service. The sellers of services like life assurance and savings funds need to develop effective promotional strategies to reach their target markets adequately. Both direct (e.g. advertising) and indirect (e.g. word of mouth) methods of communication are required to sell the benefits of their services. Where fluctuating demand is an important characteristic of a financial service then product planning, pricing and promotion challenges are offered. Non-peak usage may be encouraged by heavier promotional expenditure and lower pricing or service charges; higher prices may be charged when demand is high.

3.32 Some Empirical Evidence on Marketing of Services

It is of course difficult to generalize, across such a large sector, whether organizations within it are, or are not, market oriented. Ultimately one has to rely upon empirical evidence. What one finds in practice through discussion with service executives and observation of the way some service organizations behave is that marketing is much more in evidence in some service sectors and some service organizations than in others.

As far as the published literature on the marketing of services is concerned there is of course a good deal of advice around for the beginning service marketor. It is normally of three kinds:

(*a*) arguments for adopting the marketing concept;
(*b*) advice on how to implement the marketing concept;
(*c*) identifying problems of implementing the marketing concept.

Arguments for Adopting the Marketing Concept

There are many exhortations to adopt the marketing concept covering a wide range of services. Examples include architects' services,[13] banks,[14] libraries,[15] and professional services in general[16].

Advice on How to Implement the Marketing Concept

Advice on how to implement the marketing concept is offered to many different kinds of service organizations. However marketors in fields like non-profit organizations,[17] professional services,[18] and tourist markets[19] are particularly well provided for.

Identifying Problems of Implementing the Marketing Concept

A wide range of problems are identified for those service organizations which adopt the marketing concept. These problems cover fields like professional services,[20] publicly-provided services,[21] and transport services[22].

In addition to the above there now exist a number of reported studies which have examined the status of marketing in particular service organizations or in a similar group of services. In North America in particular the status of marketing in banking,[23] the Canadian postal service,[24] and United States utilities has been examined[25]; the latter using a series of longitudinal studies.

The writer's own investigation of the application of marketing to the public provision of recreation and leisure services uncovered three interrelated reasons for a lack of market orientation in the forty-nine organizations surveyed.[26] These were as follows.

(a) The 'General' Constraints

Most of marketing's development and application has taken place in the United Kingdom in businesses during the past twenty years or so, and the available literature has, until recently, assumed economic growth. Only latterly has attention been given to equilibrium or declining situations. What we know about marketing, in other words, has been developed in profit-making contexts under economic conditions which in general differ from those of today.

The development of sport, leisure and recreation centres on the other hand has been a much more recent phenomenon coinciding with burgeoning public expenditure in the early 1970s, reorganization of local government in 1974 and 1975, and a general restraint on expenditures in the recreation and leisure sector since then. Thus the local authority situation in which marketing might have been applied has changed quite rapidly from one of expansion to one of restraint. The marketing literature has only recently begun to examine the implications of no growth and the adjustments that may therefore be required in marketing practices. In such a situation therefore, it is not surprising that local authorities have found difficulty in understanding and adapting marketing ideas to the conditions under which they have had to operate. Also the question can be raised of whether marketing is as relevant in times of scarcity and restrictions as it is in times of growth.

(b) The 'Institutional' Constraints

A second set of explanations stems from the nature of local authority management, personnel and organizations.

Most of the managers interviewed did not receive their 'schooling' in business situations. Typically they were ex-physical recreation teachers or specialists, ex-military training personnel or local authority employees who had worked in other departments within the local government field. They were largely untrained in management in general and marketing in particular, and a number seemed to be employed for their physical education skills rather than for their managerial skills.

Also local authorities in general operate differently from business. Profit as a measure of success rarely dominates thinking as it may so often do in business. The paradox is that while the local authority should serve the community it frequently does not. Providing for everybody's needs may make good political sense; it is unlikely to make sound marketing sense where segmentation is in vogue. Organizational structures too are so often extended and are rarely designed for a speedy response to the markeplace. Political interests cloud issues, the committee system can delay decision-making, local authorities interpret their sport, leisure and recreation responsibilities differently. Some interpret their field to cover a narrow range of mainly physical recreation services, while others interpret their field to cover a wide range of leisure and recreation services, which they often regard as 'social' services.

Perhaps then, there are basic problems in trying to apply marketing ideas without adaptation in and to institutions which are different in kind from business institutions, and which regard their consumers in different ways.

(c) The 'Services' Constraint

A third possible explanation is that what is being provided or sold by local authority recreation and leisure centres is a service rather than a product. While at a general level the differences between goods and services may not be substantial, at the specific level it does seem that differences do emerge and are important. In the same way that early texts in marketing were inadequate in explaining the distinctive differences involved in industrial marketing, so now are many existing works inadequate in explaining the distinctive differences involved in marketing specific services in profit and in non-profit-orientated contexts. The nature of what is being sold may thus account for the limited evidence of marketing's application in local authority settings.

The absence of substantial marketing practice within local authority recreation and leisure centres visited, *should not necessarily be seen as a criticism of them.* The fact that marketing was not being practised does not mean that it should have been practised. On the other hand the organization, politics and decision-making problems in local authorities could be considered as an excuse rather than a reason for marketing's limited adoption.

One of the earliest studies of marketing in United States service industries employed case studies, personal interviews, trade publications and trade associations.[27] The investigator concluded that many service organizations were not market orientated. Indeed there appeared to be three areas in which management had failed:

(*a*) they did not have a complete marketing approach;
(*b*) they failed either to recognize marketing problems, or to act when they realized a problem existed;
(*c*) there was little co-ordination of the marketing efforts of various groups with service firms.

The investigator concluded his report: 'marketing must no longer be the forgotten function as it has been for many service firms in the past'.

Macnamara's[28] later study of the status of the marketing concept in United States industry excluded services. This was left to be covered by another piece of empirical work surveying similarities and differences between services and manufacturing which was also undertaken in the United States.[29] As yet there are no similar reported studies for the United Kingdom. The results of the United States survey suggest that there are many similar kinds of marketing activities undertaken in both types of organization. With respect to the product or service offer, for example, both kinds of organizations undertook the activities of:

determining which new product or services to offer;
estimating the size of the market for new product/services possibilities;
establishing written short-term goals and policies;
establishing written long-term goals and policies;
defining specific target groups within the total market;
determining the uniqueness of products/services offered by the firm for potential customers;
periodic re-examination of goals, policies and procedures;
developing an overall marketing plan for the firm.

Similar patterns of activity were reported in the pricing area, in advertising and promotion activities. There were differences in detail between the types of companies sampled and in particular there were differences in terms of where the activities examined were undertaken (e.g. in the marketing department or in some other internal or external department). The authors of the survey suggested the following major findings.

Service firms were:

less likely to have marketing mix activities carried out in the marketing department;
less likely to perform analysis in the offering area;
more likely to handle advertising internally than go to outside agencies;
less likely to have an overall sales plan;
less likely to develop sales training programmes;
less likely to use marketing research firms and marketing consultants;
less likely to spend as much on marketing when expressed as a percentage of gross sales.

On the other hand there appeared to be no significant differences between service and manufacturing firms in their approaches to goals, policies, audits and overall plans for their offerings. What emerged in fact was a pattern of similarities in terms of activities reportedly undertaken although:

the marketing function was less structured in service companies;
marketing activities were less likely to be assigned to marketing departments alone;
marketing activities in service firms were more fragmented than in manufacturing firms. This could make control of the marketing function more difficult and could reduce the effectiveness of the total marketing effort.

But the suggestion by the authors that service firms were less market-orientated than manufacturing firms is open to dispute.

3.4 Conclusion

Over the last few years greater interest has been shown by managers in the services sector in the relevance and applicability of marketing concepts to their particular fields. This chapter suggests that marketing does have relevance to the services sector but that our knowledge of the status of marketing in the services field is patchy and still developing. At this stage general guidelines only are available to those marketing services. In the light of what we do know from existing empirical evidence two factors are important:

(*a*) Frameworks that have been used in the past to generalize across all services may not be of specific value to operational marketors of services because of the variety of processes and activities embraced by the designation of 'services'. Marketors need to select and adapt from what is available those schemes that are relevant to their particular service industry. This consideration should be borne in mind when reading future chapters.

(*b*) It may also be of value to focus upon the similarities and the commonalities of product and service marketing as much as upon the supposed differences. Some product marketing guidelines are generalizable to 'service' situations.

For example, when a marketing strategy is being developed for an organization in the service sector the same factors have to be considered as in marketing tangibles. Questions like who are the customers? What benefits are they seeking? How best can they be served?

The next chapter considers some of the similarities and differences involved in forming a marketing strategy and in developing a marketing mix for a service organization.

3.5 Summary

1 Managers in most kinds of organizations can use the marketing concept as a general guide to their thinking and their actions.
2 There is limited evidence on the status of marketing in the service sector. Much of the empirical evidence is derived from North American Studies.
3 Studies are available in only a limited range of service settings.

Questions for Discussion

1 What is the marketing concept?
2 What is the difference between the marketing concept and marketing management?
3 What factors may interfere with the implementation of a market orientation in a service organization of your choice?
4 What criteria would you use to assess how market orientated a service organization might be?
5 Give three examples of market-orientated service organizations. What do they do to be market orientated?
6 Give three examples of product-orientated service organizations. What do they do to be product orientated?
7 What steps should a service organization take to implement the marketing concept?
8 'Traditionally marketors of services have not been market orientated'. What evidence is there for this statement?
9 'The marketing concept cannot be applied to service marketing.' Discuss.
10 Why is a market orientation desirable for a service organization? In what circumstances is a market orientation inappropriate?

References and Notes

1 This section is based on the author's paper 'The Marketing of Services', *Managerial Finance*, Vol. 5, No. 3, 1980, pp. 223–31.

2 Christopher, M. G., Kennedy, S. H., McDonald, M. M. and Wills, G. S. C. *Effective Marketing Management*, Gower, Aldershot, 1980.
3 This section is based on Levitt, E., 'Marketing and the Corporate Purpose', in Backman, J. and Czepial, J. A. *Changing Marketing Strategies in a New Economy*, Bobbs-Merrill, Indianapolis, 1977, p. 27.
4 Stanton, W. J. *Fundamentals of Marketing*, McGraw-Hill, New York, 1981, p. 446.
5 Donnelly, J. H. 'Marketing intermediaries in channels of distribution for services', *Journal of Marketing*, Vol. 40, No. 1, Jan. 1976, pp. 55–70.
6 Eiglier, P. 'A note on the commonality of problems in Service Management: a field study', in Eiglier, P., *et al.* 'Marketing Consumer Services: New Insights', Marketing Science Institute, Boston, 1977.
7 Gronroos, C. 'An applied service marketing theory', Working Paper No. 57, Swedish School of Economics and Business Administration, Helsinki, 1980.
8 Shostack, Lynn C. 'Breaking free from product marketing', *Journal of Marketing*, Vol. 41, No. 2, April 1977, pp. 73–80.
9 See, for example, Cannon, T. *Basic Marketing: Principles and Practice*, Holt, Rinehart & Winston, New York, 1980.
10 Rathmell, J. M. *Marketing in the Service Sector*, Winthrop, Cambridge, Mass. 1974.
11 Wilson, A. *The Marketing of Professional Services*, McGraw-Hill, London, 1972.
12 For a recent report on this see Watson, I. 'The adoption of Marketing by the English Clearing Banks', in Turnbull, P. and Lewis, B. (eds) *The Marketing of Bank Services, European Journal of Marketing*, Vol. 16, No. 3, 1982, pp. 23–30.
13 Garratt, B., *et al.* 'Marketing Architectural Services', *The Architects Journal*, 12 March 1980, pp. 545–8; 26 March 1980, p. 639; 16 April 1980, p. 783.
14 Waterworth, D. 'Banks behind bars', *Marketing*, November 1973, pp. 65–7, 84.
15 Bellardo, T. and Waldhart, T. J. 'Marketing products and services in academic libraries', *Libri*, Vol. 27, No. 3, Sept. 1977, pp. 181–94.
16 Kotler, P. and Connor, R. A. 'Marketing Professional Services', *Journal of Marketing*, Vol. 41, No. 1, Jan. 1977, pp. 71–6.
17 Kotler, P. *Marketing for Non-Profit Organisations*, Prentice-Hall, Englewood Cliffs, 1982.
18 See, for example, Bachner, J. P. and Khosla, N. K. *Marketing and Promotion for Design Professionals*, R. E. Krieger, Huntingdon, N.Y. 1981: Mahon, J. J., *The Marketing of Professional Accounting Services*, J. Wiley and Sons, New York, 1978.
19 See for example Wahab, S., Crampon, L. J. and Rothfield, L. M. *Tourism Marketing*, Tourism International Press, 1976.
20 Dornstein, M. 'Some imperfections in the market exchanges for professional and executive services', *The American Journal of Economics and Sociology*, April, 1977, Vol. 36, No. 2, pp. 113–28.

21 Houston, F. S. and Homans, R. E. 'Public Agency Marketing – Pitfalls and Problems', *MSU Business Topics*, Vol. 25 (Summer) 1977, pp. 36–40.

22 Hovell, P. J. 'Applying the marketing concept to public transport planning', *British Journal of Marketing*, Vol. 3, Autumn, 1969, pp. 152–63.

23 Stall, R. B. 'Marketing in a service industry', *Atlanta Economic Review*, Vol. 28, No. 3, 1978, pp. 15–18.

24 Barnhill, J. A. 'Developing Marketing orientation in a Postal Service', Optimum No. 3, 1974, pp. 36–47.

25 Warshaw, M. R. 'Effective marketing – key to public utility growth', *University of Michigan Business Review*, Nov. 1962, pp. 16–20 and the later follow up studies 'Re-appraising Public Utility Marketing', *University of Michigan Business Review*, May 1976, pp. 18–22.

26 This section is based on the author's paper 'Marketing in Local Authority Sport, Leisure and Recreation Centres', Local Government Studies, July/Aug. 1979, pp. 31–43.

27 Johnson, E. M. 'An Introduction to the problems of Service Marketing Management', The Bureau of Economic and Business Research, University of Delaware, 1964.

28 McNamara, C. P. 'The present status of the Marketing Concept', *Journal of Marketing*, Vol. 36, Jan. 1972, pp. 50–7.

29 George, W. R. and Barksdale, H. C. 'Marketing activities in the service industries', *Journal of Marketing*, Vol. 38, Oct. 1974, pp. 65–70.

4. *MARKETING STRATEGY AND THE MARKETING MIX IN SERVICE MARKETING*

4.1 Introduction

Marketors in service organizations who adopt the marketing concept outlined in the previous chapter have to make the idea operational. They have to put marketing into practice. It was indicated in Section 3.2 that organizations which attempt to service customers' needs would be unlikely to do so by instinct or by accident. A more sensible way would be to adopt a systematic approach to serving customers. Part of this more systematic approach would be the use of the marketing planning process defined as 'the planned application of marketing resources to achieve marketing objectives'.[1]

In outline the marketing planning process comprises the following steps:[2]

Gathering information on the external environment and the organization internally;

Identifying the major strengths and weaknesses of the organization and opportunities and threats externally (SWOT);

Formulating basic assumptions about key determinants of marketing success;

Laying down market objectives for the organization, based on the information gathered, the SWOT analysis and the assumptions made and formulating strategies;

Devising detailed plans and programmes to accomplish objectives;

Measuring progress towards achievement of objectives, reviewing and amending the plan as necessary.

Figure 4.1 illustrates this process showing the main steps involved.

In practice the content of marketing plans will vary considerably in terms of their detail and their sophistication. There has been much interest in marketing planning in recent years and a wide variety of suitable material is now available to guide the marketor interested in adopting marketing planning procedures.[2] The content of any specific marketing plan ultimately will be influenced by the key questions and issues the planner addresses (e.g. about markets; about current and future resources; about environmental changes). Whatever its content, however, a key element in any planning will be the development of an effective marketing strategy. This topic is the concern of this chapter.

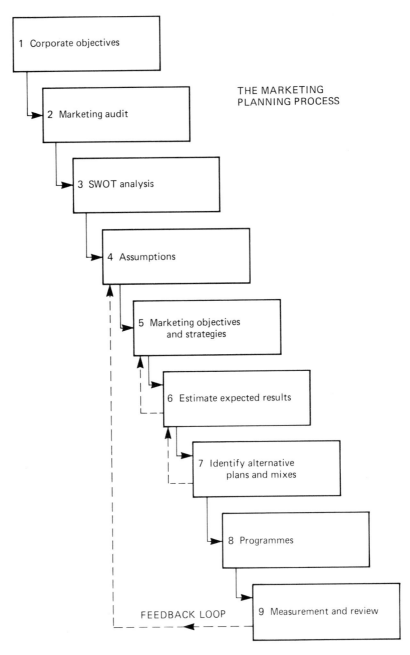

Figure 4.1 The Marketing Planning Process

Source: McDonald, M. and Gattorna, J. 'Marketing: An Introduction for Accountants', Institute of Chartered Accountants, Milton Keynes, 1980, p. 77

4.2 Developing a Marketing Strategy

Developing a 'marketing strategy' in the limited sense in which the term is used here involves two related tasks.[3] These are:

- (*a*) selecting a target market or target markets in which the enterprise is to operate; and,
- (*b*) developing a 'marketing mix' for each target market selected.

4.21 A Target Market

This consists of a group of customers sharing some similar characteristics towards which an enterprise may direct its products and services. Once a target market has been identified, the marketing process involves close examination of the target population. It may be divided into groups or 'market segments' along some further relevant dimensions or characteristics which enable more detailed and sensitive analysis of the target market that is being served (e.g. income, spending habits, location).

4.22 A Marketing Mix

This is the set of controllable elements the organization can use to influence customer response (e.g. price, promotion). A major task of marketing management in an enterprise is to blend together these elements of the marketing mix in such a way that they fulfil the needs of selected target markets. The blending process has to take account of many uncontrollable variables. Typically these uncontrollable variables would include the resources and objectives of the enterprise, the political, legal, social, cultural and economic environment, and the actions of competitors.

4.3 Marketing Strategy and Services

It has been suggested that the strategic management of a service business is different from a non-service business (i.e. the total process of selecting and implementing a corporate strategy).[4] It is further suggested that marketing strategy planning and marketing strategies themselves are different for service organizations. Of course any marketing strategy is unique anyway because it is specific to a particular organization, whether it is marketing services or not. Having said that marketing strategies of service organizations may contain significant differences from those of other organizations. Certainly some unique aspects of services that give direction to retail service marketing strategy formulation are:

- (*a*) the dominantly intangible nature of a service may make the consumers' choice of competitive offerings more difficult;
- (*b*) where the producer of the service is inseparable from the service itself, this may localize service marketing and offer the consumer more restricted choice;
- (*c*) the perishability of services prevents storage of the product itself and may also add to risk and uncertainty in service marketing.[5]

It is generally agreed though that the *process* of marketing strategy formulation is the same for all products (tangible or intangible).[6] Differences, however, may arise in the analytical stage before proceeding to develop a marketing strategy when managers have to resolve a number of questions. The questions are fairly common but the answers for service organizations are often unique.[4] Some examples of these questions are;[7]

4.31 Do we Understand Fully the Type of Service Business we are in?

In Chapter 2 it was indicated that services can be classified in many ways. (*see* Section 2.34) and that classification and description of the business is initially a useful tool for developing marketing strategies. Unlike those organizations where the essentially tangible nature of the product may provide a base on which to build an appropriate business description, the question may be more difficult to answer for abstract intangibles.

An example of one way of classifying service businesses is on the basis of whether they are 'equipment based' or 'people based'.[4] According to this classification 'equipment-based' businesses may be automated (e.g. car washes) monitored by relatively unskilled operators (e.g. dry cleaners) or operated by skilled operators (e.g. computers). 'People-based' businesses in turn may use skilled (e.g. appliance repair), unskilled (e.g. cleaning services) or professional labour (e.g. accountants). Positioning a business in this scheme depends upon answers to two questions:

(*a*) How is the service rendered?
(*b*) What type of equipment or people render the service?

Complex service businesses may be placed in a number of positions on this spectrum. Using this example some implications for people based businesses might be to build upon the buyer–seller relationship as a deliberate strategy. It might be possible to strengthen the relationship through deliberate and sustained attention to the personal element in the business relationship. This may be particularly important with professional services for example.[8]

4.32 Who are our Customers: How can we Identify them; and What Benefits are they Seeking?

An important step in strategy development is the identification of target markets, understanding the needs of customers and the bases they use in the choices they make. Clearly these problems are common to all market-orientated organizations. Service organizations' problems though may be different. For example there are many theoretical explanations of consumer behaviour but few models explain the basis of consumer-decision-making and choice for services.[9] Some important insights have been given for specific kinds of services. For example the purchaser of a professional service buys the capabilities of the seller. Therefore he can be expected to evaluate the behaviour and characteristics of the manager of the service firm or its representatives when making a purchase decision. He will also evaluate the firm itself, its location, reputation and appearance.[8]

Service marketors need to develop fuller and richer understanding in this complex and under researched area. So far there is little hard evidence for managers to use although there are two recent significant developments.

Work on Perceived Differences between Goods and Services

On the evidence of a few small-scale studies consumers do seem able to perceive differences that exist between goods and services across many of the differentiating characteristics proposed in the services marketing literature.[10]

Work on the Perceived Differences between Services

Exploratory research undertaken in this area has tried to establish whether there are broad dimensions which apply across services but which consumers may use in choosing between services (e.g. amount of human contact). Initial results which considered a number of consumer services (petrol retailing, meals at quick service restaurants, retail banking services, snack and beverage services in hotels and motels, baggage services on airlines, and sale of travellers' cheques) do suggest that consumers distinguish between services across some of the dimensions used in the study. The dimensions were:

total amount of time required;
customer control over the situation;
amount of effort required by the customer;
customer dependence upon others;
efficiency of service;
amount of human contact involved;
risk of something going wrong.[11]

Further work of both kinds would contribute greater insights for service marketing strategy formulation.

4.33 How can we Defend our Business from Competitors

Every service organization has to consider how to enter a market and then build and protect its competitive position. There are a number of ways in which distinctive positions can be developed and maintained. They are often more difficult to accomplish in service businesses because of the absence of a strong tangible core to the service offer. A key way to building a strong competitive position is through 'service differentiation' which creates a clear image of the service organization and its services in the eyes of consumers and can lead to distinctive positioning in the market (i.e. the consumers' notion or images of the comparative positions of service products and service organizations in the marketplace). Strong competitive positions can be developed by building barriers to competitive action by various means. Examples include developing a 'reputation' through the kind of service provided in a people-based service or through using proprietary technology in an equipment-based service.

4.34 How can we Obtain more Cost-efficient Operations?

Many labour intensive service operations have attempted to improve the efficiency of their operations through mechanization, specialization, use of technologies and the use of systems approaches in service design (*see* Chapter 16). The problems of accomplishing more cost-effective operations in services can be more substantial than in manufacturing. For example, it is possible to use the traditional solution of substituting capital for labour in some service organizations but not all; particularly those where the human element of service is an important component of what is provided. The strategic challenges here are often of a different kind for service marketors.

4.35 What Efforts will be used to Develop and Test new Service Offerings?

Product planning and development is an important problem in a service organization because of the difficulties there may be in building a defendable competitive position. This is particularly so with highly intangible services which are more abstract in nature. Product planning is also important because of the need for service organizations to provide a balanced range of services for customers.

   In general, research and development and product planning are not as well developed in service organizations as in manufacturing (*see* Chapter 7). There is though no reason why a structured approach to research and development in service organizations should not be adopted. There are difficulties of course in testing, developing and specifying services – particularly people-based services but so often there is a lack of real innovation in services and a great deal of imitation (e.g. in airlines and banking). Strategic challenges for service organizations include how to introduce more systematic new service development procedures.[12] Also how to design highly intangible and novel services.[13]

   Service development may be accomplished through acquisition. An associated question therefore is whether acquisition is an appropriate strategy to adopt. This is dependent on the type of business under consideration. Different criteria may be required compared with acquisitions in say the manufacturing sector:

> 'Growth through acquisition in service businesses is a risky proposition, but the risk varies. It is generally riskier as one moves down the spectrum toward people based businesses, and within people based businesses the risk increases when the service is provided by professionals or highly skilled persons. Any company that wants to acquire service businesses must make sure that it can attract and keep skilled service-oriented managers to run them.'[4]

4.36 How do Decisions about Marketing Strategy influence Decisions in other parts of the Service Organization? And how do Strategic Decisions in other parts of a Service Organization influence Marketing Strategy?

Marketing strategies, production strategies and personnel strategies cannot be separated from each other in service organizations. The trade-offs between decisions made in the different parts of the organization and their interactive effects must be understood. Often these inter-relationships between different functional parts of an organization are stronger for services.

For example, attempts to improve production efficiency in a service business by introducing equipment in place of people may have a harmful effect upon marketing efficiency. Customers may interpret such a change, with perhaps a decrease in the amount of personal service given, as a reflection of a general decline in standards of service. The effects may go deeper. Customers may interpret the change as a change in the 'nature' of the service itself. They may re-assess the extent to which the service now meets their needs. Functional strategies in service organizations are often more closely enmeshed. Production decisions for example often have marketing effects – and vice versa.

When these and other critical questions have been answered the service organization has to consider another stage in its marketing strategy, that is the formulation of its marketing mix.

4.4 The Marketing Mix

An essential element of any marketing strategy is the marketing mix. The process of mix formulation and balancing is unique to each organization and product. As in marketing planning there is nothing distinctive about the process, as such, for services. Where there does appear to be a difference for services though is in the elements that make up the marketing mix.

The utility of the inherited marketing mix framework for service business situations has been subjected to criticism in recent years by writers on service marketing management. One author suggests that service firms may need a new approach to the marketing mix.[14] Another that the conventional idea of the marketing mix should be dumped altogether for service businesses.[15] In this section the concept of the marketing mix is re-examined and adaptations to it are suggested for its use in services marketing management situations.

4.41 The Origins of the Mix*

The origins of the concept of the marketing mix are described by Borden in his classic paper.[16] He attributes the phrase to a paragraph in a research bulletin on the subject of the Management of Marketing Costs written in 1948 by an associate James Culliton. In his study of marketing costs Culliton referred to the business executive as a 'decider', an 'artist', 'a mixer of ingredients'. Borden writes: 'I liked his idea of calling a marketing executive a "mixer of ingredients", one who is constantly engaged in fashioning creatively a mix of marketing procedures and policies in his efforts to produce a profitable enterprise.'

*This section is based on a paper given by the author 'The Marketing Mix for Services Marketing', at Lancaster University, Marketing Educators Group Conference, July 1982.

Culliton's 1948 study was his second attempt to find out, amongst other things, whether there were any operating uniformities within sampled companies that would give helpful common expense figures. It was felt that such common expense figures could have significance as standards to guide management. Borden however, indicates that in the Culliton study and in an even earlier Culliton study (the results of which were published in 1929) no uniformities emerged. Neither did they from his own work on advertising nor during the process of gathering marketing cases at the Harvard Business School in that period. He commented:

> '. . . there was a wide diversity in cost ratios among any classifications of firms which were set up; no common figures were found that had much value. This was true whether companies were grouped according to similarity in product lines, amount of sales, territorial extent of operations, or other bases of classification.'

The absence of operating uniformities did not prevent Borden from recognizing that while the particular blend of marketing policies and programmes might be unique to each organization, and while the forces that influence a particular firm might have particular effects, it was nevertheless possible to:

> '. . . proceed from a realization of the existence of a variety of "marketing mixes" to the development of a concept that would comprehend not only this variety but also the market forces that cause managements to produce a variety of mixes. It is the problems raised by these forces that lead marketing managers to exercise their wits in devising mixes or programs which they hope will give a profitable business operation.'

This led him to develop a list of elements making up the marketing mix together with a list of market forces bearing on the marketing mix of manufacturers. The list of elements that Borden used in his original description of the marketing mix is shown in Exhibit 4.1.

Exhibit 4.1
Elements of the Marketing Mix of Manufacturers

1 *Product planning.* Policies and procedures relating to
   (a) product lines to be offered – qualities, design, etc.
   (b) the markets to sell – whom, where, when and in what quantity.
   (c) new product policy – research and development program.
2 *Pricing.* Policies and procedures relating to
   (a) the level of prices to adopt.
   (b) the specific prices to adopt (odd-even, etc.).
   (c) price policy – one price or varying price, price maintenance, use of list prices, etc.
   (d) the margins to adopt – for company; for the trade.
3 *Branding.* Policies and procedures relating to
   (a) selection of trade marks.
   (b) brand policy – individualized or family brand.
   (c) sale under private brand or unbranded.
4 *Channels of Distribution.* Policies and procedures relating to
   (a) the channels to use between plant and consumer.

(*b*) the degree of selectivity among wholesalers and retailers.

(*c*) efforts to gain cooperation of the trade.

5 *Personal Selling.* Policies and procedures relating to

(*a*) The burden to be placed on personal selling and the methods to be employed in (i) the manufacturer's organization, (ii) the wholesale segment of the trade, (iii) the retail segment of the trade.

6 *Advertising.* Policies and procedures relating to

(*a*) the amount to spend – i.e., the burden to be placed on advertising.

(*b*) the copy platform to adopt (i) product image desired, (ii) corporate image desired.

(*c*) the mix of advertising – to the trade; through the trade – to consumers.

7 *Promotions.* Policies and procedures relating to

(*a*) the burden to place on special selling plans or devices directed at or through the trade.

(*b*) the form of these devices for consumer promotions, for trade promotions.

8 *Packaging.* Policies and procedures relating to

(*a*) formulation of package and label.

9 *Display.* Policies and procedures relating to

(*a*) the burden to be put on display to help effect sales.

(*b*) the methods to adopt to secure display.

10 *Servicing.* Policies and procedures relating to

(*a*) providing service needed.

11 *Physical Handling.* Policies and procedures relating to

(*a*) warehousing.

(*b*) transportation.

(*c*) inventories.

12 *Fact Finding and Analysis.* Policies and procedures relating to

(*a*) the securing analysis, and use of facts in marketing operations.

Source: Borden, N. H. 'The Concept of the Marketing Mix', in Schwartz, G. *Science in Marketing*, J. Wiley and Sons, Chichester, 1965, pp. 386–97

In Exhibit 4.2 are shown the forces 'that bear on the marketing operation of a firm and to which the marketing manager must adjust in his search for a mix . . . that can be successful.'

Exhibit 4.2
Market forces bearing on the Marketing Mix of Manufacturers

1 *Consumers' Buying Behaviour*: as determined by

(*a*) their motivation in purchasing.

(*b*) their buying habits.

(c) their living habits.

(d) their environment (present and future as revealed by trends, for environment influences consumers' attitudes toward products and their use of them).

(e) their number (i.e., how many).

(f) their buying power.

2 *The Trade's Behaviour.* Wholesalers' and retailers' behaviour, as influenced by

(a) their motivations.

(b) their structure, practices, and attitudes.

(c) trends in structure and procedures that portend change.

3 *Competitors' Position and Behaviour:* as influenced by

(a) industry structure and the firm's relation thereto (i) size and strength of competitors, (ii) number of competitors and degree of industry concentration, and (iii) indirect competition – i.e., competition from other products.

(b) relation of supply to demand – oversupply or undersupply.

(c) product choices offered consumers by the industry: (i) in quality, (ii) in price, and (iii) in service.

(d) degree to which competitors compete on price versus non-price bases.

(e) competitors' motivations and attitudes – their likely response to the actions of other firms.

(f) trends technological and social, portending change in supply and demand.

4 *Governmental Behaviour – Controls over Marketing.*

(a) regulations over products.

(b) regulations over pricing.

(c) regulations over competitive practices.

(d) regulations over advertising and promotional methods.

Source: Borden, N. H. 'The Concept of the Marketing Mix', in Schwartz, G. *Science in Marketing*, J. Wiley and Sons, Chichester, 1965, pp. 386–97

Borden's original list of marketing mix elements has since been re-grouped and represented by others. One of the most popular frameworks in the marketing literature is presented by McCarthy[16] as the four 'P's'

Product

Place

Promotion

Price.

McCarthy's idea of the marketing mix, which emphasizes the inter-relationship between the elements of which it is composed has become one of the most widely used simplifications of Borden's original idea. It usually forms the heart of the structure of most marketing management textbooks.

4.42 Adapting the Marketing Mix for Services

In his original description of the marketing mix Borden recognized that others may assemble a different set of elements. What is interesting to note is how few marketors appear to have done so. His original version and the abridged McCarthy version have been employed irrespective of content.[17] Yet it does seem that Borden's original scheme may need to be adapted if it is to be usefully employed in service marketing situations.

There are three reasons why adaptation is required for services:

(*a*) the original marketing mix was developed for manufacturing companies;
(*b*) there is patchy empirical evidence that marketing practitioners in the service sector find the marketing mix may not be inclusive enough for their needs;
(*c*) there is growing evidence that the dimensions in the marketing mix may not be comprehensive enough for service marketing.

The Original Marketing Mix was developed for Manufacturing Companies

The original list developed by Borden was derived from research, cases and studies of manufacturing organizations, that is organizations producing products (i.e. tangibles). The elements that he describes in his marketing mix relate specifically to manufacturing. They are not specifically listed for services organizations. They do not necessarily accommodate services organizations where the characteristic of intangibility of the service product may be so fundamental. As item 11 in Exhibit 4.1 shows, for example, the notion of tangibility is assumed by the inclusion of 'physical handling' with its associated policies and procedures relating to warehousing, transportation and inventories. In service marketing while such policies and procedures may be appropriate they are more likely to apply to the physical items that facilitate services marketing rather than to the service products themselves. Also item 5 (a) (i) refers specifically to 'manufacturers'. It does not include 'non-manufacturers' like those providing or performing services.

The list developed by Borden was also primarily intended for situations in which manufacturing organizations were operating; by implication, profit motives were paramount. In the service sector of course many organizations (e.g. public services), do not have profit objectives as conventionally used in manufacturing settings. (The Price element of the marketing mix so often fits unsatisfactorily in such cases.) Also many public sector organizations excluded in Borden's analysis may be typically involved in the performance of services (e.g. health, education, leisure), rather than in the production of goods.

There is patchy Empirical Evidence that Marketing Practitioners in the Service Sector find the Marketing Mix may not be inclusive enough for their Needs

A number of studies are available which indicate that managers in service organizations do perceive and can identify a number of distinctive differences they have to cope with compared with managers of goods organizations.[18, 19] Common examples of such differences are:

problems of maintaining the quality of a service;
people who 'perform' the service may be part of the 'product';
services cannot be patented;
service firms cannot inventory the service product itself.

Some of these differences are reflected in the interviews reported in *Advertising Age*[20] where four managers with experience in marketing both services and packaged goods commented on what they saw as some distinctive differences. Selected extracts include:
    On quality:

'A major difference between product (goods) marketing and service marketing is that we can't control the quality of our product as well as a P & G control engineer on a production line. . . . When you buy a box of Tide, you can reasonably be 99 and 44/100ths percent sure that this stuff will work to get your clothes clean. When you buy a Holiday Inn room, you're sure at some lesser percentage that it will work to give you a good night's sleep without any hassle, or people banging on the walls, and all the bad things that can happen to you in a hotel.'

'When I was working on products I knew exactly what the product was made of and, as a consequence, what it would do. . . . In a service business, you find that you're dealing with something that is primarily delivered by people – to people. Your people are as much part of your product in the consumer's mind as any other attribute of that service. People's performance day in and day out fluctuates up and down. Therefore, the level of consistency that you can count on and try to communicate to the consumer is not a certain thing.'

    On people who deliver the service:

'(In the Postal Service) we came to the conclusion that we could not conduct over-the-counter marketing until we had wholesale restructuring and training of the over-the-counter customer service situation. We found that we were driving people to the counter and then driving them away because clerks were not fully aware of the product line. . . . In package goods marketing, the marketing management group doesn't have anything to do with managing checkout clerks. . . . What product (goods) marketing people going into the service marketing environment must know and must learn is the concept of customer service and customer interface.'

'You have to sell the benefits of a service to the operations group, too. In a package goods company, when you say (to manufacturing) we need X quantity of Y by September 1st, and we want the fragrance permutations to be 1–2–3, that's a direct order. If you were to adopt the same mentality in financial services, you would be amazed how many times the support system would be down or nonfunctioning. You somehow have to get that side of the house, particularly, to think from a marketing standpoint and not just internal efficiency.'

On the marketing mix:
'The number of variables in the marketing mix is normally larger in a service business than for a stable product. The real intangible is the human element which, with the best will in the world, most of us cannot control to anywhere near the same degrees that a product manager controls the formulation of a beauty soap, for example.'

Much other evidence suggests that practitioners in services situations face somewhat similar problems which require the adaptation of marketing approaches.

There is Growing Evidence that the Dimensions in the Marketing Mix are not Comprehensive enough for Services Marketing

There now exists enough evidence to suggest that the marketing mix needs to be adapted for service marketing. For example, people who perform or deliver services are not taken account of in the existing framework and setting, atmosphere and layout may be important influences in the purchase of some services. There are in fact a range of elements the traditional marketing mix framework does not accommodate.[14,15]

4.5 A Revised Marketing Mix for Services

The three criticisms given in the previous section suggest that a revised marketing mix framework for services marketing management may be required. Service marketors should not continue to use unquestioningly the inherited framework derived from Borden and McCarthy. However, more empirical work of the kind undertaken by Borden is required before the elements of any revised marketing mix framework for services can be established. The marketing mix framework though is a guide to action, not a theoretical idea.

In the absence of such an empirically based scheme the modifications and expansions to the existing marketing mix framework presented by Booms and Bitner[21] provide, intuitively at least, a more satisfactory guide for service marketors. Their modified and expanded marketing mix for services consists of seven elements. An adapted version of their idea is shown in Exhibit 4.3. The seven elements in this marketing mix for services are:

(*a*) Product
(*b*) Price
(*c*) Place
(*d*) Promotion
(*e*) People
(*f*) Physical evidence
(*g*) Process

Exhibit 4.3
The marketing mix for services

Product	Price	Place	Promotion	People	Physical Evidence	Process
Range	Level	Location	Advertising	Personnel:	Environment	Policies
Quality	Discounts	Accessibility	Personal selling	Training	Furnishings	Procedures
Level	Allowances	Distribution	Sales promotion	Discretion	Colour	Mechanization
Brand name	Commissions	channels	Publicity	Commitment	Layout	Employee discretion
Service line	Payment terms	Distribution	Public relations	Incentives	Noise level	Customer involvement
Warranty	Customer's	coverage		Appearance	Facilitating	Customer direction
After sales	perceived			Interpersonal	Goods	Flow of activities
service	value			behaviour	Tangible clues	
	Quality/price			Attitudes		
	Differentiation			Other customers:		
				Behaviour		
				Degree of		
				involvement		
				Customer/		
				customer		
				contact		

Source: Derived from Booms, B. H. and Bitner, M. J. 'Marketing Strategies and Organisation Structures for Service Firms' in Donnelly, J. and George, W. R. (Eds), *Marketing of Services*, American Marketing Association, Chicago, 1981

This revised marketing mix for services contains three additional elements (people, physical evidence and process). These are not brought out so explicitly in Borden's original work nor accommodated in most contemporary schemes. These seven elements could be at the heart of many service organizations' marketing programmes. Ignoring any of them could influence the success or failure of the overall programme.

The marketing concept dictates that marketing decisions should be based upon customer needs and wants. Buyers purchase goods and services to satisfy their needs and wants. Thus when a buyer engages in a market transaction he perceives a bundle of benefits and satisfactions to be derived from that transaction. However he does not usually divide the market offering into its component parts. From the sellers' viewpoint however the market offering can be divided into its component parts. The marketing mix is the convenient means of organizing all the variables controlled by the marketor that influence transactions in the marketplace. It is a 'checklist approach' where marketors attempt to list and organize the variables under their control which may be important in influencing transactions in the marketplace.

The formulation process of marketing mixes in services markets is much the same as in other types of markets. Typically this involves:

(*a*) separating the offering into its components or sub mixes;
(*b*) co-ordinating the sub mixes into the marketing mix.

The specific marketing mix adopted by a particular organization will of course vary according to circumstances (e.g. level of demand, age of service being offered). The marketing mix process then is a constant one of fashioning and reshaping the component elements in response to changing market circumstances and needs. Inevitably there is much overlap and interaction between the various components of a marketing mix. Decisions cannot be made on one component of the mix without considering their impact upon the other components. Also the precise elements and their importance within any marketing mix at any one point in time will vary. The outline that follows therefore indicates some of the key areas to which marketing managers need to devote their attention in formulating their marketing mixes for services markets. It is illustrative not comprehensive. Service organizations will almost certainly need to adapt it in their strategy planning. Each element is considered in more detail in subsequent chapters.

4.51 Product

The service product requires consideration of the range of services provided, the quality of services provided and the level of services provided. Attention will also need to be given to matters like the use of branding, warranties and after-sale service. The service product mix of

such elements can vary considerably and may be seen in comparisons of
service range between a small local building society and one of the largest
in the country; or between a steak bar offering a limited menu range and a
four star hotel offering a wide range of meals (*see* Chapters 6 and 7).

4.52 Price

Price considerations include levels of prices, discounts, allowances and
commissions, terms of payment and credit. Price may also play a part in
differentiating one service from another and therefore the customers'
perceptions of value obtained from a service and the interaction of price
and quality are important considerations in many service price sub mixes
(*see* Chapter 8).

4.53 Place

The location of the service providers and their accessibility are important
factors in services marketing. Accessibility relates not just to physical
accessibility but to other means of communication and contact. Thus the
types of distribution channels used (e.g. travel agents) and their coverage
are linked to the crucial issue of service accessibility (*see* Chapter 10).

4.54 Promotion

Promotion includes the various methods of communicating with markets
whether through advertising, personal selling activities, sales promotion
activities and other direct forms of publicity, and indirect forms of
communication like public relations (*see* Chapter 9).

These are the traditional mix elements. Service marketors may also need
to include more explicitly elements like people, physical evidence, and
process.

4.55 People

Borden accommodates people in his original idea of the marketing mix
only under personal selling. What his guidelines fail to include is at least
two further aspects of the 'people' element.

(*a*) First that people who perform a production or operational role in
service organizations (like clerks in a bank or chefs in a steak
house), may be as much a part of and contribute to the service
product (as perceived by customers) as the more obvious sales staff.
A feature of many service organizations is that operational staff
may occupy the dual role of both performing a service and selling a
service. How service performers operate in a service organization
can be just as critical to the selling of the service as conventional
selling activity. As Brundage and Marshall[22] suggest:

'In the service organisation, the distinction between selling and service delivery is
blurred. . . . In other words, the service itself is also the product and all functions visible
to the customer in delivering the service are part of the service offering – the perceived

product. Because the customer frequently has access to all parts of the service organisation, operations, product, sales and marketing personnel are deeply involved in "selling" the service. . . .'

In that sense marketing management is involved in the operational aspects of performance and therefore in influencing and controlling certain dimensions of the relationship between customer and staff. The critical role of staff particularly in what Chase[23] calls 'high contact' service operations means that marketing management has interests in the areas of employee selection, training, motivation, and control. Davidson[24] suggests that 'In a service industry the secret of success is recognition that customer contact personnel are the key people in the organisation.'

(b) An associated aspect in certain service operations is the relationship between customers. That is a customer's perceptions of the quality of a service product may be formed and influenced by other customers. For example the particular 'chemistry' of a tour group or the behaviour of other diners in a restaurant can influence the shape and quality of the service product which is obtained. The problem managers face in such situations is in 'quality controlling' the nature of the interactions between customers and in managing such relationships (*see* Chapter 11).

4.56 Physical Evidence

There are few 'pure services' where physical evidence plays no part in a market exchange. Thus components of the physical evidence available will influence consumers' and users' judgements of a service marketing organization. Physical evidence includes elements like the physical environment (furnishings, colour, layout, noise) the facilitating goods that enable the service to be provided (e.g. the cars used by a car rental company) and other tangible clues like labels used by an airline or 'packaging' of cleaned goods used by a dry cleaning company (*see* Chapter 12).

4.57 Process

The behaviour of people in service organizations is critical. So too is the process – the how – of service delivery. Cheerful, attentive and concerned staff can help alleviate the customers' problems of having to queue for service or soften the blow of the breakdown of technology involved in service production. They cannot however compensate entirely for such problems. How the overall system operates – the policies and procedures adopted, the degree of mechanization used in service provision, the amount of discretion employees have, the customers' involvement with the process of service performance, the flows of information and service, the appointments and waiting system, the capacity levels available – these are typically operational management concerns. However the importance of these aspects of service to customers' perceptions of satisfaction with the services offered make them also areas of interest to marketing management. This may seem to be an encroachment on traditional areas of operational management concern but performance, people and process are inseparable in many service operations.[25] Marketing management has to be concerned with the process of service performance and delivery, and the marketing mix should accommodate this interest.

This of course has implications for the organization of marketing activity in service businesses. The traditional separation of production or operational roles and of marketing roles may no longer apply. Managers in service operations so often perform general managerial roles embracing personnel, production, marketing and financial responsibilities (*see* Chapter 13).

Thus the marketing mix framework for services presented in this chapter differs from that conventionally presented in marketing textbooks. It includes seven main elements rather than four. Some readers may regard this revised framework as unhelpful. It should certainly be used with caution for two reasons:

(*a*) The first reason is fundamental. The marketing mix presented here is intuitively based rather than empirically based. We need more research into the factors marketing managers actually take into account in creating their marketing policies and programmes in specific services before the elements of a revised marketing mix can be defined more precisely. Even then as Borden suggests it can only provide a guideline for action for the forces influencing an organization vary and therefore the mix response to them.

(*b*) The second reason is semantic. It may be argued that some aspects of these elements are already accommodated implicitly under the original marketing mix, particularly under the 'product' or 'offering' dimension in its augmented or peripheral sense (*see* Chapter 6).

What is important though is that the marketing mix framework for some services contexts needs to incorporate more explicitly the elements presented here. Semantic arguments should not obscure the fact that we ought not to continue to use, without amendment, a framework developed out of work in manufacturing situations.

Chapters 6 to 13 in this book are devoted to examining these elements of the marketing mix in more detail. However as Borden rightly indicated in his original idea of the marketing mix, deriving it is both an art and a science. This blending of 'a mixture of intuition and research' is implicit in the multi-step approach to building a marketing mix in Cannon's[26] figure of the steps involved shown in Figure 4.2.

Certainly marketing managers in services markets need to undertake research about the markets and market segments for which their respective marketing mixes are shaped. Wherever possible the services marketing manager will need to research and analyse the characteristics of the markets served. It is these problems of conducting such analysis and research that we now examine.

4.6 Summary

1 Developing a marketing strategy involves two tasks. These are selecting target markets and formulating marketing mixes.

2 In services marketing adaptations and adjustments may be required,

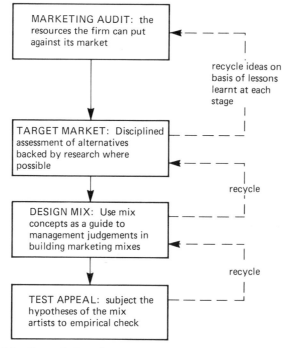

Building the marketing mix.

Figure 4.2 Building the Marketing Mix
Source: Derived from Cannon, T. *Basic Marketing: Principles and Practice*, Holt, Rinehart & Winston, New York, 1980, p. 159

although the processes of devising marketing strategies and formulating marketing mixes are similar irrespective of market type.

3 In the analytical stage preceding strategy formulation, common questions posed about all products may give rise to different answers for services.
4 The marketing mix may have to be revised for use in services contexts. In particular people, processes and physical evidence may have to be incorporated into the marketing mix framework.

Questions for Discussion

1 Explain how an organization's marketing mix is related to its overall strategic plan.
2 What are the outline steps involved in the formulation of a marketing plan?
3 Why is marketing strategy formulation likely to be different for service organizations?

4 Is the traditional marketing mix a useful operational tool for managers in the service sector?
5 'Because of the characteristics of services (e.g. intangibility) the task of developing a marketing programme in a service industry is often uniquely challenging.' Discuss.
6 What are the arguments for revising the marketing mix for services?
7 How might a service organization (of your choice) answer the question what service business are we in?
8 How can a service organization build a defendable market position?
9 What difficulties do service organizations face in 'innovating'?
10 Devise two alternative marketing strategies for a service business of your choice.

References and Notes

1 McDonald, M. and Gattorna, J. *Marketing: An introduction for Accountants*, Institute of Chartered Accountants, Milton Keynes, 1980.
2 McDonald, M. *Handbook of Marketing Planning*, MCB Publications, 1980.
3 McCarthy, E. J. *Basic Marketing: A managerial approach*, 6th Edn Richard D. Irwin, Homewood, Ill. 1978.
4 Thomas, D. R. E. 'Strategy is different in service businesses', *Harvard Business Review*, July/Aug. 1978, pp. 158–65.
5 Bessom, R. M. and Jackson, D. W. 'Service Retailing: A Strategic Marketing Approach', *Journal of Retailing*, 51, Summer 1975, pp. 75–84.
6 See, for example, Enis, B. M. and Roering, K. J. 'Services Marketing: Different Products, Similar Strategy', paper presented at the AMA Service Marketing Conference, Florida, Nov. 1981.
7 This discussion is based on Thomas, D. R. E. (reference 3 above): Bessom, R. M. and Jackson, D. W. (reference 4 above): Hise, R. T., *Product/Service Strategy*, Petrocelli/Charter, 1977, and Markin, R. *Marketing: Strategy and Management*, 2nd Edn, J. Wiley and Sons, New York, 1982.
8 Wilson, A. *The Marketing of Professional Services*, McGraw-Hill, London, 1972.
9 For a useful brief critique on consumer behaviour see Tuck, M. *How do we Choose?*, Methuen, London, 1976.
10 See, for example, Blois, K. J. 'How do consumers distinguish between products and services?' in Hanne Hartvig Larsen and Soren Heede, Proceedings of the European Academy for Advanced Research in Marketing. pp. 1606–32, 1981: Smith, M. F. and Dixon, D. F. 'Consumers Perceptions of Goods and Services', Marketing Department, Temple University, Philadelphia, Working Paper, 1981.
11 Langeard, E., Bateson, J. E. G., Lovelock, C. H. and Eiglier, P. *Services Marketing: New Insights from Consumers and Managers*, Report No. 81–104, Marketing Science Institute, Aug. 1981.

12 Konrad, E. 'An R & D approach for service industry develops responsiveness to consumer demands', *Business Horizons*, Oct. 1968, pp. 73–8.
13 Shostack, G. Lynn, 'How to design a service', *European Journal of Marketing*, Vol. 16, No. 1, 1982, pp. 49–63.
14 Shostack, G. Lynn, 'The service marketing frontier', in Zaltman, G. and Bonoma, T. *Review of Marketing*, American Marketing Association, Chicago, 1979, pp. 373–88.
15 Lovelock, C. H., 'Theoretical contributions from services and non-business marketing' in Ferrell, O. C., Brown, S. W. and Lamb, C. W. Jnr; *Conceptual and Theoretical Developments in Marketing*, American Marketing Association, Chicago, 1979, pp. 147–65.
16 Borden, N. H. 'The concept of the marketing mix', in Schwartz, G., *Science in Marketing*, J. Wiley and Sons, New York, 1965, pp. 386–97.
17 See, for example, Kotler, P. *Marketing for Non-Profit Organisations*, Prentice-Hall, Englewood Cliffs, 1975.
18 George, W. R. and Barksdale, H. C. 'Marketing activities in Service Industries', *Journal of Marketing*, vol. 38, Oct. 1974, pp. 65–70.
19 Eiglier, P., Langeard, E., Lovelock, C. H., Bateson, J. and Young, R. A. *Marketing Consumer Services: New Insights*, Marketing Science Institute, Boston, 1977.
20 Knisely, G. *Advertising Age* (15 Jan. 1979: 19 Feb. 1979: 19 March, 1979: 14 May, 1979).
21 Booms, B. H. and Bitner, M. J. 'Marketing Strategies and Organisation Structures for service firms', in Donnelly, J. and George W. R. (eds) *Marketing of Services*, American Marketing Association, Chicago, 1981, pp. 47–51.
22 Brundage, J. and Marshall, C. 'Training as a Marketing Management Tool', *Training and Development Journal*, Nov. 1980, pp. 71–6.
23 Chase, R. B. 'Where does the customer fit into a service organisation?', *Harvard Business Review*, Nov.–Dec. 1981, pp. 137–42.
24 Davidson, D. S. 'How to succeed in a service industry. . . . Turn the organisation chart upside down', *Management Review*, April, 1978, pp. 13–16.
25 Sasser, W. E., Olsen, R. P. and Wyckoff, D. D. *Management of Service Operations*, Allyn and Bacon, Boston, Mass. 1978.
26 Cannon, T. *Basic Marketing: Principles and Practice*, Holt, Rinehart & Winston, New York, 1980.

5. *MARKET ANALYSIS AND MARKETING RESEARCH FOR SERVICES*

5.1 Introduction

A number of writers on marketing suggest that market analysis and marketing research are as applicable to products as to services. Cooke[1] for example, suggests that 'In so far as logical and procedural considerations are concerned there is no meaningful substantive difference to be drawn between the process of defining and analysing a market for a product and a market for a service.' While Stanton[2] confirms 'Market analysis is essentially the same whether a firm is selling a product or a service'.

Of marketing research Hardin[3] believes 'In many ways, marketing research techniques apply more readily to service industries than to product companies'.

This chapter considers these two aspects of market analysis and marketing research for services.

5.2 Market Analysis

Market analysis is undertaken to determine the opportunities existing in a particular market and there is much similarity between the process of analysing a market for a product and analysing a market for a service.[1] This is because the elements involved – defining the market, describing the market, analysing the market – are concerned essentially with human needs and wants. The fact that a 'product' or a 'service' may be the means of meeting such wants is irrelevant to the analytical processes involved. Marketors of services need to understand why customers want – or do not want – their services; the motives underlying purchase; the determinants effecting customer behaviour, like incomes or population growth; the buying patterns which operate like where, when and how customers buy and who influences buying decisions.

In this context a market refers to a particular set of human wants and needs sufficiently homogeneous that they may be satisfied by a service offer through a marketing exchange. Clearly both products and services can contribute to mutually satisfying exchanges.

A number of frameworks are available for use by service marketors for analysing their markets.[4] One involves obtaining answers to a number of questions including[1]:

1 Does a set of needs and wants exist?
2 On what scale does it exist?
3 What economic value will buyers attach to the satisfaction of these wants?

4 What costs (including selling costs) are involved in providing satisfaction of these wants?
5 In what sense and to what degree are these wants unsatisfied or inadequately satisfied?

It is rare that explicit answers can be obtained to these questions. It is therefore necessary to pose an additional question. That is, what degree of confidence may be placed in the answers obtained? Three particularly common problems in undertaking market analysis for a new service are:

5.21 Identifying Needs and Wants

Needs and wants that are undetermined, unestimated and unfulfilled may be ascertained in a number of ways, none of them mutually exclusive.

(*a*) They may be arrived at intuitively. A successful service operation may simply develop from a good idea based neither upon customer demands nor careful marketing research. The initial insight may depend upon nothing more than personal knowledge and experience (e.g. Berni Steak Bars).

(*b*) They may be derived by formal marketing research where an orderly and logical approach is used in gathering data and systematically analysing and interpreting results obtained. This approach is the complete opposite of the intuitive approach and in Figure 5.1 the distinctions are drawn between intuition and research in marketing decision-making.

   In practice both research and intuition, based upon experience and personal judgement, are used.

(*c*) They may be derived through a process of trial and error. Intelligently applied, with careful sampling of the market before a full-scale commitment is made, this method may ensure ultimate market success.

5.22 Assessing the Scale of Demand and Cost-Price Relationships

Assessing the scale of demand and cost-price relationships is difficult. This is a multi-variate problem in which, at the very least, the factors of demand, costs and prices must be considered and the relationships between them understood. In practice of course these three elements are influenced by many other factors.

Assessing the existing and future scale of demand is an integral part of the task of market analysis. A wide array of techniques is available to assist the service marketer with this phase.[5] We are not concerned here with the techniques available and the many ways in which they can be applied. We need only note that they are much the same for service organizations and are increasingly used in services marketing today: '. . . the view still exists that it is not possible to probe the demand for services in the same depth and with the same accuracy as for products. Experience shows the contrary.'[6]

Table 5.1
*Distinction between Research and Intuition in Marketing
Decision-making*

	Research	*Intuition*
Nature	Formal planning and predicting based on scientific approach	Narrow and immediate preference based on personal feelings
Methods	Logic, systematic methods, and statistical inference	Experience and demonstration
Contri- butions	General hypo- theses for making predictions, classifying relevant variables, and systematic description and classification	Minor problems solved quickly through consider- ation of experience and practical consequences

Source: Pride, W. M. and Ferrell, O. C. *Marketing: Basic Concepts and Decisions*, 3rd edn, Houghton Mifflin, Boston, Mass. 1983, p. 107

5.23 *Assessing the Extent to which Needs and Wants are Unfulfilled*

There are two aspects to this question. They are:

(*a*) the likely competitors and their response;
(*b*) the extent to which differentiation is possible in the market.

(*a*) Most service markets suffer from competition. Exceptions include those where regulation affects the marketing process and thereby reduces or distorts the range of competition or services that may be offered (e.g. Government or Institutional Regulation).
        Service activities may be regulated in two main ways.

Self Regulation

This is where an industry has a self-appointed body composed of its own members (e.g. doctors, accountants, dentists). They may set ethical standards, fees, limitations on advertising and other competitive practices (e.g. doctors cannot advertise).

Public Regulation

Central or local government, in this case, may establish the regulations and oversee them. In the United Kingdom public utilities (e.g. Electricity

Boards) and major nationalized industries may have to seek approval for major policy decisions and sometimes on price increases.

Even where no formal self-regulation or public regulation applies directly, an industry may be affected by other environmental factors which restrict or delimit competition in some way (e.g. safety and health requirements). Market analysis must take account of these factors.

(b) A major decision for a service organization concerns how to differentiate its offerings from those of competitors. Marketors of intangibles, in the absence of strong tangible cues, have the difficult task of service product differentiation. Lack of patent protection in services means that some innovations may be easy to imitate. A current example (1983) is the intense competition between the airlines for business class travellers. Much emphasis in current advertising campaigns is placed upon factors like seat width, comfort and travel connections at the destination to induce use of particular carriers. In such competitive situations a main way in which service organizations can differentiate their offerings is through their employees and through emphasizing the quality of interactions between customers and employees. (This topic is dealt with more fully in Chapter 11.) It is in respect of this factor in particular that market analysis for services differs from market analysis for products:

'In so far as market analysis is concerned, the consequential difference between service markets and product markets rests in the fact that effective differentiation of the marketing offer is significantly more difficult to obtain in service markets. This phenomenon is related centrally to the fact – as it is sometimes put – that services are not purchased by customers but by clients. In other words, the single most important marketing fact – one which the analyst of service markets will overlook only at considerable peril – is that a "service" is ultimately an interaction between people. Marketing success or failure in a service industry will ordinarily be determined by the quality of that interaction.'[1]

In service organizations people can have a great influence on the degree to which customers' needs and wants are fulfilled.

5.3 Marketing Research

It was suggested in the previous section that one way of obtaining analytical marketing data would be through the use of marketing research. In fact a logical implication of the implementation of the marketing concept by a service organization is that some type of information flow will need to be established between customers and the organization. Thus market research may be defined as: 'The means used by those who provide goods and services to keep themselves in touch with the needs and wants of those who buy and use those goods and services'.[7]

For our purposes we use the broader term marketing research which can be research into any aspect of the marketing process: 'It is the systematic process of gathering analysing and interpreting relevant information for decision making'.[8]

The purposes of marketing research are:

(*a*) to reduce uncertainties involved in the decision making process about marketing activities in general and about specific aspects of marketing;
(*b*) to monitor and to help control the performance of marketing activities.

In sophisticated service marketing organizations the marketing research system will be a component of a wider marketing information system. Some airlines, banks and insurance companies are examples of service businesses developing the sort of system where marketing research is now one element in a broader marketing and management information system.

As well as marketing research such integrated systems would incorporate inputs from the internal accounting system (e.g. profitability analysis on service lines) general marketing intelligence (e.g. information about general environmental conditions from a trade association), and attempts to comprehend the reality of the world in which the service organization operates through the process of model building (e.g. models of consumer decision making processes).

For most service organizations, however, integrated marketing intelligence systems are pipe dreams to be developed rather than systems currently in operation although some examples of them are beginning to appear.[9] Stanton contrasts the characteristics of marketing research and marketing information systems. The latter, he indicates, can handle internal and external data; prevent and solve problems; have other sub-systems besides marketing research; operate continuously, and are often computer-based processes.[2]

5.31 The Marketing Research Process

There is general agreement that the marketing research process is much the same for organizations marketing products and services. In one of the current best United Kingdom books on that process Crimp suggests:

'The service offered to consumers by banks, tour operators, local authorities and research agencies (to quote some examples) are the products of these bodies and they are susceptible to substantially the same marketing research treatment as the goods we call "products".'[10]

In marketing research no two projects are necessarily the same. Thus there is no standard procedure that can be followed in all investigations. Therefore Figure 5.1 is representative only of the general research process which may be used by service organizations. This or similar frameworks are adequately described in detail in many standard marketing and marketing research texts.[11]

5.32 The Scope of Marketing Research in Services Markets

The scope for the use of marketing research in services markets is considerable. One list of the types of areas for which marketing research is

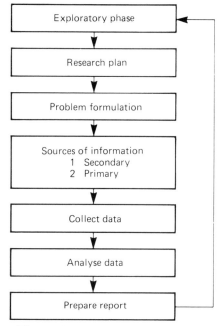

Figure 5.1 The Research Process

appropriate has been in use for some years in the context of product markets:

1 Research on markets:
   (*a*) analysing market potentials for existing products and estimating demand for new products;
   (*b*) sales forecasting;
   (*c*) characteristics of product markets;
   (*d*) analysing sales potentials;
   (*e*) studying trends in markets.
2 Research on products:
   (*a*) customer acceptance of proposed new products;
   (*b*) comparative studies of competitive products;
   (*c*) determing new uses of present products;
   (*d*) market-testing proposed products;
   (*e*) studying customer dissatisfaction with products;
   (*f*) product-line research;
   (*g*) packaging and design studies.
3 Research on promotion:
   (*a*) evaluating advertising effectiveness;
   (*b*) analysing advertising and selling practices;
   (*c*) selecting advertising media;
   (*d*) motivational studies;
   (*e*) establishing sales territories;

(*f*) evaluating present and proposed sales methods;
(*g*) studying competitive pricing;
(*h*) analysing salesmen's effectiveness;
(*i*) establishing sales quotas.
4 Research on distribution:
   (*a*) location and design of distribution centres;
   (*b*) handling and packing merchandise;
   (*c*) cost analysis of transportation methods;
   (*d*) dealer supply and storage requirements.
5 Research on pricing:
   (*a*) demand elasticities;
   (*b*) perceived prices;
   (*c*) cost analysis;
   (*d*) margin analysis.

Source: Crisp, R. D. *Marketing Research Organization and Operation*, Research Study No. 35, American Marketing Association, Chicago 1958

Another which shows research objectives for professional services markets is of general relevance to a wider range of services. It illustrates some of the key areas upon which research objectives for a range of service organizations might focus. *See* Table 5.2 opposite.

The suggestions below are narrower in focus concentrating as they do on Financial Services:

1 What are the characteristics of those segments of the public who
   (*a*) buy the service from the marketer's company;
   (*b*) buy it from competitive sources;
   (*c*) do not buy it?
2 Why do they behave in this way?
3 How satisfied are users with the service provided by the company and its competitors? Does the service satisfy all or only some of the relevant users' needs? Is it generating repeat or 'once only' business?
4 Which of the customer and non-customer categories are, or are likely to be, the most profitable for the company over a reasonable time-span?
5 What can the company do to encourage customers or potential customers to modify their behaviour to the company's advantage: or prevent them from modifying it to the company's disadvantage?
6 What recent or predictable changes in the situation of customers or potential customers are likely to create new needs which the company can satisfy?
7 What changes in the economic, legislative or social environment are likely to create new problems or opportunities with which the company can assist its customers?

Source: McIver, C. and Naylor, G. *Marketing Financial Services*, Institute of Bankers, 1980

The scope for the use of marketing research is wide. But what of usage?

Table 5.2
Research Objectives

Identification and measurement of the markets
- total markets
- significant segments of individual markets
- market coverage – new markets for existing services, new services for existing markets, new services for new markets

Analysis of the characteristics of the markets
- customer needs for services, function of services
- desirable service features
- customer practices in seeking services
- customers' attitudes and activities
- competitive conditions, share of market, marketing service costs, and related practices
- required commercial conditions
- market, facilities, and competitive trends

Projection of the markets (5 or 10 year period)
- basic growth or decline forces
- Identification of 'top out' conditions
- trends or changes in customers, type of new competing services
- environmental changes – social, economic, technical, political
- projection of total market value

Critical factors for successful operations in individual markets
- nature of the service market (industry-merchandized, selected account development)
- range of services to be offered
- key functions necessary to operate service
- costs, systems, and related factors

Projection of available share of the market
- projection of market share based on market trend
- degree to which competitive strengths and weaknesses may affect position
- extent to which improved operations can contribute to higher market share
- development of market share for 5 and 10 year period

Market development programme
A statement of objectives of programme
- functional requirements to implement programme
- organization for implementation
- action programmes related to organization facilities, business development, advertising, and promotion, etc.

Source: Wilson, A. *The Marketing of Professional Services*, McGraw-Hill, London, 1972, p. 74

5.33 Use of Marketing Research in the Service Sector

No reliable figures are available which give an accurate picture of the use of marketing research in the service sector.

In the United States one survey published in 1974 found that service firms were reported to undertake the activities shown in Table 5.3.[12]

Table 5.3
Service Firms: Research Activities Undertaken

Activity	Firms	Performed %	Not Performed %
Study of why people buy the services	152	74.3	25.7
Study who are the key influences on buying the services offered	149	79.5	21.5
Define firms image among customers and the general public	150	86.0	14.0
Study profit trends by service categories, customer categories or markets	150	78.7	21.3
Evaluate customers' needs or wants	155	95.4	4.6

Source: Adapted from George, W. R. and Barksdale, H. C. 'Marketing Activities in the Service Industries', Journal of Marketing, Vol. 38, Oct. 1974, pp. 65–70

These data confirm that some service firms do devote considerable efforts to marketing research activities and conflicts with the often held view that service firms do not place as much emphasis on marketing research as manufacturing firms. What the survey did find however was that service firms were less likely to use market research firms and consultants. The author's therefore suggested that a fruitful area for further development of marketing activities by service firms would be to give more consideration to the use of external agencies for consulting and for research.

No comparable data are available for the United Kingdom. However an analysis of the users of marketing research by Simmons[13] based upon membership of the Market Research Society is presented in Table 5.4. This indicates that during the period 1966–76 users of marketing research in service organizations included in his analysis (i.e. service trades, advertising agencies, media, academic institutions and the public sector) accounted for around 50% of all users. During the period concerned total user members increased from 1,100 to 1,400. Within the range of service organizations included in this analysis, a smaller proportion of research was commissioned by advertising agencies, a stable proportion by the media while the proportion of users in the other sectors increased between 1966 and 1976 (i.e. service trades, academic institutions, the public sector). Based on this analysis Simmons concluded that: 'As a reflection of the

Table 5.4
Users of Market Research 1966–76

	1966	1974	1976
Total user members	1,100	1,400	1,400
Organization	%	%	%
Food, drink and tobacco	19	19	22
Other manufacturing companies	32	28	28
Service trades	3	7	6
Advertising agencies	30	19	15
Media	8	9	8
Academic institutes	4	9	10
Public sector	4	9	11

Source: Simmons, M. 'The British Market Research Industry', *Journal of the Market Research Society*, Vol. 20, No. 3, July 1978

widening frontiers of market research, the main growth among users has been among government and academic institutes where research is now widely used as an aid to business decisions by retailers and financial institutions.'

More recent data from AMSO (the Association of Market Survey Organizations) show that service organizations account for a significant portion of AMSO revenues. The twenty-five member companies of AMSO account for over two-thirds of the total commercial research in the UK (i.e. syndicated continuous panel services and other large scale shared cost surveys). A comparison of their sources of revenue for 1978/1982 show organizations which may be broadly classified as service organizations accounted for 23% of revenues in 1982. These data are shown in Table 5.5.

AMSO combined sales in 1982 were in excess of £80m so spending by service organizations on this portion of reported commercial research was around £20/25m in 1982. Some interesting trends are the decline in central and local government and nationalized industries/services spending from over 10% to less than 5%. Media expenditure too declined to around 5% of the total. Projecting the sort of totals shown here suggests that services markets account for expenditures of around £30/40m at present in the United Kingdom.

There are now a large number of reported applications of marketing research in the service sector. They reflect the diverse range of tasks for which marketing research is being used. One review of applications in the United Kingdom quotes examples of marketing research usage in banking, unit trusts, building societies, merchant banking, public sector services and for a wide range of social research purposes. The author concludes his review:

'The diversity of research studies . . . reflects the new horizons of marketing research. These increasingly involve the service industries and extend into medical and social areas of human activity where, in a comparatively short period of time, positive contributions have been made. To some extent, the old prejudices about using . . . marketing research for investigating the market for services, both commercial and public sector welfare, may have become less marked, but there is still a long way to go before there is wholehearted acceptance of the value of objective field surveys. Practitioners of a relatively new discipline like marketing research cannot expect to have easy access to professions such as medicine and banking which are characteristically "closed".[14]

A small unrepresentative sample of United Kingdom service organizations contacted by the author in late 1982 showed that marketing research was reportedly being undertaken on a wide range of problems including:

How consumers choose between competing service organizations.
How the buying decision is made for a particular service.
Use of information sources in service choice.
Price elasticity of quality (i.e. what consumers were willing to pay for extra service quality).
Service product study (i.e. bundle of utilities derived from a service).
Use of advertising agents.
Checks on public awareness of a current advertising campaign.
Study of effectiveness of different forms of advertising.
Market share study.
Service quality checks.
Use of mystery shoppers to check service quality.
Satisfaction with services survey.
Survey of current customers' attitudes to investment in a particular investment vehicle.

Industries represented included transport, car rentals, hotels, leisure services, advertising, dry cleaning, and utilities.

Table 5.5
AMSO Source of Revenue Analysis 1978/82

Source of Total Revenue	1978	1982
Services	%	%
Media	7.2	5.1
Advertising agencies	3.7	5.0
Retailing	2.9	3.7
Central and local government	7.1	3.1
Commercial/financial	1.7	2.3
Tourism/travelling	1.8	2.2
Nationalized industries/services	3.0	1.6
SUB-TOTAL	27.4	23.0
Other* SUB-TOTAL	72.6	77.0
TOTAL	100.0	100.0

*Includes Food and soft drinks: Alcoholic drink: Health and beauty: Motoring: Pharmaceutical/medical: Household products: Tobacco: Other Consumer goods: Industrial: Household durables/Hardware: Agricultural: Other sources.

Source: *Market Research Society Newsletter*, April 1983, data re-grouped by author

5.34 Differences between Marketing Research for Services and for Products

This chapter has so far indicated that there are many similarities between marketing research for services and for products. These similarities apply particularly in terms of the process of marketing research, in terms of the purposes of marketing research, and in terms of the utility of marketing research for decision making. There are similarities too in terms of all the weaknesses that marketing research has as a decision-making aid. For example, marketing research is a powerful decision aid in respect of the study of existing services; it is less potent as an aid in respect of new services: '. . . research is a powerful tool for measuring customer reaction to their experience as customers. It is a rather weak tool when it attempts to get customers to project a reaction to a hypothetical experience.'[1]

But there are also a number of differences between marketing research for services and for products. Some of these differences are now outlined:

(*a*) attitudes in service organizations towards marketing research;
(*b*) quality of secondary sources on services;
(*c*) problems deriving from the characteristics of services;
(*d*) problems in researching new services.

(a) Attitudes in Service Organizations towards Marketing Research

Although the use of marketing research in service organizations has grown there is still resistance to its use in some quarters. Some of the reasons for this resistance are:

Ethical

Some service organizations regard it as unethical to practice marketing and therefore to use marketing research as one aspect of marketing in the conduct of their business. This applies particularly to many kinds of professional services. Ethical objections strengthen the product orientation of professions which fail to regard what they provide as a service and their clients as a market to be served.

Size

Some service organizations are too small in size and too local in character to justify expenditure on marketing research and to conduct work at other than the most elementary levels. Consequently they rarely obtain anything more than the most basic information about their markets.

Economic

Some service organizations cannot justify the financial outlays involved in marketing research particularly where survey techniques may be appropriate.

Monopolistic Organizations

Some monopolistic organizations have justified their low level of usage of marketing research in the past based on absence of competition. Marketing research is often regarded as unnecessary expenditure by such organizations where there are no immediate competitors.

Managerial

Some managers in service organizations lack training in marketing and therefore fail to appreciate the benefits of marketing research. Or they lack skills in the interpretation and use of marketing research data.

Customer Contact

Some service organizations justify their low level of expenditure on marketing research because they are often in direct contact with their customers (e.g. personal services). Organizations in direct contact with their customers claim they can get to know their needs better and can use their own staff to provide feedback on customers. So the gap between service organization and customer may not be as wide in services marketing. Nevertheless there remains the danger that contact will still be too unplanned and too informal for decision-making purposes.

(b) Quality of Secondary Sources on Services

A particular problem with research in the service sector is the dearth of secondary sources of information for desk research purposes. Also the information that does exist is often fragmented and scattered amongst specialist fields (e.g. library services, tourism, transportation, professional services) and can be relatively inaccessible to the uninitiated market researcher. The overall problem of the relatively poorer quality and quantity of information about services is aggravated by the problem of the lack of a clear definition of what are services anyway (*see* Chapter 2).

(c) Problems Deriving From the Characteristics of Services

Some differences between marketing research for services and for products stem from the characteristics of services themselves. Some characteristics of services and their suggested impacts for the use of marketing research particularly for new service development research designs are:

Characteristic	*Effects upon Marketing Research*
Intangibility	(*a*) Where a dominantly intangible service, home use tests not appropriate.

	(*b*) Often appropriate to move directly from concept testing to test marketing in new product development.
	(*c*) 'Researchability' problem for dominantly intangible services.
Patenting difficult	(*a*) Reduces incentives for large R & D investment.
	(*b*) More focus on 'me too' services.
	(*c*) Tendency towards service improvement rather than innovation.
	(*d*) Ease of competitive entry influences viability of new service concepts.
Standardization difficult	(*a*) Difficult to develop accurate concept descriptions.
	(*b*) Problems in concept testing.
Direct relationship between service performer and client	(*a*) Judgements of service product influenced by who performs the service and the client's involvement in performance.
No clear lines of demarcation between a service product and the place in which it is delivered, the process and the people	(*a*) Concept testing difficult because of need to assess impact of performer and physical evidence on service itself.

(d) Problems in Researching New Services

Many of the difficulties stated above apply particularly to marketing research for new services. The general problems of researching services with their often elusive, ephemeral and intangible qualities are aggravated when new services are being researched. Both the fuzziness and ambiguity of the service; the difficulty the customer may have in articulating what benefits are sought from a service innovation and what elements the service should consist of provide a 'researchability' problem for the market researcher. In Chapter 2 one scheme for representing a service as a constellation of tangible and intangible attributes was outlined. A particular problem in new service development is to identify, weight and rank the separate elements that make up a service offer. These are difficult judgements for researchers to obtain from customers for existing services. They become even more difficult with new services (*see* Chapters 6 and 7).

The very nature of services means that researchers and users have to be prepared to use 'soft', qualitative data particularly in conceptualizing a service. Because services possess the characteristics of perishability and intangibility their value is more often judged in terms of benefits rather than features. This can mean that in order to determine what a service entity is to a market, a marketor must conduct more initial marketing research than in product marketing. Also a tight service specification may be difficult to produce.

These problems of measurement have led to the development of new techniques in marketing research. They have also led to attempts to clarify the concept testing process for services. One suggested framework for concept testing a service which outlines the steps involved is shown in Figure 5.2.[16]

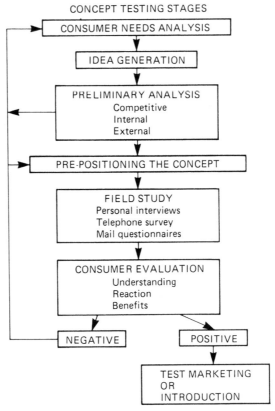

Figure 5.2

Source: Murphy, P. E. and Robinson, R. K. 'Concept Testing for Services' in Donnelly, J. H. and George, W. R. *Marketing of Services*, American Marketing Association, Chicago, 1981, p. 218.

In this framework concept testing goes through a number of steps. The service idea starts with consumer needs analysis. Then ideas are generated to meet these needs. Ideas are then subjected to a preliminary analysis during which the competitive environment is considered; ideas are examined internally and subjective judgements are made about the market; and a preliminary external reaction from potential customers and suppliers is obtained. The 'positioning' of the service product in the market is then considered and field studies are undertaken to present the concept specifically to a carefully selected sample of potential customers. Finally the concept is evaluated. In particular, customer understanding of the concept is sought; customer buying and usage intentions are sought; and customer benefits are sought. Unfavourable results may mean concept revision; favourable results may mean test marketing (where applicable) or direct introduction of the service product (where possible.) The overall purposes of this framework are thus to find out whether a potential customer

- understands the idea of the proposed service;
- reacts favourably to it;
- feels it offers benefits to meet unmet needs.

Concept testing processes for services have been a relatively neglected area of marketing management. However the growing interest in service marketing and the importance of clearer definitions of service products, suggest this will be a significant area of development over the next few years.

Some further differences with services in fact offer advantages to the marketing researcher compared with products. First the researcher has the opportunity to evaluate services before the sale, after the sale and during the sale (i.e. during the performance of the service). Unlike a product which is produced and then consumed, some services are consumed as they are being produced. The performer can thus obtain feedback while the service is being produced and make appropriate adjustments where these are required by customers. One study has shown that participating in a marketing research investigation on site does not actually interfere with enjoyment of a service. However, the consumers' evaluation of being a respondent is sensitive to the costs and rewards of participation and the service organization needs to maintain the goodwill of the respondent.[17]

Secondly, direct customer involvement with many services does allow the user to give a direct specification of what service is required to the seller or performer:

'Most companies selling services start out with an enormous market information advantage over the consumer product company; the service company knows a lot about its customers. With the increasingly effective use of internal data processing and computer applications, most service companies can effectively provide their customer characteristics entirely with internal data.'[3]

Thirdly the relatively more recent use of marketing research by service organizations has given them certain advantages. They are able to use proven techniques of marketing research developed in other contexts. They can benefit by avoiding earlier mistakes and misapplications of marketing research techniques in product fields.

5.4 Marketing Research and Public Services[18]

The application of marketing to public services – that is government agency organized, operated and sponsored services – presents a challenging testing ground amongst those who feel that one can legitimately justify the extension of marketing ideas and practices to this area. The rationale for a marketing orientation by government agencies is stated by Kotler.[19]

Government agencies like other organizations are surrounded by several publics with whom they must maintain good relations. While they may provide their services as a monopolist there may be substitutes that the public can resort to if the public service offering is poor. Even if not, the public agencies that do a poor job of meeting the needs of their clients are subject to criticism from public interest groups and the media as well as the withdrawal of client patronage. Thus marketing has a role to play in helping to understand and establish public needs, in developing, communicating and distributing public services and in assessing the degree of satisfaction with them and the public service delivery system.

The extension of general marketing ideas and practices to public services therefore means that the basic marketing activity of marketing research has an important role to play. Although many public policy issues have been decided without recourse to marketing research in the past, and although this will no doubt be the case with many public policy issues in the future, the argument for the use of marketing research and the role it can play in public policy decision-making is strong.[20]

Few marketing professionals would need persuading that if public policy is to be developed in a way which takes account of the public viewpoint and the public response to such policy, then market and social research offers an important way, although not the only way, of ensuring this. This is not to suggest that public policy is or should be based necessarily upon the public view. It is often the responsibility of public policy decision-makers to make and implement decisions which are contrary to the public view (e.g. abolition of capital punishment in this country). Nevertheless, market and social research provides a mechanism which can help public policy formulators better understand the public's views and improve the quality and impact of their decisions, particularly by helping to clarify the issues and assumptions underlying them, however popular or unpopular the decisions themselves may be.

In this country the use of marketing research in the development of public policy is not new. Chisnall[21] outlines the long standing linkage between market research and social surveys for public purposes. In the United States too, Dyer and Shimp[22] suggest that policy makers there have a growing interest in, and are receptive to, contributions from market and consumer research while Barnhill[23] has illustrated in a number of case studies dealing with consumer protection, environmental protection and consumer services how marketing research serves to link government to its publics.

There are however, some general differences between the public sector and the private sector which have implications for the use of marketing and market research[20] and may therefore require adaptation of marketing principles, ideas and techniques.

5.41 *Marketing's Acceptability*

For all its development and impact in business, marketing is regarded still by many in public agencies as being inappropriate for public bodies to use.

Its associations with 'selling', 'advertising' and 'profit' in the past perhaps imply that its use in public sector situations has to be carefully controlled to overcome any sense of discomfort and unease which may be felt by both public provider and public user. A further aspect of the relative neglect of marketing in public policy development is reflected in the formal training programmes for public policy makers and officials which rarely incorporate marketing and marketing research as subjects of study. There may be problems in understanding marketing and in using and interpreting marketing research.

5.42 Public Policy Innovation

For all the criticisms publicly financed and organized bodies receive, many of the services they offer are often highly innovative in nature. Government services are frequently provided at the frontiers of social change and the public sector may often establish precedent. The marketor and market researcher may then be dealing with highly innovative services with all the attendant problems that real innovation may bring.

5.43 Public must Benefit

The need to provide services which are in the public interest and for the public at large may mean that all sectors of the community have to be considered. Often this implies that policies of market segmentation commonly practised in the private sector and which concentrate effort on only a proportion of the market may be inappropriate and may be viewed as discriminatory. There are particular problems of providing different market offerings, charging varying price levels and delivering differing qualities of experience while avoiding charges of elitism, favouritism and discrimination.

5.44 Policy Formation

We have only limited knowledge of public policy formation. Managers may require different skills in this sector and certainly the range of criteria they use in evaluating proposals is likely to be different from the fundamental drive of the profit motive which operates in the private sector where much marketing and market research experience has so far been gained. Social considerations as much as financial and market considerations are more likely to influence thinking.

5.45 Ethical Problems

There are also issues raised by public agencies using marketing research. One problem derives from charges of intrusion when surveys and studies are undertaken for government purposes; marketing research used for public purposes raises the delicate question of whether the taxpayer's money will be used to pry into private affairs. There is also the problem of the political use which may be made of any findings and whether research data may be used for manipulative ends rather than to improve public services and their efficiency. These ethical issues are likely to become more important as research use in, and for, public agencies expands.

All the above then, have an influence upon the scope and discretion for the use of marketing research in determining public policy. The kinds of adaptations to marketing research in public services varies from service to service. Easy generalization about all public services is not possible.

5.5 Summary

1 The broad principles of market analyses are much the same for services and products. Market analysts in the service sector do however face problems in differentiating their offerings from those of competitors. People may be important in the differentiation process.
2 The processes, tools, techniques and scope of marketing research are much the same in service markets.
3 Some differences in the service sector occur due to attitudes towards marketing and marketing research, the quality of secondary data for services, problems due to the characteristics of services and problems in researching new services.
4 Most sub-sectors of the service economy present further differences and challenges e.g. the public sector.

Questions for Discussion

1 Are the principles of marketing research the same in service industries as in other industries?
2 If service organizations are close to their customers why do they need to use marketing research?
3 Suggest a framework that may be used by the market analyst examining a service market?
4 What problems arise in concept testing a service?
5 Undertake a review in the library of marketing research studies undertaken during the past two years in a service industry of your choice?
6 Why should those in the public sector have objections to the use of marketing research?
7 What problems may arise in a small service company considering hiring a marketing research agency?
8 Can you test a service like you can test a product?
9 Why is marketing research a weaker tool when researching a service market for a new service than for an existing service?
10 Comment on the difficulties marketors have in differentiating their services from those of competitors?

References and Notes

1 Cooke, B. 'Analysing Markets for Services' in *Handbook of Modern Marketing*, Edited by Buell, V., McGraw-Hill, New York, 1970, pp. 2–41 to 2–51.

2 Stanton, W. J. *Fundamentals of Marketing*, McGraw-Hill, New York, 1981.
3 Hardin, D. K. 'Marketing Research for Service Industries' in *Handbook of Modern Marketing*, edited by Buell, V., McGraw-Hill, New York, 1970, pp. 6–39 to 6–48.
4 See, for example, the framework proposed by Konrad, E. 'An R & D approach for service industry', *Business Horizons*, Oct. 1968, pp. 73–8.
5 See, for example, Green, P. E. and Tull, D. S. *Research for Marketing Decisions*, Prentice-Hall, Englewood Cliffs, 1974.
6 Wilson, A., *The Marketing of Professional Services*, McGraw-Hill, 1972.
7 *The Market Research Society Yearbook*, The Market Research Society, London, 1979/80.
8 Murphy, P. E. 'Marketing Research for the Arts' in Mokwa, M. P., Dawson, W. M. and Prieve, E. A. (Editors) *Marketing the Arts*, Praeger 1980, p. 169.
9 McDermott, D. R. 'A Service Organisations Marketing Information System', *Industrial Marketing Management* Vol. 7, No. 3, June 1978, pp. 178–85.
10 Crimp, M., *The Marketing Research Process*, Prentice-Hall, Englewood Cliffs, 1981.
11 See, for example, reference 2 and reference 10.
12 George, W. R. and Barksdale, H. C. 'Marketing Activities in the Service Industries', *Journal of Marketing*, Vol. 38, Oct. 1974, pp. 65–70.
13 Simmons, M. 'The British Market Research Industry', *Journal of the Market Research Society*. Vol. 20, No. 3, July 1978, pp. 135–65.
14 Chisnall, P. M. *Marketing Research. Analysis and Measurement*, 2nd Edn McGraw-Hill, New York, 1981, Chapter 15.
15 Wind, Y. J. *Product Policy Concepts Methods and Strategy*, Addison-Wesley, Reading, Mass. 1982.
16 Murphy, P. E. and Robinson, R. K. 'Concept testing for Services' in Donnelly, J. H. and George, W. R. (eds) *Marketing of Services*, American Marketing Association, Chicago, 1981.
17 Swan, J. E., Trawick, I. F. and Carroll, M. G. 'Effect of participation in marketing research on consumer attitudes toward research and satisfaction with a service,' *Journal of Market Research*, Vol. 18, Aug. 1981, pp. 356–63.
18 This section is based on the author's paper 'The Role of Public Policy in the Field of Recreation and Leisure', *Journal of the Market Research Society*, Vol. 23, No. 2, 1981, pp. 72–83.
19 Kotler, P. *Marketing for Non-Profit Organizations*, Prentice-Hall, Englewood Cliffs, 1975.
20 Ritchie, J. B. and Labreque, R. L. 'Marketing Research and Public Policy – a functional perspective', *Journal of Marketing*, Vol. 69, July 1975, pp. 12–19.
21 Chisnall, P. M. 'Market surveys and social planning,' *The Quarterly Review of Marketing*, Summer 1977, pp. 7–9.

22 Dyer, R. F. and Shimp, T. A. 'Enhancing the role of marketing research in public policy decision making', *Journal of Marketing*, Vol. 41, No. 1, Jan. 1977, pp. 63–7.
23 Barnhill, J. A. 'Developing marketing orientation in a postal service', *Optimum 3*, 1974, pp. 36–47.

6. *THE SERVICE PRODUCT*

6.1 Introduction

The service product and an understanding of the dimensions of which it is composed is central to the success of any service marketing organization. As with goods customers derive benefits and satisfactions from service products. Service products are bought and used for the benefits they offer, for the needs they fulfil and not for themselves. However the notion of what is a service product is complex. It is an area of service marketing research which is beginning to receive attention.[1] Also it is an area of service marketing research which has strong links with operations management,[2] and physical distribution management.[3] It is the objective of this chapter to examine more fully the idea of what is a service product.

6.2 The Service Product

Central to any definition of a service product, from a marketing viewpoint, is the linkage that must be established between the service product from the consumers' or users' viewpoint and the service product from the providers' or performers' viewpoint. Services marketing organizations may find it helpful in tracing this linkage to analyse their service product(s) at four levels. These levels are:

(*a*) the consumer benefit concept
(*b*) the service concept
(*c*) the service offer
(*d*) the service delivery system.

and they are shown in Figure 6.1.
Each level of analysis will be examined in turn.

6.21 *The Consumer Benefit Concept*

This terminology is used by Bateson.[4] He argues that it is only from the idea of a consumer benefit that the service concept can be defined. The consumer's view, so the marketing concept suggests, should be central to the shaping of any good or service for offer. As Bateson says:

> 'The true nature of a product can be perceived only by the consumer. That is, the manufacturer can specify the function of the product. He can even specify the kinds of psychological benefits that will be offered in advertising. The consumer, however, takes away from the product only that part of the bundle he/she needs at that point of time.'

The distinction between what the service organization offers and what benefits the consumer derives from the offer is important. Thus, for

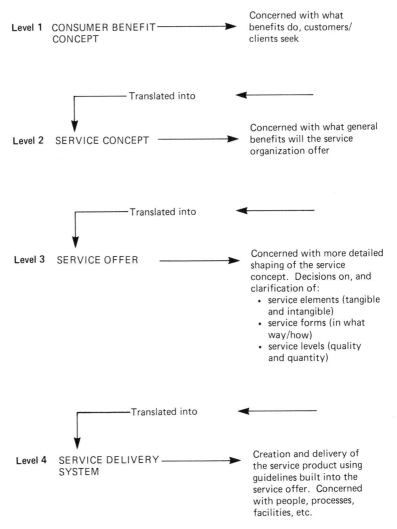

Figure 6.1 Conceptualizing The Service Product

example, a consumer obtains from a restaurant and its facilities and amenities a particular mixture of the possibilities offered in terms of food, drink, service, atmosphere and so on. Also the consumer, in a sense, helps manufacture his own 'product' from the range of possibilities offered.

Bateson continues: '. . . For any firm, then, the "consumer benefit concept" will be a bundle of functional, effectual and psychological attributes. It is important to separate this consumer benefit concept from the product itself'.

There are two suggested features of the consumer benefit concept identified by Bateson as far as services are concerned. First that it differs from a good in that it cannot exist without a service delivery system. Hence the importance of the design and operation of the service delivery system as an essential element in the definition of a service product. Secondly, and following from this, the consumer benefit concept will dictate what should or should not be quality controlled within the service delivery system. While there are some exceptions to these principles, the service product and service delivery system are usually inseparable.

The clarification, elaboration and translation of the consumer benefit concept poses a number of problems for service marketors. First the services offered should be based upon the needs and benefits sought by consumers and users. But consumers and users may be clear or unclear about what they require, articulate or inarticulate in the expression of their requirements. Difficulties may stem from their ignorance of what to expect, inexperience of what is required or basic inability to elucidate latent need. Secondly, benefits sought may change over time through good or bad experiences in service use, through new expectations' sets, through sophistication in service usage and consumption. Thirdly there are practical measurement problems for service marketors in deriving consumer-based measures of the importance of services' benefits sought, preferences between them and changes in their importance. Also it may be necessary to measure the trade-offs between elements of services offered that consumers are prepared to make.

The definition and monitoring of the consumer benefit concept however, is of central importance to all service product design and delivery decisions. The constant task of the service marketor is to try to come to grips with what benefits customers seek; benefits which are so central to the success of the service marketing operation, but so elusive to define. In the literature on marketing professional services for example, the initial insight provided by Wittreich[5] that the purchase of professional service was the purchase of uncertainty reduction has since spawned a most valuable literature on professional services marketing which builds upon this initial insight in some conceptual and practical detail.[6]

It is interesting that what consumers obtain through services are benefits or intangibles; what service marketors offer are intangibles. In theory there should be less danger of product orientation in services marketing because of the relative unimportance of tangibles. Yet paradoxically, Levitt's classic article 'Marketing Myopia'[7] used two service industries – movies and railroads – as examples of myopic marketing.

6.22 *The Service Concept*

The service concept is the definition of the general benefits the service organization offers based on customer benefits sought. At a general level it helps answer the questions

What business are we in?
What needs and wants do we attempt to meet?

The service idea or service concept is used in different ways in the literature on services marketing. Some of the different methods of usage are examined to illustrate the confusion in current services marketing terminology. The discussion however should not divert the service marketor from the basic task that the stage of defining the service concept has to be followed by the translation of the concept into a service offer and into the design of a service delivery system.

Gronroos[8] suggests that the service concept is the core of the service offering. He argues that at least two levels of service concept are possible. The 'general' service concept refers to the essential product being offered (e.g. a car hire company offers solutions to temporary transportation problems). In addition there will be 'specific' service concepts at the core of specific services (e.g. candle-lit dinners or oriental foods for restaurants).

The service concept has to be translated into what Eiglier and Langeard[1] call 'the service formula'. This translation process, according to them, implies not only a clear definition of the service concept (i.e. what consumer benefits is the service firm aiming to serve; which service attributes best express the consumer benefit). It also demands attention to

the service process; that is the ways and means the service is produced, distributed and consumed;
the market segment has to be identified;
the organization – client interface has to be organized in a network;
the service image has to facilitate clear communication between the service organization and its potential clients.

Sasser *et al.*[2] put it slightly differently. They suggest that the service concept is the definition of the offer in terms of the bundle of goods and services sold to the consumer plus the relative importance of this bundle to the consumer. This they suggest is important because it enables the manager to understand some of the intangibles, elusive and implicit that affect the consumer decision and to design and operate his organization to deliver a total service package that emphasizes the important elements of that package. They stress the importance of the process in creating the product; it is one dimension of it (i.e. the consumer interacts with the workforce, equipment, physical environment) and the delivery system must be designed with the presence of the consumer in mind. In contrast the manufacturing process is isolated from the consumer and is designed for the effective production of the physical good that is the output.

6.23 The Service Offer

Again there is a variety of terminology used to describe the service offer. Some of the schemes used to define the service product are shown in Table 6.1.

The array of terminology reflects the differing views there are in the field of services marketing and the absence, as yet, of a generally acceptable way of describing the service concept and the service offer. It is inappropriate to add further to the terminology in use. What is required is

Table 6.1
Terminology used to Describe the Service Product

Core product	Substantive service	Elementary services	Core service
What is the buyer buying?	The essential function of the service	1 Core services (a) Main reason why customer buys (b) Main output that the company provides	Consists of *general* service concepts and *specific* service concepts
Tangible product	*Peripheral service*	2 Peripheral service offered around core service and adds to it some value	*Auxiliary service*

Making the core product tangible to the buyer through:
 	
  quality level
  features
  styling
  brand name
  packaging
	Service that surrounds the substantive service		Service used as a means of competition 'Extras'. Not essential but can become an integral part of the offer

Augmented product		*Global service*	
Additional benefits and services offered with the tangible products		Set of core and peripheral services which constitute the service offering	
Source:[1] Kotler, P. *Principles of Marketing*, Prentice-Hall, Englewood Cliffs, 1980, pp. 368–9	Source:[2] Sasser, W. E., Olsen, R. P. and Wyckoff, D. D. *Management of Service Operations – Text and Cases*, Allyn and Bacon, Boston, Mass. 1978	Source:[3] Eiglier, P. and Langeard, E. 'A conceptual approach of the service offering' Working paper No. 217, iae Aix en – Provence, pp. 6–9	Source:[4] Grönroos, C. 'An applied service marketing theory', Swedish School of Economics and Business Administration. Working Paper 57, 1980, pp. 12–14

standardization rather than proliferation of terminology in use in services marketing.

The service offer is concerned with giving more specific and detailed shape to the basic service concept notion. The shape of the service offer stems from managerial decisions concerned with what services will be provided, when they will be provided, how they will be provided, where they will be provided, who will provide them. Although this stage is treated separately for presentation purposes it is emphasized that decisions on the service offer are intertwined and indissoluble from decisions on the service delivery system and are derived from the service concept.

Management of the service offer is concerned with making decisions and thinking through the implications of actions affecting at least three components.[9]

These are:

(a) service elements;
(b) service forms;
(c) service levels.

Service Elements

The service elements are the ingredients of a total service offer; they are the particular bundle of tangibles and intangibles which compose the service product. It is in describing the composition of a service product that the terminology (e.g. core, peripheral, global, etc.) referred to in Table 6.1 is most widely used. Service managers face two particular problems in defining the composition of a service offer. First there is the difficulty of articulating all of the elements that could make up a service offer. It is usually easier to articulate the tangible elements than the intangible. Secondly there is the difficulty of deciding upon the particular set of elements the service organization will actually use in its service offer.

A further problem is that in practice some of the elements making up a service offer are *not* in fact provided by the service performer. They could for example be provided by customers and thus they may be more difficult to control. To illustrate, a package holiday may be enjoyed by those who experience it not just because of the quality of the hotel where the holidaymakers are based, the promptness of the flight and the courtesy of the travel operators staff but also because the holidaymakers 'get on' together as a group. The particular chemistry of the party may ultimately determine the success or otherwise of the holiday from the consumers' point of view. Conceptually then a service offer consists of both tangible and intangible elements: some of which are controllable and some of which are uncontrollable by the provider of the service. (*See* top of Figure 6.2.)

The management and the marketing of a service operation is largely about the management of the tangible and intangible elements of the service offer. Management must try to control the tangible and intangible elements that make up the service offer to ensure that they conform with standards laid down. So the cleanliness of a hotel or the size of food portions served in a restaurant are controllable elements of a service. So too is the attention given by an air hostess to passengers or the speed with which telephones are answered in a car rental branch.

But some elements of a service offer are less controllable. Management can ensure that all guests signing in at a hotel reception desk are formally greeted by the receptionist. There is less control over the warmth of the greeting. Nevertheless management must try to anticipate some of these uncontrollable elements and ensure that the climate of the organization contributes to rather than detracts from the service offer. For example, a tour bus company can try to ensure that a party of holidaymakers will get on together (e.g. by organizing an introductory party or by separating smokers and non-smokers when desired). In practice though there are elements of the offer which are beyond management control and which cannot always be anticipated. Some may turn out to be desirable (e.g. like-minded guests sharing the same hotel); some may be undesirable (e.g. noisy guests occupying a hotel room and interfering with the enjoyment of other guests). *See* bottom of Figure 6.2.

These elements of a service offer are shown in Figure 6.2

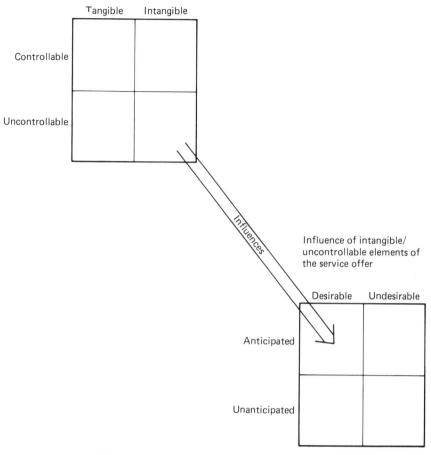

Figure 6.2 Elements of The Service Offer

By way of example[2] the bundle of goods and services offered at an expensive restaurant can be seen to consist of:

1 the physical items or facilitating goods (e.g. food, drink);
2 the sensual benefits or explicit services (e.g. taste, aroma, service);
3 the psychological benefits or implicit services (e.g. comfort, status).

Operationally it's usually easier to manage the physical elements of a service offer. Shostack[10] in fact argues that the 'management of tangible evidence' should be a primary priority of service marketors. She suggests that products are dominated with varying degrees of tangibility and intangibility and that as a product decreases in its tangible dominance attempts to position it in the marketplace should move from intangible to tangible evidence. Her conceptualization of this process is shown in Figure 6.3.

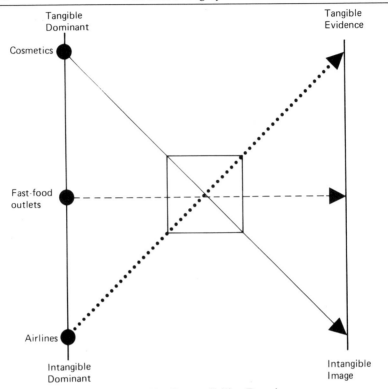

Figure 6.3 Model of Tangibility/Intangibility Dominance

Source: Shostack, G. L. 'Breaking Free from Product Marketing', *Journal of Marketing*, Vol. 41, No 2, American Marketing Association, April 1977, pp. 73–80

Levitt[11] too stresses the importance of managing tangible evidence in the sale of intangibles. He suggests that in getting customers for intangibles it is important to create surrogates or metaphors for intangibility (e.g. standards of dress or layout) (*see* Chapters 11 and 12). And in keeping customers it is important to remind them and show them what they are getting so that relative failures in delivery are seen as unimportant. Tangibilizing the intangible, managing the evidence and restating the presence and performance of services he suggests are important because: 'Customers don't usually know what they're getting until they don't get it.'

There are dangers in this approach, for tangible evidence might be given undue emphasis at the expense of intangible evidence. Service marketors should not lose sight of the fact that intangibles are the fundamental part of the service product.

Service Forms

Service elements are offered to the marketplace in different forms. For example, how the different service elements are priced is an illustration of the differing service forms possible. Eiglier and Langeard[1] suggest that there are three possibilities managers can adopt to underpin their pricing system:

1 charge a unique package for the whole set of services;
2 charge separately for each service;
3 a combination of the two.

More specifically Kotler[9] suggests that a television set manufacturer pricing its repair services has three pricing options:

1 offer free television repair services for a year with the sale of its set;
2 offer the customer the option to buy a service contract;
3 decide not to offer any repair service, leaving this to independent television repair specialists.

Related to this example is the question of how the repair services should be provided. Again there are a number of options such as the use of one's own repair staff, using the services of appointed distributors or leaving it to independent companies.

Service form then is concerned with examining in detail the various options relating to each service element. The particular decision taken on the precise form of each service element will depend upon a number of factors including market requirements, competitors' policies and the need to obtain balance within, and between, the various elements that make up the service product offer – what is called 'cohesiveness and coherence of the set of services offered'.[1] An additional consideration is to try to achieve the lowest level of complexity from the customer and service marketing organization points of view. Service products with a high degree of complexity are difficult to manage from the service marketors' perspective (e.g. in terms of quality control, staff knowledge of options) and difficult to understand from the users' point of view. The array of fare options presented by British Rail and transatlantic airlines are illustrations of this latter point.

Service Levels

Service users may have expectations of the elements of service they will obtain and the form of such elements particularly where repeat purchases are involved. They also expect a certain service level. At its most general, service level refers to the judgements made by consumers and users of the quality of the benefits they receive and the quantity or amount of the benefits they receive. These two dimensions of service quality and service quantity are examined further.

Service Quality

Service quality is of fundamental importance in the design of a service product. More than any other factor service organizations are likely to be judged by the 'quality' of service provided. Basic marketing decisions thus have to be made on service product quality because:

1 quality will influence both the volume of demand for a service and who makes that demand;
2 quality will be a major positioning tool in relation to other competitors in the marketplace.

However service quality presents a number of problems. First it is an elusive concept to define in the context of a service product. Quality is an overall measure composed of a number of dimensions like reliability of service, grade of service and accuracy of service. Some dimensions of quality may be capable of objective measurement (e.g. turnround time for a consumer repair) while others may depend upon much more subjective evaluations. Thus for the provider or producer of the service 'unbundling' all the elements is difficult. For the user making conscious evaluations and comparisons between service product elements is also difficult. Both are likely to use surrogates for quality (e.g. price). So problems of measurement follow from the problems of definition.

Secondly there are problems of designing, building into, standardizing and maintaining quality in many kinds of service marketing organizations, particularly in those service settings where there is a high degree of contact between buyer and seller. It is difficult to inspect quality (e.g. motor repairs) and systems may have to be developed to ensure it. There may be difficulties if too much quality is offered – just as much as too little quality. Also where organizations develop multi-branches or multi-units problems may arise in maintaining consistency between them.

Thirdly quality standards are ultimately defined by how the customer defines them. It is customer perceptions of quality that matter not performer perceptions. This demands an understanding of what attributes a customer takes into account in judging quality and how such attributes will change according to circumstances. Additional difficulties of quality design and control stem from the fact that service is defined differently by individual customer organizations and according to the role position of the respondent.[3]

Strategically service product quality has two important implications for the organization providing the service. First decisions must be made on the basic level of quality which will be provided to match the level of quality desired by customers and the variations within a service product range (e.g. as in restaurants and airlines). Secondly decisions have to be made on the management of quality over time. Whether to maintain, lower or increase quality are decisions with significant implications for the offering organization. This can amount to changing the product.

The importance of quality in service operations and the centrality of staff involved in service delivery is often mentioned in marketing literature on services. Hostage[12] stresses that the quality of service offered depends upon the quality of people hired and describes the quality programme of the Mariott Corporation as the control and development of their management personnel. Sasser and Pettway[13] show that how employees in service operations perceive and perform their jobs can promote or undermine the success of their organizations: thus issues of motivation and reward are important to service quality (*see* Chapter 11).

A model of service quality where the total quality of a service is a function of three components has been proposed:[8] The components are:

Corporate image   the overall image the organization has and its overall attractiveness.

Technical quality   whether the service provides the appropriate technical attributes (e.g. a haircut; the bank deposit box is safe).

Functional quality   how the service is rendered.

Which component of quality is most dominant from the consumers' viewpoint is not made clear. An outstanding image may help excuse minor deficiencies in other quality components. One proposal is that there are three models of how consumers make judgements about services.[2] They are that:

1 there may be one over-powering attribute that forms that basis of judgement about a service;
2 there may be a single attribute but with accompanying threshold minimum levels on other attributes;
3 there may be a weighted average of attributes across a range, thought to be important.

Eiglier and Langeard[1] recognize the importance of service product quality by their observations that:

1 The performance of each service element can influence the quality of the performance of other elements. A client can evaluate the whole service on the basis of his evaluation of one element (core or peripheral) of which it consists.
2 Some services are indispensable for the execution of the core service while others are there to improve the quality of the core service.
3 Even those which are peripheral to the core service can influence its quality.
4 Of central concern is how customers view the service(s) and what distinctions they perceive to be central in their choice and evaluation of service offerings.

Service Quantity

Closely related to service quality is the idea of service quantity or the amount of service provided to users or customers. Like service quality it is a difficult dimension to set and to manage. It is often difficult to disentangle the elements of service from consumer and provider viewpoints. Decisions required, as far as service quantity is concerned, relate to:

the volume of service delivered in a service product;
the timing of service delivered in a service product;
the flow of service delivered in a service product.

Thus a waiter in a restaurant may on quality dimensions of discretion, appropriateness and sensitivity deliver service of the right quality level.

However he may be found wanting in terms of the amount of attention he gives and of its timing.

6.24 *The Service Delivery System*

The final level of analysis necessary to define the service product is consideration of the service delivery system. As stated earlier the process of service product performance and delivery is an integral component of a service product. Unlike a tangible item in which manufacturing and marketing are separate processes, in services marketing the two are often inseparable. The service performance and delivery system both creates the service product and delivers it to the customer. One feature that particularly distinguishes systems which produce services rather than goods is the role that the consumer or user plays in the production process. (The implications of this for productivity measurement and improvement are considered in Chapters 11 and 16.) Specifying the system and the elements of which it is composed is an essential ingredient in defining the service product.

Two key elements of many service delivery systems are:

1 people (*see* Chapter 11);
2 physical evidence (*see* Chapter 12).

In some service settings other characteristics may be important and influence the service product such as natural phenomena like climate, terrain or geographic setting. For our purposes here we will focus on these two prime elements.

People

People involved in service product performance and delivery include the organization's own personnel. Their attitudes, skills, knowledge and behaviour can have a critical impact on the levels of satisfaction the user derives from service product consumption. All types of people may be involved in that they have impact on the service product, its form, its character and its nature. They include organization personnel in contact with the customer and those not in contact; they include personnel visible to the client and those not visible to the client.[1] Other parties may work on behalf of the service organization too and influence the service product. These include spokespersons like public relations agencies, agents, intermediaries, volunteers and personalities involved in sponsorship.

So important are people and their quality to some organizations which market services that 'internal marketing' is considered to be an important management role to ensure that all staff are customer conscious (*see* Chapter 11).

Another vital group of people are consumers, past, existing or potential. They play a part in producing the service and therefore influence the process: they also affect and influence each other. The quality of a user's experience of, say, a restaurant or a package tour will be influenced by other consumers using the restaurant or using the same hotel and tour operator. Also from the viewpoint of the service performer the nature and type of people who use and consume the service effects the image that the service develops and maintains. A high-class restaurant needs high-class clientele: an upmarket management consultancy needs nationally and internationally known clients.

Consumers of course talk about their experiences of service organizations and 'word of mouth' can be a most potent force in the shaping of a service organization's image–for good or for ill. Thus other consumers, their knowledge, skills, attitudes, behaviour, appearance and the roles they play have an influence upon the service product.

Physical Evidence

Physical objects consist of buildings, plant, equipment, tools, the layout of facilities, and tangible elements of the services from airplanes to labels, documents and forms. Gronroos[8] calls these the 'physical/technical resources'. 'The customer experiences such resources either when he comes to the service company to buy and consume a service or when the service employee comes to him to deliver the service.'

Rathmell[14] used the terms 'facilitating goods' and 'support goods' to describe some of the tangible elements involved in service delivery. He suggests that many services require facilitating goods that enable service performance and production. These include the house that is rented, the car that is rented and the telephone that is hired.

He also suggests that there is often a substantial support goods component involved in the production and consumption of services. Investments in goods necessary before a service can be produced include air terminals, hotel rooms and leisure centres. Such support goods are not inventories but are more analogous to factories providing the means of services production or place for service performance. Support goods vary in their degree of essentiality to the performance of particular services and they may be owned, hired, leased, borrowed or rented.

Such support goods and facilitating goods are tangible elements of service provision and of course may be used up during the process of service production and consumption and need maintenance repair and possibly replacement.

The context in which such physical objects are set will also influence service product performance and delivery. Intangible qualities like 'atmosphere' and 'image' may derive from the physical objects, the people providing the service and the setting, economic, geographic, cultural. The 'total experience' which consumers may derive from service product usage may be due to a host of influences. Thus a package tour's success may depend upon the exotic location or the climate as much as upon the other participants or the hotel complex (*see* Chapter 12).

6.3 Need for Integration

From the above it is clear that a service product is a complex phenomenon. It consists of an array of elements each of which has to be considered by the service manager in operating his organization. `Managing a service organization requires a clear understanding of these elements and the relationships and interactions between them. Successful management of a service organization can only be achieved by the sensitive integration of the elements comprising the service product from the provider's viewpoint, with expectations and perceptions of the service product from the consumer's viewpoint. This is a difficult task.[15] It is made even more so by the fact that few service organizations have only one service product. Most offer a range of service products.

6.4 Service Product Organizations

When does a good become a service and vice versa? A car is a good but, when Avis rent it, it becomes a service. Following from this is the issue of when does an organization become one selling service products? Does it depend upon employees involved in service provision compared with goods production; or sales attributable to each; or profits accruing from each type of activity? Clearly there are no simple answers to such questions and categorizing organizations using such dimensions has difficulties. Sasser *et al.*[2] have suggested that as firms grow there is a tendency to move along a spectrum with goods and services as the bi-polar points. They give examples of trends observable in business organizations which have moved along the spectrum such as the 'prepackaging' or 'premanufacturing' of services (e.g. do-it-yourself kits; self instruction courses) or the 'consumerization' of a service (i.e. the transfer of part of the production of a service to the consumer) like self service.

The notion of a goods-service continuum is conceptually attractive but presents problems in putting it into practice. Yet it is important for organizations to try to:

1 understand where they currently lie on this continuum;
2 understand the direction in which they are moving.

For certainly organizations with any major involvement in the service sector have ultimately to face the issue of how do they define their service product or products. It is a problem in which some of the concepts presented in this chapter may have utility.

6.5 Summary

1 Service organizations need to establish linkages between the service product as perceived by customers and what is offered by the organization.
2 In doing so it is helpful to distinguish between the:
    consumer benefit concept;
    the service concept;
    the service offer;
    the service delivery system.
3 A service offer has three components:
    service elements;

service forms;
service levels.
4 The process of service product performance and delivery is an integral component of a service product. A number of components are important in most service delivery systems including people and physical objects.

Questions for Discussion

1 What is a service product?
2 Can a service product be separated from the service delivery system?
3 Distinguish between 'core' services and 'peripheral' services.
4 What is the relationship between 'the consumer benefit concept' and 'the service concept'?
5 What are the key components of a service offer?
6 What uncontrollable elements may influence a consumer's perception of a service product?
7 Identify six main factors which will influence a service organization's 'product design'?
8 What are the differences between service quantity and service quality?
9 Distinguish between the tangible and intangible elements of the service product offer of an organization with which you are familiar.
10 What difficulties may arise in translating a 'service concept' into a 'service offer'?

References and Notes

1 Eiglier, P. and Langeard, E. 'A conceptual approach of the service offer', Working paper No. 217, iae Aix-en-Provence, April 1981.
2 Sasser, W. E., Olsen, R. P. and Wyckoff, D. D. *Management of Service Operations – Text and Cases*, Allyn and Bacon, Boston, Mass. 1978.
3 Christopher, M., Schary, P. and Skjott-Larsen, T. *Customer Service and distribution strategy.* Associated Business Press, London, 1970.
4 Bateson, J. 'Do we need service marketing?', Marketing Consumer Services: New Insights, Report 77–115, Marketing Science Institute, Boston, Nov. 1977.
5 Wittreich, W. J., 'How to buy/sell professional services,' *Harvard Business Review*, Vol. 44, March–April 1966, p. 127.
6 See, for example, Wilson, A., *The Marketing of Professional Services*, McGraw-Hill, London, 1972.
7 Levitt, T., 'Marketing Myopia', *Harvard Business Review*, Vol. 38, July–Aug. 1960, pp. 24–47.
8 Gronroos, C. 'An Applied Service Marketing Theory', Working Paper No. 57, Swedish School of Economics and Business Administration, Helsinki, 1980.
9 Kotler, P. *Principles of Marketing*, Prentice-Hall, Englewood Cliffs, 1980.
10 Shostack, G. L. 'Breaking Free from Product Marketing', *Journal of Marketing* Vol. 41, No. 2, April 1977, pp. 73–80.

11 Levitt, T. 'Marketing intangible products and ´product intangibles', *Harvard Business Review*, Vol. 59, May–June 1981, pp. 94–102.

12 Hostage, G. M. 'Quality control in a service business', *Harvard Business Review*, Vol. 53, July–Aug. 1975, pp. 98–106.

13 Sasser, E. W. and Pettway, S. H., 'Case of Big Macs pay plans', *Harvard Business Review*, Vol. 52, July–Aug. 1974, pp. 30–46 and 156–8.

14 Rathmell, J. M. *Marketing in the Service Sector*, Winthrop, Cambridge, Mass. 1974.

15 For one suggestion on how to set about this see Shostack, G. L., 'How to design a service', *European Journal of Marketing*, Vol. 16, No. 1, 1982, pp. 49–63.

7.   SERVICE PRODUCT PLANNING AND DEVELOPMENT

7.1 Introduction

Customers derive benefits and satisfactions from the service products they consume. The decisions therefore that are associated with the planning and development of the service product are central to the success of service marketing organizations. Further, the selection and development of a service product and the range of services offered are strategic decisions and have an influence on many other decisions in the organization whether to do with the kind of personnel employed or with the integration of other elements of the marketing mix with the service product mix. It follows then that service product strategies are no less important to service marketing organizations than they are to organizations marketing goods. Characteristics like intangibility and the involvement of the consumer in service production and performance do not invalidate the relevance of product planning and development to service settings.

This chapter examines the relevance of some of the concepts conventionally employed in the context of the product planning and development of tangibles and considers their validity for services settings. First there is an examination of the Product Life-Cycle Concept. Secondly the ways in which organizations may grow is considered. There then follows a discussion of New Service Product Development, Modification and Elimination.

7.2 The Product Life-Cycle

One of the most common ideas in marketing is the concept of the Product Life-Cycle. Almost without exception basic marketing texts refer to and illustrate the meaning of this concept. Briefly, it is suggested that products pass through a number of stages over time. These are usually described as[1]:

Introduction

Sales of new products increase slowly at first. Factors influencing the growth of sales at this stage include the relatively small number of innovative customers, problems of building effective distribution, technical problems of assuring quality and reliability and limited production capacity. Profits too may be low or non-existent at this stage because of factors like the promotional costs involved in promoting sales.

115

Growth

In this stage sales growth develops. More consumers follow the lead of innovators, the market broadens through policies of product differentiation and market segmentation, competitors enter the market, and distribution broadens. Profit margins peak as experience effects serve to reduce unit costs and promotional expenditures are spread over larger sales volumes.

Maturity

In this stage sales growth slows down with market acceptance and even market saturation. Growth is increasingly governed by factors like population growth or attempts to stretch the cycle through market segmentation strategies. Profits too decline because of the number of competitive offerings, cost reductions become more difficult and smaller specialist competitors eat into the market.

Decline

In this stage sales decline through factors like changing tastes and fashions and technical advances causing product substitution. Declining sales are accompanied by reducing profit margins as too many competitors fight for the remaining market. Price cutting may be active and marginal competitors fall out of the industry.

This classic product life-cycle is illustrated in Figure 7.1. It shows the two key elements in the life-cycle, sales and profits, and the relationship, over time, between them. Further as Doyle[1] indicates:

'the primary economic conclusions from these patterns are first that management must develop new products to fill the "gap" and sustain sales and profit growth. . . . Second,

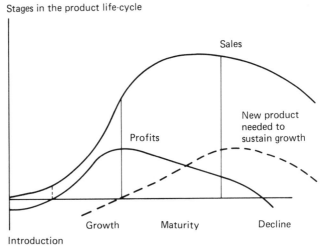

Figure 7.1 The Product Life-Cycle

each stage of the cycle offers distinct opportunities and problems with respect to marketing strategy and profit potential.'

Hise[2] suggests that the sales volume history of many products and services may not accord with the generalized model illustrated. He illustrates some of the likely mutations to the basic concept. These are shown in Figure 7.2.

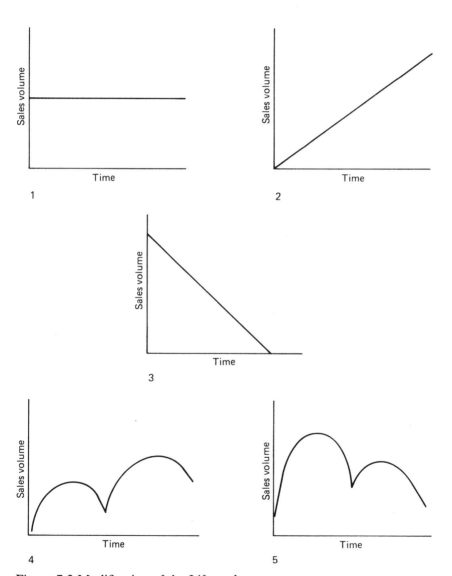

Figure 7.2 Modification of the Life-cycle
Source: Hise, R. T. *Product/Service Strategy*, Petrocelli/Charter, New York, 1977

The first example is a product or service which establishes its place in the market from the very beginning and continues sales at much the same level. The second example represents a product or service with advantages over competitors and continues to pick up new customers and repeat business. The third example is of a product or service which starts with an advantage over competitors' offerings but is then made obsolete by others judged to be superior. The fourth example is where a product or service which has progressed into the decline stage is rescued by a promotional campaign or price cut which leads to the development of an even more favourable sales curve. The fifth example is of a product or service revitalized during the decline stage although the second life-cycle in this case is not as successful as the first cycle. The examples shown only present the sales curve and do not focus on the pattern of profit growth and decline in each case.

7.21 Relevance to Service Products

The underlying logic and attractiveness of the life-cycle concept to service marketors is undeniable. Intuitively therefore one cannot but agree with Rathmell[3] that: 'Services, like goods, have life cycles' and he suggests that services in the growth segment of the life-cycle include telecommunications, health maintenance delivery systems, leasing and forms of outdoor recreation. Services which appear to have passed their peak of growth include the cinema, watch repairing, domestic services and single sex educational institutions.

The concept is widely referred to in other services marketing contexts. For example, McIver and Naylor[4] suggest that it is generally applicable to the marketing of financial services; Kotler[5] suggests that it is generally applicable to marketing for non-profit organizations; Laczniak[6] specifically suggests its applicability for arts organizations. Two areas of services marketing where the concept is particularly quoted as of relevance are tourism and air transport. Wahab *et al.*[7] suggest that tourism products have short lives (Montparnasse) or long (Madame Tussaud's). Those that have taken on a new lease of life include transatlantic liners (for cruises), branch railway lines (run by clubs of amateurs) and canal barges (used for holidays rather than moving goods). With others, they suggest, changes in fashion and in social mores have resulted in permanent decline:

> 'The assembly rooms in Bath were handsomely restored after their wartime bombing, but they have not been filled with the spectacles for which they were designed in the 18th century. Monarchs no longer meet at Marienbad. And the Orient Express witnesses a confusion of huddled Turks, rather than the downfall of Hungarian countesses.'

The transatlantic airline industry is believed to have progressed to the maturity phase of the life-cycle.[8] The introductory stage, involving competition with sea travel from the end of the Second World War until 1958 was on the basis of speed and convenience rather than price. The introduction of jet passenger transport and air economy fares in 1958 led to the growth phase of the life-cycle and much harsher competition for sea transport. The maturity phase from the early 1970s to the present time has been marked by increasing price sensitivity and the growing success of charter flights and cheap fare offers.

An interesting illustration of the life-cycle is that applied by Sasser *et al.*[9] to the multisite service firm. They generalize that based on experience of multisite companies like McDonalds, Holiday Inns and Hertz the multisite firm passes through five stages. These stages are:

entrepreneurial;
multisite rationalization;
growth;
maturity;
decline/regeneration;

Each stage of the life-cycle is described and examined in the context of the five major functional areas of the firm:

finance/control;
operations;
marketing;
development;
administration.

From their examination of each stage of the life-cycle and these main functional areas they believe that by identifying a company's position in the life-cycle, the major objectives, decisions, problems and organizational transitions needed for the future can be anticipated. They develop their analysis further to consider how a firm's costs might behave as it passes through the life-cycle (e.g. economies may flow from learning and volume increases).

The lessons service managers can extract from their analysis, the authors suggest, are that the successful growth of a multisite firm depends upon the ability of its executive to manage the present and the future. As the firm progresses through the life-cycle the following management actions must be undertaken:

(*a*) management must understand there are four basic functions to manage (new unit development, operations, marketing, concept development);
(*b*) the founder(s) must delegate;
(*c*) the management team must develop or acquire the competencies required to manage a larger firm;
(*d*) management motivation must be maintained;
(*e*) sloppy (i.e. haphazard) growth must be avoided;
(*f*) the firm must change a mature concept;
(*g*) the firm must not diversify too quickly. Communication channels must be kept open.

The detailed argument and analysis, presented by Sasser *et al.*[9] represents an important contribution to the literature on life-cycles and service operations and is worthy of further refinement and more detailed empirical evaluation. In particular how to implement some of their suggested managerial actions, and the utility of some of their concepts to a United Kingdom setting and contexts other than service firms, are areas deserving further research.

Another example of the use of a form of the life-cycle concept is that of Urwin[10] in what he termed 'customized communications'. He believes that service industries go through two phases of an industrial life-cycle. In the first phase jobs are done by hand and the service is personalized and diversified to meet the needs of individual customers. In the second phase the service industry begins to rationalize, mechanize and streamline its services. Urwin argues that knowing which stage of the cycle an industry is in has implications for the communications mix that will be used and he suggests that the purpose of the communications efforts, the types of appeals made (e.g. building awareness, motivating use) the form of such appeals (e.g. use of emotional themes) and whether services will be promoted separately or together varies according to the stage of the cycle.

On the basis of some of this evidence it would seem that the product life-cycle concept is of relevance to the service sector. However there are a number of criticisms that must be noted.

7.22 *Problems with the Product Life-Cycle Concept*

In spite of the examples given in the previous section there are problems in applying the Product Life-Cycle concept to service products. These problems are of three kinds:

(*a*) general criticisms of the life-cycle and of its relevance to services;
(*b*) definitional problems;
(*c*) lack of empirical evidence of its validity.

General Criticisms of the Life-cycle and of its Relevance to Services

It is not surprising that the life-cycle concept has critics. Some attempts to derive the conventional S-shaped curve of the cycle with its stages of introduction, growth, maturity and decline have not been altogether convincing.[11] In fact some authors have even gone so far as to suggest that the idea should be forgotten altogether.[12] Carman and Langeard[13] argue that using the life-cycle concept to build a product portfolio in services contexts is not very helpful. While it may be useful for a company to balance its tangible products by stage of the life-cycle as part of its planning process, they argue that with some exceptions (e.g. banks,) most service organizations have only a very small number of core services or do not have the flexibility for combining different services belonging to the same category. They also highlight the importance of defining in what context the term product life-cycle is used. This gives rise to a second set of problems.

Definitional Problems

There are two issues here. First it is necessary to distinguish between the different ways in which the Product Life-Cycle concept is used. It may refer to a product class (e.g. cigarettes) a product form, (e.g. filter cigarettes), or a brand (e.g. Senior Service). Also the concept may be used to describe the life-cycle of a firm (*see* Sasser *et al.*[9]). Figure 7.3 shows the cycles for a product class (total sales of cigarettes), two product forms (plain or filter), and a brand (Guards filter). Product classes have the longest life-cycles; product forms tend to be like the standard S-shape while brands may show an erratic picture because of changing competitive policies.

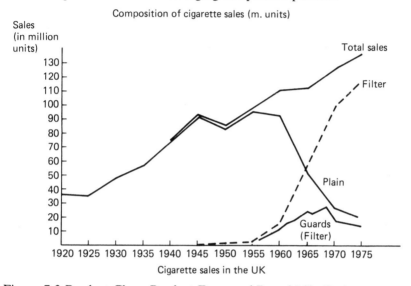

Figure 7.3 Product Class, Product Form and Brand Life-Cycles

Source: Doyle, P. 'The realities of the Product Life Cycle', *Quarterly Review of Marketing* – Summer 1976, pp. 1–6

Secondly in addition to these issues of classification, Doyle[1] suggests that sales data used to establish Product Life-Cycles need to be adjusted for seasonal and erratic movements, the effects of inflation and for population growth if technically useful life-cycles are to be derived.

Lack of Empirical Evidence of its Validity

A final and telling criticism voiced by Doyle[1] that: 'there has been no comprehensive empirical research on its validity'. While there is evidence that most products do follow a broad life-cycle pattern the patterns do not seem to be regular enough to allow the use of the product life-cycle as a forecasting tool. Even more significant from the viewpoint of service product marketors is the dearth of studies relating to services. Much of the empirical evidence that is available concerns products like cigarettes, drugs, capital goods, grocery products and health products.

On the basis of the above criticisms therefore and, until there is more substantial evidence of the validity of the Product Life-Cycle concept in service product situations, caution must be exercised in its use. It would seem that one is prevented from making statements, other than those which are most carefully defined and supported by empirical evidence, about the use of the concept in service product marketing situations.

7.3 Growth Directions

An important influence upon an organization's service product planning will be its service product/market strategy.[14] This relates to the decisions taken in the organization regarding the target markets it chooses to go after and the service products it offers to those markets. A simple version of this idea for services is provided by Wilson[15] who sets out the service product/ market options available to an organization in terms of the situation it is attempting to achieve and the implications for its resources (capabilities, facilities and markets). These options and their implications are shown in Table 7.1.

Table 7.1
New Service Options

Situation	*Resource*
1 Attempting to sell more existing services to existing clients	Existing capability, facilities, and market position
2 Attempting to sell existing services to new clients	Existing capabilities and facilities. No market resources
3 Attempting to sell new services to existing clients	Market resources, no existing capability or facility resource
4 Attempting to sell new services in new markets	Nil

Source: Wilson, A. *The Marketing of Professional Services*, McGraw-Hill, London, 1972

A more elaborate version in terms of directions for growth an organization can take along the two vectors of product development and market developments is shown in the matrix in Table 7.2.[16] This matrix provides a useful framework for marketors of services suggesting a wider range of options than Wilson though using product terminology. Before giving examples to illustrate the matrix in services contexts it is important to emphasize three aspects related to it. These are firstly the notion of what is a 'new' service product; secondly the importance of its resource base to any service organization adjusting the range of services it offers or considering moves into new markets; thirdly the importance of a service product range and associated make or buy decisions.

7.31 New Service Products

It is necessary to define what is meant by a new service product. Wilson[15] argues for a definition which is as wide as possible and he includes:

Table 7.2
Growth Vectors

Market	Present	Product modification quality style performance	Product range extension size variation variety variation	New products in related technology	New products in unrelated technologies
Present	Market–penetration strategies	Product–reformulation strategies	Product range–extension strategies	Product–development strategies	Lateral–diversification strategies
New	Market–development strategies	Market–extension strategies	Market–segmentation–product differentiation strategies	Product–diversification strategies	Longitudinal–diversification strategies
Resource and/or distribution markets			Forward or backward integration strategies		

Source: Christopher, M., McDonald, M. and Wills, G. *Introducing Marketing*, Pan, London, 1980

second and subsequent generation service products;
service products new to a service organizations range but already available in the market;
service products already available but adapted for a new market;
totally new service products.

Rathmell distinguishes two key elements, the service offer and the service delivery system.[3] He suggests that a distinction can be made between a new service and a new method of delivering a service though expresses doubt about whether the latter is a new service product as such. The conceptual difficulty of defining what is new and the problems which exist in attempting to distinguish whether sampled new and improved products are in fact new or improved products or new or improved means of delivering an existing product, are illustrated in the list he presents in Table 7.3.

7.32 Resource Base

Opportunities in the marketplace provide the impetus for service product policies. However such policies must be based on careful consideration of the resources which a service organization has or can acquire. The capabilities of a service organization are both a creator and a limiter of the opportunities of which a service organization may take advantage. Marketing involves the matching of opportunities with an organization's

Table 7.3
Examples of Service Product Innovations

Nature of Service	New Service Product	Service Product Improvement
Communications	Communication satellite	Free-standing public telephone
Consulting and business facilitating	Equipment leasing	Overnight TV rating service
Educational	Three-year degrees	New Curricula
Financial	Bank credits cards	'Bank by mail'
Health	Treatment with lasers	Intensive care
Household operations	Laundromat	Fuel budget accounts
Housing	Housing for the elderly	Motel Swimming pool
Insurance	National health insurance	No-fault insurance
Legal	'Divorce Yourself' kit*	Legal services for the poor
Personal	Physical fitness facilities	—
Recreational	Dual cinema	New play
Transportation	Unit train	Flight reservation system

*Under court injunction in New York but being appealed.

Source: Rathmell, J. M. *Marketing in the Service Sector*, Winthrop, Cambridge, Mass. 1974

abilities. The service product is the vehicle through which service organizations achieve this matching.

A problem many service organizations face is that they may be unaware of all the capabilities they have. This applies particularly to those service organizations where the tangible elements of the service product are a small component of it and where the intangible elements – particularly human skills and aptitudes – are a large component. Writing of professional services Wilson[15] says: 'It is truly surprising how rarely well organized and managed firms have failed to audit all the areas in which they have capability. This is because of the intangibility of this capability.'

An understanding of an organization's abilities is therefore an important step in identifying realistic service product/market strategies.

7.33 Service Product Range

Few service marketing organizations offer only one service. They usually offer a mix of services for use or purchase. The idea of the service product range concerns the set or mix of all service products offered by an organization. Table 7.4 shows a partial list of services offered by U.S. banks to corporate and to retail markets.

Table 7.4
List of Typical Services offered by U.S. Banks to Corporate and Retail Customers

	Corporate	Retail
Funds using services		
Current loans	√	
Term loans	√	
Export financing	√	
Overdrafts	√	√
Consumer financing		√
Credit card	√	√
Mortgage loans	√	√
Installment loans		√
Acceptances	√	
Discounted trade bills	√	
Commercial credits	√	
Factoring	√	
Equipment leasing	√	
Non-fund using credit		
Commitments	√	
Clean credits	√	
Acceptances	√	
Commercial credits	√	
Funds-generating services		
Checking accounts	√	√
Regular savings		√
Club accounts		√
Passbook savings		√
Time deposits	√	√
Offshore time deposits	√	
Certificates of deposit	√	√
Treasury tax and loan personal pension	√	
Commission services		
Domestic collection	√	√
Foreign collection	√	√
Freight payment	√	
Lockbox	√	
Cash management	√	
Automatic pay deposit	√	√
Bill paying services	√	√
Personal custodian	√	
Corporate custodian		√
Credit reports	√	
Investment advisory	√	√
Merger/acquisition	√	
Account reconciliation	√	√

	Corporate	Retail
Foreign exchange	√	√
Travellers cheques		√
Travel services	√	√
Automated services	√	
Budgeting services		√

*From Wat Tyler, 'Organizing the Critical Tasks in Bank Marketing.' in Leonard L. Berry and L. A. Capaldini, eds., *Marketing for the Bank Executive*, (Petrocelli Books, New York, 1974), p. 84–5.

Source: Berry, L. L. and Donnelly, J. H. (Jnr) 'Marketing for Bankers', American Institute of Banking, 1975

The particular range of services offered will be developed in response to internal needs or to external influences. For example a leisure organization with highly seasonal patterns of usage may decide to add additional services to its range to help overcome these seasonal sales patterns. Or the same organization may add additional services to its range in response to expressed customers' wishes or as a reaction to competitors' actions.

A typical service product range has width and depth. Width refers to the number of different service product lines offered while depth refers to the assortment of items within each service product line. For its part a service product line is a group of service product items which share similar characteristics in terms of say customers, end use, sales methods or price range. Table 7.5 illustrates the concepts of service product range, width, depth and service product line using simple customer-based categories for a local authority leisure centre. The basis of the width of the product range in Table 7.5 could have been different. In this instance, for illustrative purposes, it is customer based but there is scope for more imaginative service product range bases which can be linked with market segments. Customer and user perceptions of product lines can often give service marketors useful insights into ways in which the service product mix should be extended or reduced or service product lines stretched or shortened. Morrill[17] for example, indicated how life insurance spending patterns in the 1950s had not kept pace with income growth and instanced some of the new or multi-line selling approaches possible as a result (e.g. family life policies, easier methods of payment, simpler procedures, property insurance development).

In designing a service product range careful attention needs to be devoted to:

1 What the optimum range of service should be. There is no foolproof way to do this and most organizations rely on trial and error.
2 The positioning of the range of services provided against competitors' offerings.
3 The length and width of the range and the complementarity of separate service products within it; and the synergistic effects of range developments.

Table 7.5
Illustrative Service Product Range

	Infants	Children	Mixed Adults	Single sex Adult Groups	Pensioners
	Creche	Swimming lesson	Badminton classes	Weight training	Exercise group
	Socialization groups	Football league	Squash coaching	Karate	Bowls
	Mother and child classes	Tennis tournaments	Squash league Hockey teams	Slimming clubs	Social group

4 In commercial services contexts, the profitability of the range of services. In most organizations the Pareto principle – the 80/20 principle – applies. 80% of profits come from 20% of customers and so on. However service marketors should remember that there is nothing immutable about the principle. It is not a natural law but one based upon empirical evidence. That does not necessarily make it a guiding principle for action.

7.34 Make or Buy Decision

A related decision faced by service marketing organizations is whether to invest in capital, people and training in order to develop additional service products through one's own efforts and resources or whether to buy in the resources of others. Thus a restaurant could buy in prepared foods or produce its own special dishes; a consultancy could train its own managers or buy in staff from outside; an advertising agency could buy in staff to provide additional specialist services like specialist photography or continue to sub-contract work to outsiders. The make or buy decision for service products, at its most general level, resembles the decision in relation to channel choice which revolves around the issue of cost versus control.

On a larger scale, make or buy decisions become a form of intra-service sector competition. Thus banks have broadened their range of services in recent years and this has now brought them into direct competition with other financial service organizations. They compete with insurance companies for some of their personal and pension scheme arrangements; they compete with building societies in the home loans market. Airlines own and operate their own hotels and terminals. Such examples illustrate some of the diversification growth which has occurred in the service sector.

They also reflect the growth of the idea of systems selling where an organization (like a bank) attempts to provide a total system of benefits for customers relating to their financial affairs.

Of course many goods producing companies have also expanded into the service sector. Rathmell[3] identifies several patterns of diversification into services:

> 'First, conglomerates have not hesitated to acquire service businesses. A review of the reports of larger conglomerates shows that very few have failed to invade one type of service industry or another. A second pattern is a selective and judiciously planned entry into services, not by conglomerates, but as a strategy of product line extension. Third, the systems selling pattern is becoming increasingly evident as firms manufacturing capital goods enter into long term contracts with customers to service the capital goods they sell. Fourth, some firms are capitalizing on internal know-how; if skills work for the firm, and are of a non proprietary nature, they are a marketable intangible product. Finally, some manufacturers have broken into the service sector for a variety of reasons ranging from social responsibility to public relations.'

Such moves have been commonplace amongst manufacturing and commercial organizations. Mapel[18] recognizes that many service businesses are outgrowths of product businesses. Cars need insurance, repairs and financing; houses need maintenance, repair, insurance and financing. He suggests that an opportunity for those who produce products lies in converting the product into a service.

7.35 Illustrations of the Matrix in Services Contexts

Table 7.2 shows a number of growth directions available to organizations based on the two vectors of product development and market development. Some examples which are drawn from services contexts illustrate the use of the matrix as a framework for developing service product/market strategies.

Market Penetration

American Express encourage current subscribers to recommend new subscribers through the offer of free goods for each new subscriber enlisted.

Market Development

A British hotel chain has opened up a new market by offering 'leisure learning' weekends in its hotels.[16]

Service Product Reformulation

Criticisms of standards of comfort and flight service on airlines by businessmen have led to the introduction of better seating and a standard of service different from that available for economy passengers.

Market Extension

British banks have attempted to reach new markets through developing a special range of services for students who open accounts with them.

Service Product Range Extension

The Production Engineering Research Association (PERA) offered a management consultancy service for members.[15]

Market Segmentation

A holiday tour company designed a different kind of holiday for older people. This opened up a new market segment in the holiday market.

Product Development

A good deal of growth in the banking industry has come from offering existing customers new services like financial counselling, investment plans, investment advice and insurance.[2]

Product Diversification

Airlines have secured additional revenues by offering new travel packages and setting up their own travel and hotel companies.[2]

Lateral Diversification

A successful French company in the materials handling market acquired a small warehouse design consultancy which then enabled the company to offer a complete package to its customers.[16]

Longitudinal Diversification

An Irish TV rental company successfully launched an office equipment leasing company into an area hardly known before. Hitherto, office equipment was purchased. Leasing became an attractive and profitable alternative for both customers and the company.[16]

Forward Integration

A British building society increased its deposit and savers substantially by a planned expansion of its high street retail outlets.

Backward Integration

A dry cleaning company acquired the company making the equipment which it used in its cleaning outlets.

In general service organizations should develop alternatives which cost the least to pursue but which are compatible with its areas of competence and growth and profit objectives. This probably means starting with existing markets and existing services and moving into less familiar ground when opportunities for improvement in these areas have been exhausted.

7.36 Criticisms of the Service Product/market Matrix

Criticism of the service product/market matrix and its uncritical use in service marketing situations has been expressed by Carmen and Langeard.[13] In their examination of the logical, minimum risk growth strategy paths for service firms and low technology product firms with a high service component they argue that the growth strategy paths are different. Their suggested growth paths for service-oriented firms and product-oriented firms are shown in Table 7.6.

Table 7.6
Comparison of Growth Paths for Service and Product-oriented firms

Service-Oriented Firm	Product-Oriented Firm
Penetration	Penetration
Geographic market expansion	Geographic market expansion
Innovative redesign of existing services	Sociodemographic market expansion
New core service development	Innovative redesign of existing products
or	Product development
Concentric diversification	Expand to out-of-country markets
Expand to out-of-country markets	Concentric diversification
Conglomerate diversification	Conglomerate diversification

Source: Carman, J. M. and Langeard, E. 'Growth Strategies for Service Firms', Proceedings of the 8th Annual Meeting of the European Academy for Advanced Research in Marketing, Groningen, 1979

The point of departure between the two strategies comes at the stage where a service-oriented firm, like a product-oriented firm, might be expected to pursue a policy of market segmentation in its growth path. They suggest that a service firm does not have the same flexibility as a product-oriented firm both to change the conceptualization of its 'core' service to fit the new market segment and to isolate existing market segments from information about such a new conceptualization. The strong relationship between the service product and the service delivery system (*see* Chapter 6) create structural problems for this particular strategy. Better alternatives to market segmentation are the development of new core services to be sold to existing market segments, selling the existing service overseas and concentric diversification (i.e. where there is some commonality between the new venture and the old like a similar process or marketing approach, though it is not a common market or product).

Although the authors do not support their arguments with anything more than general evidence, their work does reflect a necessary and healthy criticism of the too-ready acceptance of the conventional wisdom in marketing. This applies particularly to the marketing of services where the assumption is made too readily that ideas and concepts developed in goods contexts may be applied indiscriminately in services contexts.

7.4 New Service Product Development

'In general, new product development for services does not appear to be a highly developed art. Most service firms have not established formal new product development departments'.[2] It is possible to question this statement for there is evidence that many service organizations like banks, travel companies and insurance companies do take product development seriously. Yet it is also true that many service organizations do not consider the opportunities available through developing new services. Writing of professional services Wilson said[15]

> 'often the initial mistake . . . is to restrict its perspectives and to limit its consideration of market opportunities by taking the existing service "product" as the basic target in planning marketing activities. If, however, the service "product" is seen as a means of reaching the sales targets, the need for analysis of "product" alternatives and the constant search for new "product" ideas is highlighted.'

All too often because service organizations take too narrow a view of their skills the issue of developing new service products is often neglected. This is shortsighted and in the longer term can be dangerous.

Some reasons suggested for the relatively elementary stage reached in the service sector on organized new service product development include:[2]

(a) the limited resources (e.g. financial, human) of many service firms;
(b) public sector organizations with little competition may lack the motivation to innovate;
(c) services subject to government regulation and control may provide limited opportunities for innovation because of these constraints;
(d) the relative newness of the service sector and small amount of attention it has received may partly explain lack of progress as far as new service product development is concerned.

In addition it has been suggested that the development of new service products is a much more difficult art than the development of new products and that this too could be a limitation on the stage of development reached so far in this area in the service sector 'the successful development of a new service . . . is so difficult it makes new product development look like child's play'.[19]

Service marketing organizations cannot continue to rely on their existing service products for their success. It is obviously necessary for them to develop new kinds of services. Some of the reasons why this is so include the following.[2]

The Need to Remain Competitive
New services are required to maintain present sales success as well as to capitalize on changing requirements in the marketplace.

Replacing Service Products Eliminated from the Portfolio
New service products need to be introduced to replace those which have become outdated and whose sales are declining.

Utilizing Excess Capacity

New service products will be introduced to take advantage of spare capacity like spare theatre seats or unused facilities in a sports centre.

Smoothing out Seasonal Fluctuation

Many service organizations (e.g. in the tourism field) may have seasonal sales patterns. New service products may be introduced to even out fluctuations in sales.

Risk Reduction

New service products can be introduced to balance an existing sales pattern where heavy dependence may be placed on a few services offered in the service product range.

Exploiting New Opportunities

New opportunities may arise through a competitor dropping out of the market or through changing customer needs.

Whatever the reasons for introducing new services products they may be obtained in two ways. First they may be acquired externally through acquisition or through licensing, a strategy common in international marketing (*see* Chapter 14). Secondly they may be obtained internally through the process of new service product development, the focus of discussion here. Both strategies of course are risky and there are a number of illustrations and insights into the reasons for new product failure.[2] In the service product sector however there is much less substantial evidence about why new service products fail. What is available is much more fragmentary.

7.41 Failure of new service Products

Eiglier and Langeard[20] suggest that the lack of success of a new service offering is based upon management inability in handling four key decisions and the relationships between them. Basing their judgement upon observations across a range of service industries they suggest that the four key decisions are as follows.

The Service Concept

This has to be clearly defined. It must consider what customer benefits the service firm is intending to serve, the service attributes expressing the customer benefits, and the ways and means the service is produced, distributed and consumed.

The Market Segment

The dimensions used to define the market segment must take account of the needs people have for a specific service and the trade-offs they are willing to make in terms of accessibility (e.g. time versus money).

The Organization–client Interface

The interface has to be organized as a network. Two key considerations are the participative behaviour expected from clients and, with the development of large service networks, the control of interface complexity.

The Service Image

The service image is dependent not only on the use of the conventional mass media but also upon the way in which the whole image is created and sustained through clients interacting with the service organization and clients themselves spreading an image when sharing their experiences with others.

They suggest that there must be coherence and cohesiveness within and between these four key elements.

In the context of bank services, Berry and Donnelly[21] argue that the failure of many new bank services can be attributed to the failure of bank marketors to:

visualize new products from the perspective of the consumer;
engage in creative research for uncovering unfulfilled needs within various market segments;
effectively minimize the psychological discomfort associated with new products requiring substantive behavioural change of the consumer;
clearly and graphically communicate the benefits of new products to the market segments towards which they are directed.

Wilson[15] suggests that in respect of professional services creative problem solvers find it difficult to be consistently creative. This may account for the high rate of failure of new service companies and generally low profit levels.

What the evidence does confirm is that service products are as likely to fail in the marketplace as any others. Organizations concerned with their marketing may try to reduce the risks involved by utilizing the approach suggested to be of relevance for goods. This consists of adopting procedures to contain risk – as far as possible – in the new product development process.

7.42 New Service Product Development Procedures

Rathmell[3] says that: 'The conventional steps of exploration, screening, business analysis, development, testing and commercialization apply to services as well as goods' and there is some evidence that this is so. While the terminology of new product development and the range and order of steps included in the process varies, the underlying notions behind the use of systematic procedures does not. These are first to create as many good ideas as possible, secondly to reduce the number of ideas by careful screening and analysis so ensuring that only those with the best chances of success get into the marketplace.

Idea Generation

Ideas may be generated in many ways. They can arise inside the organization and outside it; they can result from formal search procedures (e.g. marketing research) as well as informally: they may involve the organization in creating the means of delivering the new service product or they may involve the organization in obtaining rights to the service product, like a franchise. The sources of such ideas are many and have been illustrated by Oliver[22] as shown in Figure 7.4.

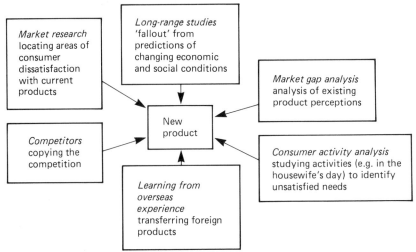

Figure 7.4 External Sources of New Product Ideas

Source: Oliver, G. *Marketing Today*, Prentice-Hall, Englewood Cliffs, 1980

Excluded from this figure are ideas generated through the internal creative process. The creative process of developing new ideas has intrigued marketors although the process itself still defies detailed understanding. This has led, in some cases, to the adoption of techniques, like 'synectics', brainstorming and lateral thinking to help improve the creative dimension of new product development. Wilson[15] for example, outlines the synectic method in his study of professional services but notes that, though it is a method sometimes used to help client problem-solving, it seems to be rarely used to solve professional services organizations' own service mix and marketing problems. He further suggests in this context that: 'In the development and use of structured approaches to creativity . . . the opportunity exists to move to the forefront of marketing thought and activity, since all marketors are still on the lower slopes of this development.'

Idea Screening

This stage is concerned with checking out which ideas will justify the time, expense and managerial commitment of further research and study. Two features usually associated with the screening phase are:

1 The establishment or use of previously agreed evaluative criteria to enable the comparison of ideas generated (e.g. ideas compatible with the organization's objectives and resources);

2 the weighing, ranking and rating of the ideas against the criteria used.

Screening systems range from the highly sophisticated involving the collection and analysis on computers of a mass of data to simple checklists of a few factors considered to be vital. O'Meara[23] for example, produced a widely quoted set of screening criteria for products which have since been used by many organizations. But it is important to stress that no single set of criteria is appropriate for all organizations. Organizations have to develop and adapt their own set of criteria to their particular circumstances. Wilson[15] gives a partial example of what is involved in this screening process. It relates to a search for new opportunities by a service industry skilled in establishing and operating local services and seeking to exploit this capability. However the criteria established for the first screening excluded consideration of any activity with a gambling or gaming element, undertaking, and services linked with the motor industry cycle. Any business with an actual or potential market exceeding £10m was considered. To quote Wilson:

> 'These were then compared with each other and against the firms criteria for the development of their services and corporate direction and growth. The most suitable services were then isolated and probed in depth. From this probing the marketing and "product" strategy was developed.'

A number of markets were studied for the selected business using the broad indicators of market size, market growth, level of service required and competition, as part of this screening process. They included security and protection, road haulage, furniture removal and storage, conference facilities, leasing, employment agencies and television rental (see Figure 7.5).

Concept Development and Testing

Ideas surviving the screening process then have to be translated into product concepts. In the service product context this means concept development and concept testing.

(a) Concept Development

This phase is concerned with translating the service product idea, where the possible service product is defined in functional and objective terms, into a service product concept, the specific subjective consumer meaning the organization tries to build into the product idea. Thus a building society in attempting to sell the idea of regular saving to young, unmarried people might attempt to market the idea on the basis that participants would be saving towards house purchase and might receive preferential treatment with a later mortgage application.

(b) Concept Testing

Concept testing is applicable in services' contexts as well as in goods' contexts. Concept testing consists of taking the concepts developed after

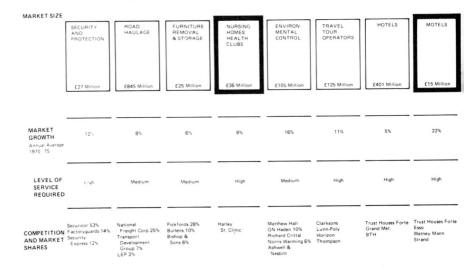

MARKET SIZE

	SECURITY AND PROTECTION	ROAD HAULAGE	FURNITURE REMOVAL & STORAGE	NURSING HOMES HEALTH CLUBS	ENVIRON-MENTAL CONTROL	TRAVEL TOUR OPERATORS	HOTELS	MOTELS
	£27 Million	£845 Million	£25 Million	£36 Million	£105 Million	£125 Million	£401 Million	£15 Million

MARKET GROWTH Annual Average 1970-75	12%	8%	6%	9%	16%	11%	5%	22%

LEVEL OF SERVICE REQUIRED	High	Medium	Medium	High	Medium	High	High	High

COMPETITION AND MARKET SHARES	Securicor 53% Factoryguards 14% Security Express 12%	National Freight Corp 25% Transport Development Group 7% LEP 3%	Pickfords 28% Bullens 10% Bishop & Sons 6%	Harley St. Clinic	Matthew Hall GN Haden 10% Richard Crittal Norris Warming 6% Ashwell & Nesbitt	Clarksons Lunn-Poly Horizon Thompson	Trust Houses Forte Grand Met. BTH	Trust Houses Forte Esso Watney Mann Strand

Figure 7.5 The UK Market for selected
figures adjusted to preserve

Source: *English Accountancy 180*

the stages of idea generation and idea screening and getting reactions to them from groups of target customers.

A number of studies have been reported in both profit contexts and in non-profit contexts. Wills[24] for example reports on the merits of three different types of life assurance proposal compared in a small pilot group. The study is interesting not only because it is concerned with a service but also because it employs a tool meriting wider development in service contexts, Lewin's 'vector analysis', to enable the measurement of strength of feeling towards various service dimensions and attributes. Moriarty and Venkatesan[25] describe an application of concept testing for the introduction of new financial aid management services in a non-profit context. They conclude from their study that concept evaluation procedures are applicable in a wide variety of settings. Further that segmentation analysis for new concepts can aid in planning and marketing of services by non-profit organizations before they are introduced. Mauser's[26] study, which is tangential to the field of service marketing, is interesting in that it shows how marketing research techniques developed for the evaluation of new product concepts were used to screen alternative conceptualizations of campaign strategy for a political candidate – although the candidate did lose!

Novel examples of concept testing in a high technology context are described by Blois and Cowell.[27] In one particular study they describe how a piece of specialist equipment developed by scientists thought to have

CONFERENCE FACILITIES	HOLIDAY & SIGHTSEEING COACHING	SAILING & BOATING	TELEVISION RENTAL	EMPLOYMENT AGENCIES	MANAGEMENT CONSULTANCY CONFERENCES SEMINARS	MICRO-FILMING DUPLICATING PHOTO-COPYING	LEASING	CAR HIRE	CATERING
£18 Million	£10 Million	£41 Million	£185 Million	£38 Million	£41 Million	£46 Million	£32 Million	£35 Million	£480 Million
11%	NIL	12%	12%	12%	11%	9%	25%	11%	6%
High	Low	Low	Medium	Medium	High	Low	Low	Medium	High
...ank ...ust Houses Forte	Wallace Arnold 18% Frames 8%	Lymington Marina Gosport Marina	Thorn 32% Rediffusion 16% Granada 12%	Brook St. Bureau 21% Alfred Marks 11% Conduit 15%	Urwick Orr 8% AIC 9% PE 7% Chartered Accountants PA Associated Business Programmes	Rank Xerox	Mercantile Leasing 30% Lloyds & Scottish 10% Bowmaker Commercial 15% Astley Leasing 10% United Dominions 5%	Hertz 18% Avis 15% Godfrey Davis 31%	Trust Houses Forte Mecca

...ervice businesses, 1969, (all
...ropriety information)
1954, Gee, London, 1954, pp. xiii

service applications in the area of fine measurement in fact turned out to be of much more relevance to provide a service in the area of non-destructive testing.

An associated stage of the development of the service product idea is that of service product positioning. Service product positioning is a concept increasingly widely referred to though it remains imprecisely defined, loosely used and difficult to measure. Essentially positioning is the visual presentation of the image of an organization's service product in relation either to competitive service products or to other service products in its own mix. The principle underlying this method of presentation is that it enables service product attributes to be compared with competitive offerings and with the customer's perceptions of products relative to his or her needs.

It is now widely employed in consumer goods markets but is also finding increasing use in services markets Coplin,[28] for example, argues that the joint application of consumer research and product positioning can assist in improving investor relationships. He suggests that the companies' stock should be viewed as a product that should be carefully positioned in the marketplace. A further illustration in a services context is the work of Wind and Robinson[29] who illustrate how visual mapping can be used for positioning a new bank service and the occupations of those likely to use the service, in a joint space map (*see* Figure 7.6).

Comparison of the services and the perceptions of the occupations of

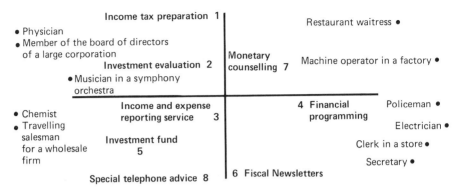

Figure 7.6 Joint Space Configuration of Eight Financial Services and Twelve Occupations

Source: Wind, Y. and Robinson, P. J. 'Product Positioning: An application of multi dimensional scaling' in Haley, R. I. (Ed.) *Attitude Research in Transition*, American Marketing Association, Chicago, 1972

persons who will use them reveals the existence of prestige and non-prestige services which give useful insights for developing a promotional programme.

Some services are best positioned directly against competition (e.g. tour operators). Other companies have developed effective strategies by deliberately not confronting competition directly. For example Avis admitted it was number two in the car rental market in the U.S. and advertised that it must try harder. On the other hand economy motels in the United States such as Motel 6 Inc., Scottish Inns, Days Inns and Econo-Travel, have stressed low cost lodging, eliminated swimming pools and restaurants and used pay television in positioning themselves against rivals with more elaborate services.[2]

Business Analysis

This stage is concerned with translating the proposed idea into a firm business proposal. It involves undertaking a detailed analysis of the attractiveness of the idea in business terms and its likely chances of success or failure. A substantial analysis will consider in detail aspects like the manpower required to implement the new service product idea, the additional physical resources required, the likely estimates of sales, costs and profits over time, the contribution of the new service to the range on offer, likely customer reaction to the innovation and the likely response of competitors. Obviously it is not possible to generate accurate forecasts and estimates and it is customary to build some degree of tolerance into the analysis to allow for the uncertainties and ambiguities involved. This stage may typically involve some initial technical and market research and initial timings and costing for a new service product launch.

Development

This stage requires the translation of the idea into an actual service product for the market. Typically this means that there will be an increase in investment in the project. Staff may have to be recruited or trained, facilities may have to be constructed, communications systems may need to be established. The tangible elements of the service product will be designed and tested. Unlike goods the development stage of new service product development involves attention to both the tangible elements of the service product and the service product delivery system.

Testing

Testing of new service products may not always be possible. Airlines may introduce a new class of service on a selected number of routes or a bank may make a new service available initially on a regional basis like automated cash dispensers. But some new service products do not have such an opportunity. They must be available and operate to designed levels of quality and performance from their introduction. Flack[30] indicates how the American Express Bank after the conduct of detailed prior research which indicated that opening a London branch would be successful, had ultimately to take the plunge and go ahead by establishing a branch with a range of services.

Commercialization

This stage represents the organization's commitment to a full-scale launch of the new service product. The scale of operation may be relatively modest like adding an additional service to an airline's routes or large scale involving the national launch of fast service footwear repair outlets operating on a concession basis. In undertaking the launch Kotler[31] suggests four basic decisions apply:

(*a*) when to introduce the new service product;
(*b*) where to launch the new service product, whether locally, regionally, nationally or internationally;
(*c*) to whom to launch the new service product usually determined by earlier exploration in the new service product development process;
(*d*) how to launch the new service product. Unit trusts for example may offer a fixed price unit on initial investments for a certain time period.

With highly novel and innovative service products, organizations may be guided by the extensive literature and experience on innovation and diffusion. However like many areas of marketing most documented experience in this area has focussed upon tangibles rather than intangibles[32] and innovation and diffusion knowledge in the service sector requires further empirical study.

A feature of new product development practices in recent years has been the growing experimentation and application of mathematical models and other quantitative techniques to this area. For example PERT (programme evaluation and review technique) and CPA (critical path analysis) are two techniques used for scheduling and co-ordinating the activities involved in the new product development process. Statistical decision theory too has been increasingly used in this area and there seems to be no reason why such approaches should not find utility in service product marketing. However the small scale and relative unsophistication of many service marketing organizations does militate against their universal use.

7.43 New Service Product Development – Illustration

To illustrate the process in a service context Northfleet's[33] example describing how a large multibank holding company conducts its new product development activity is of interest.

Idea Generation

There is a formalized employee idea generation program, with cash incentives being awarded for ideas which survive the initial screening process. In addition to this program the bank closely follows product lines of other banks throughout the country, encourages product feedback from officers attending conferences, and thoroughly reviews trade publications. Consumer research as a means of generating ideas has been employed on a limited basis.

Evaluation and Development

The product development department within the marketing department initially screens ideas with an eye more toward originality than toward feasibility. This liberal approach is employed to reduce the chances of a potentially good new product being eliminated too early in the cycle. While commercial products follow the same path, product development is primarily concerned with retail-oriented ideas.

Ideas deemed worthy of further evaluation are listed and ranked by product development. Product ranking is used to guide management in recommending services for development. The list is reviewed by the 'retail marketing council', which is composed of an executive from each of the bank's four regions. This body authorizes product development to research no more than three services at any one time.

A product brief is finally submitted to the retail marketing council, and, if approved, the brief is presented to the top executive committee in the organization. This executive body either approves, rejects, or requests additional information on the product.

Executive approval gives product development the authority to organize a task force. The task force is committed to creating a total package and each concerned function in the organization is represented. Product planning here serves to guide and co-ordinate the progress of the task force. Both the retail and management councils are given periodic updates on task force progress.

Testing

The bank has tried to eliminate the possibility of product failure through testing wherever possible. Concept testing via direct consumer research and 'focus group' interviews are often used by research to determine the probable acceptability of the product. If the service involves a significant financial exposure, it is not unusual for the bank to conduct an actual market test. This avenue is being utilized more and more as a means of reducing failure, correcting product flaws and establishing proper market segments.

Introduction

Although the product development area is responsible for the entire cycle, introduction often becomes a total marketing responsibility. During this phase the bank embarks on extremely complete sales and skills training programs. It is not unusual to tie a product launch to an employee incentive campaign. Sales promotion efforts may link a premium campaign to the new product. Each affiliate has the opportunity to recommend a media program which will most effectively sell the product in its community. This selection involves primarily the media mix, not the creative strategy. The bank recognizes the critical nature of the introduction phase and strives for maximum effectiveness by directing the right mixture of promotional tools at the right market.

7.44 New Service Product Features

The buyer's choice of a new service product may be influenced by features associated with it. These features may be seen as a fundamental part of the 'core' service by the consumer or as 'peripheral' to the core service (*see* Chapter 6). In tangible product marketing the brand, the colour, the design or the package may be important contributory factors to the consumer's purchase decision. Generally such elements are less conspicuous features in service product marketing but they may nevertheless be integral components of some forms of service product planning. The relevance of some of these features is described.

Service Product Branding

Johnson[34] suggests that: 'branding, brand development and brand acceptance are usually not prominent in the marketing of services'.

Certainly branding is difficult because of the problems of maintaining consistency of quality in service settings. Livesey[35], for example in his study of brand loyalty in the context of the TV rental market, found there was no one reason why customers terminated rental agreements or maintained or renewed their agreements. A combination of factors such as service speed, the quality of the TV set, the appearance of the staff appeared to be important. However it would seem that branding is not used as much as it should be in services marketing. This is surprising for, given the intangible nature of services and the difficulty of distinguishing one service from another, branding provides a significant method for achieving some degree of service product differentiation.

Service Product Patents

The intangibility of services means that there are no patents. It is thus difficult to prevent competitors from copying service innovations though trade names can be protected. This means that innovations can have short life-cycles because they are easy to copy. Banks and airlines are examples where the absence of patent protection has brought large-scale copying of practices e.g. classes of air travel available. Judd[36] identified lack of patent protection as an important difference in the retailing of services and Eiglier and Langeard[37] confirmed the absence of patent protection as one of the characteristics which present unique problems to service organizations and their clients in their study in distribution, hotel, transportation and banking. On the other hand the British Invisible Exports Council has pointed out that with regard to certain services, the expertise they require makes them difficult to copy quickly.

Service Product Warranty

Warranties are usually related to product sales. However they can be an important element in the strategy of service marketors. In law a warranty is an undertaking on the vendor's part that the thing sold is the vendors and is fit for use or fulfills specified conditions. Such undertakings are of two kinds, implied and express. An implied warranty is one that exists through legislation and applies whether the vendor extends express warranties or not. An express warranty is one that is explicitly provided by the vendor. Express warranties have been used in the past for both sales promotion and vendor protection reasons. However recent legislation (Unfair Contract Terms Act, 1977) appears now to limit the vendor from claims once protected by express warranties.

Warranties can be of importance in marketing certain services. For example investment schemes which guarantee payments in spite of changes in external conditions can be a useful factor in marketing financial services. Also organizations which carry out warranties and go beyond what is legally required (e.g. airlines in their treatment of delayed passengers) can benefit in the longer term by retaining customers and building goodwill.

Service Product After-sale Service

After-sale service is usually associated with the sale of tangibles. However it too has relevance to services markets. For example, an airline can assist passengers to arrange hire cars and book hotels as part of their service; an insurance company can advise clients on changes they should make to their policies as their personal circumstances change; a stockbroker can assist a client to re-adjust a portfolio of shares; a dentist can provide a check-up some time after providing dental treatment.

After-sale service can be an important element of the service marketing mix. Its availability can help get a sale in the first place; it can maintain and develop customer loyalty and goodwill; it can provide a means of obtaining feedback about service performance; it can provide a means for obtaining suggestions for new and improved services.

7.5 Service Product Elimination

In the previous section the relevance of systematic procedures for new service product development was emphasized. There is also a similar rationale for systematic procedures for service product elimination. The evidence for the existence of such elimination practices in the service sector is scanty however. The Hise[2] study, in which he commented that: 'In general, the product elimination programs examined proved to be highly unstructured, unsophisticated and ineffective' was confined to 96 manufacturing companies in the U.S. and therefore did not deal with the service sector as such. Berry and Donnelly[21] however suggest that there is no evidence that banks, for example, are any better at service product elimination than industry in general.

The reasons for such unsystematic approaches are understandable:

sheer sentimentality and vested interest;
the hope that things will improve;
lack of adequate data on which to base decisions;
the disruptive consequences which may follow elimination;
the inter-relationships that exist between sales of different service products.

But they are far outweighed by the benefits that accrue:

improved profitability;
time can be devoted to more successful service products;
marginal service products tie up other resources like personnel and advertising budgets;
weak service products may delay the search for new ones.

The elimination of service products of course is not easy and indeed organizations may adopt a number of strategies before doing so like selling overseas, optimizing profitability over whatever life remains or revitalizing the offering in some way. But these moves do not ultimately remove the need for systematic procedures to assist with decision making in this area. As Stanton[38] says: 'Knowing when and how to abandon products successfully may be as important as knowing when and how to introduce new ones. Certainly management should develop a systematic procedure for phasing out its weak products.'

7.6 Summary

1 The service product life-cycle concept is intuitively attractive to service marketors. However care must be exercised in its use. More substantial evidence of the validity of the life-cycle in service product situations is required.

2 Service organizations can grow in many ways and the full range of options should be explored.
3 New service product development does not seem to be as well organized in service organizations. New product development procedures do appear to be of relevance to service organizations.
4 Systematic procedures for service product elimination are also required in service marketing organizations.

Questions for Discussion

1 What considerations should a service firm take account of when deciding whether to expand its service product line?
2 What considerations should a service firm take account of when deciding whether to contract its service product line?
3 Comment on the use of the product life-cycle concept for service marketors.
4 What are the benefits of a systematic approach to new service product development?
5 Identify and describe eight ways in which service organizations can grow?
6 Comment on the relevance of:

    (*a*) branding
    (*b*) packaging
    (*c*) warranties
    (*d*) after sales service

for service marketors.
7 Describe the sources service marketors may use to generate ideas for new service products.
8 Comment on the relevance of the life-cycle concept to multisite service operation.
9 What is meant by a 'new service product'?
10 Identify five genuinely new services introduced in the past few years.

References and Notes

1 Many textbooks and articles give full descriptions of the life-cycle concept. The material here is based upon an article by Doyle, P. 'The realities of the Product Life Cycle', *Quarterly Review of Marketing*, Summer 1976, pp. 1–6, which is a most useful critique of the concept as well as a description of it.
2 Hise, R. T. *Product/Service Strategy*, Petrocelli/Charter, New York, 1977. A useful book on the whole area of Product/Service Strategy which makes an attempt to incorporate services as well as products in its analysis.
3 Rathmell, J. M. *Marketing in the Service Sector*, Winthrop, Cambridge, Mass. 1974.

4 McIver, C. and Naylor, G. 'Marketing Financial Services', Institute of Bankers, 1980.

5 Kotler, P. *Marketing for Non-Profit Organisations*, Prentice-Hall, Englewood Cliffs, 1975.

6 Laczniak, G. R. in Mokwa, M. P., Dawson, W. M. and Prieve, E. A. (eds) *Marketing the Arts*, Praeger, New York, 1980.

7 Wahab, S., Crampon, L. J. and Rothfield, L. M. 'Tourism Marketing', Tourism International Press, London, 1976.

8 Klug, J. R. and Brumwell, R. A. 'Air Travel as a Commodity' in Rathmell, J. M. *Marketing in the Service Sector*, Winthrop, Cambridge, Mass. 1974.

9 Sasser, W. E., Olsen, R. P. and Wyckoff, D. D. *Management of Service Operations – Text and Cases*, Allyn and Bacon, Boston, Mass 1978.

10 Urwin, S. 'Customized Communication – A concept for Service advertising', *Advertising Quarterly*, Summer 1975, pp. 28–30.

11 Polli, R. and Cook, V. 'Validity of the Product Life Cycle', *Journal of Business*, Vol. 42, No. 4, Oct. 1969, pp. 385–400.

12 Dhalla, N. K. and Yuspeh, S. 'Forget the Product Life Cycle Concept', *Harvard Business Review*, Vol. 54, Jan. 1976, pp. 102–12.

13 Carman, J. M. and Langeard, E. 'Growth Strategies for Service Firms', Proceedings of the 8th Annual Meeting of the European Academy for Advanced Research in Marketing, Groningen, 10–12 April, 1979.

14 Ansoff, I. *Corporate Strategy*, Penguin, Harmondsworth, 1968, sets out this idea.

15 Wilson, A. *The Marketing of Professional Services*, McGraw-Hill, London, 1972.

16 Christopher, M., McDonald, M. and Wills, G. *Introducing Marketing*, Pan, London, 1980.

17 Morrill, T. C. Creative Marketing of Life Insurance, *Journal of Marketing*, Vol. 24, Oct. 1959, pp. 11–16.

18 Mapel, E. B. 'The Marketing of Services' in Buell, V. P. *Handbook of Modern Marketing*, McGraw-Hill, New York, 1970.

19 Shostack, G. Lynn 'Breaking free from Product Marketing', *Journal of Marketing*, Vol. 41, No. 2, April 1977, pp. 73–80.

20 Eiglier, P. and Langeard, E. 'A conceptual approach of the service offering', Working Paper No. 217, iae Aix-en-Provence, April 1981.

21 Berry, L. L. and Donnelly, J. H. 'Marketing for Bankers', American Institute of Banking, 1975.

22 Oliver, G. *Marketing Today*, Prentice-Hall, Englewood Cliffs, 1980.

23 O'Meara, J. T. 'Selecting Profitable Products', *Harvard Business Review*, Jan.–Feb. 1961, pp. 83–9.

24 Wills, G. S. C. 'The Marketing design of Life Assurance Proposals', *British Journal of Marketing*, Vol. 1, Autumn 1967, pp. 21–8.

25 Moriarty, M. and Venkatesan, M. 'Concept evaluation and market segmentation', *Journal of Marketing*, Vol. 42, No. 3, July 1978, pp. 82–6.

26 Mauser, G. A. 'Positioning political candidates – an application of concept evaluation techniques', *Journal of the Market Research Society*, Vol. 22, No. 3, pp. 181–91.

27 Blois, K. J. and Cowell, D. W. 'Marketing Research for new product ideas arising from R & D Departments', *R & D Management*, Vol. 9, No. 2, 1979, pp. 61–4.

28 Coplin, R. A. 'Marketing concepts can improve your investor relations', *Financial Executive*, Nov. 1977, pp. 32–4.

29 Wind, Y. and Robinson, P. J. 'Product Positioning: An Application of Multidimensional Scaling', in R. I. Haley, (Ed.) *Attitude Research in Transition*, American Marketing Association, Chicago, 1972.

30 Flack, M. 'Research for financial and investment marketing decisions', *Journal of the Market Research Society*, Vol. 20, No. 1, Jan. 1978, pp. 14–29.

31 Kotler, P. *Principles of Marketing*, Prentice-Hall, Englewood Cliffs, 1980.

32 See, for example, Midgley, D. F. *Innovation and New Product Marketing*, Croom Helm, London, 1977.

33 Northfleet, R. F. 'Product development in large banks', Thesis, Rutgers University, 1974. Quoted in Berry, L. L. and Donnelly, J. H. – *see* reference 21.

34 Johnson, E. M. 'An introduction to the problems of Service Marketing Management', The Bureau of Economic and Business Research, University of Delaware, 1964.

35 Livesey, F. *Pricing*, Macmillan, London, 1976.

36 Judd, R. C. 'Similarities and Differences in Product Service Retailing', *Journal of Retailing*, Winter 1968, pp. 1–9.

37 Eiglier, P. and Langeard, E. 'A New approach to Service Marketing', Marketing Consumer Services: New Insights Report 77–115, Marketing Science Institute, Boston, 1977.

38 Stanton, W. J. *Fundamentals of Marketing*, McGraw-Hill, New York, 1981.

8. PRICING OF SERVICES

8.1 Introduction

Pricing decisions are of major importance in service marketing strategy. As with other marketing mix elements, the price of a service should be related to the achievement of marketing and organizational goals and should be appropriate for the service organization's marketing programme. Like many other fields of service marketing included in this book, pricing has not yet received the attention it deserves:

> 'In Britain, in the United States as in some other similarly developed economies more people are employed in the provision of services than in the direct production of material goods, yet the marketing of services in general and their pricing in particular are relatively neglected aspects of management studies.'[1]

This means that, in the main, service pricing principles and practices tend to be based on principles and practices used in pricing goods. As with goods, easy generalizations about pricing are difficult to make. There is as much diversity in the service sector as in the goods sector.

Table 8.1
Price Terminology for Selected Services

Terminology	*Typical Service*
Admission	Theatre entry
Charge	Hairdressing
Commission	Stockbroking service
Dues	Union membership
Fare	Transport
Fee	Legal service
Honorarium	Guest speaker
Interest	Use of money
Premium	Insurance
Rate	Municipal services
Rent	Property usage
Retainer	Consultants' services
Salary	Employee services
Subscription	Membership
Tariff	Utilities
Toll	Road use
Tuition	Education
Wage	Employee services

Compiled from various sources

The great variety of environments in which service pricing decisions are made and the diversity of pricing practices which may apply, is partly reflected in the different terms used to describe the prices of services. Some price terminology for selected services is shown in Table 8.1.

This chapter discusses characteristics of services and their influence upon pricing, a classification of services for pricing purposes, the relationship between pricing and marketing strategy, methods of pricing services and price tactics in service markets.

8.2 Characteristics of Services and their Influence upon Service Prices

The characteristics of services referred to in Chapter 2 may influence prices set in services markets. The influence of these characteristics will vary according to the type of service and market situation under consideration. They are however an added consideration when examining the traditional main forces influencing price; costs, competition and demand. Some impacts of these services characteristics include these five categories.

(*a*) Service perishability, the fact that service cannot be stored and that fluctuations in demand cannot be met as easily through using inventory, has price implications. Special price offers and price reductions to use up spare capacity may be used· and marginal pricing may be more commonplace. This may happen in markets like airline travel and package holidays. Constant use of these forms of pricing may lead to increasing customer sophistication: buyers may deliberately hold off from purchasing certain services with the expectations that price reductions will occur. Sellers for their part may try to compensate for this effect by offering advantageous reductions on orders for services placed early. Again the holiday tour market exhibits some of these forces at work.

(*b*) Customers may be able to delay or postpone the performance or use of many services. Alternatively they may be able to perform certain services for themselves. These features can lead to keener competition amongst sellers of services. They can also encourage a greater degree of price stability in certain markets, in the short term.

(*c*) Intangibility has many price implications. First-time users may have great difficulty understanding what they get for their money but this may be influenced by the material content of the service product. The higher the material content, the more will prices set tend to be based on costs and the greater the tendency towards more standard prices. The smaller the material content the more customer orientated and the less standard will prices be.

Service intangibility also means that services provided may be more easily varied than physical products. Thus service level, service quality and service quantity can be adjusted to meet particular customer requirements. Prices may ultimately be determined by negotiation between buyer and seller.

(*d*) Where services are homogeneous (e.g. car washes, dry cleaners) then pricing may be highly competitive. On the other hand regulatory agencies may discourage price cutting through pre-scribed fees and charges (e.g. trade associations or government agencies). The more unique a service then the greater the discretion of the seller to vary price according to what buyers in the market are prepared to pay. In such situations price may be used as a quality indicator and the reputation of the individual or organization offering the service may give considerable price leverage.

(*e*) The inseparability of service from the person providing it may place geographic limits or time limits on markets that can be served. Equally buyers of services may search for service provision within certain geographic or time zones. The degree of competition operating within these limits will influence prices charged.

8.3 Classification of Services for Pricing Purposes

In Chapter 2 a number of alternative schemes for classifying services were outlined. Another scheme is presented here for pricing purposes.[2] There are three categories of services:

(*a*) services subject to public regulation;
(*b*) services subject to formal self regulation;
(*c*) services subject to regulation of the marketplace.

8.31 Services Subject to Public Regulation

Communications services, educational services, health services and trans-port services are examples where price is chiefly publicly regulated. Rail fares, for example, are controlled by government policy. In these examples the price element of the marketing mix is uncontrolled by the marketor and reliance has to be placed on other non-price elements to achieve marketing policies.

One complication with the public regulations of prices is that political and social considerations will take precedence over purely economic considera-tions. Basic public policy decisions are required on whether price is intended to recover costs or whether it is a tool for achieving some political or social ends. Thus health charges may be kept as low as possible to permit wide use of the health service while traffic parking fines in central city areas may be kept high to discourage traffic.

Another complication with public services is that the tax system may be used to fund services. Prices of some public services may be based on ability to pay (e.g. National Insurance) or location (e.g. rates). The contribution from direct and indirect taxes towards public service provision is determined by political, social and economic factors.

A final complication with public services is cost determination. Econo-mic costs alone are an insufficient basis for price determination. While some novel attempts have been made to move towards marginal pricing with some services (e.g. rail travel) cost determination and cost assignation is a major difficulty in pricing public services.

8.32 Services Subject to Formal Self Regulation

Many services are subject to regulation by institutional pressures of various kinds. Professional service fees may be institutionally determined; air fares may be subject to IATA agreements; sea freight rates may be determined by shipping conferences. In some professions regulation of entry to the profession as well as regulation of fees may apply. Again marketors may have to place greater reliance upon non-price elements in formulating competitive marketing mixes.

A recent example of weakening institutional pressure on prices is the commission price war which has broken out among some companies in the Life Assurance industry. This illustrates that formal self regulation is dependent upon an appropriate regulatory body having the power to fix prices and price ranges. That power only exists as long as members value the benefits of membership.

One argument against self-regulation is that prices may be based upon cost structures of the least efficient members of a profession. On the other hand self-regulation does largely ensure that the chances of excessive charging policies are reduced. In the United Kingdom some professions have precise charging scales (e.g. stockbrokers) whereas other professions operate on recommended guidelines for fees.

Wilson observed that some service industries are governed by rules of practice laid down and policed by many professional services for the very reason of avoiding price competition. He felt that '. . . discussion on price for many services would appear to be largely academic'. While price fixing has been 'roundly condemned and outlawed for almost all goods', charges for services continue 'standard' (which is a euphemism for 'fixed') in many professions; conveyancing charges by solicitors, property sales commissions by estate agents, scales of fees by architects and many types of insurance premiums and for some bank services. Besides those prices which are enforceable legally, or by professional associations, there is a whole structure of 'accepted' prices, e.g. the major management consultants opt for per diem charges, literary and advertising agencies for commission, and doctors for consultation.

'. . . Nevertheless, even with these restricted fields, there is room for more profitable option by the use of pricing as a marketing tool or weapon, depending on how the service companies regard price. Outside the areas of fixed, standard or customary prices, the use of pricing in the marketing mix remains primitive and awaits only intelligent application for substantial rewards to be reaped.'[3]

8.33 Services Subject to Regulation of the Marketplace

This method applies to many kinds of services. Prices charged depend on a range of factors including economic conditions, consumer feelings about prices, competition in the marketplace, level of demand, the degree to which customers 'begrudge' purchases of certain services, 'buyer need urgency' and many other factors. Prices charged depend upon what the market will bear.

Bank charges, dry cleaning rates, private school fees, housing rentals and garage repairs are examples of service prices largely determined by marketplace forces. Sometimes some element of regulation (public or institutional) may also apply to the broad level of charges imposed (e.g. building society general interest rates; but not to the specific rates charged by a particular society).

8.4 Pricing and Marketing Strategy

Integrated marketing strategies imply that the various elements of the marketing mix are formulated and implemented with the objectives of those strategies clearly in mind. Pricing decisions are no exception to this principle. In setting price objectives for services a number of factors must be considered.[4] The more significant of these are:

(*a*) the planned market position for the service product;
(*b*) the stage of the life-cycle of the service product;
(*c*) elasticity of demand;
(*d*) the competitive situation;
(*e*) the strategic role of price.

The Planned Market Position for the Service Product

Market position means the place the service product is intended to take up and does take up in the customer's eyes and in comparison with competitors. It refers to the customer's perceptual positioning of the service product: in other words how the service product is 'seen' in relation to others available. Clearly price is an important element in the marketing mix influencing this position. Tangible products may occupy a particular position by virtue of their physical characteristics (e.g. a grade of industrial steel tubing). Services, on the other hand, are more often 'positioned' on the basis of their intangible attributes. Gitlow,[5] for example, suggests that price quality relationships may exist in a market like that for abortion services. Price would influence market position.

The Stage of the Life-cycle of the Service Product

The price of the service product will also relate to its life-cycle. For example in introducing a new service an organization could opt to set low prices to penetrate markets and gain rapid market share (e.g. Laker's original Skytrain service). Alternatively an organization could opt to charge high prices to make as much profit as possible in a short time (skimming policy). This strategy is only possible if there is no immediate competition and a high level of buyer need urgency (e.g. windscreen replacement services). However the value of the life-cycle as an analytical tool in services marketing was questioned earlier and the weaknesses identified there should be borne in mind (*see* Chapter 7).

Elasticity of Demand

The discretion a service organization has to determine its pricing objectives will be influenced by elasticity of demand in the market. Elasticity of demand refers to the responsiveness of demand to changes in price. In some markets demand is much influenced by price changes (e.g. urban bus services) in others this is less so. Clearly it is vital for a service organization to understand how elastic or inelastic demand for its services is in response to price change. For example, if a service company reduces its prices and demand is elastic then the effect would be to reduce margins with no compensating increase in demand. Elasticity may impose limitations on certain price options.

The Competitive Situation

The strength of competition in the market influences a service organization's discretion over its prices. In situations where there is little differentiation between service products and where competition is intense (e.g. a seaside resort during a poor tourist season) then price discretion is limited. Competition of course has a number of dimensions apart from interbrand or intertype competition. In transport services, for example, there is competition between different modes of transport (e.g. rail v. road) different brands (e.g. Pan Am v. TWA) as well as alternative uses of the potential customers' time and money (e.g. not to travel at all). Nevertheless a degree of price uniformity will be established in those markets with little differentiation between service products and strong levels of competition. In other settings tradition and custom may influence prices charged (e.g. Advertising agencies commission system).

The Strategic Role of Price

Pricing policies have a strategic role aimed at achieving organizational objectives. Thus the pricing decision on any particular service product should fit in with strategic objectives. For example, a new holiday company intent upon establishing itself in the package holiday market might use a deliberate policy of low prices to obtain substantial market share although this could mean unprofitable trading for some time. Maximum sales would be won through penetration pricing as a deliberate policy. Any pricing strategy must of course fit in with the way in which other elements of the marketing mix are manipulated to attain strategic ends.

8.5 Methods of Pricing Services

There are few schemes available which deal with pricing practices in services markets.[6] Below is one of the more popular.[1] Services organizations may use:

(i) Cost-based Pricing

    (*a*) Profit orientated – aiming at a minimum profit target. Prices fixed by professional and trade associations belong to this category. If entry is severely restricted, prices will be related more to the customer's ability and willingness to pay and less to costs. In this case (ii)*b* below is a more appropriate category.

(*b*) Government controlled prices – aiming at consumer protection by fixing prices on a cost-plus-a-modest-margin basis.

(ii) Market-orientated Pricing

(*a*) Competitive – either accepting the going rate or maintaining or increasing market share by an aggressive pricing policy.

(*b*) Customer oriented – prices set with regard to consumers' attitudes and behaviour. Quality and costs of services may be varied to remain in harmony with prices.

A full description of these various methods need not concern us here as they are comprehensively covered elsewhere.[1] However some problems with cost-based systems should be noted. In service businesses it is often difficult to establish, for cost purposes, what a 'unit' of service is, let alone to calculate its cost. Particular difficulties occur with highly intangible services where people are the chief element of cost. For example it may be difficult to measure the time spent in performing a service; also overhead allocation may be problematic. Yet it is difficult to develop a pricing strategy for a service business without some clear idea of costs; if only to establish how costs act as a constraint on the lower limit of price discretion available to the price maker. People-intensive services like professional services have to develop more accurate methods of identifying and allocating costs to overcome the problems of costing in such service businesses i.e.

the product is difficult to describe and measure;
costs are primarily people costs;
other costs (e.g. rent, travel) are people-related costs;
people are more difficult to cost than machines.[7]

Cost accounting problems are not confined to professional firms. Fields like banking too present problems of cost allocation, activity measurement and capacity assessment.[8] These difficulties have led to suggestions that traditional cost accounting methods are inappropriate for services and that alternative methods of product profitability analysis should be used.[9]

Another problem with cost-based systems is that where costs are used as the only basis for calculating prices then there may be reduced incentive actually to control costs.

8.6 Price Tactics

Many of the tactical price techniques used to sell tangibles can be used to sell intangibles. In both cases the particular tactics used are dependent upon the kind of service involved, the target market and general conditions prevailing in that marketplace at the time (e.g. supply shortages therefore possible over-demand for service products). Some of the frequently used pricing tactics in services markets are now considered. They are:

(*a*) differential or flexible pricing;
(*b*) discrete pricing;
(*c*) discount pricing;
(*d*) diversionary pricing;
(*e*) guarantee pricing;
(*f*) high price maintenance pricing;
(*g*) loss leader pricing;
(*h*) offset pricing;
(*i*) price lining.

Differential or Flexible Pricing

Differential pricing is the practice of charging different prices according, for example, to customers' willingness to pay. It is used chiefly to:

(*a*) build primary demand particularly for non-peak time service use;
(*b*) even out fluctuations in demand which may occur in many services and to reduce the influence of 'perishability' of a service.

Some forms of differential pricing include:

(*a*) price-time differentials (e.g. as used in holiday, utilities and telephone services);
(*b*) customer ability to pay differentials (e.g. used in management consultancy; professional services; bank loan rates);
(*c*) service product type differentials (e.g. used for different models of telephone rental);
(*d*) place differential (e.g. used in hotel room pricing and in theatre seat pricing).

The ability to use differential pricing tactics is dependent upon a market being segmentable on a price basis, low chance of resale or re-allocation of a service to another, and minimum customer resentment towards the practice.

Differential pricing seems to be one of the most common practices in the service sector. It is particularly used in those services where a bespoke price is quoted. One study of the pest control industry found that differential pricing was the most common price fixing tactic. Indeed about 58% of sample respondents claimed to use differential pricing; that is customers were charged different prices for the same work.[10]

Some problems which can occur when differential pricing is used are:

(*a*) customers may delay their purchases and wait for differentials to be exercised (e.g. holiday markets are increasingly experiencing this growing customer sophistication).
(*b*) customers may come to expect discounts as a regular feature of a service product offer where differential prices are used (*see* discount pricing).

For these reasons some service organizations deliberately resist differential pricing. Instead they use uniform price practices, charging the same price to all customers irrespective of time, place or ability to pay.

Discrete Pricing

Discrete pricing means setting the price so that it is pitched at a level that brings it within the competence of the decision-making unit which is sympathetic towards a particular service or organization. Practised in a number of organizational markets for services like contract catering and plant maintenance it demands a clear knowledge of price limits within which decision makers have authority to work (e.g. purchasing officers may be able to order projects to a value of £10,000 without further approval).

Discount Pricing

Discount pricing occurs in most markets. Discounts in services marketing serve two purposes.

(*a*) They are a payment or reward for services undertaken which enable service production and consumption to take place (e.g. fees paid to intermediaries in financial markets)
(*b*) They are promotional devices to encourage actions like early payment, bulk purchase or off peak usage.

Examples of the former include commission payments to insurance brokers or unit trust advisers for services rendered. Examples of the latter include cash discounts offered by advertising agencies for prompt payment; quantity discounts offered by ferry operators for group travel; temporal discounts for off-peak daily use of a service (e.g. British Rail discounts) or for use at a particular time of the week or season of the year (e.g. Breakaway weekends); promotional discounts (e.g. short-term price reductions offered by a dry cleaning service or special offers made by a franchisor to a franchisee). These discounts may be on top of differential pricing practices that are operating in a market.

Most service organizations can offer special reductions or payments of these kinds. What is less well understood is that these payments erode the margins available to the service producer. Discounts have traditionally been regarded as tactical pricing adjustments. Increasingly though they are seen to have strategic importance. Sometimes margins must be used as devices to gain service exposure, and larger than traditional margins may be offered to buy exposure and support (e.g. the recent collapse of the Life Insurance Offices commission system). A new area of marketing, 'margin management' is emerging. It is concerned with the trade-off decisions which determine how the total channel margin should be split between intermediaries and customers involved in the process. It is as relevant to the marketing of services as it is to the marketing of goods.

Diversionary Pricing

This occurs where a low basic price may be quoted for a service or parts of a service to develop an image of a low price structure. Restaurants may offer a basic meal at an attractive price to encourage custom though most diners may finish up eating from other higher priced menus; a garage may offer a reduced rate standard service in the expectation of picking up additional, higher priced repair work.

Guaranteed Pricing

This occurs where payment is made only if certain results are guaranteed. Employment agencies may only charge fees when clients obtain suitable employment; estate agents may only take commission if a property actually sells. It is an appropriate tactic for a service organization to use when:

(a) the specific promises inherent in a guarantee can be determined and assured;

(b) when high quality service operators are finding it difficult to compete in a competitive cut price competitive environment;

(c) the customer is seeking some clear assurance of results (e.g. rust proofing; guaranteed return on investments).

High Price Maintenance Pricing

This practice is used where consumers associate the price of a service with its quality. In these circumstances some service organizations will deliberately pursue a high quality, high price posture. Those organizations that have cultivated a particular market segment or established a particularly prestigious reputation may use this approach of using price as an index of quality. Evidence of this approach occurred in the pest control study cited earlier. A small segment of this industry was able to maintain higher prices: '. . . they seem to be the major participants in the industry, able to hold out against the price threat of the low priced sellers.'[10]

Loss Leader Pricing

Loss leader pricing means charging a reduced price for the first order or contract in the hope of getting further business from a customer at better prices. It is an appropriate practice in those markets where:

(a) customers are dissatisfied with existing suppliers;

(b) buyers are relatively unsophisticated;

(c) market prices are competitive.

The chief disadvantage is that an initially low price may become a price ceiling. Customers may resist further price increases once that ceiling has been established. Nevertheless it is used in marketing consultancy and management education services.

Offset Pricing

A practice similar to diversionary pricing in which a low basic price is quoted but 'extras' carry relatively higher charges. For example, a management consultant may quote a price for his time but exclude the extras associated with an assignment like travel and hotel costs.

Price Lining

Price lining is where prices are not varied but the quality, quantity and level of service is to reflect cost changes. It is not normally recommended as a way of dealing with cost changes. It is more appropriate in circumstances where a fixed set of charges can apply to a range of standard services. Leasing firms use price lining and dry cleaning establishments have recently introduced pricing practices which reflect attempts at price lining. A problem with this practice is that quality, quantity and level of service product differentiation has to be relatively easy for customers to appreciate (e.g. as in airline travel on long haul flights). Price lining can therefore be difficult to implement in repair services. One study has shown that customers do not expect to receive a lower quality repair service on lower cost products than higher cost products. The 'value' of a repair is not necessarily related to the value of the product being repaired.[11]

8.7 Additional Aspects of Service Pricing

In addition to the tactical variations of price considered above there are other aspects of service pricing which should be noted. These are concerned with:

(*a*) price negotiation;
(*b*) competitive bidding;
(*c*) price awareness.

Price Negotiation

Price negotiation is a common feature of service pricing in a number of service industries. For example prices are negotiated in many professional services transactions. It is common practice too in consumer services like car repairs, foreign travel and financial assistance (e.g. bank loans). Certain specialized business services, like plant rentals, insurance and market research are also priced by negotiation.

Competitive Bidding

Some service contracts, particularly in organizational markets, may be awarded on the basis of competitive bidding or tenders. A bid is an offer price. It is based on expectations of how competitors will price their services. If a bidding company wants to gain a contract it will also need to consider its costs to determine the minimum price level at which it should bid. Currently a number of models are applied in bidding to take account of competitors' likely bids and they attempt to estimate expected profits at various bid prices. More sophisticated models take account of past bidding data in deriving bid prices.

One study which has examined the problems of competitive bidding from a buyer and a seller point of view identifies a number of disadvantages for both parties in service markets.[12] From the seller's point of view the time, effort and cost involved, the possibility of ideas being borrowed and transferred to competitors and difficulties of knowing how bids are appraised are seen as arguments against their use. While for the buyer the time involved, problems with the timing of proposals and considerations regarding whether the specification is tight or flexible, also suggest that alternatives may be more satisfactory (e.g. rotate jobs among contacts).

A later study of over 100 marketing research agencies showed that relatively few marketing research projects were awarded on the basis of competitive bidding.[13] In fact price was an unimportant facet of many research firms' marketing programmes and non-price competition (e.g. quality of work, experience of the business, understanding of the client's problem) were more potent factors.

These other aspects of service have been found to be significant in other service market situations. One study of the TV rental market showed 26% of subscribers who had terminated their agreement had done so because of unsatisfactory servicing of their sets and a further 15% because the administrative arrangements were unsatisfactory. Similar findings have been reported in industrial services markets (e.g. use of freight transport). The concept of service in many service markets is made up of a number of elements which customers evaluate in their overall judgement of a service (*see* Chapter 6). For a car repair not only the quality of the repair but also aspects like minimum waiting time, provision of credit or prompt attention to complaints may matter. With a transport service it may be speed of service, reliability of service mode and comfort.[14]

Price Awareness

There is no evidence to suggest that price awareness in services markets is any different in its diversity from price awareness found in markets for goods. Low price awareness has been found in settings as diverse as professional services, freight transport and funerals. Where price awareness is low in a service market then two strategies are relevant for price makers:

(*a*) exploit the low level of awareness through the price discretion it offers;
(*b*) make the market more aware of price levels thereby attacking competitive services (e.g. airline fares on the North Atlantic route).

Price awareness studies are an example of where marketing research may be used in service markets. Price adjustments may often be made once awareness studies have been conducted and there is evidence to suggest that the 'buy-response' method of analysis, used in many goods markets, may be suitable for services like dry cleaning services and travel agents.[1]

8.8 Pricing in Practice

There are few reported studies of pricing in service industries and this is a fertile area for further research. One of these found that in practice many factors complicate the method used for price determination:

'The most widespread method employed is cost-plus-mark-up. The actual selling price selected is dependent upon the firm's perception of its market segment and competitive position. Elasticity of demand is not seen as a market factor to which respondents could profitably react, apart from other considerations. Survey data suggest that there may indeed be several price and market segments, with minimal competitive overlap between them. Since the intangibility and uniformity of the service provide little basis for differentiation between sellers, market segments possibly may be defined in terms of customer motivation and/or company image. In any case, the price function plays an active role in the marketing strategy of the firm.'[10]

The author of this study suggested that to improve their competitive positions and ultimate profitability marketors in this service industry should:

set annual total profit and sales volume goals;
keep a definite profit margin in mind when quoting jobs;
have good knowledge of costs;
review price schedules regularly;
try to secure higher, rather than lower or average, prices;
tend to be flexible in pricing.

This list suggests what price makers already know; that prices emerge out of a series of separate decisions each dealing with a set of sub-problems. Also pricing decisions are not all the same. Launching a new type of service like a high quality dry cleaning service or a new cheap airline travel service is as difficult and uncertain as adjusting prices for an existing range of services with many competitors and substitutes. The complexity of these problems for service marketors is no different than for marketors of goods. The classic multistage approach to pricing still provides an appropriate framework for making some sense of this complexity.[15] *See* Figure 8.1.

Nevertheless it must recognized that no one framework is suitable for all decisions. Every pricing decision has to take account of existing circum-

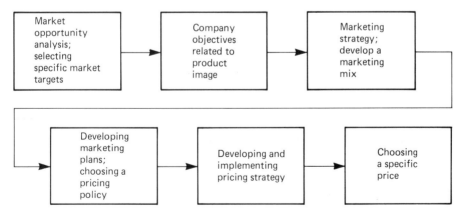

Figure 8.1 Multistage Approach to Pricing
Source: Based on Oxenfeldt, A. R. 'Multi-stage approach to Pricing', *Harvard Business Review*, July–Aug. 1960, p. 125–33

stances, cost, demand, competition, the service product and its characteristics, and the situation in the marketplace. Pricing for services, as for
goods, still remains largely a combination of good management, experience, trial and error, intuition and good luck.

8.9 Summary

1 Service pricing principles and practices tend to be based on principles
  and practices used in pricing goods.
2 Characteristics of services create some differences for pricing in the
  service sector compared with goods.
3 Services may be classified for pricing purposes according to whether they
  are subject to public regulation, subject to formal self regulation or
  subject to regulation of the marketplace.
4 In setting price objectives for services a number of factors must be
  considered including the planned market position for the service
  product, the life-cycle, elasticity of demand, competition, the strategic
  role of price.
5 Methods of pricing services may be cost based or market based. Within
  these categories prices may be profit orientated, government controlled,
  competitive or customer orientated.
6 Many price tactics are available to service marketors including differential pricing, discrete pricing, discount pricing, diversionary pricing,
  guarantee pricing, high price maintenance pricing, loss leader pricing,
  offset pricing and price lining.
7 Other aspects of service pricing include price negotiation, competitive
  bidding and price awareness.
8 In practice, service pricing has all the complexity of goods pricing.

Questions for Discussion

 1 How can prices be fixed for services?
 2 Comment on the importance of price-quality relationships in services
   marketing.
 3 Can price discrimination be used as a marketing tool by service
   industries?
 4 What price do users 'pay' for services?
 5 Why is pricing of services difficult?
 6 Explain the importance of demand elasticity in the pricing of services.
 7 Illustrate the ways in which five different kinds of discounts may be
   used in service pricing.
 8 'Pricing of services is more flexible than pricing of goods.' Discuss.
 9 What problems are involved in preparing a competitive bid for a service
   like market research?
10 Comment on the roles of 'regulation' and 'tradition' ·in the pricing of
   services.

References and Notes

1 Gabor, A. *Pricing Principles and Practice*. Heinemann Educational Books, London, 1980. See Chapter 10, pp. 168–76 for one of the few treatments of services pricing.
2 Rathmell, J. M. *Marketing in the Service Sector*, Winthrop, Cambridge, Mass. 1974.
3 Wilson, A. *The Marketing of Professional Services*, McGraw-Hill, London, 1972.
4 This discussion follows Christopher, M. G., Kennedy, S. H., McDonald, M. M. and Wills, G. S. C. *Effective Marketing Management* Gower, Aldershot, 1980, pp. 108–9.
5 Gitlow, H. S. 'Abortion Services: time for a discussion of marketing policies', *Journal of Marketing*, Vol. 42, April 1978, pp. 71–82.
6 For one of them see Sibson, R. E. 'A Service' in *Creative Pricing* (Ed. E. Marting) American Marketing Association, Chicago, 1968, pp. 147–51.
7 McDonald, E. H. and Stromberger, T. L. 'Cost control for the professional service firm', *Harvard Business Review*, Jan.–Feb. 1969, pp. 109–21.
8 Sloan, L. 'Managing Bank Costs', *The Bankers' Magazine*, Dec. 1973, pp. 248–52.
9 Dearden, J. 'Cost accounting comes to service industries', *Harvard Business Review*, Sept.–Oct. 1978, pp. 132–40.
10 Schlissel, M. R. 'Pricing in a Service Industry', *M.S.U. Business Topics*, Vol. 25, Spring 1977, pp. 37–48.
11 Adler, L. and Hlavacek, J. D. 'The relationship between Price and Repair Service for Consumer Durables', *Journal of Marketing*, Vol. 90, April 1976, pp. 80–2.
12 Myers, J. H. 'Competitive bidding for Marketing Research Services', *Journal of Marketing*, Vol, 33, July 1969, pp. 40–5.
13 Haynes, J. B. and Rothe, J. T. 'Competitive bidding for Marketing Research Services: fact or fiction', *Journal of Marketing*, July 1974, pp. 69–71.
14 Livesey, F. *Pricing*, Macmillan, London, 1976.
15 Oxenfeldt, A. R. 'Multi-Stage approach to Pricing', *Harvard Business Review*, July–Aug. 1960, pp. 125–33.

9. *PROMOTION AND SERVICES*

9.1 Introduction

This chapter deals with the promotion of service products. Here promotion includes the following.

  (*a*) Advertising – defined as any paid form of non-personal presentation and promotion of services by an identified individual or organization.

  (*b*) Personal selling – defined as the personal presentation of services in a conversation with one or more prospective purchasers for the purpose of making sales.

  (*c*) Publicity – defined as the non-personal stimulation of demand for a service by obtaining commercially significant news about it in any medium or obtaining favourable presentation of it in any medium that is not paid for by the service sponsor.

  (*d*) Sales promotion – marketing activities other than advertising, personal selling or publicity that stimulate customer purchasing and use and enhance dealer effectiveness (e.g. competitions, coupons).

These four types of promotion are the traditional marketor-dominated ways of influencing sales for service products. Between them they offer the service organization a wide range of possibilities for promoting services in the marketplace. Astutely used they can be most effective tools of communication and influence. However two important qualifications should be noted. First, service organizations promote themselves and their service products in other ways than the four forms considered here. Though this chapter deals with 'personal salesmen' as part of 'promotion', in many services markets the 'selling' of services and the 'performance' of services cannot be separated. Indeed there may not be a separate sales force as such. So this separation of the 'selling role' may be unrealistic in practice. The comments about people in this chapter should be seen alongside the 'other service personnel' who can influence promotional effort dealt with in Chapter 11. Also physical evidence will influence customer response to service products (*see* Chapter 12).

  Second, there is increasing research evidence that in some kinds of services markets these marketor dominated ways of influencing sales for service products may not necessarily be the most effective. For example, a study covering eight different types of retail services (dry cleaning, hairdressing, car loan finance, dentistry, photography, carpet shampoo, car repair, gynaecological services) showed that customers of retail services do not rely on the more traditional information sources considered here. Instead, they prefer to use more personal sources of information from friends and other contacts. Also location is a key factor in the final purchase decision.[1] The importance of personal recommendations has been confirmed in the life insurance market too. Customers in this market have been shown to rely heavily on the opinions and influences of others through word of mouth communication.[2]

9.2 Promotional Objectives

The general purposes of promotion in services marketing are much the same as in other kinds of marketing to:

(*a*) build awareness and interest in the service product and the service organization;

(*b*) differentiate the service offer and the service organization from competitors;

(*c*) communicate and portray the benefits of the services available;

(*d*) build and maintain the overall image and reputation of the service organization;

(*e*) persuade customers to buy or use the service.

Ultimately the purpose of any promotional effort is to sell the service product through informing, persuading and reminding.

Clearly these general objectives vary according to the nature of each service industry and service product. For example, the kinds of promotional objectives that are considered to be relevant in the transport and distribution business include:

(*a*) creating awareness of the firm's service among potential users;

(*b*) generating detailed knowledge of the firm's product and service including details of cost-benefit relationship, price and other pertinent information;

(*c*) improving the firm's image among existing and potential users so as to improve the customers' attitude towards it. The main objective is to prepare the firm's target group towards being more receptive to the new service which will be launched in the near future;

(*d*) eliminating perceived misconceptions;

(*e*) advising existing and potential customers of special offers or modifications of the service;

(*f*) advising the marketplace of new channels.[3]

Clearly the specific objectives for any particular service in any service product/market situation will vary. So too will use made of the elements of the promotion mix.

When the three British banks, Lloyds, Midland and National Westminster, launched their major credit card, Access, co-ordinated use was made of all kinds of promotion. Accomplishing the task of recruiting 3 million card holders and recruiting 60,000 retail outlets in the pre-launch phase of their programme placed heavy demands upon the promotional element of the marketing mix. One particular problem was how to help customers understand the concepts of 'instant finance and flexible repayment' at a time, in the early 1970s, when credit card usage was still relatively new. An outline of the thinking that led to the development of the launch slogan is shown in Exhibit 9.1.

Exhibit 9.1
Role of Promotion in 'Access' Credit Card Launch

The basic marketing tasks
With this commitment there were four basic marketing tasks to be accomplished during the pre-launch period:

1 to recruit 3 million card-holders;
2 to recruit 60,000 retail outlets;
3 to create the advertising and promotional platform and programme for the launch;
4 to select a name for the new credit card (Access was chosen after duly diligent research).

Just as important as the four marketing tasks was the task of establishing the necessary computer operation facilities. This went on in parallel with the marketing activities.

Advertising and promotion
All the appropriate media for delivering persuasive messages to potential or existing customers, such as press advertising, leaflets and direct mail were considered, as also were the point-of-sale support materials, such as display material in shops.

What had to be recognised was that the new card-holders in most cases would have had no previous experience of using a credit card; so their knowledge and acceptance of the benefits to be gained from intelligent use of the card would be low. The prime task of the advertising and promotion would be to encourage use both of the card itself and of the extended credit facility which it represented.

Analysis of the consumer research, supplemented by creative imagination, suggested that the intangible concepts of instant finance and flexible repayment could be made more tangible when expressed in terms of the things that people want and of when they want them.

Things have a value over and above their intrinsic worth – the value which is conferred on them by being available at a particular time; they can be more valuable at certain times than at others – what was called 'the time utility of money'. A refrigerator, for example, tends to be more valuable in summer than in winter, and a family holiday is more valuable when the children are on holiday from school than two months later. And winter clothes must be bought in good time, even if, say, a car repair bill arises suddenly.

The new credit card, it was concluded, could provide access to things when they are needed, when they are most valuable. From this, and involving the name of the new credit card, came the launch slogan 'Access takes the waiting out of wanting'.

Source: McIver, C. and Naylor, G. *Marketing Financial Services,* Institute of Bankers, 1980, pp. 221–2.

9.3 Differences in Promoting Services

The promotion of goods and services has many similarities. Thus we do not need to discriminate between the two when considering matters like:

the role of promotion in marketing;
the problems of creating effective promotions;
the managerial problems involved in executing promotional efforts;
the broad methods and media available for promotional efforts;
the institutions available to assist with promotions.

These similarities however tend to obscure some of the differences that exist between promoting goods and services. These differences are of two kinds due to the characteristics of (*a*) service industries; (*b*) services.

9.31 *Differences due to the Characteristics of Service Industries*

Service industries (as Chapter 2 indicates) are very heterogeneous. This makes it problematic to identify differences that apply in all cases. The factors listed here are then indicative of some of the reasons why there may be variation between goods and services promotion. They have relevance in some cases but not necessarily in all cases.

Lack of Marketing Orientation

Some service industries are product orientated. They are unaware of the possibilities that the practice of marketing would offer in their industries. They see themselves as producers of services and not as organizations serving customer needs. Managers are untrained, unskilled and unaware of the role that promotion could play within marketing.

Professional and Ethical Constraints

There may be professional and ethical constraints placed upon the use of certain marketing and promotional methods. Tradition and custom may prevent the use of certain forms of promotion. They may be regarded as 'inappropriate' by the industry or to be in 'bad taste'.

Small Scale of Many Service Operations

Many service operations may be small in scale (e.g. one man businesses). They may not regard themselves as large enough to warrant expenditure on marketing in general and promotions in particular.

Nature of Competition and Market Conditions

Many service organizations may not need to promote their services extensively because of their inability to cope with present workloads. They do not see that even in this situation promotional effort may have a longer term role to play in maintaining a secure market position.

Limited View of Promotion Methods Available

Service organizations may have a limited view of the very wide range of promotional methods available. They may only consider mass advertising and personal selling and ignore the scores of other methods which may be appropriate, are just as effective and may be less costly.

The Nature of the Service

The nature of the service may itself limit the use of certain promotional devices on any large scale. For example, advertising agencies rarely use mass media advertising. The kind of service, the traditions in the particular service industry, the limitations of some methods of promotion for certain kinds of services may constrain the use of promotions.

9.32 Differences Due to the Characteristics of Services

Some features of services which have marketing implications were identified in Chapter 2 (i.e. intangibility, inseparability, heterogeneity, perishability). These factors can assume importance when differences between goods and services are examined from the buyer's viewpoint.

Few studies are available on whether goods and services marketing are perceived to be different from the customer's viewpoint. What evidence there is suggests that many similarities exist in buyer behaviour for the two categories. Yet there are some important differences. These differences are to do with:

(*a*) consumer attitudes;
(*b*) needs and motives for purchase;
(*c*) buying process.

Consumer Attitudes

Consumer attitudes are a key influence upon purchase decisions. With services intangibility is an important quality in marketing them. Consumers are more likely to rely upon subjective impressions of the service and of the performer or seller of the service when purchasing. This reliance on subjective impressions may be of less importance in the purchase of tangible goods. Two dimensions of consumer attitudes towards service sellers and service industries on which services are different from goods are:

(*a*) services are perceived as being more personal than goods;
(*b*) consumers are sometimes less satisfied with purchases of services.

Needs and Motives for Purchase

Needs and motives for the purchase of goods and services are much the same. The same kinds of needs are satisfied whether through the purchase of tangibles or intangibles. However, one need that is important – in both situations – is the desire for personal attention. Satisfying this need for personal attention is one way in which service sellers can differentiate their service products from competitors. Though in some services like plant maintenance and computer bureaux, need for personal attention may be less important than other factors.

Buying Process

Differences between goods and services are more noticeable in the buying process. Some service purchases are regarded as riskier partly because it may be more difficult for buyers to evaluate quality and value. Also consumers are more likely to be influenced by others, such as friends and neighbours who have experiences of purchase and use. This more dominant role for personal influence in the buying process has implications for services marketing. In particular the need to develop a professional relationship between service suppliers and their customers; and the need for promotional efforts to build upon word of mouth communication. These are two of a number of guidelines which can be suggested to help make service promotional efforts more effective.

As far as industrial services purchases are concerned a number of differences have been noted between the purchase processes for capital equipment and for services. In one of the few major studies recorded of industrial services purchases they usually involved:

fewer levels of the corporate hierarchy than capital equipment purchases;
fewer same level departments than capital equipment purchases;
fewer individuals in the firm overall;
generally more communication than did the purchases of capital equipment.[5]

These findings suggest that the social influences in firms on purchases of industrial services may be less extensive vertically (formally) and laterally (informally). Such less extensive social networks in turn suggest that the possibility of influencing a firm is less complex for services than for capital equipment. On the other hand the smaller degree of diversity may limit the number of options available to influence purchases.

This same study also confirmed the importance of intangibility as an influence upon purchasing practices. It did seem that 'reputation of the vendor' was an important consideration in the development of a bid list because of the intangible nature of a service. Also, in a number of cases, potential bidders were involved in talks to clarify and answer questions about the bids. Details of exact needs were often discussed because of the difficulty of writing a tight specification for an intangible.

9.4 Guidelines for Improving the Promotion of Services

The differences between goods and services can have some implications for promotional effort. This section gives general guidelines which may be appropriate for service organizations in attempting to improve the effectiveness of their promotion mix. Each element of this mix is examined.

9.41 Advertising

Advertising by service organizations is not new. It has been used for many years in sectors like housing, entertainment, transport, the arts and insurance. What is new is the larger sums of money now being spent on advertising in some service industries (e.g. banking, building societies, travel). Another change is that restrictions on advertising by many professional services are being amended or removed. Greater awareness now exists of the advantages and weaknesses of this form of promotion.

In the United States a number of studies dealing with the attitudes of different professional groups towards advertising have been published. One study showed there was a significant difference in attitudes of accountants, lawyers, dentists and doctors regarding advertising by professionals. All four groups had negative attitudes towards it though accountants and lawyers were more positive to the potential role advertising could play.[6] A study of the attitudes of financial executives towards proposed advertising by accountants indicated that in general they, as potential or existing customers for accountants services, were in favour.[7] A further study examining advertising by lawyers, from a consumer point of view, confirmed a number of significant points for professional service marketors.[8] These included:

  professional choice is an important decision for consumers;
  services are not seen as homogeneous;
  personal information sources dominate in the selection process;
  consumers appear to be responsive to advertising;
  there is an information gap when selecting legal counsel.

The study also confirmed that advertising alone was not likely to be helpful to consumers. Personal interaction was needed in the choice process in which verifiable data, like age and experience, could be confirmed. However whatever measures are taken it still remains difficult for consumers to confirm two main attributes before the choice is made: these attributes are quality and integrity.

In the United Kingdom the four professional accounting associations amended their rules from 1 October 1981 to permit their members to advertise (i.e. the Chartered Accountants bodies of England and Wales, Scotland, Ireland and the Association of Certified Accountants). The Councils of these bodies now implement guidelines on the medium, form and content of advertisements and require that advertisements:

(*a*) should not contain explicit or implicit criticisms of the professional services of others;

(*b*) should be factual and not be likely to mislead;

(*c*) should not refer to fee levels but must include a statement to the effect that the fee basis will be discussed before an assignment is accepted;

(*d*) should not make claim to any particular expertise and should be restricted to all or any of the following: accountancy, auditing, book keeping, trusts, personal and/or corporate taxation and advisory services related to the foregoing;

(*e*) should be of a style and content appropriate to the profession.[9]

We are likely to see many more service organizations lifting their restrictions on advertising in the next few years. We are also likely to see wider use of advertising by many kinds of services who may not have used it in the past (e.g. medicine). Given that service advertising may become more widespread and faced with the inherent problems posed by the characteristics of services what measures can service advertisers take?

There are a number of guidelines that advertisers of services can use to ensure more effective impact.[10] The guidelines included here apply to goods too but may be more critical for services.

(a) Use Clear, Unambiguous Messages

A major difficulty with service advertising is that of communicating the range, depth, quality and level of services provided in simple written or illustrated form. Some service advertising can use pictures or symbols to help convey the advertising message. Other services however may have to present more detailed explanations of their services (e.g. professional services). This can lead to 'wordy' advertising which may interfere with advertising effectiveness. Advertising agencies face considerable creative problems in developing clear and simple messages which neatly encapsulate the richness and dimensions of many service offerings.

(b) Emphasize the Benefits of Services

Attention getting and influential advertising should emphasize the benefits of services advertised rather than their technical details. The emphasis on benefits is in accord with the marketing concept and its concern with fulfilling customer needs. It is important though that benefits stressed should be in line with benefits sought. The benefit appeals used should therefore be based on a clear understanding of customer needs to ensure maximum favourable impact.

(c) Only Promise what can be Delivered

The promise of benefits which can be obtained through service use should not be unrealistic, raise excessive expectations in customers and be incapable of delivery by the service organization. Service organizations must be able to fulfil advertising promises. This may be difficult with highly labour intensive services where performance may vary according to who delivers the service. This means that methods have to be used to ensure minimum consistent standards of performance (*see* Chapter 11). Undue pressures should not be placed on employees by promising standards of service which cannot be fulfilled or maintained (e.g. hotel groups, consultants). It is better to ensure that the minimum standard of service promised is achieved so that, when it is exceeded, customers will be even more pleased.

(d) Advertise to Employees

Employees are particularly important in many people-intensive services and in many services where the interaction between service employees and customers is central to customer satisfaction. This means that employees are a potential audience for service advertising: 'When the performances of people are what customers buy the advertiser needs to be concerned not only with encouraging customers to buy, but also with encouraging employees to perform.'[10]

Advertising can thus be an important tool for reaching employees and motivating and influencing them on how service should be provided; as well as a tool for reaching customers.

(e) Obtain and Maintain Customer Co-operation in the Service Production Process

Service marketors face two challenges in their service advertising. The first, common to goods and service advertising, is how to obtain and maintain customer patronage as users of the services in question. The second, unique to many services, is how to obtain and maintain customer collaboration and co-operation in the service production process. Customers play a role in the production and performance of many services (*see* Chapter 13).

> 'In services . . . the customer frequently plays an important role in production. Sometimes, as in the barber's chair, the role is essentially passive . . . But in the supermarket and laundromat the consumer actually works, and in the doctor's office the quality of the medical history the patient gives may influence significantly the productivity of the doctor.'[11]

Well-conceived advertising will thus sometimes focus on how to obtain and maintain the compliance and co-operation of the customer in service production.

(f) Build on Word-of-mouth Communications

In the introduction to this chapter it was indicated that non-marketor-dominated sources may be more influential in determining service organization and service product choice. One strong influence is word-of-mouth communication; service advertisers should therefore build upon this form of communication. Some ways in which this may be done include:

persuade satisfied customers to let others know of their satisfaction;
develop material that customers can pass on to non-customers;
direct advertising campaigns at opinion leaders;
encourage potential customers to talk to existing customers.

These approaches are used in service marketing settings as diverse as new town developments, management education programmes, credit cards, airline travel and hotels.

(g) Provide Tangible Clues

Service advertisers should use tangible clues wherever possible to strengthen their promotional efforts. It is interesting that much tangible product advertising emphasizes abstract, intangible associations in its appeals (e.g. Heineken beer). On the other hand, services are already abstract and to add further intangible associations to an already abstract concept could be counter-productive: 'The service advertiser . . . is often left with describing the invisible, articulating the imaginary and defining the indistinct.'[12]

In advertising services therefore it is advantageous to translate the range of intangible attributes of a service into something more concrete. This more concrete communication evidence can act as a surrogate or a metaphor for intangibility. Well-known personalities and objects (e.g. buildings, aircraft) are often used to provide tangible evidence about services that the services themselves cannot provide.

(h) Develop Continuity in Advertising

Service organizations can help overcome two disadvantages they may face – intangibility and service product differentiation – through using consistent and continuous symbols, themes, formats or images in their advertising. The British Airways successful 'Fly the flag' campaign enjoyed these qualities of continuity and consistency. Some brands and symbols can become so well known that consumers recognize the organization by the symbol (e.g. Visa, Lloyds Bank, P and O, British Rail). One study of advertising themes used by service organizations found several major themes stood out. These were 'efficiency', 'progressiveness', 'status', 'prestige', 'importance' and 'friendliness'. Most service firms sampled attempted to add at least one of these characteristics to their service through the use of advertising.[12]

(i) Remove Post-purchase Anxiety

Consumers of goods and services are subject to doubts about the soundness of their purchases. With goods some tangible object is available for post-purchase evaluation, with services this may not be so. In service marketing more effort must usually be spent in reassuring the buyer of the soundness of choice and in encouraging customers to tell others about the benefits derived from service purchase and use. Advertising is one means of doing this. However, it is much more potent if during the buying process customers enjoy considerate, sympathetic, adaptive and courteous personal service from those in the service organization with whom they come into contact. Personal selling has a major role to play too.

These guidelines are particularly appropriate in the marketing of consumer services. It has been suggested that a major difference between marketing consumer products and marketing consumer services is the degree of interaction between the consumer and personnel or equipment of the marketor.[13] For consumer products interaction levels can vary considerably from no interaction to high levels of interaction depending upon the product. For consumer services, on the other hand, interaction levels are relatively high. Because of these relatively higher levels of interaction services advertising's role is to act as a surrogate for the marketor. Five roles for services advertising have been identified:

(a) Creating the company's world in the mind of the customer.
 This involves describing the world in which the company operates; its activities; what is special about its services; the values of the company.
(b) Building an appropriate personality for the company.
 This involves long-term efforts to shape the customers' ideas and expectations about the company and its services and to get the customer to feel favourably towards the company.
(c) Identifying the company with the customer.
 This involves getting customers to identify strongly with the service company. The company image and services should be relevant to the needs, values and attitudes of its customers.
(d) Influencing company personnel on how they deal with customers.
 Services advertising has two audiences, customers and company personnel. Services advertising needs to represent and reflect company employees' views, and be understood by them if they are to support company marketing effort.
(e) Helping to open doors for sales representatives.
 Services advertising should form a favourable backcloth against which company sales representatives can operate. Favourable customer predispositions towards a company and its services can help sales representatives calling on prospects.

9.42 Personal Selling

Like advertising, the principles, procedures and methods of personal selling are similar for services as for goods:

'The sales job must be defined; qualified salesmen must be recruited, selected and trained; effective compensation plans must be designed and administered; and the sales force must be supervised and controlled. However, although the major activities are similar, the means by which these activities are performed are frequently quite different for service markets.'[14]

One difference is that, in some services markets, organizations may use 'professionals of the specialism' rather than professional salesmen to sell their services. Another is that like advertising differences are due to the characteristics of services (e.g. intangibility). These characteristics may impose rather different requirements on service salesmen. For example, one study in the life assurance industry of how consumers perceive the purchases of services; how they behave when purchasing services; and how the purchase of services differs from the purchase of goods, revealed the insights summarized in Table 9.1. The implications of these findings for service selling are that selling services can be more difficult than selling goods because of the number of subjective and intangible variables affecting a customer's decision.

Table 9.1
Differences between Selling Goods and Services

Consumers purchase perception of services
Findings
Customers view services as having less consistent quality than goods
Services purchases have higher risks than goods purchases
Service purchasing is a less pleasant buying experience
Services are bought with greater consideration given to the particular seller
Perception of the service company is an important factor when deciding to buy a service

Consumers purchase behaviour with services
Findings
Customers may do less price comparisons with services
Customers give great consideration to the particular seller of services
Customers are likely to be less influenced by advertising and more influenced by personal recommendations

Personal selling of services
Findings
Customer involvement is greater in purchasing services
Customer satisfaction is influenced by the salesperson's attitude and personality
Salespeople may have to spend more time reducing customer uncertainty about purchase

Source: Adapted from George, W. R. and Myers, T. A. 'Life Underwriters Perceptions of differences in Selling Goods and Services', *CLU Journal*, April 1981, pp. 44–9

While this study relates specifically to Life Assurance it should be noted that the findings confirm and conform with other published studies on the marketing of services. The importance of personal contact and the influential role of people in the marketing of services is confirmed elsewhere.[4] Personal selling and personal contact is invariably the backbone of much service marketing. Other studies have shown that lower levels of satisfaction may be derived from services purchases compared with goods.[15] Also, it has been shown that relatively higher risks are involved in purchasing some services and different risk reduction strategies may need to be adopted compared with purchase of goods.[16] These findings have implications for promotional measures used by service organizations. They have particular importance for the personal selling job. They tend to confirm the assertion that: 'In service markets the "official" sales force tends to be more important than it is in industrial markets. Although the definition of a salesman is far broader, his role is significantly more substantial.'[17]

In-service settings, there are therefore a number of guidelines which may be used for service selling.[14]

(a) Develop Personal Relationships with Customers

Good personal contacts between employees and customers can lead to mutual satisfaction. The image of personal attention and personal interest that a service organization may try to convey through its advertising programmes has to be supported by real personal interest and attention in the marketplace. However, a high level of personal interest and attention is not without its problems. First it can be expensive to implement. Secondly, more staff may need to be employed with increased risks of more variability in staffing performance. Thirdly, there are organizational implications. A service organization intent on giving high levels of personal attention has to be organized and resourced to do so (e.g. back-up facilities, detailed knowledge of customer service levels required). Fourthly, personal attention usually takes place at the expense of standardization. This has implications for opportunities for improving productivity in services (*see* Chapter 16).

(b) Adopt a Professional Orientation

The customer in most service transactions must have confidence in the seller's ability to deliver the expected results. A professional approach to business can assist this process. Selling services means people have to be thoroughly competent in their jobs as sellers (e.g. sound knowledge of services available). They must also be perceived by customers to act and sound like professionals. The sellers' appearance, actions, behaviour and attitudes must conform with customers' views of how 'professional' sales people are expected to conduct themselves.

(c) Use Indirect Selling

Three general forms of indirect selling are suggested:

1 *Create derived demand by measures like promoting and selling related goods and services and helping customers use existing services more effectively and efficiently.*

Thus airlines can sell holidays, hotels sell local tourist attractions, Gas and Electricity Boards sell appliances to boost gas and electricity sales. Cross relating services with other services or products provides many opportunities for the seller or services in fields as diverse as insurance, banking, dry cleaning and tourism.

2 Use referees, testimonials and opinion leaders in the customer choice process
In many services the customer may rely on others for help and advice (e.g. insurance brokers, travel agents, investment consultants, management consultants, tourist boards). Sellers of services should ensure indirect selling by exposure to these sorts of referees, sources of advice, opinion influencers and influentials.

3 Self selling
This practice is common in the field of professional services where more direct forms of selling may be frowned on. More informal ways of gaining exposure may be used like speaking in public, involvement in community affairs, membership of professional organizations and attending conferences and courses.

(d) Build and Maintain a Favourable Image

Effective marketing depends upon the creation and maintenance of a favourable image. People and organizations will develop and have images anyway. What marketing activities (e.g. advertising, public relations) try to ensure is that the image develops in a way consistent with how the individual or organization would like to be seen; and in a way which is congruent with customer perceptions of what that image should be. The impressions that customers and non-customers have of an organization and its staff will greatly influence their patronage decisions.

Image building and maintenance is an important element in service marketing because high levels of intangibility in a service mean reliance must be placed on reputation and subjective impressions of the service. Second non-marketor sources of influence (e.g. word-of-mouth) are important in service marketing. Other users or non-users are an important contributor to service selling and the image formed.

Thus the personal selling effort contributes to the overall image of a service organization. Customers may judge a company by the quality of its sales people. The courtesy, efficiency, attentiveness and skill of sales people will contribute to and enhance the image formed; supplemented by the other methods of image creation like advertising and publicity.

(e) Sell Services not Service

In selling core services, organizations can benefit from having a range of support services surrounding the core services. These make it easier, more convenient and less trouble for the customer to purchase. Package holidays provide a convenient example of how a range of services can be rolled into one straightforward purchase from the customer's viewpoint. Insurance companies, airlines, banks and retail organizations have extended the range of services offered (e.g. financial arrangements). All these supplementary services can strengthen the impetus to purchase the core service (e.g. travel, risk reduction, credit).

(f) Make Purchase Easy

Service products may be conceptually difficult for customers to understand. This may be because the customer is making an infrequent purchase (e.g. buying a house). It may also be that in certain circumstances the customer is under great emotional strain (e.g. using the services of a funeral director). In these circumstances professional service sellers will make it easy for the customer to purchase. It implies looking after all arrangements in a professional way while keeping the customer informed of progress in the performance of the service. Minimal demands are imposed on the customer.

A recent model of seven guidelines for the personal selling of services has been developed.[18] This was derived from empirical data on the differences between selling goods and services as perceived by representatives of both goods and services firms. The model was then validated by comparison with a bank marketing programme. The seven guidelines in this model are:

1 *Orchestrate the service purchase encounter*
   Input
      solicit buyer needs and expectations;
      assess knowledge of evaluative criteria.
   Processing
      apply technical expertise;
      recognize the representative as a surrogate for the service;
      manage the impressions of the buyer–seller and buyer–producer interactions;
      elicit positive customer participation.
   Output
      a pleasant, satisfying service purchase experience long term.
2 *Facilitate quality assessment*
      establish reasonable levels of expected performance;
      use established expectations as a basis for judging quality after purchase.
3 *Tangibilize the service*
      teach what the buyer should look for;
      educate the buyer on comparing alternative services;
      teach the buyer about the uniqueness of the service.
4 *Emphasize organizational image*
      assess the customer's awareness level of the generic service, the firm and the representative;
      communicate relevant image attributes of the service, the firm and the representative.
5 *Utilize references external to the organization*
      encourage satisfied customers to become involved in the communication process (e.g. word-of-mouth advertising);
      develop and manage favourable publicity.
6 *Recognize the importance of all public contact personnel*
      sensitize all personnel to their direct role in the customer satisfaction process;

minimize the total number of people interacting with each specific customer.

7 Recognize the customer's involvement during the service design process to generate customer specifications by asking questions, showing examples, etc.

9.43 Publicity

There is no fundamental difference between publicity for services and for goods. Methods of obtaining editorial space may vary, the purposes for which publicity is used may vary, the importance that organizations attach to publicity may vary. Ultimately though, in all contexts, the appeal of publicity is the same and is based on three distinctive qualities.[19] These are:

(a) Credibility

News features and stories may have higher credibility than directly sponsored reports.

(d) Off guard

Publicity is presented as news rather than as a direct attempt to sell or advertise which may catch potential users off guard.

(c) Dramatization

Publicity has potential for dramatizing a service or service organization.

Publicity is part of the more general field of public relations whose tasks typically include press relations, product and service publicity, organizational communications (internal and external), lobbying and providing a general information role for an organization.

The major decisions in publicity:

(a) establish objectives;
(b) choose the publicity messages and vehicles;
(c) evaluate the results;

are common to all organizations. Publicity is important in many service organizations. One advantage it has for smaller service organizations with small marketing budgets is that it can be a cheap method of gaining exposure. Yet it can be a potent tool for building awareness and preference in the marketplace.

9.44 Sales Promotion

Some commentators on services marketing dismiss sales promotion in a few sentences: 'Sales promotion in the traditional sense of sampling, demonstrations, and point of purchase display are severely limited . . .'[20] and sales promotion is not usually regarded as an important tool. Nothing could be further from the truth. Of course certain kinds of sales promotion may be irrelevant in particular kinds of service setting (e.g. sampling of a solicitor's services). Also, certain kinds of sales promotion may be incompatible with purchase and use of some services. But despite this the increase in sales promotion activity in many service markets in the last ten to fifteen years has been one of the major changes which have taken place in marketing. Like those changes which took place earlier from around 1960 with the increased use of sales promotions in many consumer goods markets, the upsurge in sales promotions for services has been largely uncharted. Particular forms of activity have received more scrutiny than others (e.g. sponsorship of sport and leisure); but overall it is a field of marketing awaiting further detailed attention.

One of the leading commentators on sales promotion in the United Kingdom has written in one of the few sources which give attention specifically to services (e.g. retailing, professional services, transport agencies and tourism):

> 'It must not be thought that . . . sales promotion is the prerogative of manufacturing firms. Those selling a service have just as much, if not more, of a problem on their hands. . . . There are still the same set of marketing problems to be faced, but they are sometimes complicated and sometimes eased by special factors applying only to the service industries.'[21]

Some of those special factors include the following.

(a) Problems due to the Characteristics of Services

For example, services cannot be stored so this has particular implications for the use of sales promotional practices which spread the load of service use more evenly (e.g. off-peak attractive pricing schemes).

(b) Problems which are Specific to Certain Service Sectors

For example, there may be ethical constraints on the use of certain sales promotion practices or their use may be regarded as too brash by a professional group. In practice most sales promotion schemes apply though they are often 'disguised' and go under other names. A solicitor may waive his fee for certain minor services (a price cut as a reward for loyalty), an estate agent may offer 'no sale – no fee' terms, a management consultant may offer an amount of time free of charge (sampling), advertising agencies may offer free advice on related services (e.g. publicity), stockbrokers and unit trust groups may provide regular clients with a statistical service and regular private investment letters. All of these are forms of sales promotion.

The difference between goods and services as far as sales promotions are concerned is not that they may not be used, but that the forms of activity will be different given the characteristics of target audiences and the appropriateness of the devices available. Reasons for use remain the same and include the following:

| (a) Demand problems | Where demand fluctuates and there is wasted capacity |

(b) Customer problems	Where there are not enough of them using the service
	Where they are not buying enough of the service
	Where they need help in choice before purchase/use
	Where they perceive risk in purchase/use
	Where they have payment problems
(c) Service product problems	Where new service products are launched
	Where services are not being talked about
	Where services are not being used
(d) Intermediary problems	Where dealers are not giving enough attention to an organization's services
	Where dealers are not giving enough support to an organization's services
(e) Competition problems	Where competition is strong and intense
	Where competition is promoting heavily
	Where competition is launching new services

Ultimately sales promotion is one element of the service organization's promotion mix. The most effective promotional efforts are those which fit in with overall promotional strategy and is, in turn, seen as one element in overall marketing mix strategy.

9.5 Summary

1 Service organizations can use four methods to formally promote their service products. They are advertising, personal selling, publicity and sales promotion.
2 The principles of promotion are the same for goods and services. However, some differences are due to (a) the characteristics of service industries; (b) the characteristics of services.
3 Both factors have implications for promotion of services. Some general guidelines may be used to improve the effectiveness of advertising and personal selling.
4 Publicity and sales promotion is much the same for services as for goods.

Questions for Discussion

1 Why is promoting of services difficult?
2 What is the role of personal selling in the marketing of services?
3 Suggest three guidelines that marketors of services can use in their advertising?
4 Suggest three guidelines that marketors of services can use in their personal selling?
5 Suggest a list of ten different sorts of publicity campaign that could be used in a service industry of your choice?
6 What differences exist in using sales promotions in:

(*a*) retailing?
(*b*) professional services?
7 Identify six special skills required in a personal salesman selling:
(*a*) an industrial service (e.g. fleet hire)?
(*b*) a personal service (e.g. life insurance)?
8 How important is systems selling in the marketing of services?
9 Why do some professions limit the use of advertising?
10 In what other ways does a service organization communicate with its
markets besides advertising, personal selling, publicity and sales
promotions?

References and Notes

1 Davis, D. L., Guiltinan, J. P. and Jones, W. H. 'Service Characteristics, Consumer Search and the Classification of Retail Services', *Journal of Retailing*, Vol. 55, No. 3, Fall 1979, pp. 3–23.
2 George, W. R. and Myers, T. A. 'Life Underwriters' perceptions of differences in selling goods and services', *C L U Journal*, April 1981, pp. 44–9.
3 Majaro, S. *Marketing in Perspective*, George Allen and Unwin, London 1982.
4 This section is based on Johnson E. M. 'Are goods and services different? – An exercise in marketing Theory' unpublished DBA dissertation, Washington University, 1969.
5 Johnston, W. J. and Bonoma, T. V. 'Purchase process for Capital Equipment and Services', *Industrial Marketing Management*, Vol. 10, 1981, pp. 253–64.
6 See, for example, Darling, J. R. and Hackett, D. W. 'The advertising of fees and services: a study of contrasts between and similarities among professional groups', *Journal of Marketing*, Spring 1978, pp. 23–4.
7 See, for example, Carver, M. R., King, T. E. and Label, W. A. 'Attitudes towards advertising by accountants', *Financial Executive*, Oct. 1979, pp. 27–32.
8 Smith, R. E. and Meyer, T. S., 'Attorney Advertising: A Consumer perspective', *Journal of Marketing*, Spring 1980, Vol. 44, No. 2, pp. 56–64.
9 Office of Fair Trading, Annual Report of the Director General of Fair Trading 1981, HMSO July 1982.
10 This section includes ideas from George, W. R. and Berry, L. L. 'Guidelines for the Advertising of Services', *Business Horizons*. Vol. 24, July–Aug. 1981, pp. 52–6.
11 Fuchs, V. R. *The Service Economy*, Columbia University Press, New York, 1968.
12 Urwin, S. 'Customized Communications: a concept for Service Advertising', *Advertising Quarterly*, Summer 1975, pp. 28–30.
13 This section is based on Firestone, S. H. 'Why advertising a service is different' in *Emerging Perspectives on Services Marketing* (Edited by

Berry, L. L., Shostack, G. Lynn and Upah, G. D.) American Marketing Association, Chicago, 1983.

14 Johnson, E. M. 'The Selling of Services' in *Handbook of Modern Marketing* (Ed. Buell, V. P.) McGraw-Hill, New York, 1970, pp. 12–110.

15 George, W. R. 'The Retailing of Services – a challenging future' *Journal of Retailing*, Fall, Vol. 53, No. 3, 1977, pp. 85–98.

16 See for example Guseman, D. W. 'The perception of risk in consumer services – a comparison with consumer products' D.B.A. Dissertation, University of Colorado (Boulder) 1977; Lewis, W. F. 'An empirical investigation of the conceptual relationship between Services and Products', PhD Dissertation, University of Cincinnati, 1976.

17 Cannon, T. *Basic Marketing: Principles and Practice*, Holt, Rinehart & Winston, New York, 1980.

18 This section is based on George, W. R., Kelly, J. Patrick and Marshall, Claudia E., 'Personal Selling of Services' in *Emerging Perspectives on Services Marketing* (Eds. Berry, L. L., Shostack, G. Lynn and Upah, G. D.) American Marketing Association, Chicago, 1983.

19 Kotler, P. *Principles of Marketing*, Prentice-Hall, Englewood Cliffs, 1980.

20 Markin, R. *Marketing: Strategy and Management*, 2nd Edn. J. Wiley and Sons, New York, 1982.

21 Spillard, P. *Sales Promotion*, Business Books, London, 2nd Edn, 1975 (see Chapter on Sales Promotion in the Service Industries).

10. *PLACE DECISIONS AND SERVICES*

10.1 Introduction

All organizations – whether producing tangibles or intangibles – are concerned with place decisions. That is how to make their offerings available and accessible to users. In Chapter 4 therefore place was shown as one of the seven elements of the marketing mix for services. In general, this element of the marketing mix has been neglected as far as services are concerned for most texts deal with place decisions in the context of the movement of physical items.

Discussion of place decisions for physical items has spawned a range of terms used to describe the area of concern. These include:

Channels;	Distribution;
Place;	Location;
Delivery;	Coverage.

These terms are often used interchangeably when describing product marketing. Their transfer to the area of services marketing, without clarification, can cause conceptual problems. Shostack[1] suggests that the subject of place decisions for services is confused as people grapple with the concept of a 'distribution channel' for items which are intangible, often inseparable from the person performing the service and perishable, in the sense that inventory cannot be carried. The subject is further confused because the generalizations made about services (e.g. no inventory carried) do not always apply in specific situations. For example, while the characteristic of intangibility means that physical distribution problems are less important in a service like professional accountancy, where inventory is largely restricted to supplies of support materials; in other services physical distribution can be a problem. A group of plant hire contractors have to cope with inventory problems; a hire car company like Avis have to cope with inventory problems; even hotel groups with spare rooms (inventory) or airlines with spare seats (inventory) have inventory problems.

In this chapter place decisions are limited to: 'any extra – corporate entity between the producer of a service and prospective users that is utilized to make the service available and/or more convenient'.[2] The chapter focuses upon two aspects of place decisions. These are the outlets through which services may flow to reach the user; and the location of these outlets.

10.2 Methods of Distributing Services

A distribution channel for our purpose is the sequence of firms involved in moving a service from producer to consumer. The usual generalization made about service distribution is that direct sale is the most common method and that channels are short. Direct sale certainly is common in some services markets (e.g. professional services); but many service channels contain one or more intermediaries. It would be incorrect to suggest that direct sale is the only method of distribution in services markets. Intermediaries are common. Some of these intermediaries assume ownership risks; some perform roles that change ownership (e.g. purchasing); some perform roles that enable physical movement (e.g. transporting). In fact, as Rathmell[3] suggests: 'there is no uniformity in the functions performed by intermediaries'. This lack of uniformity however should not conceal the fundamental truth that organizations operating in services markets have two main channel choice options.

These options are the same for producers of physical items. They are:

(*a*) Direct sale;
(*b*) Sale via intermediary(ies).

In practice organizations may use both options.

10.21 Direct Sale

Direct sale may be the chosen method of distribution for a service through choice or because of inseparability of service and provider. Where direct sale is selected through choice then the service marketor does so presumably to derive specific marketing advantages such as:

(*a*) maintaining better 'control' over how the service is provided or performed. Loss of control may be a disadvantage of dealing through an intermediary;
(*b*) obtaining distinguishable service product differentiation in what are otherwise standard and uniform markets through real personal service.
(*c*) obtaining direct feedback from customers on their existing needs, how those needs are changing and their perceptions of competitors' market offerings.

To illustrate, some investment advisors or accountants may deliberately limit the number of clients they take on to provide individual service: some owner-managed gastronomic restaurants limit the number of bookings they accept to maintain their personal high standards of service.

Where direct sale is due to the inseparability of service and provider (e.g. as in legal services or certain kinds of household services) then the provider of the service may face problems. Among these are:

(*a*) problems of expanding the business and coping with high workloads where the services of a particular individual may be in demand (e.g. a distinguished defence lawyer);

(*b*) sometimes direct sale means limited geographic market coverage; particularly where a large personal element of service is involved and technology cannot be used, to any great extent, to bridge the gap between the service organization and its customers.

Direct sale may of course be accomplished by the customer going to the service provider (e.g. a hairdresser, tourists making use of an information centre) or by the provider going to the customer (e.g. a mobile bank; a plumber or a drain cleaning service). Many personal and business services are characterized by the direct channel between service organization and customer. Direct channels are found in personal and business service fields like beauty shops, photographic studios, shoe repair shops, funeral service firms, consultants, security services and plant rental.

10.22 Sale via Intermediary(ies)

The most frequently used channel by service organizations however is that which operates through intermediaries. Service channel structures vary considerably and some are now complex. Figure 10.1 illustrates the array of channels used to distribute what are called 'money products'.[4]

Some of the more novel channel forms for distributing money products have emerged because service organizations have developed or taken advantage of new products to overcome the problem of inseparability. The bank credit card is an example of a physical representation of a service offered:

> 'the bank credit card is a tangible representation of the service of credit though it is not the service itself. As such it has enabled banks to overcome the inseparability problem and use the retail merchant as an intermediary in the distribution of credit. The credit card has also made it possible for banks to expand their geographic markets by maintaining credit customers far outside their immediate trading areas, since it enables subscribers to maintain an 'inventory' of the bank's credit for use at their convenience.'[5]

Many forms of intermediary are now common in services markets. They include:

(*a*) *Agents.* Common in markets like tourism, travel, hotels, transport, insurance, credit and employment and industrial services.
(*b*) *Dealers.* Intermediaries trained to perform or provide a service and franchised to sell it (*see* Section 10.42).
(*c*) *Institutional middlemen.* Arise in markets where services must be or are traditionally provided by intermediaries like the stockmarket or advertising.
(*d*) *Wholesalers.* Intermediaries in wholesale markets like merchant banks or laundry and dry cleaning services for industry.
(*e*) *Retailers.* Examples include photographic studios and shops providing dry cleaning services.

The possible forms of intermediary are many. In some service transactions a number of service organizations may be involved. For example an individual taking on the long-term rental of a house could be involved with

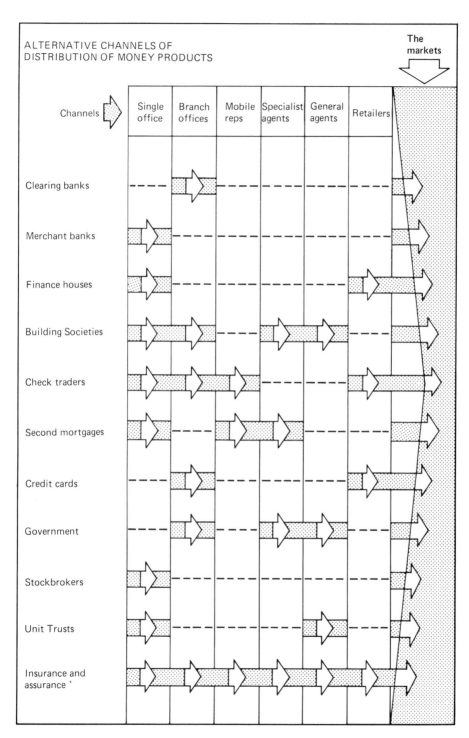

Figure 10.1 Alternative Channels of Distribution of Money Products
Source: Ornstein, E. J. *The Marketing of Money*, Gower, Aldershot, 1972

estate agents, surveyors, solicitors, banks, building societies and so on. Also in many service markets intermediaries may represent buyers and sellers e.g. auctioneering. Some of the possible permutations which may apply in particular service sectors are outlined below. They serve to illustrate the variety in service channel structure that may be possible. They do not of course provide a comprehensive outline of all permutations possible.

Financial Services

Banks provide a wide range of services to individuals and organizations. Current accounts, deposit accounts, credit, financial advice, estate planning, capital loans, are some of the products available and of course many users deal direct with the bank. But use of intermediaries too is common. For example credit may be handled through middlemen like retailers and finance houses. Credit cards are now widely used and the bank may act as a clearing house between the seller accepting a credit card for payment (like a retail outlet) and the credit card company itself which processes the credit slips. Both bank and seller may receive commission for their role in providing the service. Another current example is where an employer transfers funds through his own bank to pay wages and salaries of employees who may use other banks; the banks co-operate in the funds transfer process. Banks have recently developed a number of new ways of distributing some of their services. Apart from temporary branches on novel sites (e.g. trade fairs; race meetings; university campuses), banking by post and the use of automatic teller machines in a range of locations are becoming more common.

Insurance Services

Direct sale of insurance is common. It may also be sold through merchants, agents, brokers or some combination of intermediaries. Some trading companies, like the Co-operative Society, may have their own insurance companies. Other outlets like travel agents may act for a number of companies as part of their insurance travel services to customers. Brokers typically serve a number of insurance companies and are important intermediaries in insurance channels. Vending machines are increasingly used to sell insurance (e.g. at airports) and group insurance (e.g. BUPA) is common in many work settings. Also an insurance agent may write a group insurance policy operated by an employer to cover employees (e.g. for accidents at work).

In developing a channel strategy in the field of insurance Majaro[6] suggests that some of the following questions are pertinent:

If we could start life afresh, what kind of distribution system would be compatible with our marketing objectives? How do the ideal channels we identify compare with what we currently have?

Have we analysed the various middlemen we use and their relative performance?

What do the middlemen think of us?

How does our commission system compare with our competitors' systems?

Do we use budgetary control to monitor the performance of our channels of distribution?

Do we take steps to create customer loyalty?

Do we allocate sufficient funds towards training and developing our channels of distribution and their personnel?

Do we maintain an efficient and effective communication system with our distributors?

Hotels

Hotels increasingly utilize indirect channels of sale in spite of the traditionally direct nature of their services. Some of the growing range of intermediaries in the hotel industry are shown in Figure 10.2.

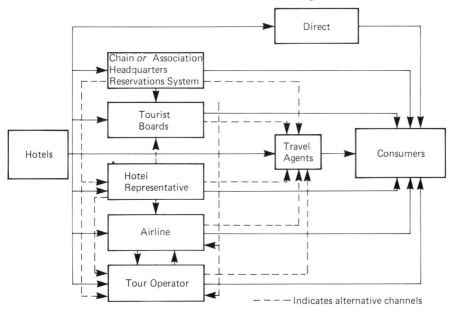

Figure 10.2 Hotel Service Channels

Source: Derived from Rathmell, J. M. *Marketing in the Service Sector*, Winthrop, Cambridge, Mass., 1974

The examples shown include the following.

(a) Travel Agents

Travel agents may contract with a hotel on behalf of customers. Increasingly though they deal through other intermediaries who may hold blocks of rooms or act as agents for the hotels (e.g. tourist offices).

(b) Tour Operators

Tour operators reserve blocks of rooms to sell through their retailers (e.g. Travel Agents) or direct to the Public (e.g. Portland Holidays).

(c) Tourist Boards

Tourist boards may act as booking agents for hotels competing in a particular regional market.

(d) Hotel Representatives

Hotel representatives act as sales agents, usually for non-competing hotels (e.g. resorts).

(e) Airlines

Many hotel groups are now integrated with airlines to provide a complete package. Integration may involve ownership or a close working relationship.

(f) Centralized Reservation Systems

Many franchised groups (e.g. Best Western) or chain hotels (e.g. Reo Stakis) use centralized reservation systems.

In addition to the above, hotels themselves may act as intermediaries to sell other services like car rentals, tour guides, theatre and concert seats.

10.3 Service Channel Development

Two writers on service channels suggest that they develop in two ways either as independent channels or as combined channels.[7]

Independent Service Channels

Independent channels emerge to fulfill a specific need and are not necessarily associated with another product or service. Thus a consulting company or a travel agent not linked with any other company and operated separately from other firms are examples of independent service firms. Independent service firms may of course make use of other intermediaries (e.g. as in film distribution).

Combined Service Channels

Combined service channels on the other hand emerge when the service is integrated with a channel that distributes a product. Combined service channels can arise through:

 (*a*) Combination by Acquisition – this is where services may be offered as part of a total product mix (e.g. finance for consumer durable purchases);

(b) Combination through Concessions – this is where services may be offered and operated within the facilities of another firm. The concessionaire pays rent and perhaps some percentage of sales on the space occupied to the firm granting the concession (e.g. Debenhams and Texas Homecare grant concessions);

(c) Combination through a Tie in Agreement – this is where two or more independent companies come to some contractual agreement to co-operate in the marketing of a service. Thus finance companies and car dealers may operate tie-in agreements. Two current examples in the United Kingdom are the tie up between Robert Fleming the Bankers and the Save and Prosper Group in marketing a high interest bank account. Also in 1982 the Prudential Assurance Company and the National Giro test marketed a scheme to sell travel assurance over the counter at Post Offices.[8]

What is not made clear in the above suggestions is why these sorts of patterns may emerge. This is an area of service marketing requiring further research. One possible framework for such analysis is the life-cycle presented in Chapter 7. There it was presented in the conventional way as a model for understanding and analysing service products and service organizations. An interesting and thoughtful model of the potential use of the life-cycle as an instrument for analysis and possible explanation and prediction has been proposed.[9] This deals with multi-site service firms (e.g. Hertz, Holiday Inns) and suggests how the pre-occupations, interests, objectives and strategies of such firms change as they move through the life-cycle from entrepreneurial stage to decline/regeneration. Considerations of the place element of the marketing mix are included in the description of the model.

10.4 Innovations in Methods of Distributing Services

There have been considerable innovations, in recent years, in methods of distributing services. This contrasts with views expressed some years ago that service marketors had lagged in using innovative marketing practices.[10] Four examples are included here to illustrate the nature of some of these innovations. They cover new service developments and new service institutions. The examples are:

(a) the growth of rental services;
(b) the growth of franchising;
(c) the growth of service integration;
(d) quasi-retailing.

10.41 The Growth of Rental Services

An interesting phenomenon of the service economies is the growth of rental services. That is many individuals and organizations have moved and are moving away from the ownership of goods to the renting or leasing of goods. Purchases are shifting from the goods sector to the service sector. This has meant that many organizations selling goods have added leasing and rental arrangements to their services. Also new kinds of service institutions have emerged to service the rental market.

In industrial markets it is now possible to rent or lease items like cars, lorries, plant and equipment, aircraft, containers, office equipment of all kinds, uniforms, overalls, towels and so forth. In consumer markets too flats, homes, furniture and TV, sports goods, tents, tools, paintings, films, videos and social companions are amongst the range of items available for rental. A number of organizations traditionally involved in goods production have developed a service arm to their operations through renting and leasing their equipment and banks and finance houses play an important role in this market as third parties to many leasing and rental agreements.

Some products do not lend themselves to renting, particularly consumable items like food, medicines and oil. Also in many situations it is more beneficial to own a product – because it is more convenient to do so – or because financially the costs of renting are higher particularly when the residual value of an asset is taken into account.

There are however a number of advantages in renting for both the renter and the rentee. The importance and predominance of these will vary according to the nature of the market (e.g. consumer or industrial). For the renter some advantages are:

(*a*) income obtainable after repair costs and maintenance and service charges may be higher than could be obtained by selling the product;

(*b*) renting may enable the renter to tap markets that could not be reached otherwise because of capital costs involved;

(*c*) renting equipment may give the renter leverage in the sale of products associated with it (e.g. photocopiers and paper);

(*d*) rental arrangements can assist with the launch and distribution of new products and complement arrangements based on purchase and ownership by the customer.

For the rentee some advantages of rental arrangements include:

(*a*) Capital is not tied up in assets. Such capital can be used for other purchases.

(*b*) In industrial markets there may be tax advantages to renting or leasing rather than owning goods.

(*c*) Less capital outlay is required to enter business or markets where goods may be rented rather than acquired by purchase.

(*d*) New designs may become available to those who rent thus avoiding the risks in purchase of obsolescence and style change.

(*e*) In situations where seasonal demand or sporadic use only is made of a product (e.g. harvesting) then renting equipment may be a more sensible and economically sound strategy than ownership.

(*f*) The problems of service – maintenance, repair, breakdown – are usually the responsibility of others under many rental arrangements.

(g) Renting removes the risk of incorrect product selection and anxieties which may follow purchase.

(h) For many, renting or leasing is the mechanism which permits consumption and use which would not otherwise be possible (e.g. because of costs or practical problems of surveillance and maintenance as with holiday homes).

Berry and Maricle[11] have suggested that 'consumption without ownership' has great possibilities for expansion in consumer markets. They also suggest that some of the more likely implications of this trend in terms of its impact on marketing and business are as follows.

(a) Increased investment in inventory for those leasing and renting. This will be coupled with lower stock turnover rates, greater demands for storage and facilities for maintenance, repair, renovation and repackaging of stock.

(b) The larger amount of inventory in turn requires different financing arrangements. This has led to financial institutions themselves assuming the ownership function within channels of distribution. Coupled with this though is that consumer credit requirements may be reduced as ownership is shifted elsewhere in the channel.

(c) New inventory concepts are required under conditions of leasing and renting (e.g. greater concern with 'occupancy rates' and 'capacity usage' rather than stockturn).

(d) Products rented and leased may need to be of better quality. Durability and ease of maintenance and repair are important characteristics where heavy and repeated use may occur.

(e) In addition it is suggested that leasing and renting in consumer markets affords an opportunity for salesmen to be 'consultants of consumption' occupying a greater advising role. Also there are opportunities for more 'flexible' pricing practices in situations in which goods are rented rather than owned, particularly over the life of the item in service.

10.42 The Growth of Franchising

Franchising is a growing phenomenon in those service industries where standardization of the service is possible. At a general level: 'a franchise is where one person grants rights to another to exploit an intellectual property right involving perhaps trade names, products, trade marks, equipment distribution'.[12]

The following features are found in every franchise transaction:

(a) 'The ownership by one person of a name, an idea, a secret process, or a specialized piece of equipment and the goodwill associated with it.

(b) 'The grant of a licence by that person to another permitting the exploitation of such name, idea, process, or equipment and the goodwill associated with it.

(c) 'The inclusion in the licence agreement of regulations relating to the

operation of the business in the conduct of which the licensee
exploits his rights.

(*d*) 'The payment by the licensee of a royalty or some other
consideration for the rights that are obtained.'

A business format franchise is more specific and the following must be
present in every 'business format' franchise:

(*a*) 'There must be a contract containing all the terms agreed upon.

(*b*) 'The franchisor must initiate and train the franchisee in all aspects
of the business prior to the opening of the business and assist in the
opening.

(*c*) After the business is opened the franchisor must maintain a
continuing interest in providing the franchisee with support in all
aspects of the operation of the business.

(*d*) The franchisee is permitted under the control of the franchisor to
operate under a trade name, format and/or procedure, and with the
benefit of goodwill owned by the franchisor.

(*e*) The franchisee must make a substantial capital investment from his
own resources.

(*f*) The franchisee must own his own business.

(*g*) The franchisee will pay the franchisor for the rights which he
acquires in one way or other.

(*h*) The franchisee will be given some territory within which to
operate.'

An illustrative list of some current types of business franchise operations is
shown in Table 10.1.

Table 10.1
Illustrative List of Business Franchise Operations

Accounting and tax services	Motels
Beauty salons	Nursing homes
Car rental services	Office systems
Drain cleaning services	Pest control
Employment services	Restaurants
Fast food operations	Sales training services
Glass tinting	Travel agencies
Hotels	Vending operations
Industrial services	Weight control systems
Lawn and garden care	

Source: Mendelsohn, M. *The Guide to Franchising*, 2nd edn, Pergamon,
Oxford, 1979

Until recently franchising, in the United Kingdom, was chiefly associated with manufacturer-led operations. These usually took the form of
agencies (e.g. cosmetic manufacturers' agreements with retail outlets) or
dealerships (e.g. car dealers). They are known as 'vertical franchising'
arrangements because operations on two or more different levels of

distribution are involved. A more recent development has been the emergence of 'horizontal franchising' arrangements. These are usually when retailers of products or services franchise others at the same level in the distribution channel. This kind of franchising is called 'service-sponsor-retailer franchising' and it is in this area that much recent growth has occurred. Developments have taken place in areas like coin-operated dry cleaning, employment services, tool and equipment rental and cleaning services. Many service operations now use franchising as a growth strategy. It is likely to become of more importance in service marketing because of the benefits it affords. The franchisor gains:

(*a*) expansion possibilities in spite of capital or manpower limitations;
(*b*) motivated managers in multi-site operations because they are part owners of the business;
(*c*) a means of control over pricing, promotion, distribution and consistency of the service product offering;
(*d*) a source of revenue.

The franchisee gains:

(*a*) a chance to run his own business, usually with a tested service product concept;
(*b*) the backing of mass purchasing power;
(*c*) the backing of promotional support;
(*d*) the benefits of centralized managment.

The customer gains:

(*a*) some assurance of service product quality particularly where the operation is established nationally.

10.43 The Growth of Service Integration

The growth of franchising outlined in the previous section is a manifestation of another phenomenon in the service sector – integration. Integrated corporate systems and integrated contractual systems are developing and beginning to dominate in certain fields. In hotels and motels, for example, integrated systems like Holiday Inns, Sheraton and Best Western are of increasing importance. In travel and tourism the service systems link two or more service industries like airlines, hotels, motels, car rental, tour buses, restaurants, seat booking agencies, leisure and recreation sites, ski resorts, shipping lines and so on. Some large service organizations now control the complete 'package' offered to the tourist or holidaymaker through control over horizontal and vertical service channel systems. Integration so often thought of only in manufacturing systems is an important feature of many modern service systems too.

10.44 Quasi-retailing

One of the most important intermediaries for services is the retailer. A feature of the development of the service economy in recent years has been the emergence of 'quasi-retail' outlets.[13] Quasi-retail outlets sell services rather than goods. They include:

Hairdressers;	Estate agents;	Amusement arcades;
Undertakers;	Building societies;	Launderettes;
Travel agents;	Employment agencies;	Betting offices;
Ticket agents;	Car hire agencies;	Hotels;
Banks;	Driving schools;	Restaurants.

In practice definitional problems surround the use of the term quasi-retailing. For example under the Town and Country Planning (Use classes) Order, 1972, a distinction is drawn between shops, offices and other unspecified uses. Thus as Table 10.2 shows an undertaker is classified as a shop, a bank as an office, while a Betting Office is an Other unspecified use!

Table 10.2
Classification of Shops, Offices and Other Non-Retail Services (Town and Country Planning (Use Classes) order, 1972)

Class I, Shops	Class II, Offices	Other unspecified uses
Retail shop	Bank	Amusement arcade
Hairdresser	Estate agent	Pin-ball saloon
Undertaker	Building society	Launderette
Travel agency	Employment	Betting office
Ticket agency	agency	Hotel
Post office	Car hire	Restaurant
Premises for the	Driving school	Cafe/snack bar
reception of goods to		Public house
be washed, cleaned or		Premises for sale of hot
repaired		food

Source: Kivell, P. T. and Doidge, R. A. 'Service Outlets in Shopping Centres: Problems and Policies', *Service Industries Review*, Vol. 2, No. 1, Spring 1982, pp. 22–37.

These problems of defining quasi-retail outlets, coupled with the fact that only limited work has been undertaken on this retailing phenomenon, make it difficult to give precise measures of the extent of quasi-retailing. One general indication of the growth which has taken place in this field is shown in Table 10.3 for a sample of sixty shopping centres.

This indicates that in absolute terms building societies, cafes and restaurants and travel and ticket agencies experienced the largest changes in the shopping centres sampled. However employment agencies and take-away food outlets led the way in terms of percentage increase. The three kinds of service businesses experiencing a decline in absolute and in percentage terms were launderettes, shoe repairs and dry cleaners. Reasons for the growth of some outlets and the decline of others vary. Generally they are due to shifts in consumer demand through changing patterns of employment, housing, mobility and life styles.

Table 10.3
Growth of Quasi-Retail Outlets 1965–76

Service Business	Number of Outlets 1965	Number of Outlets 1976	Absolute Change 1965–76	% Change
Building society	36	138	102	283
Cafe, restaurants	151	226	75	50
Travel & ticket agents	29	102	73	252
Estate agents	95	141	46	48
Take-away food	6	48	42	700
Betting offices	25	66	41	164
Insurance/money agents	22	48	26	118
Employment agents	3	28	25	833
Banks	222	232	10	5
Hairdressers	107	117	10	9
Post offices	29	35	6	21
Opticians/surgeries	92	95	3	3
Launderettes	29	26	–3	–10
Shoe repairs	50	35	–15	–30
Dry cleaners	190	104	–86	–46

Source: Kivell, P. T. and Doidge, R. A. 'Service Outlets in Shopping Centres: Problems and Policies', *Service Industries Review*, Vol. 2, No. 1, Spring 1982, pp. 22–7

An interesting problem faced by local authorities in controlling shopping centres is the extent to which quasi-retail outlet growth should be encouraged or restricted. Given that local authorities have an obligation to blend the mix of retail outlets in a commercial centre, questions are inevitably raised about the 'right' number, type and location of service outlets in shopping centres. Local authorities policies vary in their attitudes towards service outlets. A simplified summary of these policies is shown in Table 10.4.

There is little evidence about the impact of quasi-retail outlets on the nature of a centre as a whole. Some arguments against too great a number of such outlets in a centre include these:

(a) they can push up property values;
(b) they may create dead frontages which discourage window shopping;
(c) some service outlets may be closed on peak shopping days (e.g. banks on Saturday);
(d) some service outlets are bad neighbours (e.g. take-away food shops, amusement arcades);
(e) too many quasi-retail outlets in a centre can reduce the range of conventional retail store choice.

On the other hand arguments for encouraging quasi-retail outlet developments include these:

Table 10.4
Formal Policies towards Quasi-retail Development

Policy	Character	Drawbacks
Core area	No change of user permitted within a designated area of the shopping centre	Delimitation of area arbitrary and therefore open to question
Segregation	Directs each service use to a particular location or street	Can lead to 'service ghettoes' and declining vitality of some streets
Appropriate uses	Specification of certain quasi-retail activities as appropriate to shopping streets	Inconsistency between and within local authorities
Quota level	Accepts legitimacy of service uses but seeks to establish maximum limit (e.g. floor-space)	Entire quota may be taken by one user
Dispersal	Service uses permitted but dispersal among shops to prevent excessive dead frontages.	Used alone could lead to over-representation of service uses

Source: Kivell, P. T. and Doidge, R. A. 'Service outlets in shopping centres: Problems and Policies', *Service Industries Review*, Vol. 2, No. 1, Spring 1982, pp. 22–37

(a) many complement other retail businesses (e.g. users of facilities like banks and building societies may use shops selling goods on the same shopping trip);
(b) service outlets can have imaginative window displays to encourage window shopping.

Many quasi-retail outlets are owned by large organizations operating on a multi-site basis and are dominant concerns. For example, Sketchleys the cleaning company, is the seventh largest retailer in the United Kingdom, in terms of number of retail outlets. The problems for such organizations in mass marketing their retail services have been examined and a number of suggestions are made on how service retailers can overcome the problems they face.[14] These suggestions include the following:

(a) encourage customers to travel longer distances (e.g. by special promotions);
(b) locate service outlets near complementary facilities (e.g. multiple theatre complexes and entertainment centres);
(c) centralize service production facilities but decentralize customer contact facilities (e.g. photograph processing);

(*d*) reduce the range of needs satisfied at individual service outlets (e.g. hospital services);

(*e*) share service capacity to achieve economies in production costs (e.g. airlines share baggage handling services);

(*f*) improve efficiency in production procedures (e.g. substitute equipment for people).

Many multi-site service operations employ these suggestions. For example, banks are not likely to expand in relation to population patterns in the future. This is because the chief motivations underlying bank branch network expansion (i.e. good location and satisfying customer needs for convenience) are likely to be catered for by the use of automated teller machines.[15]

Some of the major changes taking place in retailing are now in the field of services rather than goods. The phenomenon has not been as actively studied by marketors as it deserves. As services continue to occupy a major role in developed economies in the 1980s service retailing will become a field of increasing research interest and a growing way for service marketors to reach their customers.

10.5 Location

Associated with the choice of distribution methods for services is the issue of location. Whatever the form of distribution used to reach customers, the location of intermediaries, that is the siting of service operations, will be an important factor. Location, in this context, refers to the placing of people and/or facilities to perform service operations. Banks, accountants, solicitors, restaurants, dry cleaners and launderettes face location decisions just like those firms distributing tangibles.

Location may vary in importance according to the nature of the service marketed. For a repair service conducted in the home, like emergency plumbing, then the location of the base of the performer of the service may be irrelevant in the customer decision-making process. On the other hand small-scale studies of university students' choice of bank suggest that convenience of location is a critical factor in the bank selection decision.[16]

According to Rathmell[3] services are classified by location in three ways:

(*a*) location may be irrelevant;
(*b*) services may be concentrated;
(*c*) services may be dispersed.

Location may be Irrelevant

Location may be irrelevant for services like household repairs, car breakdown services and utilities. These services are performed where the customer is. Therefore location of any service facility is of less importance than for services performed in a specific location. What is critical about such services however is their 'accessibility' or 'availability' to the customer when service is required. In this sense then location refers not just to physical proximity: though this may be important for some organizations which develop branch offices to get nearer to clients (e.g. advertising agencies, architects). An important element in the design of such services then is the communications system which should permit speedy response to customer calls on the system. In setting and operating standards in these service organizations decisions are required on the level of service which is provided.

Services may be Concentrated

Many services are concentrated (e.g. advertising in London). Here two factors – conditions of supply and tradition – act as centralizing forces. Reasons which encourage such concentration include the status associated with certain sites; low intensity of demand; customer willingness to be mobile; the historical development of complementary services in close proximity to core services and the unimportance of demand orientation.

Services may be Dispersed

Services which are dispersed locate in terms of market potential. The nature of demand and the characteristics of the service require dispersal into the marketplace. Sometimes institutions may be centralized (e.g. business consultants) but operations are dispersed (e.g. consultants visit specific customers).

These various patterns of service location are shown in Figure 10.3.

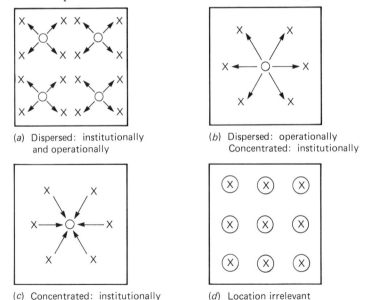

(a) Dispersed: institutionally and operationally

(b) Dispersed: operationally Concentrated: institutionally

(c) Concentrated: institutionally and operationally

(d) Location irrelevant

Figure 10.3 Service Location Patterns

Source: Rathmell, J. M. *Marketing in the Service Sector*, Winthrop, Cambridge, Mass. 1974, p. 106

The importance of location varies according to the type of service though a number of common questions should be considered by service marketors in making location decisions. These include:

(a) What does the market require? If service is not provided in a convenient location will purchase of the service be postponed or use delayed? Will poor location lead to do-it-yourself decisions by the customer? Are accessibility and convenience critical factors in service choice (e.g. bank choice)?

(b) What are the trends within the sector of service activity in which the service organization operates? Are competitors reaching out into markets (e.g. distance learning in education)? Could some competitive advantage be obtained by going against the norms operating in the sub-sector?

(c) How flexible is the service? Is it technology based or people based? How do these factors affect flexibility in location and relocation decisions?

(d) Does the organization have an obligation to locate in convenient sites (e.g. public services like health care)?

(e) What new systems, procedures, processes and technology can be harnessed to overcome weaknesses of past location decisions (e.g. growth of banking by post)?

(f) How critical are complementary services to the location decision? Are customers seeking service systems or service clusters? Does the location of other service organizations reinforce any location decision taken (e.g. services can reinforce each other in attracting custom)?

The critical importance of location in many service operations is resulting in more systematic approaches than in the past. Intuition still plays a part in management decision-making but it is increasingly being complemented by more careful and methodical analysis in service fields like banking[17] and hotels.[18] Service marketors are increasingly conscious of the importance played by location and channel choice in the marketing mix.

10.6 Summary

1 All service organizations are concerned with place decisions, particularly what outlets, if any, will be used and their location.

2 Organizations operating in services markets have the options of marketing their services direct to customers, through intermediaries or some combination of these methods.

3 A wide range of intermediaries exist in services markets.

4 Some innovations in methods of distributing in recent years include rental services, franchising, service integration and quasi-retailing.

5 Some services may be concentrated in specific locations, others may be dispersed. For some services location may be of less importance than accessibility to them and speed of response to customer requests.

Questions for Discussion

1 Suggest suitable alternative channels of distribution for;
   (*a*) health care services;
   (*b*) educational services.
2 In what kinds of situations are services likely to be:
   (*a*) concentrated?
   (*b*) dispersed?
3 What is quasi-retailing?
4 Why have rental services become more important in recent years?
5 Evaluate the importance of location in a service industry where restrictions may apply on other elements of the marketing mix (e.g. professional services).
6 What technological changes are likely to influence future channel choice decisions in a service industry of your choice?
7 Identify five kinds of services that have appeared on United Kingdom high streets in the past ten to fifteen years.
8 Identify three kinds of services that have tended to disappear from United Kingdom high streets in the past ten to fifteen years.
9 How does the 'perishability' of a service influence channel selection decisions?
10 Suggest three services for which the location of a service organization is unimportant. Why?

References and Notes

1 Shostack, G. Lynn, 'The service marketing frontier'. In Zaltman, J. and Bonoma, T. V. (Editors) *Annual Review of Marketing*, Chicago, American Marketing Association 1978, pp. 373–88.
2 Schoell, W. and Ivy, J. T. *Marketing: Contemporary Concepts and Practices*, Allyn and Bacon, 1981.
3 Rathmell, J. M. *Marketing in the Service Sector*, Winthrop, Cambridge, Mass. 1974.
4 Ornstein, E. J. *The Marketing of Money*, Gower, Aldershot, 1972.
5 Donnelly, J. H. 'Marketing intermediaries in channels of distribution for services', *Journal of Marketing* Vol. 40, No. 1, Jan. 1976, pp. 55–7.
6 Majaro, S. *Marketing in Perspective* George Allen and Unwin, London, 1982, pp. 206–7.
7 Walters, C. G. and Bergiel, B. J. *Marketing Channels*, Scott, Foresman, Glenview, Ill. 1982.
8 *The Financial Times*, 5 June 1982, p. 7.
9 Sasser, W. E., Olsen, R. P. and Wyckoff, D. D. *Management of Service Operations*, Allyn and Bacon, Boston, Mass. 1978.
10 Johnson, E. M. 'An introduction to the problems of Service Marketing Management', Bureau of Economic and Business Research, University of Delaware, 1964.
11 Berry, L. L. and Maricle, K. E. 'Consumption without ownership:

Marketing opportunity for Today and Tomorrow', *M.S.U. Business Topics*, Spring 1973, pp. 33–41.

12 Mendelsohn, M. *The Guide to Franchising*, 2nd Edn., Pergamon Press, Oxford, 1979.

13 Kivell, P. T. and Doidge, R. A. 'Service Outlets in Shopping Centres: Problems and Policies', *Service Industries Review*, Vol. 2, No. 1, Spring 1982, pp. 22–37. The authors provide a useful analysis of the quasi-retail phenomenon. Much of the material presented here draws on this paper.

14 Upah, G. D. 'Mass Marketing in Service Retailing: A review and synthesis of major methods', *Journal of Retailing* Vol. 56, No. 3, Fall 1980, pp. 59–76.

15 Pattison, J. and Quelch, J. 'Branch Banking Strategies', *The Bankers' Magazine*, Vol. 223, Jan. 1979, pp. 21–4.

16 Cowell, D. W. 'Marketing of Bank Services to University Students', Mimeograph, Loughborough University, 1977.

17 Soenan, L. A. 'Locating Bank Branches', *Industrial Marketing Management*, Vol. 3 July 1974, pp. 211–25.

18 Peters, C. H. 'Pre-opening marketing analysis for Hotels', *The Cornell Hotel and Restaurant Administration Quarterly*, May 1978, pp. 15–22.

11. *PEOPLE AND SERVICES*

11.1 Introduction

In Chapter 9 the role of personal selling in services marketing was discussed. In this chapter we consider two other groups of people who have an impact upon the 'selling' of services:

(*a*) service personnel;
(*b*) customers.

11.11 Service Personnel

Service personnel are those people who provide an organization's services for customers. The following extracts show their importance:

> 'As a client in a manufacturing company for more years than I care to mention, I have noticed a recent trend which I find very worrying, and that is towards junior people being left to run big projects. Everyone knows that experience has to be gained somewhere and that senior researchers move off the everyday running of projects, but are you agency directors sure that the people left to carry your agency's banner on a day-to-day basis are doing you justice?
>
> Manner when dealing with clients is obviously another issue, and something that comes with greater confidence but junior researchers should bear in mind the PR job they do for their companies everytime they lift a phone. In the same way as one fails to use a certain shop because the sales girls are slovenly, no matter how marvellous the manager may be; so may clients drop agencies for no apparent reason. . . . This therefore is a plea to research agency directors to take stock of your personnel, talk to your clients to see if they are happy with the contacts they make, and thereby protect the reputation and business of your agency.'

(From the *Market Research Society Newsletter*, 1983).

> 'Research continually reveals that agents regard our standards of service as low, particularly at London. Our ability to overcome technical difficulties is limited by the planned integration which will not be completed until late in the year. However, human contact with the customer is just as important. When, through personal contact with staff, the customer forms the impression that we regard him as a "necessary evil", it colours his whole image of our company to the extent that some of our unique advantages are ignored and therefore wasted.'

(From a service company's marketing plan, 1976).

> 'We are in a highly competitive business and face a somewhat unpredictable economic climate, and this means that we must more than ever give our customers better service and better value than our competitors.
>
> The strength of our business depends on the goodwill of our customers. In turn, that goodwill is determined by the service we give. Service to our customers is influenced more than anything by our attitude to customers, the ability to see things through their eyes. This has helped build out reputation in the past, and must continue to guide us in the future.'

(From the Chief Executive of a service company in his report to employees, 1982).

Service personnel are important in all organizations. However, they are particularly important in those situations where, in the absence of clues from tangible products, the customer will form an impression of the organization from the behaviour and attitudes of its staff.

Service personnel include operators (bus drivers, lift attendants, librarians) clerks in banks, chefs in steak houses, receptionists and counter clerks in hotels or hire car companies, security guards, telephonists, repair and servicing personnel and waiters. These people may perform a 'production' or 'operational' role but may also have a customer contact role in service organizations. Their behaviour may be as important in influencing the perceived quality of a service as the behaviour of formal sales staff. It is crucial therefore that these service personnel perform their jobs effectively and efficiently; also that the service organization's measures of effectiveness and efficiency include a strong element of customer orientation among its staff. The importance of staff to service organizations is widely recognized in the service marketing literature:

> 'A customer sees a company through its employees. The employees represent the first line of contact with the customer. They must, therefore, be well informed and provide the kind of service that wins customer approval. The firm must recognize that each employee . . . is a salesman for the company's service.'[1]

> 'If service personnel are cold or rude, they can undermine all the marketing work done to attract customers. If they are friendly and warm, they can increase customer satisfaction and loyalty.'[2]

What is less widely understood however is that marketing management should be involved in the operational aspects of job performance because of the importance of the varieties of types of service people to the quality of the services provided. How a service is performed can influence the nature of the relationships that exist between a service organization's personnel and its customers. It will ultimately influence the image of a service organization. These relationships should not be left to chance. They are a marketing responsibility as well as an operational responsibility.

11.12 Customers

Another factor which may influence the marketing of services is the relationships between customers. A customer's perception of the quality of a service may be formed and influenced by other customers as well as by service organization personnel. Customers may talk to other customers about service organizations. Or where groups of customers 'receive' a service at the same time (e.g. a package tour) the enjoyment of the service may be shaped by the behaviour of other customers. In services marketing management may play a role in 'quality controlling' the interactions between customers and in influencing the relationship that takes place between them. Relationships between customers are, of course, just one dimension of their behaviour as participants in the service production process and in the service consumption process. Unfortunately there are few studies available to cast light on this whole area of consumer behaviour in services markets.

This chapter examines these two additional human influences upon the service marketing process in more detail.

11.2 The Service Organization and its Personnel

It was Wittreich who observed that: 'the selling of a service and the rendering of the service can seldom be separated'.[3] Examples of situations where the service cannot be separated from the person providing the service include window cleaning, dentistry and hairdressing. It is only with mechanized and automated services that people play little part in service transactions (e.g. automatic photograph booths; vending machines).

Human beings therefore may play a unique role in the marketing and the production of services. This has important implications for the marketing function since it is clear that the human service representatives constitute an important element of any service marketing strategy and are an element in any service marketing mix.

What distinguishes service organizations from industrial goods companies is that the customer may come into contact with people whose primary role is to perform a service rather than to market a service.

> 'In industrial markets access to operations is extremely limited: the industrial customer may meet the tool and jig maker but that will probably be all. No customer expects to meet the packers in a sweet factory, let alone expect them to have any responsibility for the total product offering. In service markets, however, access is far greater. The overwhelming majority of staff have some form of direct customer contact.'[4]

Service personnel include those members of the organization who are in contact with customer – contact personnel – and those members of the service organization who are not in contact with customers. Some of these staff may be visible to the customer during purchase and consumption of a service. Some may not. Figure 11.1 illustrates the kinds of occupations falling into these categories.

	Contact with client	Non-contact with client
Visible to client	Waitress	Cook in steak house
	Service engineer	Computer operator
Non-visible to client	Telephone operator	Maintenance worker
	Airline pilot	Accountant

Figure 11.1 Organization Personnel Involved in Service Product Performance and Delivery

As far as contact personnel are concerned Davidson[5] believes that: 'customer contact personnel are the key people in the organisation'. He quotes one chief executive who believes that in a successful service organization, the organization chart should be turned upside down with the customer contact personnel at the top. But organizations vary considerably in respect of the amount of contact that takes place between service personnel and customers. In some there is a lot of contact between the service employees and customers, in others there is little contact between service employees and customers.

11.21 High Contact and Low Contact Organizations

In discussing service employees in contact with customers, Chase[6] makes a distinction between the 'extent of customer contact in the creation of a service'. In this case customer contact is the physical presence of the customer in the service system and creation of the service is the work process involved in providing the service. His interesting distinction is between high contact and low contact service systems; where high contact and low contact are roughly defined as the percentage of total time the customer must be in the system compared with the relative time it takes to service him. In this scheme high contact service systems include hotels, restaurants and schools; low contact service systems include Government administration and post offices. The various types of service systems have implications for marketing management in a number of ways. For example they influence the process of service delivery (*see* Chapter 13). In this context, because human performance can so influence the service outcome, in high contact service organizations the quality of the service product may be inseparable from the service personnel.

A further useful insight into the importance of service personnel to the type and quality of service a customer gets is the distinction between the types of service quality. The type of service a customer receives can be viewed as consisting of two elements:

(*a*) technical quality;
(*b*) functional quality.

Technical Quality

Technical quality refers to 'what' the customer receives in his interactions with service organizations: the bedrooms in a hotel; the meal in a restaurant; the transport service of a distribution company. It may be capable of objective measurement as with any product and it forms an important element in any customer's evaluation of a service.

Functional Quality

Functional quality refers to 'how' the technical elements of the service are transferred. Two important components of how the technical elements of service are provided are the process (*see* Chapter 13) and the people involved in operating the system. Functional quality may be less capable of objective measurement. It nevertheless forms an important element in any customer's evaluation of a service.[7]

The relationship between technical quality and functional quality is shown in Figure 11.2. This also shows how both contribute to the image of the organization.

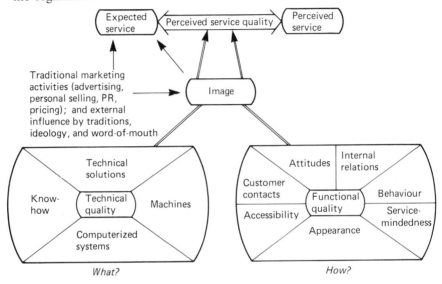

Figure 11.2 Managing the perceived service quality

Source: Gronroos, C. 'Strategic Management and Marketing in the Service Sector', Swedish School of Economics and Business Administration, Helsinki, 1982

Figure 11.2 shows functional quality consists of a number of elements:

attitudes of employees;
behaviour of employees;
the relationships between them;
the importance of employees who have contact with customers;
the appearance of service personnel;
the general 'accessibility' of services to customers;
the general service mindedness of personnel.

Thus service marketors need to be concerned with many dimensions of service personnel quality and performance. The problem is how to manage these dimensions of quality and performance. Some of the measures which can be used are suggested below.

11.22 Maintaining and Improving Service Personnel Quality and Performance

There are a number of ways in which a service organization can maintain and improve the quality of personnel and their performance. Six are examined here. They are:

(*a*) careful selection and training of service personnel;
(*b*) internal marketing;
(*c*) using practices to obtain consistent behaviour;
(*d*) ensuring consistent appearance;
(*e*) reducing the importance of personal contact;
(*f*) careful control through the service personnel audit.

These ideas are intended only to illustrate some of the measures service organizations may take. In practice there is often overlap between actions and practices in each category and a number of other possibilities may be considered.

Careful Selection and Training of Service Personnel

It is clearly important that customer contact personnel should be carefully selected and trained. The principles of good personnel and training management apply just as much to this group of employees as to any other group in the organization. The clear implication of the importance of personal contact to many services is that recruitment, selection, training and development programmes have to be tailored to the needs of the services being provided. There should be a clear understanding of the job by service personnel. This involves drawing up detailed job specifications. Also the qualities required in the people undertaking customer contact jobs should be defined. Service jobs traditionally can be classified according to the type of educational requirements, previous experience required, social skills required and so forth. One recent suggestion is that service sector employees should be divided according to the communication demands placed upon them by customers.[8] The nature and type of communication may be an important determinant of employee qualities sought. Finally attention needs to be given to how the job will be controlled and organized. Service employees in 'boundary spanning' roles (i.e. linking the organization to customers) often have to be more flexible and adaptive than other employees. Close, rigid and methodical systems may be difficult to implement and looser kinds of organizational structures and methods of operating may be appropriate. Special kinds of service personnel may be required to cope with the ambiguities and uncertainties involved in many kinds of boundary spanning, customer contact roles.

Internal Marketing

To accomplish levels of service quality and performance in keeping with the service organizations standards means that it must be concerned with 'internal marketing' as well as with external marketing.

There is nothing new about the concept of internal marketing. It is implied in the original idea of the marketing concept with its focus on the key role of the customer and the central objective for a market-orientated organization, the satisfaction of customer needs. What the internal marketing concept does is to re-emphasize the importance of marketing to people who serve external customers. Berry defines internal marketing as:

'internal marketing means applying the philosophy and practices of marketing to people who serve the external customers so that (i) the best possible people can be employed and retained and (ii) they will do the best possible work'.[9]

This interpretation implies that employees are viewed as internal customers and jobs are internal products which have to be designed to better meet the needs of customers. If the organization offers employees better, more satisfying jobs then it increases its ability to be a more effective service marketing organization. Sasser and Arbeit suggest that:[10] 'the successful service company must first sell the job to employees before it can sell its services to customers'.

A wider view of internal marketing presents it as a managerial philosophy with both strategic and tactical implications. As a managerial philosophy the internal marketing function has as its objective 'to get motivated and customer conscious employees'. At a strategic level the objective of internal marketing is 'to create an internal environment which supports customer-consciousness and sales mindedness among the personnel'. At a tactical level the objective of internal marketing is 'to sell services, supporting services, campaigns and single marketing efforts to the employees'.[7] What this can give rise to in practice is marketing measures like an advertising campaign designed to influence employees as well as customers. A summary of this wider view of the internal marketing concept is presented in Table 11.1.

Irrespective of which view is taken the value of internal marketing is undeniable. It is practised in a range of service organizations already. Shostack argues that internal marketing has been a well established, though not universal practice within service industries. 'Consumer marketing often stops at the production of materials and programs for salesmen to use; some service industries on the other hand, have long intuitively managed human evidence to larger ends.'[11]

Internal marketing is of crucial importance since staff may be reluctant to sell a service product which they do not find acceptable. This point can be illustrated by the attitude of some staff to the banks' new charging policies for credits collected for other banks. During the introduction of these policies, some staff would not accept the directive to charge customers for using the service partly due to certain long-established customer relationships. The policy had to be modified and ended in an authority to charge only when 'feasible'.

This example also illustrates one of the problems that service personnel in operational roles face in dealing with customers; namely that the service employee often has to adjudicate between the interest of the service organization and the interests of the customer. Frequently, operating personnel are required to have a dual set of often conflicting roles since 'they are the production direct labour or artisans or both and they are also the sales personnel'.[12] The employee/client interface is thus a complex area because an employee in contact with a client may be 'torn between the firm's objectives and those of the client'.[13]

To a large extent a service organization can reduce this role conflict for

Table 11.1
The Internal Marketing Concept – a Summary

Internal marketing
Overall objective: To get a motivated and customer-conscious personnel.

Strategic level
Objective: To create an internal environment which supports customer-consciousness and salesmindedness among the personnel

        supporting management methods;
        supporting personnel policy;
        supporting internal training policy;
        supporting planning and control procedures.

Tactical level
Objective: To sell services, supporting services (used as means of competition), campaigns and single marketing efforts to the employees.

        the personnel is the first market of the service company;
        the employees must understand why they are expected to perform in a certain manner, or in a certain situation actively support, for example, a given service or supporting service;
        the employees must accept the services and other activities of the company in order to be expected to support them in their contact with the consumers;
        a service must be fully developed and internally accepted before it is launched;
        the internal information channels must work;
        personal selling is needed internally, too.

Source: Gronroos, C. 'Internal Marketing – An integral Part of Marketing Theory', in Donnelly, J. H. and George, W. R. (eds), *Marketing of Services*, American Marketing Assocation, Chicago, 1981, p. 237

its employees through its marketing practices and procedures. The work of Schneider,[14] who has researched specifically in banking contexts, demonstrates how crucial is the 'climate' of a service organization. His research shows that an enthusiastic orientation to service by an organization has positive effects upon both bank customers and bank employees.

Using Practices to Obtain Consistent Behaviour

A third problem for the service organization lies in achieving consistency of behaviour among staff. The behaviour of the consumer will affect the behaviour of the human representatives of the firm and the quality of the service provided may vary since it depends very much on the individual who offers it. For example, the branches of a bank may offer identical services to their customers; but the success of individual cashiers in 'producing' these services can vary widely. Achieving consistency of human effort is an important goal of many service organizations. Clearly it is important for service organizations to establish set procedures for some of their services to ensure they are performed in a consistent way. There are dangers though that such practices can become too mechanistic. Most organizations have to strike a balance between too much rigidity in their systems and too much flexibility. Procedures have to be flexible enough to tolerate the ambiguity of customer variety. Two service businesses where the control of quality poses particular problems are hotels and car rental. Hostage[15] gives examples of how the Marriott Corporation attempts to ensure that high standards of service are set by all personnel. These efforts include:

> clear standards of performance;
> individual development programmes;
> management training;
> manpower planning;
> profit sharing schemes.

Shapiro[16] describing the particular problems posed by managing a service business and the kinds of responses management must adopt with the workforce observes that: 'todays manager of a service business has to take responsibility for all the tangibles of any other business plus the intangibles of the people business'.

The human resources of a service firm can be used as an important means of competition in service marketing. Thus continuous training – especially in communications and selling – is, usually, a much greater task and involves many more people in service industries. Indeed the selection, training and monitoring of the human service representatives is a vital part of the service marketing function.

As far as training is concerned banks, for example, run courses for employees at all levels in the firm's hierarchy. This training now emphasizes the manner of contact with the customer, as well as the range of services which the bank can offer. The most important part of the bank cashier's job is frequently stated to be the identification of the needs of customers, and the recommendation of financial services which might be of assistance.

A less direct approach to marketing to the service employee is to allow discounts to staff on the service products sold by the company, as an incentive to try the service and therefore to recommend it from personal experience. For instance, travel firms frequently send their staff to resorts to sample the hotels and facilities offered; airline operators offer free flights to employees and supermarkets give staff discounts. In this way, staff have better knowledge of the advantages of certain service products and their use.

An outline of one service company's recent campaign plan to improve its service to customers, including training of existing staff, is shown below.

'Customer Service Campaign Plan

1 Communication with Management and Staff

There is a need for staff to concentrate their efforts in work to their highest level of competence and this depends to a great extent in involvement in corporate objectives. To this end it is necessary to produce a planned, professional approach to staff communication. This requires an investigation into the appropriate medium to be used.

2 Training

Customer service training is vital but it is prerequisite that arbitrary nominations are not made for any such courses.

It is necessary therefore to identify units where customer service training is appropriate and take the action required in programming courses and staff lists. It should also be made clear to staff nominated that the whole point of any course is to increase standards of customer service.

3 Management/Staff Relationships

The other facet besides involving staff in company policies is to make people feel wanted and show that the company is interested in their problems. This requires on the part of management and supervisors the necessity to get amongst the staff on the "shop floor".

4 Customer Service Improvement

An important part of this campaign involves making improvements. This can take the form of either changing a procedure/introducing a new service or can be attitude development. We should therefore identify many of the limitations and obstacles with which we confront our customers and have a plan to remove them.

5 Link Major Changes to Customer Service

It will be difficult to get commitment to a customer service campaign if staff do not see evidence of effort to remove some of the production inadequacies which frustrate them. There must be, therefore, a means of passing on to all personnel, information on the effects that a change has made, however small.

6 Rewards for Outstanding Individual Performance

This should be a major feature of the campaign and ranges from a supervisor saying "well done", to a special Customer Service Awards Scheme. Therefore we have to establish a policy among all section heads towards the recognition of individual performance. A method of reward scheme, possibly in the form of free tickets, should be considered, with a committee appointed to consider nominations.'

Ensuring Consistent Appearance

Bearing in mind the characteristic of intangibility of many services, the appearance of the establishment and its personnel are often the only tangible aspects of a service organization. Therefore 'the consumer can be expected to choose a service supplier whose place of business and sales personnel clearly suggest the quality of service desired for the satisfaction

of his needs'.[17] One way in which organizations attempt to create an image
and suggest quality of service is through the appearance of service
personnel.

The appearance of service personnel can be controlled by service
management. One way in which this may be accomplished is through the
use of 'uniforms' and styles of dress. Waiters in hotels, airline stewardes-
ses, motoring centre repairmen may all be required to adopt certain formal
styles of dress. The degree of formality may range from the issue of a top
coat to a complete uniform including accessories. Further standardization
of appearance may be accomplished by recruiting service personnel with
specific characteristics (e.g. of a certain height or age range). Also the
service organization may provide facilities to encourage personal care like
hairdressing salons and beauty parlours. Even when a service organization
does not require the wearing of a formal uniform for protective or
promotional purposes, an 'acceptable' style of dress may be deliberately
encouraged (e.g. amongst bankers and stockbrokers). Equally 'unacceptable' dress styles may be discouraged. Such uniforms help create standards
of 'uniformity' and thus are an important input to the overall image of a
service organization, where uniformity is required. Where uniformity is
not required, service organizations may encourage varying styles of non-
conforming dress to cultivate an unconventional image of variety (e.g. as in
advertising agencies).

Reducing the Importance of Personal Contacts

Thus far, it seems reasonable to support the proposition that the personnel
involved in service marketing and operations should be given priority
consideration in thinking about the marketing of a service. However,
alternative forms of production can be introduced into service operations
(e.g. mechanization).

> 'The solution to improved service is viewed as being dependent on improvements in the
> skills and attitudes of the performers of that service. This humanisation conception of
> service diverts us from seeking alternatives to the use of people, especially large,
> organised groups of people.'[18]

An example of a situation where a manufacturing style and technology
has been applied to a people-intensive service industry is the fast food
chain of McDonald's. We have already noted the problems that lack of
uniformity in some services may pose because individuals are integral to
the process. In the case of an airline stewardess, for example, 'when the
pressure is on, service deteriorates' states Levitt. He proposes therefore
that manufacturing style and processes, similar to those applied in
McDonald's, can be applied to other service situations to remove the
inadequacies of people intensive conditions.

An extension of this more ordered and systematic way of thinking about
service marketing is the 'industrialization' of service. This takes place most
obviously in the form of 'hard technologies' which substitute machinery or
tangible items for people intensive performance. Notable examples include
the consumer credit card, automatic car washes, automatic bank machines

and airport X-ray equipment. In thinking of service as something done by machines or systems the marketing concept for services can be broadened. However, this will change the way in which consumers interact with service producers. Although many technological innovations may offer benefits to customers, service managers cannot take consumer acceptance of them for granted. Sensitivity to the needs of the customer remains essential. It is vital to obtain the trust and co-operation of customers; and equipment needs to be tested and demonstrated so that consumers are taught how to use service innovations.

Also firms in the service sector exhibit very different characteristics. In some cases, many people in service organizations never come into contact with the consumer. These people are similar to goods factory workers.

Levitt reports that service marketors commonly look for solutions: '. . . in the performers of the task. This is a paralysing legacy of our inherited attitudes. We see service as invariably and undeviatingly personal, as something performed by individuals directly for other individuals.'[18]

This attitude may limit innovative thinking about methods to tailor the service to the customer's needs and to extend marketing techniques to the management of service operations. Traditionally, service operations have been people intensive. Yet people-intensive operations may not be necessary for the provision of an efficient service. Marketors may overlook this when the principles underlying the marketing of the service are considered concurrently with the present service personnel arrangements. The most important principle must be to fulfil customers' needs. Customers may have certain ideas about the performance of the service, and may identify certain service personnel as being key to the service. For example, clients speak of 'their' lawyer rather than their legal services. However, there may be some services in which the service personnel are a minor part of the offering. In these a more innovative approach to production and marketing, using equipment rather than people to control quality in production and distribution, might result in a higher level of service. Such steps may require a change in consumer attitudes as well as in the attitudes of service managers.

For example, it has been a traditional view that because services cannot be separated from the sellers or producers of the product, only direct channels of distribution are available to the marketor. However, whilst it is necessary to consider the characteristics of production and the importance of service personnel, as with goods, it may be possible to develop new forms of service delivery. Retailers can extend the credit card market as agents for credit card services; banks are often outlets for insurance; rock concerts have been transmitted to cinemas by satellite to reach a wider audience. But attempts to create new methods of distribution, must take account of the traditional marketing concerns of consumer acceptance and product characteristics. For instance, patients may consider medical centres operated by a number of doctors as impersonal if they are treated by different doctors on each visit.

Consumer acceptance becomes especially important when new methods of production and delivery imply less contact between the consumer and service personnel. Services can often be delivered by automatic means. For example, flight insurance is provided by slot machines at many airports. Likewise weight machines installed on stations do not require any service personnel and can assist in establishing a homogeneous product.

But, there are certain services, where direct contact remains paramount, like, legal and accounting services. Innovations must always be limited by the level of consumer acceptance. It is theoretically possible to create automatic bank tellers to perform all the functions that cashiers perform. However this might place demands on customers which may prove unacceptable. Furthermore, even if the practice was accepted, it might prove impossible to ensure an adequate level of accuracy to make the system effective.

Careful Control through the Service Personnel Audit

A service organization must strive constantly to create and maintain a clear and attractive image. As both employees and customers will influence and reflect the image of a service organization anyway, it is a responsibility of service management to ensure that the perceived image matches the required image. In the absence of service features themselves, which sufficiently discriminate between one service and another, the key to image formation will be the attitudes and behaviour of service personnel.

Many service organizations understand how crucial customer service is and the role of staff in serving customers. (*See* Exhibit 11.1.)

Exhibit 11.1

CUSTOMER SERVICE.

No company can or does survive for long without satisfied customers. It is our constant endeavour to ensure that our customers receive the best service possible. During the year a number of programmes have been introduced with this objective in mind. We introduced the 'Code of Practice' which lays down firm guidelines for all our staff to work to. This is prominently displayed in all Depots for our customers to study. Our unique 'No Quibble Guarantee' was introduced in September and became an immediate success.

The standard of Depot presentation and cleanliness has reached new heights but this is a field requiring constant effort if such standards are to be maintained. Customer satisfaction on this point has featured constantly in testimonials received at Head Office.

The 'Customer Services' Department has been centralized in Edinburgh and provides a very useful 'mirror' for us to judge our performance through the 'Customer Reaction Cards' now being returned in a steady flow.

We can take pride in the fact that our standards of service are an industry leader, but we do receive correspondence that indicates that there is always room for improvement, and that we must constantly be ready to respond to our customers' criticisms.

The necessary guidelines have been laid down during the year and it is now up to us all to see that the highest standards are achieved and maintained.

Source: Kwik Fit Euro statement to employees

Some service organizations go so far as:

(*a*) to establish norms and standards of service personnel behaviour;

(*b*) to establish evaluative systems to ensure those standards are adhered to.

The service personnel audit is one way of ensuring standards are set and maintained. It is a systematic, critical and unbiased review of service personnel practices. In any service organization it forms part of the marketing audit. Basically the service audit aims to take stock of the organization's total service with the goal of supporting effective marketing practices and correcting faulty behaviour.[19]

Service organizations may use a range of methods to monitor performance. Practices will vary according to the kind of service organization and numbers of service personnel involved. Five common practices are described here. They are:

(*a*) sales related systems;

(*b*) complaint systems;

(*c*) suggestion systems;

(*d*) audit visits;

(*e*) customer satisfaction surveys.

Sales-related Systems

Many organizations rely on sales related systems – sales growth, market share, profitability, repeat purchase – as measures of customer and employee satisfaction. These types of measure are clearly important but can give misleading feedback particularly when there is a little competition, where demand is rising naturally or where there is a good deal of customer inertia (e.g. to change bank accounts). Nevertheless as a surrogate measure they can provide a general indirect indication of performance.

Complaint Systems

Service organizations should make it easy for customers to complain. Many organizations fail to give enough attention to establishing easy and simple mechanisms to ensure that customer problems and complaints get heard and acted upon. Customers who are not given an opportunity to complain might reduce their business and do damage to the organization through the 'word of mouth' influence they have on existing or potential customers: 'It goes without saying that a good complaint department . . . is essential for success in any service business. The department should be responsive to complaints and diligent in finding out facts.'[5]

Suggestion Schemes

Suggestion schemes can be used to solicit customer and employee views of how a service organization performs. When tied to a reward system they can be a valuable source of ideas for service, system and organizational improvement.

Audit Visits

Audit visits may vary from routine, structured and announced to non-routine, unstructured and unannounced. The kinds of audit-routine used will be influenced by the nature of the service organization and the types of markets it serves. Some service organizations monitor telephone switch-board staff through unannounced calls and the competence of service personnel through asking a series of complex questions and enquiries. Another way to audit personnel is to use mystery 'shoppers' who are: 'generally trained, experienced interviewers and observers who have been briefed in advance about what to expect and look for, and who operate under semi-controlled conditions'.[19]

Exhibit 11.2 shows the semi-structured checklist used by one multi-site service operation with 120 branches nationwide, which is used to check Branch Managers compliance and progress with agreed Personnel and Training routines and requirements.

Exhibit 11.2
Branch Personnel and Training Audit

Branch ....   Manager ....
Date of visit ....   Assistant Manager/Senior Sales

....
Action to be taken

1   *STATUTORY FORMS*
1.1 Employers liability insurance form
1.2 Form G – Records of hours worked (or form F)
1.3 Form H – Employment of Young Persons (Abstract)
1.4 Form I (SA1) – Assistants weekly half day holidays
1.5 OSR – General Guide
1.6 OSR9b – Abstract
1.7 Accident book and related accident report forms.
1.8 Wages Council Order NF8
1.9 Health & Safety at Work Policy Statements
1.10 Fire Notice Signs (Exits)
1.11 Fire Notice – Customers
1.12 Fire Notice – Staff
1.13 First Aid Box

2   *PERSONNEL*
2.1 Application forms

2.2   Interview notes
2.3   Personnel records and record cards
2.4   Hourly paid time sheets (BNS10)
2.5   Wage Receipt Forms
2.6   Holiday Notification Forms
2.7   Absence Notification Forms
2.8   Casual Labour Records
2.9   Handbooks
2.10 Right of Search Notice
2.11 Current Wages Sheet
2.12 Job Descriptions
2.13 Offer of Employment letters
2.14 Reject letters
2.15 Dismissal Forms P11
2.16 Termination of Employment Forms P9
2.17 Change of Rate/Transfer Forms P10
2.18 Retail Division Instructions

3.   *TRAINING*
3.1   Training Policy Statement
3.2   Training Programmes – Induction
                              Basic Skills
3.3   Half hour training notes and reports
3.4   Training Record Cards
3.5   Appraisal
3.6   Training plan and progress

4   *STAFFING*
4.1   Current staff
4.2   Current Wage Costs (from published accounts)
4.3   Staff Turnover Details
4.4   Current Schedule (see separate sheet)
4.5   Comments and Recommendations

5   *WORK EXPERIENCE SCHEME*
5.1   Name of Trainee(s)
5.2   Duration of Scheme
5.3   Comments

6   *SALES TRAINING*
6.1   Staff attended
6.2   Progress
6.3   Comments

7   *FOLLOW-UP ACTION*

Signed ....   Date ....

MP/SB October 1983

STAFFING LEVELS 1982/83

Job title	Contractual hours	Monday	Tuesday	Wednesday	Thursday	Friday	Saturday
Current							
Recommended							
COMMENTS:							

Customer Satisfaction Surveys

Many service organizations use periodic surveys of customer satisfaction to check out what past customers like and dislike about services offered. Airlines, garages, management training centres and hotels have all used such surveys in the past. Many hotels for example leave questionnaires in their bedrooms and invite guests to give their comments on standards of food, accommodation, service and so on.

All of the above of course are ways of checking out whether or not a service organization services customers well. They help identify areas for improvement and corrective action. For a final observation on the role of people in service organizations it is worth returning to the work of Schneider:[14]

'Employees and customers of service organisations will each experience positive outcomes when the organisation operates with a customer service orientation. This orientation seems to result in superior service practices and procedures that are observable by customers and that seem to fit employee views of the appropriate style for dealing with customers.'

Procedures and checks are clearly important for helping to develop and maintain the 'people image' of a service organization – ultimately though it is the 'climate' of the organization that matters.

11.3 Customers

Service marketors have an interest in customers at three levels. First they are interested in customers as producers of services. Secondly they are interested in customers as users of services. Thirdly they are interested in customers because of their influence on other customers as producers and users of services. This section deals with these three aspects of service marketing.

11.31 Customers as Producers of Services

The discussion so far in this text has implied that customers are an input to the service production process. This has a number of implications for service marketing. For example: 'if the customers assume a more active role in the service production and delivery process, they effectively remove some of the labour tasks from the service organisations'.

This could result in benefits for both customers and service firms. In the production of a service the process not only creates the product but also simultaneously delivers it to the customer. So simultaneity of production and consumption is one of the distinctive characteristics of service and it has special marketing implications.

(a) The first implication is seen in the service delivery system. This is the process in which the customer may participate. Since it may be impossible to separate the customer from the production process, for example in personal and medical services, the service provider must either go to the market or bring the market to the service facility. Thus, each service facility may have a limited geographic area from which to draw customers: 'the close production-marketing interface requires that the service delivery system must be located within the market and therefore sized for the specific market'.[11]

Hence, the multi-site nature of many service operations and the managerial challenges of looking after multi-site operations (e.g. achieving uniform service standards).

(b) The second implication, resulting from the importance of the customer in the production process for services, is that: 'service systems with high customer contact are more difficult to control and more difficult to rationalise than those with low customer contact'.[6]

Examples of high-contact services include restaurants, personal services and schools. The customer can, in high-contact systems, affect the service in terms of time of demand and quality of service. Also the high degree of producer-customer interaction in the production of a service is a 'mixed blessing', since while problems of uncertainty about time and quality exist as a result of the customer's participation in the system, customers are also 'a source of productive capacity'. Customers therefore play an active role in shaping the service offering either adversely (by causing queues in a bank perhaps) or by improving quality (providing the atmosphere in a restaurant). The customer can make an input to or cause disruption in the production process.

(c) The third implication is in respect of the range of roles the customer may now be required to play in service production.[20] When an individual sets out to obtain a service he or she is first of all a buyer, getting something for which he or she or a third party must usually pay. But the customer is also involved in other relationships, for example as a worker and co-producer, giving time and effort without which the service could not be produced. The participation of the customer in the division of labour involved in the production of the service means that there is interdependence between buyer and seller of the service. The parties need to co-operate to achieve the ends of both parties. But just as there is co-operation in buyer–seller relationships so too there is conflict. This conflict has a number of dimensions:

- where a service is rendered on the basis of an explicit or implicit contract there is potential for conflict over the scope of the contract.

- there is potential for conflict over the roles in the division of labour. Some roles may be evaluated as being subordinate and more dependent compared with other roles.

- the 'expert' knowledge of the seller of services and the ignorance of consumers might create a relationship of inequality between them which may be a source of conflict. In a professional service relationship the customer may try to learn more of the knowledge of the practitioner while the latter may try to prevent the erosion of his position. Conflict between those who possess knowledge and those who depend on them for its application is commonplace. The client may feel powerless and the professional may feel contemptuous.

- there may be conflict over definitions of the service situation – what the customer defines as urgent may be seen by to provider as routine and commonplace.

The implications of the customer's role in the production of services and the conflicts that stem from them have not been studied by marketors. The customer is not just a buyer, he is a co-producer and a resource, without which the service could not function: schools must have pupils, transport companies must have passengers, hospitals must have patients. The customers' roles in services settings provide scope for their exploitation and alienation. It is therefore vital for the service marketor to have sympathy for the customers' roles and how these roles may change according to the nature of the service being provided.

Customers may find themselves in certain involuntary roles for which they have not contracted and they may therefore resent the roles they have to play in the production process. Further examination of this role of the customer as a co-producer in the services field, represents an important avenue for researchers in marketing today. Few studies have so far been undertaken on the willingness of customers to participate in the production of services and on whether there may be segments in the market of those more ready to participate. The work of Langeard et al.[21] is a welcome development in this respect.

11.32 *Customers as Users of Services*

Most texts on marketing deal, at some point, with the topic of customer behaviour. It is central to the marketing concept that they should do so. For an understanding of how customers behave and what factors influence their choice is clearly of vital importance to marketing success. A considerable body of knowledge is now available which covers the wealth of influences upon customer choice as well as the mechanisms of customer choice. Much of this knowledge has been summarized, organized and presented in the form of various models of buyer behaviour. Some sources give comprehensive coverage to the range of variables influencing consumers incorporating them into models of consumer behaviour.[22] Most basic British textbooks now include outline summaries of a number of the more common and influential models that have been developed.[23]

These models of consumer behaviour are of value for a number of reasons.

(a) They provide a framework for presenting knowledge on consumer behaviour. They enable us to present ideas in a simple and economic way; in particular to show relationships between variables thought to influence choice.

(b) They help identify inadequacies and weaknesses in knowledge of consumer behaviour and point to areas for future research and development.

(c) They require the statement of assumptions which underlie the constructs in the models. Most marketing practitioners, for example, have personal implicit models of how customers react to their marketing measures and how markets behave. The formal modelling process requires a more explicit statement of those assumptions.

Modelling activities in marketing can be categorized as comprehensive or limited.[24] Two factors are important about development to date for the marketor in a service organization.

No model, comprehensive or limited, has yet provided anything other than a partial explanation of consumer behaviour. The mechanisms implicit in the various models are not wholly understood and this is a field of continuing research in marketing.

Few models focus explicitly on the marketing of services rather than upon the marketing of physical goods.

Some writers on specific aspects of services marketing have adapted established frameworks for use in their specialist field of interest.[25] However there is growing disquiet about using models developed for goods which do not take account of the special characteristics of services. This applies particularly to more limited models which focus on how consumers choose and evaluate their offerings:

'Unfortunately, most of what is known about consumer evaluation processes pertains specifically to goods. The assumption appears to be that services, if not identical to goods, are at least similar enough in the consumers' mind that they are chosen and evaluated in the same manner.'[26]

There is now growing interest in developing models which are specifically based upon service choice and evaluation. However no comprehensive understanding is yet available which incorporates the customers' involvement in the service production process (mentioned in the previous section) and the customers' involvement in the service consumption process. For the present there are only a number of limited models in existence. Two of these limited models are mentioned here:

(*a*) The Sasser, Olsen and Wyckoff Consumer Model[12]
(*b*) The Fisk Consumption/Evaluation Process Model[24]

The Sasser, Olsen and Wyckoff Consumer Model

This model attempts to indicate how a market segment of consumers with similar needs and behaviour makes judgements about services.

The consumer is shown to have a set of needs (e.g. for substantive service such as a hotel room, for control over choice, for trust in the service performer). These needs are translated into a set of desired attributes. Some may be clear to the consumer; others will be more vague and will be clarified by the service organization's suggestions. Over time however the consumer forms a model of what is desired. These desired attributes include factors like:

security (e.g. reliability of service);
consistency (e.g. reliability of reactions);
attitude (e.g. interpersonal reactions);
completeness (e.g. array of services provided);
condition (e.g. 'atmosphere' of service environment);
availability (e.g. ease of access in time or space);
timing (e.g. length of time required for service).

Competitors also offer services containing a variety of mixes of these attributes, all of which are communicated in a variety of ways by the service organization (e.g. advertising) and perceived and judged by consumers.

Three models of how consumers make judgements between services are suggested:

(*a*) there is one over-powering attribute influencing choice;
(*b*) there is a requirement for a specific dominant attribute; and other attributes must achieve a threshold minimum level to influence choice;
(*c*) the alternatives are weighted and ranked.

Consumers may then relate services offered against price(s) charged. The authors suggest that there is a 'range of reasonable combinations' of prices and service levels within which the rational consumer will operate in exercising choice.

The merits of this model are that it attempts to portray the range of attributes that the consumer will take account of in the typical service choice decision. Also it takes account of both the service organization's attempts to communicate with the market and with the consumer's perception and judgements of different service offerings. In fact it forms a useful general scheme for further development and testing. One development could be to combine it with the consumption/evaluation process outlined by Fisk.

The Fisk Consumption/Evaluation Process Model

This model attempts to describe the consumption/evaluation process for services. The model is shown in Figure 11.3 and is divided into three stages, pre-consumption, consumption and post-consumption.

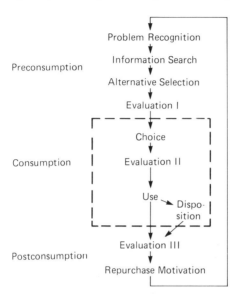

Figure 11.3 Consumption/Evaluation Process for services. $E_I = f$ (Problem Recognition, Information Search, Alternative Selection); $E_{II} = f$ (E_I, Choice); $E_{III} = f$ (E_I, E_{II}, Use).

Source: Fisk, R. P., 'Toward a consumption/evaluation process model for services', in Donnelly, J. H. and George, W. R. (Eds.) *Marketing of Services*, American Marketing Association, Chicago, 1981, pp. 191–95

The pre-consumption stage incorporates the events and actions that typically precede consumption behaviour (i.e. problem recognition, information search, the selection of alternative solutions). Evaluation I is an attempt to identify the 'best' solution.

The consumption stage is where the consumer acts by choosing the 'best' service. Evaluation II is a function of Evaluation I and Choice behaviour. Evaluation I forms expectations about the service while the choice and any experience associated with choice serve as a comparison with expectations. Satisfaction with choice leads to service use. Dissatisfaction with choice may still lead to service use or attempts to reduce dissatisfaction (e.g. complaints, non-payment). Use concludes the consumption phase of the process.

Following service use Evaluation III occurs which is a function of Evaluation I, Evaluation II and Use. If the consumer is satisfied then repurchase motivation will occur; if not then repurchase motivation will not occur and dissatisfaction may lead to complaining behaviour.

The author recognizes that the model oversimplifies the consumption/evaluation process (e.g. it takes little account of internal psychological processes or external influences). Also he recognizes the weakness that the concepts are shown as discrete elements; in practice consumption/evaluation probably occurs as a continuous process. Nevertheless it is a useful first step in conceptualizing the consumption/evaluation process. The model may be used as a framework for research on the satisfaction and dissatisfaction with services and as a stimulus to further developments in model building in the so far largely neglected area of services marketing.

Increasing interest in the field of service marketing has encouraged further research in the area of consumer behaviour. Current work is concerned with problems like how consumers evaluate services; whether these evaluation processes differ for services compared with goods; whether there is greater perceived risk involved in the purchase of services than of products. These developments promise to add further important insights into consumer behaviour in service markets.

11.33 Customers as an Influence on other Customers as Producers and Users of Services

Exhibit 11.3

Audience Participation
During tests, a note played *mezzo forte* on the horn measured approximately 65 decibels of sound.
A single uncovered cough gave the same reading.
A handkerchief placed over the mouth when coughing will assist in obtaining a *pianissimo*.

Source: Programme Note, Nottingham Theatre

Much of the interest in service marketing focuses on the relationship and interaction between service operators and customers. There is also the need to examine relationships and interactions between customers. Existing models of consumer behaviour take account of the input that other people (whether customers or not) may have on an individual's buying behaviour. Thus the influence of family, of reference groups and of other customers as information sources and influencers, is recognized. However these influences tend to be regarded as taking place in the pre-consumption or post-consumption stages of purchase or use. What is different about many services, particularly group services, is the importance of the interaction between customers *during* the service performance and consumption process. For example, enjoyment of an evening in a restaurant can be influenced by other diners; pleasure from attending a concert can be influenced by other members of an audience. (See Exhibit 11.3 above). The nature of these interactions between customers is implicitly recognized by service marketors. However more systematic empirical work is required to further our understanding of this dimension of customer behaviour before more explicit statements can be made about the impact and nature of such influences.

11.4 Summary

1 Service personnel and service customers have an influence upon the marketing of services.
2 Service personnel quality and performance needs to be maintained and improved. Service organizations can take a number of measures to do so.
3 Service marketors' interest in customers arises because of their involvement in the service production process; because of the need to understand their behaviour as customers; because customers can influence other customers during the service production and consumption process.
4 Currently there is only limited understanding, in the form of explicit models, about customer behaviour in service marketing situations. More empirical work is required in this field.

Questions for Discussion

1 How can service personnel influence the service performed by a service organization?
2 What is a 'low contact' organization?
3 Distinguish between the 'technical quality' and 'functional quality' of a service.
4 Describe four measures a service organization can take to improve the quality of service personnel and their performance?
5 What is 'internal marketing'?
6 What are the implications of the customers' involvement in service performance?
7 In developing a model of consumer behaviour for a service, identify six elements that need to be incorporated in such a model.
8 Comment upon ways in which customers can influence other customers in the service production and consumption process?
9 Develop the main elements of a training programme you would devise for a:
   (*a*) car hire receptionist;
   (*b*) waiter;
   (*c*) tour guide.
10 Should people who work for a service organization be incorporated more explicitly as an element of the service marketing mix?

References and Notes

1 Johnson, E. M. An Introduction to the problems of Service Marketing Management, Bureau of Economic and Business Research, University of Delaware, 1964.
2 Kotler, P. *Marketing for Non-Profit Organisations*, Prentice-Hall, Englewood Cliffs, 1982.
3 Wittreich, W. J. 'How to buy/sell professional services', *Harvard Business Review*, Vol. 44, March–April 1966, pp. 127–36.

4 Cannon, T. *Basic Marketing: Principles and Practice*, Holt, Rinehart & Winston, New York, 1980.

5 Davidson, D. S. 'How to succeed in a service industry . . . turn the organisation chart upside down', *Management Review*, April 1978, pp. 13–16.

6 Chase, R. B. 'Where does the customer fit into a service organisation, *Harvard Business Review*, Nov.–Dec. 1978, pp. 137–42.

7 Gronroos, C. 'Strategic Management and Marketing in the Service Sector', Swedish School of Economics and Business Administration, 1982.

8 Booms, B. H. and Nyquist, J. L. 'Analyzing the Customer/Firm Communication Component of the Services Marketing Mix', paper presented at the AMA Service Marketing Conference, Florida, Nov. 1981, pp. 172–7.

9 Berry, L. L. 'Services Marketing is different', *Business*, May–June 1980, Vol. 30, No. 3, pp. 24–9.

10 Sasser, W. E. and Arbeit, S. P. 'Selling jobs in the service sector', *Business Horizons*, Vol. 19, June 1976, pp. 61–5.

11 Shostack, G. Lynn, 'Breaking free from product marketing', *Journal of Marketing*, Vol. 41, No. 2, April 1977, pp. 73–80.

12 Sasser, W. E., Olsen, R. P. and Wyckoff, D. D. *Management of Service Operations – Text and Cases*, Allyn and Bacon, Boston, Mass. 1978.

13 Bateson, J. 'Do we need service marketing?' in Eiglier, P. *et al.*, 'Marketing Consumer Services: New Insights', Report 77–115, Marketing Science Institute, Boston, 1977.

14 Schneider, B. 'The Service Organisation – climate is crucial', *Organisational Dynamics*, Vol. 9, Autumn 1980, pp. 52–65.

15 Hostage, G. M. 'Quality Control in a service business', *Harvard Business Review*, July–Aug. 1975, pp. 98–106.

16 Shapiro, G. 'Solving management problems in the burgeoning service field', *SAM Advanced Management Journal*, April 1971, pp. 4–9.

17 Bessom, R. M. and Jackson, D. W. Jnr. 'Service Retailing: a strategic marketing approach', *Journal of Retailing*, Summer, 1975.

18 Levitt, T. 'Production line approach to service', *Harvard Business Review*, Sept.–Oct. 1972, pp. 41–52.

19 Kramer, R. 'Kramer urges Service firms to audit employee performance', *Marketing News*, 31 Jan. 1975, p. 9.

20 Gersuny, C. and Rosengren, W. R. *The Service Economy*, Schenkman, Cambridge, Mass, 1973. This section is based on this source.

21 Langeard, E., Bateson, J. E. G., Lovelock, C. H. and Eiglier, P. 'Services Marketing: New Insights from Consumers and Managers', Report No. 81–104, Marketing Science Institute, Boston, 1981.

22 Engel, J. F. and Blackwell, R. D. *Consumer Behaviour*, 4th Edn, The Dryden Press, 1982, is an example.

23 See, for example, Baker, M. J. *Marketing: an introductory text*, 3rd Edn, Macmillan, London, 1979: Oliver, G. *Marketing Today*, Prentice-Hall, Englewood Cliffs, 1980.

24 Fisk, R. P. 'Toward a consumption/evaluation process model for

services' paper presented at the AMA Service Marketing Conference, Florida, Nov. 1981, pp. 191–5.

25 Wilson, A. *The Marketing of Professional Services*, McGraw-Hill, London, 1972.
26 Zeithmal, V. A. 'How consumer evaluation processes differ between goods and services', paper presented at the AMA Service Marketing Conference, Florida, Nov. 1981, pp. 186–90.

12. *PHYSICAL EVIDENCE AND SERVICES*

12.1 Introduction

Customers of service organizations may be influenced by a range of factors in their decisions to purchase or use a specific service. Some of these factors have been considered in earlier chapters. One factor which is assuming more importance is the role played by physical evidence. Physical evidence can assist in creating the 'environment' and 'atmosphere' in which a service is bought or performed and can help shape customer perceptions of a service. Customers form impressions of a service organization partly through physical evidence like buildings, furnishings, layout, colour and goods associated with the service like carrier bags, tickets, brochures, labels and so on. Many service marketors neglect this aspect of service design and fail to take account of how they can use such physical evidence to shape the image of their organization and its services: 'Because of product marketing's biases, service marketors often fail to recognise the unique forms of evidence that they can normally control and fail to see that they should be part of marketing's responsibilities.'[1]

This chapter considers this neglected aspect of service marketing in more detail. Two aspects are considered; physical evidence closely related to a service product and physical evidence which has a more general influence upon service image and atmosphere.

12.2 Role of Service Evidence

A distinction is made in services marketing between two kinds of physical evidence:[1]

(*a*) peripheral evidence;
(*b*) essential evidence.

12.21 Peripheral Evidence

Peripheral evidence is actually possessed as part of the purchase of a service. It has however little or no independent value. Thus a bank chequebook is of no value unless backed by the funds transfer and storage service it represents. An admission ticket for a cinema equally has no independent value. It merely confirms the service. It is not a surrogate for it. Peripheral evidence 'adds to' the value of essential evidence only as far as the customer values these symbols of service. The hotel rooms of many large international hotel groups contain much peripheral evidence like directories, town guides, pens, notepads, welcome gifts, drink packs, matchbooks and so on. These representations of service must be designed and developed with customer needs in mind. They often provide an important set of complementary items to the essential core service sought by customers. Figure 12.1 is a novel illustration of the use of peripheral evidence in advertising a transport service.

One convenience other Dover Calais ferries prefer to forget.

A Channel ferry can be a decidedly inconvenient place for a baby to be caught short.
Unless you're lucky enough to be on a Sealink ferry, that is.
On all three of our Flagship Service ferries, we provide a special Mother and Baby Room. Where you will find peace and quiet, along with everything that you need to turn a damp baby into a dry one.
We also take care of your older offspring, with special children's menus, video rooms and a Children's Club to keep them amused all the way to France.
While for you, we provide bars, good food at good

prices, plus the extra comfort of sailing on the newest ships on the Channel.
It's not expensive either. You can take a family of four in a car to France for as little as £41.00. With up to twelve sailings a day, you can go when it suits you.
And, unlike some ferry companies, we can promise everyone will be dry on arrival.
For more information call (01) 200 0200 or see your travel agent, principal rail station or travel centre.

Sealink Dover·Calais
Determined to give you a better service.

Figure 12.1 Peripheral evidence
Source: *The Mail on Sunday*, 27 March, 1983

12.22 Essential Evidence

Essential evidence, unlike peripheral evidence, cannot be possessed by the customer. Nevertheless essential evidence may be so important in its influence on service purchase it may be considered as an element in its own right. The overall appearance and layout of a hotel; the 'feel' of a bank branch; the type of vehicle rented by a car rental company; the type of aircraft used by a carrier. All are examples of essential evidence.

Ultimately peripheral evidence and essential evidence, in combination with other image forming elements, (e.g. people who provide the service) influence the customer's view of the service: '. . . when a consumer attempts to judge a service, particularly before using or buying it, that service is "known" by the tangible clues, the tangible evidence, that surround it'.[1]

12.3 Managing the Evidence

Essential evidence and peripheral evidence in conjunction with personnel, promotional, advertising and public relations efforts are some of the chief ways through which a service organization can formally create and maintain its image. All are inputs to service product design. Images are difficult to define, measure and control for the fact is that image is a subjective and personal construct. Nevertheless people do form images of service products and service organizations based on an array of evidence. Therefore management of that evidence is desirable to ensure that the image conveyed conforms with the image desired. The management of physical evidence forms part of this task.

Service organizations with competing service products may use physical evidence to differentiate their service products in the marketplace and give their service products a competitive advantage. A physical product like a car or a camera can be augmented through the use of both tangible and intangible elements. A car can be given additional tangible features like a sliding sunroof or stereophonic radio equipment; a camera can be given additional tangible features like control devices which enable use in a wide variety of light conditions. A car may be sold with a long life anti-rust warranty or cost-free service for the first year of ownership; a camera with a long-life warranty or free lens insurance. Tangible and intangible elements may be used to augment the essential product offer. In fact organizations marketing tangible dominant products frequently use intangible, abstract elements as part of their communications strategy.

Service marketing organizations also try to use tangible clues to strengthen the meaning of their intangible products. They tend however to do so intuitively:

> 'The management of tangible evidence is not articulated in marketing as a primary priority for service marketors. There has been little in-depth exploration of the range of authority that emphasis on tangible evidence would create for the service marketor.'[1]

Yet managing physical evidence should be an important strategy for a service marketing organization because of the intangibility of a service. In Chapter 2 two aspects of intangibility were identified:

(*a*) that which cannot be touched; impalpable;
(*b*) that which cannot be defined, formulated, grasped mentally.

Services have both elements of intangibility. Both features present problems and challenges to service marketors who have to find ways to make the service more 'palpable' and to make it easier to 'grasp mentally'. There are a number of things service marketors can do to overcome these difficulties. They include these.

12.31 Make the Service more Tangible

One suggestion is to develop a tangible representation of the service. The bank credit card is an example of the tangible representation of the service, 'credit'. The use of a credit card means:

(*a*) the service can be separated from the seller;
(*b*) intermediaries can be used in distribution thereby expanding the geographic area in which the service marketor can operate;
(*c*) the service product of one bank can be differentiated from the service product of another bank (e.g. through colour, graphics and brand names like Visa);
(*d*) the card acts as a symbol of status as well as providing a line of credit.

A recent innovation has been the introduction of Gold Credit cards offering a range of credit and other services. These are effectively another 'brand' of upmarket credit cards. Authority to use a gold card gives the user access to a superior range of services e.g. unsecured minimum overdrafts, larger cash advances against the card, free tax and financial planning consultations, travel accident insurance.

12.32 Make the Service Easier to Grasp Mentally

There are two ways in which a service can be made easier to grasp mentally.

(a) Associate the service with a tangible object which is more easily perceived by the customer

This approach may be used in advertising messages like Figure 12.2. Here the intangible nature of the service is translated into tangible objects representing that service. These may have more significance and meaning for customers. In this case the airline is attempting to make it easier for the customer to grasp what their service means compared with competitors. With this approach it is obviously vital to:

(*a*) use tangible objects that are considered important by the customer and which are sought as part of the service. Using objects that customers do not value may be counter-productive;
(*b*) ensure that the 'promise' implied by these tangible objects in fact is delivered when the service is used. That is the quality of the goods must live up to the reputation implied by the promise.

If these conditions are not met then incorrect, meaningless and damaging associations can be created.

(b) Focus on the Buyer–seller Relationship

This approach focuses on the relationship between the buyer and the seller. The customer is encouraged to identify with a person or group of people in the service organization instead of the intangible services themselves. Advertising agencies use account executives; market research agencies assemble client teams; the Co-operative Bank uses 'personal' bankers. All encourage a focus on people performing services rather than upon the services themselves. Figure 12.3 is an example or recent advertisement stressing the personal relationship between bank and client.

Figure 12.2 Tangible elements of service
Source: Lufthansa advertisement

The assumption which underlies both these approaches is that the customer can derive some benefit from tangible clues presented in these ways about intangible services offered. Service marketors have traditionally used such symbolism in selling their services. Advertising agencies attempt to design their offices in styles which convey the personality of the agency; airlines and hotels use an array of peripheral, tangible elements to emphasize their services, from luggage labels to bags. Many service organizations instinctively presented tangible manifestations of their intangible services. However before a service organization can translate intangibles into more concrete clues it must ensure that it:

(a) knows precisely its target audience and the effect being sought by the use of such devices;
(b) has defined the unique selling points which should be incorporated into the service and which meet the needs of the target market.[2]

There have been few published studies which confirm the usefulness of tangible cues in the marketing of services. In spite of this many writers and practitioners in marketing suggest their use and several types of cues have been suggested. One study by Krentler[3] evaluated the usefulness of tangible cues in the marketing of consumer services. She investigated three types of cues:

Figure 12.3 Emphasis on the personal relationship in service
Source: Williams & Glyn advertisement (appeared Spring 1983)

(*a*) a tangible representation of the service (i.e. it reminded the customer of the service benefits);
(*b*) a cue which focused on the interpersonal relationship between service provider and consumer;
(*c*) a cue which associated the intangible service with a tangible object which was easier for the customer to perceive.

Three services were examined, savings accounts, dry cleaning and hair styling. The effect of the cues was measured by the ability of advertisements, which used the cues, to convince consumers that the benefits were forthcoming. The benefits were specific to each service and were identified by focus group interviews. The findings and methodology are not altogether convincing although the results did suggest that the effect of tangible cues may vary with the type of benefit being considered, as one might expect. As far as the provider–client interface cue was concerned it was effective with respect to benefits related to personal trust between provider and client. This emphasizes that cues do need to be related to benefits sought by customers and should not be used without consideration of these benefits. The major challenge to service organizations is to identify these benefits and then to match the benefits sought with appropriate cues. There are a variety of cues service organizations can use from the physical environment, to furnishings, equipment, stationery, general decoration, colour, lighting. All are part of the environment formed and shaped by the service organization.

12.4 The Design of a Service Environment

The design and creation of an environment should be a deliberate act for most service organizations. Exceptions might be those service organizations providing services at the customers premises or in the home. Even with these kinds of service attention must be given to equipment design, vehicle livery, stationery used and similar influences upon the 'impression' of the organization which may be formed in the customer's mind.

The environment refers to the context (physical and non-physical) where a service is performed and where the service organization and the customer interact. It therefore includes any facilities which influence the performance and communication of the service.[4] In the case of a hotel, for example, it means:

> 'The building, land and equipment, including all furniture, fittings and supplies. Thus such things as saucepans, a sheet of notepaper or an ice bucket are included as well as the obvious items beyond which a more conventional concept of design might not tend to look.'[5]

In general corporate personality and corporate identity have been treated in a narrow way in the past. The design of a service organization should be approached in a more complete way. In a total sense this is more than logos, headed notepaper and potted plants in reception areas. It means the entire shaping of a service facility in every respect. Today corporate design is a skilled business and:

> 'graphic designers working by themselves are rarely able to resolve corporate identity problems of any real complexity. The arguments for the multidisciplinary design consultancy with its designers, marketing men, psychologists, sociologists and economists is unassailable.'[5]

Thus in designing a service facility the 'meaning' of the total environment and its impact upon employees and customers must be considered. Environments are more than mere objects and the distinctions between an environment and an object have been summarized as follows.

(a) An environment surrounds, enfolds and engulfs. One cannot be a subject of an environment, one can only be a participant.
(b) Environments are always multi-model. That is to say they impact on the senses in more than one way. It would probably be impossible to build an environment that did not do this.
(c) Peripheral as well as central information is always present. The area behind one is no less a part of the environment than that in front. One is aware of those parts on which the attention is not actually focused.
(d) As an extension of this environments always provide more information than can actually be processed. Thus some of the information which they represent might conflict, contradict or be ambiguous.

(*e*) Environments imply purpose and action (roles).

(*f*) Environments contain meanings and motivational messages.

(*g*) Environments imply aesthetic, social and systemic qualities.[5]

Thus the design task in concerned with the totality of impressions conveyed by the parts and by the whole. Marketors have worked closely with product designers in the past. The impact of the service environment upon customer satisfaction with services means they ought to work together more closely in the future on environment design.

12.41 Creating the Ideal Environment

Creating the ideal physical environment and atmosphere within it is clearly a difficult task. Two particular problems service organizations face in attempting to do so are these.

(*a*) Our current knowledge of the impact of environment and particular elements within it is imperfect. How important is space, colour, shape and texture of materials? What of carpets, curtains, lighting, heating, chairs in relation to each other and in relation to the space in which they are enclosed? Judgements on these matters are inevitably largely personal and subjective. This field of work is still largely in its infancy. But it is a field of work in which service marketors are beginning to show an interest:

> 'The impact of physical environmental factors, though difficult to quantify, nevertheless merits investigation. The development of innovative approaches to help to further understand the role of physical environment in services marketing is a key research area to be pursued.'[6]

(*b*) The second difficulty is that because individuals are different, they deal with and respond to their environment in various personal ways. Service organization environments which serve a wide variety of people like hotels, bus stations or rail stations or airports are particularly difficult to design in the sense that they must be neutral enough to please everybody. Nevertheless groups of people may respond to an environment in a similar way. If the differences between groups of people responding in different ways can be identified then it may be possible to design more appropriate environments for target customers and use 'response to environment' as a psychographic segmentation variable. Some dimensions thought to influence responses to environments include age, sex, social class, creativity and intelligence.[5]

12.42 Influences upon Image Formation

Clearly there are many factors which influence the image that may be formed by a service organization. All elements of the marketing mix like price, the services themselves, advertising and promotional campaigns and public relations activities will contribute to customer and client perceptions as well as physical evidence. In the case of a retail store for example:

> 'A store image is composed of many dimensions, each interacting with the others to influence the kind of image various consumer groups hold for the store. Among the more

important dimensions of a store's image are its architecture and exterior design, its interior design, its store personnel, its lines of merchandise, its signs and logos, its advertising and sales promotion, its location, and its post purchase communications. Its services, displays, reputation, customers and name also affect a store's image.'[7]

Research undertaken in the area of retail image formation in fact contains many useful insights for marketors in the service sector. The important attributes, which determine retail store choice, have been categorized as:[8]

(*a*) physical attributes;
(*b*) atmosphere;
(*c*) location;
(*d*) nature and quality of assortment;
(*e*) price;
(*f*) advertising and promotion;
(*g*) sales personnel;
(*h*) services offered;
(*i*) nature of store clientele;
(*j*) post transaction satisfaction.

All of these attributes are interlinked although it is the first two which are of particular interest here.

Physical Attributes

Several aspects of a service organization's architecture and design have an influence on image formation. Some of the important components in retail settings are shown in Table 12.1.

Table 12.1
Some Attributes influencing Retail Store Image

External

Physical size of buildings;   Building materials used;
Shape of buildings;   Entrances;
Frontage of buildings;   Signs and logos;
Outside lighting;   Vans, lorries, parking areas.

Internal

Layout;   Lighting;
Colour schemes;   Signs and logos;
Equipment;   Aisle width;
Materials and support materials   Air conditioning;
  e.g. stationery   Heating and ventilation.

All have been found to be factors which influence image.[8] However their presence or absence also influences the perception of other individual attributes listed. In that sense they probably play more of a role in facilitating the creation and maintenance of an image rather than a determining role.

The exterior physical appearance of a service organization can influence image. The physical structure of a building, including its size, its shape, the type of materials used in construction, its location and comparative attractiveness compared with nearby buildings are factors shaping customer perceptions. Allied factors like ease of parking and access, frontages, door and window design, signposting and vehicle livery are also important. The external appearance may convey impressions of solidity, permanence, conservatism, progressiveness and so forth.

Internally the layout of the service organization, the arrangement of equipment, desks, fixtures and fittings, the seating, lighting, colour schemes, materials used, the air conditioning and heating systems, the signs and logos, the quality of visual evidence like pictures and photographs; all these factors combine to create impression and image. At the detailed level internal attributes may also include items like notepaper, stationery, brochures and display space and racks.

The combination of all of these elements into a distinctive overall personality for a service organization is a skilled and creative task. Often the 'environmental engineer' is constrained in his ability to create and express a personality for a service organization by uncontrollable factors (e.g. poor location; cost constraints; building restrictions).

Physical evidence contributes to the 'personality' of an organization – a 'personality' which may be the key differentiating feature in highly competitive and undifferentiated service product markets:

'Airlines, like banks, petrol companies and indeed very many suppliers of products and services, know that they don't differ very much in the fundamental aspects of their business. They sell approximately the same thing at about the same price and give much the same service. The main characteristic that distinguishes one airline or bank or one petrol company from another is personality, the way it presents itself, its identity.'[9]

Atmosphere

The atmosphere of a service facility too influences image. The term 'atmospherics' has been coined to define the conscious design of space to influence buyers.[10] Atmosphere, of course, also has an important influence on employees and other people who come into contact with the organization. 'Working conditions' in this sense influence how service personnel may treat customers. In relation to retail outlets:

'Every store has a physical layout that makes it hard or easy to move around. Every store has a "feel": one store is dirty, another is charming, a third is palatial, a fourth is sombre. The store must embody a planned atmosphere that suits the target market and leans them toward purchase . . . the atmosphere is designed by creative people who know how to combine visual, aural, olfactory, and tactile stimuli to achieve the desired effect.'[11]

Many service organizations increasingly recognize the importance of atmosphere. Restaurants may be known for their atmosphere as well as for their food; hotels may be regarded as warm and welcoming; retail stores may be given added attractiveness by careful attention to atmosphere; some advertising agencies are known for their careful attention to atmospheric design; banks, solicitors' offices and dental surgeons' waiting rooms can be made forbidding or welcoming by the attention given to atmosphere.

Some influences upon 'atmospherics' include:

Sight

Retailers use the term 'visual merchandising' to describe visual factors that affect the customer's perception of the store. Visual merchandising is concerned with image building and with selling. It attempts to ensure that whenever a customer is in a store these twin aims are achieved. Visual merchandisers in retailing try to ensure that whether a customer is in a lift, on an escalator or waiting to pay a bill at a counter, selling and image building continue. Lighting, layout, colour clearly are all part of visual merchandising. So is the appearance and dress of employees (*see* Chapter 11). Visual cues are a potent influence upon customer patronage of a service facility.

Scent

Odour can effect image. In retailing, coffee shops, bread shops, flower shops and perfume shops may use aroma and fragrance to sell their products. Bread shops may position fans strategically to carry the smell of fresh baked bread into the street. Restaurants, steak bars and fish and chip shops can also exploit the benefits of aroma to good effect. In offices of professionals the scent of leather and leather polish or the fragrance of polished wood panelling may help develop a particular atmosphere of luxury and solidity.

Sound

Sound is often a backcloth for atmosphere creation. Film makers have always recognized its importance and even in the days of silent movies musical accompaniment was a significant atmospheric ingredient. The background music in a teenage fashion store creates a very different atmosphere from the piped Mozart played in the lifts of upmarket department stores or the soothing melodies some airlines play to their passengers just before take-off. A 'quiet' atmosphere can be created by eliminating extraneous noise through careful partitioning, low ceilings, deep pile carpeting and the hushed tones of sales personnel. Such an atmosphere may be required in a library, an art gallery or an exclusive fur shop. A recent study of music in retail stores found that the pace of store traffic can be influenced by the type of music played. Takings were larger when slower music was played.[13]

Touch

The feel of materials like the rich texture of a heavy cloth-covered chair, the depth and feel of carpeting, the touchability of wall coverings, the woodgrain of a coffee table, the coldness of stone floors; all convey feelings and contribute to atmosphere. In some retail settings touching is encouraged through sample displays. In other settings like cut glass and china stores, antique shops, art galleries and museums, touching may be discouraged. Materials used and skill in display are important factors in both instances.

Kotler suggests that atmosphere can be a particularly appropriate competitive tool when:

(*a*) there is a large, growing number of competitors;
(*b*) product and/or price differences are small;
(*c*) products are aimed at distinct social class or life style groups.

Creating an atmosphere may therefore be a deliberate act for many service organizations. This means that when designing a service facility for the first time organizations face four major design decisions:

(*a*) what should the building look like on the outside?
(*b*) what should be the functions and flow characteristics of the building?
(*c*) what should the building be like on the inside?
(*d*) what materials would best support the desired feeling of the building?

12.5 Summary

1 Physical evidence and atmosphere can be important elements in helping to create the image of a service organization and in saying something about its services.
2 A distinction can be made between peripheral evidence (which has little independent value) and essential evidence (which is fundamental to the service offer).
3 Service organizations need to manage the evidence they use in a planned and systematic way to help overcome the problems posed by the intangible nature of services.
4 service environments require a comprehensive approach to their design and management.
5 Creating ideal environments is difficult. Many factors influence the impact environment has upon employees and customers.

Questions for Discussion

1 What kinds of physical evidence can the service marketor use to help market his service products?
2 What problems arise in managing service evidence?
3 How can problems of intangibility be overcome through service product evidence?
4 What is meant by a service environment?
5 What problems do service organizations have to overcome in managing service environments?
6 List the factors which influence retail store choice. Could these influence hotel choice? bank choice? airline choice?

7 What is 'atmospherics'?

8 Identify ten factors that contribute to the image of a retail store of your own choice? Describe the image you have of that store.

9 Describe what influence the following may have on a service environment:

(*a*) layout;
(*b*) colour;
(*c*) lighting.

10 'Images are so personal that they cannot be managed.' Discuss.

References and Notes

1 Shostack, G. Lynn 'Breaking free from Product Marketing', *Journal of Marketing*, Vol. 41, April 1977, pp. 73–80.

2 Majaro, S. *Marketing in Perspective*, George Allen and Unwin, London, 1982.

3 Krentler, K. A. 'Empirical Investigation of the use of tangible cues in the marketing of consumer services', DBA Dissertation, University of Kentucky, 1981.

4 Booms, B. H. and Bitner, M. J. 'Marketing Strategies and Organisation Structures for Service Firms', in Donnelly, J. and George, W. R. *Marketing of Services*, American Marketing Association, Chicago, 1981.

5 Doswell, R. and Gamble, P. R. *Marketing and Planning Hotels and Tourism Projects*, Hutchinson, London, 1979.

6 Upah, G. D., Berry, L. L. and Shostack, G. Lynn 'Emerging themes and directions for service marketing', Summary Paper of American Marketing Association, Chicago, 1 February 1983.

7 Delozier, M. W. *The Marketing Communications Process*, McGraw-Hill, New York, 1976.

8 Engel, J. E. and Blackwell, R. D. *Consumer Behaviour*, The Dryden Press, 1982.

9 Olins, W. 'The Corporate Personality', Design Council, 1978.

10 Kotler, P. 'Atmospherics as a Marketing Tool', *Journal of Retailing*, Winter 1973–4, pp. 48–64.

11 Kotler, P. *Principles of Marketing*, Prentice-Hall, Englewood Cliffs, 1980.

12 Kotler, P. *Marketing for Non-Profit Organisations*, Prentice-Hall, Englewood Cliffs, 1982.

13 Milliman, R. 'The use of background music to affect the behaviour of Supermarket Shoppers', *Journal of Marketing*, Vol. 46, Summer 1982, pp. 86–91.

13. PROCESS AND SERVICES

13.1 Introduction

Marketing books rarely discuss operations management in any detail. They of course acknowledge its importance and the contribution it makes to those systems in which marketing management and operations management co-exist. The usual view expressed is that marketing management and operations management need to work together if customer needs are to be satisfied. Areas of potential conflict inevitably occur e.g. what level of capacity should be planned, how broad product lines should be, what levels of support stock should be held.

Thus marketing is seen to have a role to play in the necessary forecasting and planning phases of operations management through marketing research; product specification and product design too are significant areas to which marketing management may contribute; equally the whole area of marketing logistics is one which brings together the functions of marketing management and of operations management, concerned as they both are with transport, delivery, inventory levels and customer service.

In service organizations co-operation between marketing and operations is vital. The linkage between the two functions requires more than the cursory treatment usually given in most marketing books. In service organizations marketing is too important to be left to marketing managers; and operations is too important to be left to operations managers. This is because a significant component of any service product, from the customers' point of view is, *how the process of service delivery functions.*

Customers of service organizations obtain benefits and satisfactions from the services themselves and from how those services are delivered. The way in which service systems operate is crucial. Service systems which operate efficiently and effectively can give marketing management considerable marketing leverage and promotional advantage. It is clear that a smooth running service operation offers competitive advantages, particularly where differentiation between service products may be minimal. Those service systems which make it easy for a customer to leave a car for service and collect it at some agreed time; which make it easy for a busy executive to pick up a hire car at an airport; which give reliable and prompt service in a restaurant; which allow customers to book a holiday or a hairdressing appointment with little effort; all these systems will have advantages over competitive systems which do not run to time, impose excessive demands on customers, break down while operating or simply do not deliver what they promise. Ensuring that service systems work efficiently and effectively is traditionally an operations management task. In service systems the marketing implications of operational performance are so important that the two functions have to co-operate. In services, marketing must be just as involved with the operational aspects of performance as operations managers; that is, with the 'how' and the 'process' of service delivery.

Earlier chapters examined the 'people' involved in service delivery and the 'physical' factors that influence service delivery. Both are obviously closely related to the 'process' of service delivery. Service personnel can mitigate system breakdown, to some extent, by cheerful and considerate attention to customers' problems. Pleasant physical facilities may soften the blow of having to wait longer than anticipated for an appointment with a lawyer or a hairdresser. Neither however can compensate entirely for system inefficiencies and breakdown. How well the overall system works, its procedures and policies, customer involvement in the process, the degree of standardization in the system, the capacity of the system to cope with workload fluctuations; these are marketing concerns as well as operations concerns.

The operational management literature has rather neglected service systems until recently and concentrated instead upon manufacturing operations. This traditional emphasis is now changing and specialists in operations management are giving more attention to how their skills and experience can be transferred to service systems.[1] This chapter examines the critical relationship between marketing management and operations management in service systems.

13.2 Operations Management

Operations management is not just concerned with manufacturing, although the former labelling of the area as production management did tend to give it this emphasis. Certainly most textbooks on the subject have given more coverage to manufacturing organizations than to non-manufacturing organizations in spite of the growth which has taken place in the service sector outlined in Chapter 1. Increasingly though banks, airlines, hotels, freight forwarders, quasi-retailers, leisure centres, insurance companies and many other types of service organizations are discovering that operations management ideas and practices are now an essential input to their control of costs, system improvement and levels of customer service.

Here we define operations as the means by which resource inputs are combined, reformed, transformed or separated to create useful outputs (goods and services). Operations management is concerned with planning, organizing and controlling this resource conversion process which is illustrated in Figure 13.1. The concept of useful is important; for the purpose of the process is to add 'utility' or 'value' over and above the costs incurred in obtaining system inputs and in undertaking the transformation process.

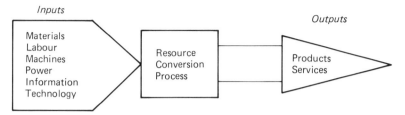

Operations management is concerned with systems design, operations
planning, execution and control.

Figure 13.1 Operations System

In managing this process some traditional areas of operations management include:

(*a*) Process planning and control
The selection and specification of operations to achieve service
outputs in terms of quality, quantity, delivery and cost to meet
customer requirements.
(*b*) Operations planning
The detailed specification of each operation to achieve service
outputs of the required quality, rate and cost.
(*c*) Facilities design, layout, materials handling and maintenance
The design, location, layout, handling of any materials involved and
the maintenance of any equipment involved to achieve a smooth
flow of materials and people through the operating system.
(*d*) Scheduling
Detailing the times at which operations should be undertaken to
allow services to be completed by agreed delivery promises,
consistent with resources available and their economic utilization.
(*e*) Inventory planning and control
Planning and control of inventory (including 'people' and
'capacity') to achieve desired and agreed levels of service.
(*f*) Quality control
Appropriate checking and control techniques and procedures used
at relevant points within a service system to ensure that prescribed
quality levels are attained.
(*g*) Operations control
Information flows into and out of service systems which ensure that
operations are undertaken at specified times, in accordance with
agreed schedules; and with monitoring of work in service systems
and implementation of alternative procedures where necessary.
(*h*) Forecasting and longer term planning
Anticipating demands placed on the service system and forecasting
the capabilities that need to be included in the system (e.g.
capacity).

All service systems would not necessarily include all the above. Also some
service systems would embrace other areas (e.g. purchasing, make or buy

decisions). The tasks shown above should be considered only as an outline of the principal areas of responsibility of operations managers. Because operations management is so interlinked with so many other functional areas (e.g. personnel, marketing) it is difficult to define precisely the responsibilities of operations managers in all types of situations. Within each of these areas an array of techniques may be used to help design and improve the capability of the service system (e.g. networking, forecasting, simulation).

13.3 Classifications of Services Operating Systems

Services operating systems may be classified in a number of ways. Two considered here for illustrative purposes are according to:

(*a*) the type of process;
(*b*) the degree of contact.

13.31 The Type of Process[2]

Three types of processes of relevance to service organizations are:

(*a*) line operations;
(*b*) job shop operations;
(*c*) intermittent operations.

Line Operations

In a line operation there is an arranged sequence of operations or activities undertaken. The service is produced by following this sequence. In manufacturing, an assembly line for domestic appliances typifies this type of process; in services, a self-service restaurant typifies this process. In the latter people move through a sequence of stages although there is no reason why customers should not remain stationary and receive a sequence of services. The high degree of interrelationship between different elements of a line operation mean that performance overall is limited by performance at the weakest link in the system and hold-ups can arise (e.g. a slow check-out operator in a self-service cafeteria). Also it tends to be a relatively inflexible type of process although tasks in the process can be specialized and made routine giving more speedy performance. This process is most suitable in service organizations with high volumes of fairly continuous demand for relatively standard kinds of service.

Job Shop Operations

A job shop operation produces a variety of services using different combinations and sequences of activities. The services can be tailored to meet varying customer needs and to provide a bespoke service. Restaurants and professional services are examples of job shop operations. While flexibility is a key advantage of this type of system it may suffer from being more difficult to schedule, from being more difficult to substitute capital for labour in the system and from being more difficult to calculate the capacity of the system.

Intermittent Operations

Intermittent operations refer to service projects which are one off or only infrequently repeated. Examples include the construction of new service facilities, the design of an advertising campaign, the installation of a large computer or the making of a major film. The scale of such projects makes their management a complex task. Such projects provide an appropriate field for the ready transfer of many project control and scheduling techniques like Critical Path Analysis. The scale and infrequency of these projects make them different in kind from line and job shop operations.

13.32 The Degree of Contact[3]

An alternative classification is based on the extent of customer contact in the creation of the service (*see* Chapter 11). Managing service operations with a high level of customer contact with the service delivery process presents different challenges compared with those systems where there is a low level of customer contact. The amount of customer contact has an effect on many of the decisions operations managers have to make.

According to Chase these kinds of systems (high contact or low contact) have an effect upon service operations and have implications for managers of service systems. Some of these are:

(*a*) high contact systems are more difficult to control since the customer can make an input to the process or even disrupt the process;

(*b*) in high contact systems the customer can affect the timing of demand and it is more difficult to balance the capacity of the system to meet demands placed upon it;

(*c*) workers in high contact systems can have a great influence upon the customers' view of the service provided;

(*d*) in high contact systems production scheduling is more difficult;

(*e*) it may be more difficult to rationalize high contact systems (e.g. by substituting technology);

(*f*) it may be beneficial to separate high contact and low contact elements of a service system and encourage staff specialization in these different functions because of the varying skills required.

Both of the schemes outlined are useful ways of classifying service systems for operational purposes. Both however imply that the sequence of operations involved in the service process can be made explicit to enable the systems to be categorized according to degree of contact. One step that service managers can take to understand their process of service delivery is to flow chart the system and the interactions with customers within that system. Flow charting offers a number of advantages including:

(*a*) providing a visual representation of the service system. It shows what activities take place and how they relate to each other;

(*b*) identifying possible bottlenecks in the process and estimating capacity required at each stage;

(*c*) identifying the steps in which the customer is involved in the process;

(*d*) identifying information requirements at each stage of the process.

Some of the key questions service managers need to consider in developing policy for service organizations emerge from this kind of analysis. They include:

What steps are involved in the process?
Are they arranged logically?
Can some steps be eliminated or combined?
Are the capacities of each step balanced?
Where are customers involved in the process?
Can unnecessary customer contact be reduced or eliminated?
Can technology be used to speed up the process?
Can some steps in the process be transferred elsewhere?

13.4 Operations Management Difficulties in Services

The previous section suggested that service systems and service processes are much like manufacturing systems and processes. Operations management principles and techniques seem to be applicable in both settings. Indeed in operations management as in marketing management no great advantage is derived from treating non-manufacturing operations as being distinctively different to manufacturing operations. The line between services and products is blurred as Chapter 2 made clear. Most productive systems produce a bundle of products and services and the analysis of the problems of operations management should recognize both aspects of the system output.[4]

Nevertheless some differences which may influence operational management problems and solutions in particular service settings have been identified.[5]

Establishing Objectives in Service Systems

In some service systems conventional measures like profit and return on investment cannot be used (e.g. public services like transport). Some alternative schemes may have to be used. In non-profit services and the social services sector in particular, establishing system objectives may be difficult and complex at both the general level and at the operational unit level. Typically objectives for public services will have to incorporate measures of the level and quality of service which is provided in some settings and these pose particular difficulties (e.g. health care, education).

Capacity Utilization

The intangibility of a service means that there are limitations on inventory building, although of course people and their skills can be inventoried (through hoarding labour) and facilities can be inventoried (to provide extra capacity when needed). Generally in services, what is unused or idle today is wasted and cannot be used to fill any overload there may be in the future. A fundamental decision in managing a service operation is what level of capacity will be provided. Too much may make the operation uneconomic; too little can cause bottlenecks in service delivery, customer resentment because of inefficiency and lost business. In some systems it is not easy to identify when peak loads will occur or to transfer them when they do (e.g. holiday resorts during a fine spring weekend). In manufacturing systems inventory acts as a buffer between the system and demands placed upon it. Most service systems do not have the luxury of such a buffer 'stock of service'. A constant difficulty then for many service operations is the balancing of supply and demand. Some ways of doing this are shown in Table 13.1.

Table 13.1
Actions to Balance Supply and Demand in Service Systems

Supply Side	*Demand Side*
1 Inventory wherever possible (e.g. spare capacity, people, etc.)	1 Have customers wait in favourable environments
2 Schedule workers according to demand (e.g. shift working, part-time employees)	2 Schedule customers (e.g. appointment systems)
3 Subcontract work to other service organizations	3 Provide substitute goods or services (e.g. automatic tellers)
4 Have peak-time efficiency routines (e.g. only do essential jobs)	4 Diversify demands (e.g. enter counter seasonal markets)
5 Increase customer participation in the production process (e.g. self-service)	5 Turn customers away during peak demand period (e.g. differential pricing)
6 Share services/facilities with other service organizations	6 Use marketing to shift demand (e.g. advertising campaigns)
7 Improve the service system (e.g. use technology where possible)	7 Change customer expectations of service (e.g. through usage)

(Based on various sources)

People involved in the Service Process

In Chapter 11 the role and influence of service personnel in service systems was considered. The point was made then that customers often judge the quality of a service and obtain satisfaction with a service, through the quality of the relationship they enjoy with service employees. Clearly the manner in which service employees conduct themselves, the quality of their training and their knowledge of the services available are important influences upon these satisfactions. But employees ultimately operate systems. Employees may do all they can to assist customers but they cannot compensate entirely for bad, inefficient and unfair systems.

In operations management there is a trade off between people and systems. Taking away discretion from service employees who operate a service system can make sound economic sense and result in a more standardized service. It may too mean cheaper service, perhaps of a uniformly more consistent quality. However it may only be achieved at the expense of employee job satisfaction. Tasks that are routinized and systematized may be less intellectually demanding and enriching for employees and may reduce their motivation. This in turn may have a harmful influence upon the quality of services they ultimately provide.

In high contact systems customers too are involved in the service delivery process. Service system design must take account of their reactions and motivation:

> '. . . consumers are involved in the production process. Consequently they are also an input to production. The thoughtful service manager should ask: How can our customers become more productive inputs to the creation of the services that we produce for them? And what marketing strategies can we use to influence their behaviour?'[6]

The demands which customers impose on service organizations determine service performers' behaviour. To modify the management of a service system it may be necessary first to modify the behaviour of service customers or to eliminate them from the system. Traditional economic theory identifies three ways in which productivity may be increased:

(a) improve the quality of the labour force;
(b) invest in more efficient capital equipment;
(c) automate tasks previously undertaken by labour.

Lovelock and Young[6] maintain that when dealing specifically with services a fourth component may be added: 'to change the ways consumers interact with service producers'. They recommend that there is a need to adopt a marketing perspective when changing service systems. For where operations management inspired changes in traditionally accepted service industry procedures directly affect customers, their acceptance of these changes cannot be assumed. Customer resistance can place a significant constraint upon the application of logical methods improvements. Even where the financial benefits from system changes may be apparent (e.g. self-service petrol stations): '. . . consumer resistance to changes in familiar environments and long established behaviour patterns can thwart attempts to improve productivity in service organisations.'[6]

Chase[3] proposes that these problems can be ameliorated, especially in high contact services, by demarcating service systems into 'technical core' or 'back room operations' and 'personal contact service'. Using this approach many significant productivity gains have been effected within the technical core (e.g. computerized bank transactions). However, even here, the customer may have some contact with technical core operations, no matter how indirect (e.g. computerized order coding). Again acquiescence to this cannot be assumed and a high degree of sensitivity to customer reactions must be maintained. Lovelock and Young[6] propose seven steps to help achieve the successful implementation of operations management changes:

(a) Develop customer trust
The willingness of customers to accept change may be a function of the organization's perceived trustworthiness.

(b) Understand customer habits
This will assist in successful presentation of the rationale for any changes.

(c) Pretest new procedures and equipment
Get an assessment of customer understanding and their reactions through field tests.

(d) Understand the determinants of consumer behaviour
Understand why customers behave the way that they do.

(e) Teach consumers how to use service innovations
Customers may be resistant to change particularly mechanization, and may need training and reassurance.

(f) Promote the benefits and stimulate trial
Acceptance is frequently a function of perceived customer benefits. If these are not apparent it is important that they should be promoted.

(g) Monitor and evaluate performance
An integral part of service system change is continuing monitoring, evaluation and modification.

These recommendations apply specifically to gaining customer approval although they could equally apply to the problem of ensuring service personnel acceptance of change.

Organizational Conflict in Service Systems

Some kinds of service systems involve managing many small units (multi-site operations), which may be dispersed geographically. Central operations may be limited to strategic decisions on matters like choosing new service sites, planning future service capacity, establishing personnel and training policies, controlling buying and financial control. But at the site or branch level managers have to operate the system. They occupy a key role with responsibilities for marketing, operations and personnel which makes service site operation much more of a 'general managerial' role. There is a good deal of influence and interdependence between functions which can lead to problems of conflict as site managers try to balance the needs of operations and marketing or operations and personnel. One major study has identified four general sources of interfunctional conflict between marketing and operations when a service firm is introducing a service innovation.[7] These are:

(a) Different motivations for change
Different functions may have varying motives for change (e.g. operations may be excited by a technical development, marketing by the possibility of increasing market share).

(b) Revenue versus cost orientation
     Operations managers tend to be concerned with efficiency and cost
     reduction, marketing managers with opportunities for increasing
     sales and revenue.
(c) Different time horizons
     Marketing may adopt a short-term orientation focusing on current
     concerns, operations a longer-term orientation to bring in new
     technology and operating procedures.
(d) Perceived fit of the new service with existing operations
     A new service product introduced by marketing may be incompati-
     ble and not fit existing operating systems.

Some ways in which service organizations try to overcome interfunctional conflict were identified in this research. They included:

(a) Interfunctional transfers
     Moving staff between different functions by job rotation.
(b) Task forces
     Task forces may be formed to integrate functional viewpoints and
     resolve interfunctional conflicts.
(c) New tasks and new people
     Redirecting existing staff and bringing in people from other parts of
     the business or from outside.
(d) Developing a marketing orientation at the field level

Field level managers can be encouraged to be more consumer orientated
by:

1 Decentralizing revenue responsibility
   Cost-based evaluations can be transformed into revenue-based evaluations.
2 Internal marketing
   Winning co-operation and acceptance of service innovations requires
   internal marketing as well as external marketing.
3 Control by procedures manuals
   Consumer-orientated procedures and controls can be developed and laid
   down in procedures manuals.

Organizational conflict may stem from the ethos and structure of a service
operation. For example, many multi-site service operations are organized
on line and staff principles. The line may be short and flat with many
operating units each with a manager. The motivation of each manager may
be influenced by how much discretion is given to run the site and how much
control and influence is exercised by the centre and those in staff roles.
Some service systems require a high level of delegation to the operating
manager on site and require high levels of initiative and motivation. Other
systems performing more standard kinds of services, may require rigid
adherence to centrally established procedures and standards and require
little in the way of managerial discretion on site. A particular difficulty in
service operations is deciding how tight control should be from the centre.

Too much control can be counterproductive and destroy motivation, too little can lead to widely varying standards of performance at each site.

Quality Control

Another difficulty, related to the previous point, is quality control. Many principles of quality control applicable in manufacturing, apply to services too.[8] Some of these include:

(a) quality control involves everyone in a service operation in visible and non-visible tasks;
(b) systems need to be used to identify quality failures, reward successes and help with improvements;
(c) quality control may be helped by replacing people with machines, particularly in routine tasks.

One American airline is said to operate service process quality standards dealing with matters like:

How long it should take for a customer to obtain a flight ticket;
How long it should take to unload baggage from planes;
How long a telephone should be allowed to ring before being answered.

The often-cited MacDonald's too has standards dealing with:

How often hamburgers are turned;
How long unsold hamburgers should be kept;
How long unsold French fries should be kept;
Cashiers should make eye contact with every customer and smile.

These unusual examples show that it is possible to establish quality control standards for service delivery processes though their development and implementation may be more difficult than in manufacturing setttings. In part many of the principles for improving productivity in service operations apply to improving quality (*see* Chapter 16). The use of mechanization, time and motion studies, standardization, specialization of labour, use of assembly line principles, better training, more job scheduling and attention to the organization of work are all principles that can be used for both purposes. Technology in particular has its uses, but also its limitations, as it is generally less flexible than people.[9]

The Systems Concept in Services[10]

The systems concept is widely used in operations management to model the fundamental nature of the conversion process in manufacturing (i.e. there is a logical sequence with inputs of raw materials passing through a conversion process in which technologies are applied, value is added and finished goods are produced). However applying this model is more difficult in some service systems because distinctions between inputs, conversions and outputs is less clear. For example, the transactional nature of many services may mean that certain steps are missed out or repeated. Also 'unintended conversions' may take place (e.g. a client may decide to run his own training programme after talking to a business school). Part of the problem is that it may not be as easy to seal off the technical core of a service system as in a manufacturing system, because tasks to be undertaken and workflow may be more uncertain. While some service systems may try to develop less open-ended systems through careful customer selection and socialization and through routinizing the conversion process; there is a danger that customer satisfaction may decrease as the service process moves towards a more closed system of operation.

There are some standard services where this problem may not occur. But clearly with some bespoke and personal services there are dangers in adopting too readily the tools and techniques of operations management without considering their impact upon the customer.

13.5 Summary

1 In service organizations co-operation between marketing and operations is vital. Both functions are concerned with how service systems operate. Customers judge services by the efficiency and effectiveness of service processes.
2 Operations management ideas and practices can be used in a variety of service organizations.
3 Service operating systems can be classified according to the type of process used and according to the degree of contact between customer and system.
4 Some operations management difficulties in services include establishing objectives, capacity utilization, people may be involved in the process, interfunctional conflict, quality control, the systems concept may not be easy to apply.

Questions for Discussion

1 Why should marketing be involved in operational aspects of service system performance?
2 Describe two ways in which service systems may be classified.
3 What difficulties are likely to occur, from an operational point of view, in high contact systems?
4 Describe the benefits of flowcharting a service system.
5 What difficulties do operations managers face in managing service systems?
6 Why does interfunctional conflict occur in service systems?
7 How might interfunctional conflict be resolved?
8 How do people influence service processes?
9 What problems occur in using technology to deliver services to customers?
10 'Service systems are more open than closed.' Discuss.

References and Notes

1 Some examples include Sasser, W. E., Olsen, R. P. and Wyckoff, D. D. *Management of Service Operations*, Allyn and Bacon, Boston, Mass. 1978; Buffa, E. S. *Elements of Production/Operations Management*, J. Wiley and Sons, New York, 1981.

2 This discussion is based on Sasser, W. E., Olsen, R. P. and Wyckoff, D. D. *Management of Service Operations*, Allyn and Bacon, Boston, Mass. 1978, pp. 81–6.

3 This discussion is based on Chase, R. B. 'Where does the customer fit in a Service Operation?', *Harvard Business Review*, Nov.–Dec. 1978, pp. 137–42.

4 Buffa, E. S. *Elements of Production/Operations Management*, J. Wiley and Sons, New York, 1981, p. 6.

5 Constable, C. J. and New, C. C. *Operations Management A Systems Approach*, J. Wiley and Sons, New York, 1976.

6 Lovelock, C. H. and Young, R. F. 'Look to customers to increase productivity', *Harvard Business Review*, Vol. 57, No. 2, 1979, pp. 168–78.

7 Langeard, E., Bateson, J. E. G., Lovelock, C. H., Eiglier, P. 'Services Marketing: New Insights from Consumers and Managers', Report No. 81–104, Marketing Science Institute, Cambridge, Boston, 1981.

8 'Towards service without a snarl', *Fortune*, 23 March, 1981, pp. 58–66.

9 'Services grow while the quality shrinks', *Business Week*, 30 Oct. 1971.

10 This section is based on Mills, P. K. and Moberg, D. J. 'Perspectives on the technology of service operations', *Academy of Management Review*, Vol. 7, No. 3, July 1982, pp. 467–78.

PART 3
**International Marketing of Services, Competition
Policy, Consumer Protection and Services
and Improving Productivity in Services**

14. *INTERNATIONAL MARKETING OF SERVICES*

14.1 Introduction

Britain is a trading nation depending for her livelihood on her ability to sell goods and services overseas. Yet nowhere is the neglect of services marketing more apparent than in the scant attention devoted to the services element of this overseas trade in works on marketing and overseas marketing. As Cateora and Hess[1] point out:

> 'When thinking of exporting or foreign marketing an image of some tangible product (a consumer durable, a piece of machinery or clothing) generally comes to mind. The intangible product or business service i.e. legal services, advertising, consulting, contractors, accountants, etc. is frequently overlooked as a subject of study.'

This lack of attention to services marketing overseas would be understandable if it formed a minor element of our overseas trade. But this is not the case. Services in fact account for a not insubstantial part of Britain's overseas earnings. While the trade in physical imports has tended to exceed the trade in physical exports over the years, it has been the income derived from the so-called 'invisibles' trade which has helped to make good the trade imbalance in physical items. Furthermore invisible trade is of great importance in world trade. While many activities in the service sector do not result in international transactions it is estimated that invisibles that do now account for between one-quarter and one-third of all current international payments.

This chapter outlines some of the main items contributing to Britain's trade in services; considers some of the barriers to trade in services; and indicates some of the main ways through which services organizations may operate in international markets.

14.2 Invisible Trade

The British Invisible Exports Council[2] define invisible trade as:

> ' "Invisible" earnings are basically earnings (whether in foreign currency or in sterling) from the provision of services to people living abroad ("invisible" exports) in direct contrast to "visible" exports which are derived from the sale of tangible goods abroad.'

> ' "Invisible" exports arise from a variety of activities, primarily in two ways. Either they are interest, profits or dividends earned by individuals or companies here from investments in foreign enterprises; or they are money received from foreigners in return for the provision of services. These are many and varied. The shipping of foreign goods by a British vessel, the insurance of a foreign factory, accounting advice given to a foreign client, the raising of capital in London by a foreign borrower, the performance of a British

play on Broadway: all are "invisible" and all lead to the earning of currency from foreigners.'

Another group of items usually covered by the term 'invisibles' are 'transfers'. Transfers refer to transfers of money between Britain and countries overseas like immigrant workers sending money home or government contributions to the European Economic Community. Such items are not relevant to our purpose here.

Table 14.1

World Invisible Trade: Total Invisible Receipts (excluding miscellaneous government transactions)

	1979 (U.S. $m)	% of World Total	1980 (U.S. $m)	% of World Total
United States	93,838	20.9	108,038	19.9
France	39,750	8.9	50,993	9.4
United Kingdom	42,867	9.6	49,963	9.2
West Germany	34,690	7.7	41,518	7.6
Belgium/Luxembourg	23,495	5.2	32,475	6.0
Italy	23,166	5.2	27,753	5.1
Netherlands	21,439	4.8	27,460	5.1
Japan	19,651	4.4	26,147	4.8
Switzerland	12,313	2.7	13,671	2.5
Spain	10,496	2.3	11,747	2.2
Austria	9,100	2.0	11,115	2.0
Canada	8,107	1.8	9,862	1.8
Mexico	6,659	1.5	8,415	1.6
Sweden	6,888	1.5	7,560	1.4
Singapore	4,850	1.1	6,213	1.1
Egypt	3,997	0.9	5,268	1.0
Australia	3,428	0.8	4,167	0.8
Yugoslavia*	3,432	0.8	4,062	0.7
Greece	3,441	0.8	3,980	0.7
South Africa	2,707	0.6	3,452	0.6
Brazil	2,658	0.6	3,078	0.6
Venezuela	1,919	0.4	3,057	0.6
Saudi Arabia	2,735	0.6	3,005	0.6
Argentina	1,810	0.4	2,718	0.5
Iran	4,137	0.9	2,668	0.5
Nigeria	1,297	0.3	1,976	0.4
Others	59,183	13.3	72,479	12.3
World Total	448,053	100.0	542,840	100.0

Exchange Rates: 1979   1.2920 U.S. $/SDR
             1980   1.3015 U.S. $/SDR

*Including miscellaneous government transactions.

Source: British Invisible Exports Council formerly the Committee on Invisible Exports, Annual Report, 1981–2, London, July 1982[3]

Table 14.2
World Invisible Trade (Net Receipts) Net Invisible Receipts
(excluding miscellaneous government transactions)

	1979 (U.S. $m)	1980 (U.S. $m)
United States	45,104	48,468
United Kingdom	10,997	10,443
France	6,755	7,444
Switzerland*	5,912	6,493
Italy	5,947	5,546
Spain	5,050	4,318
Singapore	2,218	2,752
Egypt	2,093	2,583
Greece	2,145	2,579
Austria	2,044	2,350
Belgium/Luxembourg	1,607	551
New Zealand	—1,194	—1,419
Libya	—1,539	—1,706
Yugoslavia*	—1,313	—1,839
Iran	—2,570	—2,408
Malaysia	—2,125	—2,896
Venezuela	—3,651	—3,122
Argentina	—2,362	—3,671
Sweden	—2,402	—3,263
South Africa	—2,531	—3,759
Nigeria	—2,874	—3,981
Algeria	—3,765	—4,311
Australia	—4,207	—4,792
Mexico	—2,870	—5,414
Indonesia	—4,873	—6,008
Canada	—8,389	—9,367
Brazil	—7,302	—9,846
Saudi Arabia	—8,760	—14,451
Japan	—14,212	—16,047
West Germany	—17,226	—18,780

*Including miscellaneous government transactions.

Source: British Invisible Exports Council formerly the Committee on Invisible Exports, Annual Report, 1981–2, London, July 1982

The world-wide trade in invisibles is huge amounting to nearly $550,000 million in 1980 as Table 14.1 shows. These data exclude transfers and certain government transfers (e.g. for keeping troops abroad). Table 14.1 shows the United States heads the league in countries involved in World Invisible Trade with around 20% of the world total. Britain, France, and West Germany account for about another 25% of the total; while the countries mentioned so far together with Belgium/Luxembourg, Italy, the Netherlands, Japan, Switzerland and Spain account for over 70% of the world total.

However not all of these countries have a surplus on their invisible trade. Interestingly West Germany and Japan, two of Britains sternest competitors in international markets, are among the list of countries which have a deficit on their invisible trade as Table 14.2 indicates. It is worth noting in contrast that the United Kingdom is second only to the United States in terms of the value of Net Invisible Receipts. The United Kingdom has been consistently a net creditor in her invisible trade account. In fact the importance of trade in invisibles to the United Kingdom balance of payments has been vital. It is estimated that in less than a dozen of the last two hundred years or so has the United Kingdom exported more goods than she has imported. Further the surplus on invisible earnings has usually made up the loss on visible trade. Currently invisible trade accounts for around one-third of total United Kingdom export earnings and import payments.

14.21 Major Contributors to the United Kingdom Invisible Trade

The importance of Invisible trade to United Kingdom performance in international markets is revealed in Table 14.3. This shows invisibles in the United Kingdom current account for the six years from 1976 to 1981. Noteworthy is that in each of these years the trade balance on Net Private Invisibles was in surplus and even taking account of Net Government Invisibles, there was still an Invisibles surplus each year. The visible trade balance on the other hand was only in surplus in 1980, largely due to the impact of the development of North Sea oil reserves.

Table 14.3
Invisibles in Britain's Current Account

(£ millions)	1976	1977	1978	1979	1980	1981
Gross Private Invisible Receipts*	14,279	15,865	17,516	21,902	23,397	26,472
Gross Private Invisible Payments*	9,128	11,050	12,013	15,958	18,215	19,836
Net Private Invisibles*	+5,151	+4,815	+5,503	+5,944	+5,182	+6,636
Net Government Invisibles	−2,103	−2,572	−3,016	−3,431	−3,234	−3,165
Invisibles Surplus (Private & Government)	+3,048	+2,243	+2,487	+2,513	+1,948	+3,471
Visible Trade	−3,929	−2,284	−1,542	−3,449	+1,185	†
Current Account Balance	−881	−41	+945	−936	+3,133	†

*Including public corporations.
†Figures not available

Source: British Invisible Exports Council formerly the Committee on Invisible Exports Annual Reports, 1981–2, London, July 1982

A breakdown of some of the main items contributing to the United Kingdom's invisible earnings is shown in Table 14.4. Excluding the surplus derived from Interest, Profits and Dividends (that is income arising from inward and outward investment like interest on money borrowed abroad or dividends produced by overseas investments), the prime earning sectors were Tourism, the City of London, Shipping and Construction work overseas.

Table 14.4
Some United Kingdom invisible earnings

(£ millions)		1976	1977	1978	1979	1980	1981	1982
Interest, Profits and Dividends (Private and Public Corporations)	Gross	3,718	3,648	4,457	7,063	7,435	9,356	10,175
	Net	2,013	837	1,207	1,422	420	1,925	2,377
Tourism to the UK*		1,768	2,352	2,507	2,797	2,961	2,970	3,184
UK ships† (net)		1,014	1,025	975	1,144	1,150	1,123	1,044
UK airlines (net)		316	337	438	341	350	323	358
UK construction work overseas:								
Consulting Engineers		214	305	370	401	423	487	565
Contractors and others‡		372	452	552	554	468	508	534
Royalties, licences, etc.		387	423	460	494	517	599	640
Telecommunications and postal services		119	165	210	155	316	284	334
Advertising		28	32	35	40	48	69	55
Films and television		59	84	107	114	156	128	147
The City of London§		1,813	1,807	2,388	1,983	2,292	3,514	4,369

*Totals exclude fares paid by foreign tourists to UK carriers.

†Ships owned by UK operators.

‡Covering fees of architects and quantity surveyors engaged on projects overseas, and the net earnings of UK building and civil engineering contractors (after deducting their local expenses) on projects managed direct from the UK.

§Some earnings in this category are also included in Interest, Profits and Dividends above.

Source: Compiled by author from the British Invisible Exports Council, formerly the Committee on Invisible Exports: Annual Report: 1981/82 London, July 1982 (for the years 1976 to 1979) and British Invisible Exports Council Information Card, October 1983 (for the years 1980 to 1982).

Tourism

In 1969 The Development of Tourism Act provided government support and assistance for Britain's tourism industry. Four statutory boards were established and one of them – the British Tourist Authority – is responsible for promoting Britain in overseas markets and has a general responsibility for tourism in Britain. The English, Scottish and Wales Tourist Boards are responsible for tourism in the respective countries. Tourism is an important and consistent earner of money for Britain and provides employment for hundreds of thousands. As Table 14.4 shows tourism earned Britain over £3,000 million in 1982 and it is estimated that around 12½ million visitors came to Britain. Also it is believed that about 1.5 million jobs are directly or indirectly supported by tourism in Britain.[4]

The City of London

The intermediary and financial services provided for international trading and marketing by United Kingdom financial and related institutions make a major contribution to the invisible trade balances as Table 14.4 reveals. Most of these services are provided by the City of London which is still regarded by many as the major banking and insurance centre of the world. The city has an unrivalled reputation for the provision of worldwide banking services. This is reflected in the worldwide connections it has through the many overseas banks and financial institutions represented in London whether as branches, representative offices, subsidiaries or consortia. For example, in 1980 there were 380 banks directly represented in London of which 75 were from America, 60 from non-E.E.C. countries, 55 from the E.E.C. and 25 from Japan.

The wide range of services available in the banking sector is backed by the power of the comprehensive and competitive insurance services available in the City. It is estimated that British insurers handle around 20% of business placed on the world market and the London market has become the world's leading centre for insurance. Most of it is provided by mutual or joint stock insurance companies or Lloyds' underwriters, although some of it is provided by banks and other organizations like friendly societies. There are over 800 companies authorized to carry out one or more categories of insurance business in Britain of which about 170 are overseas companies. Most of the large companies regard themselves as international insurers obtaining most of their premium income from international rather than purely domestic business. Around 300 companies belong to the British Insurance Association. They account for about 95% of worldwide business of the British Insurance companies market and about 55% of the general (non-life) business is carried on overseas.

Lloyds is an incorporated society of private insurers: it is not a company but a market for insurance where business is transacted by individual underwriters on their own account and at their own risk in competition with each other but in a strictly regulated way. There are over 18,000 underwriting members of Lloyds grouped into around 400 syndicates. Insurance may be placed through Lloyds' brokers who negotiate with the underwriters on behalf of the insured. Lloyds activities were originally based upon marine insurance business and it is in this context together with its worldwide intelligence system on shipping on which its reputation is based. However a substantial market for other insurance risks has grown up e.g. aviation and Lloyds now operates a worldwide market for a range of insurance business. The scale of these insurance operations together with other services earning invisible trade for Britain is shown in Table 14.5.

In addition to the fields of banking and insurance other activities based on London account for its stature as the major world financial services centre. The London Gold market whose five members meet twice a day to establish a London fixing price for gold acts as a reference point for gold dealings worldwide. The London foreign exchange market – providing

Table 14.5
What the City of London earns overseas

£ millions		1973	1980	1981	1982
Banking		159	457	1,340	1,656
Insurance:	Companies	157	297	321	366
	Lloyd's	139	341	382	475
	Brokers	60	238	302	362
Less:	Debits*	–9	–28	–29	–29
		347	848	976	1,174
Pension Funds		9	87	107	287
Baltic Exchange		53	181	287	254
Merchanting†		55	160	200	234
Commodities		110	180	160	215
Other Brokerage		21	123	137	146
Investment Trusts		33	82	91	116
Solicitors		13	61	68	75
Leasing		—	14	43	70
Unit Trusts		6	33	39	61
Stock Exchange		18	43	34	44
Lloyd's Register of Shipping		7	23	32	37
Total		831	2,292	3,514	4,369

*Direct investment income due to overseas parents of UK branches, etc.
†Profits on non-commodity third-country trade

Source: British Invisible Exports Council, formerly the Committee on Invisible Exports, Information Card, October 1983

those engaged in worldwide trade with foreign currencies for their transactions – is one of the most important in the world. Britain is an important international centre for transactions in many commodities like copper, cocoa, grain, sugar, coffee, tin, lead and zinc although many of the sales negotiated never pass through London. The location of these markets is more influenced by the availability in London of the 'external economies' associated with the links with finance, transport and insurance services rather than with London's importance as a centre for the physical movement of such commodities.

To some extent Britain's success in the field of marketing financial and related services internationally, particularly banking services, relies upon skills developed over the years and an inherited reputation. However it is an arena which has become much more competitive over the last decade. Writing of financial services McIver and Naylor[5] suggest that:

'No longer is international banking a relatively comfortable business of providing facilities for expansionist British firms and teaching the locals the rules of the game through overseas offices and correspondent banks. It is on the contrary a fiercely competitive

business in which the British banker operating from the base of a shaky economy has few
competitive advantages apart from his inherited reputation and professional skills.'

In the corporate market, for example, overseas banks operating in Britain
have established themselves and now provide around 30% of corporate
loans.[4] British banks have had to react defensively by concentrating on
customers most at risk from the inroads of overseas banks. They have also
mounted aggressive overseas efforts by developing business with non-
British clients in these markets as opposed to British originated international clients.

But it is not only the banks who have had to face stiff competition in
recent years. A service industry which has been on the defensive for a
number of years now is British shipping.

Shipping, Air Transport and Related Freight Services

An efficient transport and freight system is a necessity as well as an asset
for a country like Britain so heavily dependent on international trade.
Over the years a considerable invisibles trade market has been developed
through the experience and expertise obtained in moving goods and
people. Although the British merchant fleet has declined in size over
recent years through the world recession in shipping and intense
international competition (e.g. from the Soviet Union and Third World
Countries) it is still impressively large and modern. Britain has the fourth
largest merchant fleet in the world after Liberia, Greece and Japan (at 1
January 1980), there were over 1,500 United Kingdom owned and
registered vessels in the fleet and the average age was less than 7 years by
dead weight (at 1 July, 1979). Also Britain has a fleet with much
sophisticated tonnage capable of handling cargoes like liquified gases,
chemicals, refrigerated goods and nuclear material. In addition Britain
played and still plays an important role in the container revolution as more
and more trades are containerized.

The United Kingdom owned and registered fleet contributed over
£1,000 m net in 1982 to the balance of payments. This represents receipts
from abroad less payment abroad for bunkers and port and cargo handling
charges. Also a large part of these earnings are derived from 'cross trades'
i.e. carriage entirely away from the United Kingdom. What Britain has to
pay for foreign ships on charter to United Kingdom operators and to
overseas operators in practice reduces this net contribution to the smaller
net figure of around £60 m (for 1979). In addition to these earnings derived
from shipping London still acts as the largest centre for the chartering of
ships of all nationalities through the Baltic Exchange shown in Table 14.5.[6]

A large market in transportation too is provided through civil aviation.
Payments by overseas residents for fares, freight, mail and charter hire and
expenditures by foreign operators for airport landing fees, handling
charges and so on find their way into this category of earnings. Over 15%
of all world trade by value is now carried by air and in Britain's case (in
1979) around 20% of the value of all exports were carried by air and 17%
by value of all imports.[7]

Construction Work Overseas and other Services

This group includes a miscellany of items and it is in these industries that the largest growth occurred in the decade 1970–80 and in which there is the most substantial balance on the invisibles account. Included in this group, some of which are not shown in Table 14.4, are advice and consultancy offered abroad by advertisers, accountants, solicitors, architects, designers and builders. Technical expertise and skills whether provided by civil, electrical, electronic, mechanical and mining engineers or through the services of experts in agriculture make a substantial contribution. So too do services provided by colleges, universities and polytechnics. Royalties accrue on scientific, literary and artistic work: gambling brings in substantial sums. What are so often regarded as small and unimportant contributions to invisibles trade cumulatively are responsible for a large portion of the British surplus. In 1980, for example, film and television companies earned record sums from exports of their material.[8]

14.3 Problems Connected with Marketing Services Internationally

The principles of marketing services internationally are the same as those which apply to domestic markets. Clearly the notions of setting clear marketing objectives, defining and selecting target markets, developing appropriate marketing strategies and marketing mixes and controlling marketing efforts are the same. What is different are the environmental contexts – social, political, economic, legal and cultural – to which marketors need to adjust. The nature of such environmental forces are given detailed treatment in many texts on international marketing – albeit in product marketing settings – and will not be repeated here.[1] Their absence is in no way a measure of their unimportance. There are however few illustrations of how such influences affect service organizations specifically. Three strands of evidence which are available relate to:

(*a*) the risks of international marketing for service organizations;
(*b*) problems of adaptation to and operation in overseas markets;
(*c*) barriers to trade in services.

The Risks of International Marketing for Service Organizations

Carman and Langeard[9] have suggested that while internationalization represents a growth strategy for service firms they also believe that:

(*a*) out-of-country expansion is a more risky strategy for a service firm than, for example, concentric diversification or new service development in existing markets;
(*b*) out-of-country expansion is more risky for a service business than it is for a manufacturer of physical items.

They base their argument for the relatively greater risks involved for service businesses in out-of-country expansion on the fact that out-of-country expansion by ·product manufacturers can be undertaken more gradually. Manufacturers can learn from their gradual experience. Service marketors on the other hand: '. . . must go to the country, face the customer, and produce the service. With simultaneous production and receipt, exporting is out. The seller must produce on foreign soil and must deal directly with the customer.' Added to this difficulty are the problems of establishing immediate on-site quality control, personnel difficulties and know-how difficulties which they believe are greater for service organizations; again because gradual learning about an out-of-country market cannot be accomplished so easily. Gronroos[10] also shares these views.

Problems of Adaptation to and Operation in Overseas Markets

Carmen and Langeard also suggest that service marketors may have a more difficult time with the host government than product marketors:

'the service firms rank just behind the raw material extractors as the firms that take the most out of a country and leave little. There is little capital inflow into the country, little or no technological transfer, and the service firm usually does little to upgrade the training of workers.'

This is an interesting but a controversial view and requires most empirical evidence to substantiate the claims made. Gaedeke[11] identified problems that applied particularly to advertising, consulting and legal firms. These were the lack of qualified staff to meet needs below the level of the key positions. Also:

'Adjusting to foreign business practices, client expertise and the culture in general; gaining client confidence; and overcoming national hostilities were additional challenges faced by all firms initially. As a group, the adjustment to overseas business practices and client expertise was the greatest barrier faced by advertising firms, while consulting firms experienced most difficulties in gaining client confidence and law firms had to meet the problems of overcoming national hostilities.
'A major problem encountered today by both consulting and law firms is the maze of host government laws and industry rules.'

Barriers to Trade in Services

In the previous section the terms 'invisibles' and 'services' were used somewhat interchangeably. In discussing barriers to services trade it is necessary to distinguish further between:[12]

(a) the flow of currently produced services;
(b) the movement of capital which is the source of these services;
(c) the earnings of direct foreign investment concerned with the production of goods;
(d) interest payments on short-term capital movements.

A more appropriate distinction for our purposes is between the flow and marketing of currently produced services and the movement of capital which may or may not be concerned only with services. Thus services in this context refers to part of the area covered by the term invisibles. The barriers to services marketing with which we are concerned here are those which relate specifically to foreign produced services and cover discriminatory measures in the fields of banking, insurance, transport, consultancy services and so forth. Also of general significance are the restrictions which may operate on capital movements, like investing in a foreign country or the remission of earnings on such investments or on private portfolios. Where these restrictions are more general in kind it is recognized that such constraints can have discriminatory side effects on efforts to market services. For example restrictions on capital movements may deter a service company from setting up a service operation in an overseas country in the first place, just as they may deter a manufacturer from building a factory.

In a major study which examined the barriers to trade in services and other invisibles the following general restrictions were identified.[12]

(a) Restriction on Foreign Competition

A service organization may be excluded by law, by a restrictive licensing system, by tariffs (i.e. taxes), by takeover or by nationalization. Examples include bilateral arrangements on use of shipping between various South American countries: legislation in various countries prohibiting insurance abroad for certain kinds of risks and the limitation in most countries that internal routes are reserved for domestic airlines.

(b) Government Procurement

Discrimination practised in favour of national producers e.g. for services like shipping by the United States.

(c) Exchange Control

Limitations exercised over the purchase of foreign exchange for buying foreign produced services e.g. restrictions on the amount of foreign currency for overseas travel.

(d) Constraints on Choice of Product Mix

Constraints may be placed on the product mix foreign firms can offer e.g. in shipping services which may be offered.

(e) Constraints on Choice of Factor Input Mix

The amount of capital or local labour that must be employed may be specified e.g. in the employment of local nationals in a service like banking.

In addition to the above controls may be exercised over the payment of interest on deposits, on the amount of foreign borrowing and lending, taxes may be set to prevent the outflow of capital and higher bank reserve requirements may be specified for non-residents than residents.

Such barriers to trade of course have their equivalents in the marketing of tangibles where tariffs, quotas and embargoes may be employed to limit the extent and the impact of foreign competition. Also the arguments in favour of their imposition are much the same in both contexts:

the need to protect infant industries;
the need for certain industries to remain under domestic control;
the need for a means of retaliation by one country against the discriminatory practices of another;
the need to improve the balance of payments for particular countries instituting such barriers.

However the recognition of the role of 'invisible barriers to invisible trade' has led in recent years to a growing interest in the extent to which the trade in services may be made more free. For its part the British Invisible Exports Council formed a new Committee, the Liberalization of Trade in Services Committee (LOTIS) with a membership drawn from banking, insurance, shipping and consultancy sectors. Its initial role consists of trying to co-ordinate the views of the United Kingdom service industries on reducing trade barriers. By doing so it will act as a source of advice and counsel to Government Departments and official negotiators representing the United Kingdom in international meetings where trade liberalization is discussed like the GATT ministerial meeting in November 1982.

14.31 Free Trade in Services

A move towards freer trade in services is the policy of the current U.S. administration and the British government. Both could benefit, as indeed could other industrialized countries from greater liberalization in the field. Although American attempts to remove barriers to international trade in services in the early 1970s met with little success, it has been suggested that the opening up of trade in services in the 1980s could be as important as was the Kennedy Round of multilateral trade negotiations in the 1960s or the Tokyo Round of multilateral trade negotiations in the 1970s.[13] There are though a number of important problem areas to be resolved if freer trade is to be encouraged. Three of importance are:

(*a*) What constitutes a trade restriction in the service sector?
An actor who cannot appear in London because of restrictive practices, it can be argued, is just as much a victim of protectionism as is an airline prevented from operating on a certain route or a bank unable to set up operations in another country. The diversity of the service sector makes it difficult to generalize about trade restrictions.[12]

(*b*) What is an appropriate forum where such issues can be raised?
G.A.T.T., O.E.C.D., and the International Chambers of Commerce have all at one time or another looked at the area of services though it is generally felt that G.A.T.T., with its experience of trade liberalization for goods may make a more appropriate forum for discussion on freer trade in services.

(*c*) What is the best way of developing a more liberal policy?
Is it better to look across the board at all services trading which

seems to be the U.S. approach and laying down a set of principles for them or to take a sector by sector approach? Would bilateral arrangements on a sectoral basis set the ground for development of a wider basis?

An illustration of the difficulties, which can occur, is the United Kingdom attempts within the E.E.C. to create a free market for services. So far this has not met with success though the signs are that a freer trade in non-life insurance may develop in the E.E.C. over the next few years. Ministers agreed in 1981 to remove the necessity for insurance companies to win an 'authorization' from another Government if they want to establish business in the country concerned. Instead the right to establish will be presumed and it will be up to the host Government to 'verify' that the proper procedures are being followed.[14] If such liberalization of trade in services does occur in the E.E.C. in insurance and in other fields then it will give the member countries experience of the sorts of difficulties that may occur in practice but also make it easier for them to negotiate internationally with other non-E.E.C. Governments.

14.4 Obtaining Overseas Business

Overseas markets may offer attractive opportunities for services marketors and the reasons for entry are varied. It may be because:

market share is being lost in domestic markets as a result of increased competition (e.g. in the corporate banking sector);
saturation of the domestic market and the need to seek new customers (e.g. franchise operations);
inducements to seek overseas customers (e.g. through Government aid and awards like the Queens Award to industry);
there is potential unsatisfied demand overseas.

In Britain the British Invisible Exports Council specifically undertakes promotional activities overseas. These are usually in the form of conferences, missions and top level discussions to promote Britain's services. In cataloguing some of the impacts of such activities the Council reports on a range of achievements like:[2]

setting up banks;
making leasing finance arrangements;
obtaining insurance contracts;
advising on the establishment of a stock exchange;
opening up an air route;
obtaining a contract for a City Solicitor;
financing a hydro electricity project;
tourist developments;

in settings as diverse as South Korea, Canada, the Phillipines, Brazil, Italy, Venezuela, Denmark, Malaysia and Portugal. Also it was reported that fourteen invisible exporters were among the winners of the Queen's Award for Export Achievement in 1981. The winners came from many fields including three engineering consultants and contractors, a Lloyds Under-writing agency, an aircraft overhaul company, a haulage company, a construction company, two commodity brokers and traders, a freight forwarding company, a firm of computer consultants, a company engaged in fire protection, a racing car design company and a firm specializing in the operation and maintenance of oil fields. In 1982 there were 15 invisible exporters who received the Queen's Award for Export Achievement. Their range of activities covered engineering and civil engineering consultants, aircraft overhaul, shipping, hotels, merchant banking, a law college, medical and pharmaceutical research, computer software and systems, computer consultancy and educational films.[3]

Gronroos[10] quotes the case of a Swedish publicly-owned consulting company which discovered an international demand for government administrative systems. Projects on which it was or expected to be working included a tax system for Venezuala, an administration system for Trinidad and automobile and driving licence register systems for several Middle East States. Also Gaedeke[11] indicated in a U.S. study of advertising, consulting and legal firms that following existing clients abroad was a prime reason for expanding overseas. Nearer home, the encouragement of overseas tourists to visit Britain by the British Tourist Authority and the attempts to encourage foreign direct investment by a local authority[14] are reminders that marketing to overseas customers may mean bringing them to the domestic market as well as setting up a service operation overseas. Whatever the reasons for selling, overseas organizations have a number of initial market entry strategies open to them.

14.41 Direct Export

Direct export represents one way in which services may be offered in overseas markets. A consultant, a designer, a teacher, a catering company may be given an overseas assignment based on hearsay, experience, books, articles, publications and so forth. In all these cases the provider of the service may be approached by the potential buyer. This method of entry may involve working out of the home market or it may involve establishing an overseas office as in the case of a consultancy organization.

14.42 Joint Ventures

Joint ventures represent another way in which service organizations can get involved in overseas markets. A joint venture is the formation of a partnership and association with someone in the overseas market. A number of types of joint venture are appropriate for service marketing operations.

(a) Licensing

This term covers a range of agreements relating to the sale or leasing of a process, trademark, formula, secret or some other item of value by one party to another. Payment may be made in a number of forms for a licence such as a direct fee for know-how, an annual flat rate payment for usage, a fee or royalty based on sales or profits or some cross-licensing agreement such as the mutual interchange of expertise. From the licensor's viewpoint this can be a relatively easy and low risk way to gain market entry. It may require little capital investment though care is needed over the drafting of the licensing agreement and the maintenance of service product quality. There are the ultimate dangers that the licensee may not make the most of opportunities available in the overseas market thereby attracting competitors; on the other hand when the licensing agreement expires the licensor may have a strongly entrenched competitor where the licensee has been actively market orientated. The skill with licensing is to maintain the mutual advantages of working together thus ensuring continued interdependence. This can usually be achieved by the licensee maintaining a regular flow of ideas, innovations and help to the licensor.

Users of the licensing system of entry to overseas services markets include Scientific Methods Inc., whose licensors acquire the rights to use the Managerial Grid concept and Sales Grid concept for use in management and sales courses.[10] Also Manpower Inc. (whose service is the provision of temporary office help) have been successful in licensing its operations. Winter[15] suggests that while licensing may present problems (e.g. legal difficulties) it offers a chance to set up local operations in more nationalistic countries. Elements contributing to the success of a licensing operation he suggests include a strong name, a well-designed marketing strategy, a complete operational system including management training, recruitment assistance, advertising advice, and a substantial opportunity for profit for the licensor. Licensing a service operation requires know-how which is tried and tested.

(b) Franchising

Franchising is a form of licensing where the franchiser provides the package of products, operational systems, management services and advice and the franchisee the capital, market knowledge and personal involvement in the management of the operation. It differs from licensing in that it provides a greater degree of control over the ingredients and system and service components in use. It usually applies to smaller scale operations, more widely represented in the overseas market and is effectively a form of vertical integration with the advantages of centralized control over skills and knowledge but decentralized operational networks.

Franchising in the United Kingdom is most commonly associated with food organizations like MacDonald's, Wimpy and Kentucky Fried Chicken. However many services are now supplied by franchise organizations including hotels, motels, equipment rentals, employment services, dry cleaning stores, launderettes and car rentals. In addition franchising operates in markets like vehicle repairs, drain clearing and building and window cleaning services. Franchising in Britain is by no means an

American invention although many services operated here are imported systems. But British developed systems have been exported too and though these are primarily associated with retail organizations of different kinds like Marks and Spencer and hotel groups like Trust House Forte, notable franchise organizations operating overseas include the Tack Organization – the sales and management training business – as well as that peculiarly British export, the prefabricated British pub. Franchising presents an opportunity for service organizations to enter overseas markets. One of the newest of such organizations to enter Britain is Realty World Corporation (UK) which is introducing estate agent franchising during 1982[16] a concept that is already well-established in America. The conservative reaction of the Royal Institute of Chartered Surveyors to this move is indicative of the kind of problems that can arise in attempting to transfer a soundly-based franchise concept into a different market overseas!

(c) Joint Ownership Ventures

This provides another way in which service organizations can enter overseas markets. Two or more organizations may work together in an overseas market a strategy which may be necessary because of the costs of going it alone in a new market, because of local political requirements (e.g. joint ownership as a condition of market entry) or because of limited resources available (e.g. management). Some of the main weaknesses with this approach are the conflicts that may occur over managerial decisions between the interested parties, together with differences of culture, business practices, style of management and communication breakdown arising from language and distance problems. It is suggested however that where a service company joins with a local company both potentially may benefit from such an arrangement. The local company may acquire know-how, ideas and capital while the overseas party will gain the advantages of local knowledge of the market and a ready-made base for service operations.[10]

(d) Management Contracting

Management contracting is where an organization provides management skills only in the overseas market in return for fees or some share of profits or sales. A method which offers low risk entry into overseas markets, gives a quick return and uses existing skills: its disadvantages are the possibilities of interference by locally based investors and the fact that the scarce management skills could be used elsewhere, more productively and profitably. Examples of this method of operation are commonplace. Hilton Hotels manage hotels throughout the world under this system while the services of educational administrators and academics who help to establish practices and systems in overseas institutions provides another example. Mr Ian McGregor's tenure as Chairman of British Steel also is typical of such a contractual arrangement.

(e) Acquisition

Purchasing all or the majority of the shares in an organization overseas is another way for service organizations to move into international markets. There may be restrictions (e.g. legal) on such a move or there may be opposition from the overseas shareholders to such a manoeuvre. But if it is possible it offers the immediate prospect of market entry and revenue earning through an organization that is already established with staff, contacts and market knowledge. In a study of internationalization of U.S., advertising agencies Weinstein observed that agencies adopting an acquisition strategy did so to learn about local work conditions and customers.[17] Gronroos[10] indicates that the Danish cleaning company, International Service System A/S has frequently used this strategy. In 1981 examples of British companies acquiring overseas organizations included the Midland Bank acquisition of the U.S. based Crocker Bank and the Legal and General Insurance Company acquisition of 66% of the shares of the U.S. based Government Employees Life Assurance Company, giving it an entree to the life insurance market in that country.[18]

14.5 Future of Invisible Trade

Invisible trade makes a substantial contribution to Britain's trade balances. Some forecasters suggest that Britain's economic future is in fact likely to be more closely linked to performance in the service sectors included in this business rather than in manufacturing industries. Whether this is so is uncertain. What is more predictable however is:

(*a*) The surplus on private invisible trade is likely to fall in the short-term because of the large part of North Sea Oil owned by foreign companies and the profits and dividends that will be paid to these overseas companies. On the other hand the visible trade balance should improve because of the need to import less oil and the growth of oil exports.

(*b*) Britain will face increasing competition in invisible trade as local capacity overseas grows particularly from new trading countries such as Hong Kong and Singapore as well as more established competitors like the United States. Britain's dominance of sea transport has been eroded over the years and her strong position in other service sectors will come under pressure. Whether Britain can maintain or increase her present share of world trade in invisibles will depend upon many factors including:

(i) Government support and recognition of the importance of invisible trade as a major contributor to wealth production e.g. through incentives to encourage tourism.

(ii) Nationalistic tendencies in overseas markets which may give preference to locally provided services.

(iii) More efficient and effective operation in international markets. To some extent this will be influenced by the strength of the £ and its exchange rate e.g. in sectors like tourism.

(iv) How much new investment is made abroad e.g. through North
Sea Oil revenue, to boost interests, profits and dividends from
abroad.

(v) Opportunities taken to reduce Government expenditure abroad
through, for example, reductions in military expenditure and
through further cuts in our contribution to the E.E.C.

(vi) The easing of restrictions on the freer marketing of services, by
professions, governments and international organizations (e.g.
the E.E.C.).

As far as the world outlook for invisibles is concerned the British Invisible
Exports Council recognize that the global market in services and return
on overseas investment – about 25% of world trade – are dependent upon
overall economic growth. While the immediate prospects for growth are
mixed between different service sectors experience suggests that any
upturn in invisibles trade follows a year or so after an upturn in economic
growth.

14.6 Summary

1 Invisible trade is an important element of Britain's overseas trade
earnings. Britain is near the top of the world league table in world trade
in invisibles.

2 Major contributions to invisible trade include tourism, the City of
London, transport and construction work overseas.

3 Problems of marketing services internationally include greater risks,
adapting to overseas environments and barriers to trade.

4 Methods of obtaining overseas business for services include direct export
and joint ventures of various kinds.

5 Britain is likely to face increasing competition in invisible trade. There
will be a number of influences upon whether she can maintain her
current share of world invisibles trade.

Questions for Discussion

1 How important are services to Britain's balance of payments?

2 Is marketing services internationally different from marketing goods?

3 What limitations operate on selling services internationally?

4 What methods of entering overseas markets may be used by service
marketors?

5 If Britain declines as an exporter of goods, can she expect to be able to
increase her exports of services to compensate?

6 What is the difference between 'invisibles' and 'services'?

7 Which sectors of the service economy contribute most to Britain's
invisible exports?

8 What future do you think Britain has in the sectors you have identified?

9 Do services require separate treatment in any analysis of International
Trade? Why?

10 What new kinds of services might Britain export in the next decade?

References and Notes

1 Cateora, P. R. and Hess, J. M. *International Marketing*, Irwin 1975, p. 380.
2 The British Invisible Exports Council formerly the Committee on Invisible Exports, Annual Report, 1980–1 London, July 1981.
3 The British Invisible Exports Council, Annual Report, 1981–2, London, July 1982.
4 *British Business*, 26 Sept. 1980, p. 131.
5 McIver, C. and Naylor, G. *Marketing Financial Services*, Institute of Bankers, 1980, p. 233.
6 Some of this material is derived from the British Shipping Review for 1979 and for 1980 both published by the General Council of British Shipping 30–2 St Mary Axe, London EC3A 8ET.
7 *Britain 1981*, H.M.S.O., 1981.
8 *Daily Telegraph*, report 4 Sept. 1981.
9 Carman, J. M. and Langeard, E. 'Growth Strategies for Service Firms', Paper presented to the 8th Annual Meeting of the European Academy for Advanced Research in Marketing, Groningen (The Netherlands), 10–12 April 1979.
10 Gronroos, C. Service Oriented International Marketing Strategies: an overview, Working Paper No. 16, Swedish School of Economics and Business Administration, Finland, 1979.
11 Gaedeke, R. M. 'Selected U.S. Multinational Service firms in perspective', *Journal of International Business Studies*, Spring 1973, pp. 61–6.
12 Much of this material is based upon Professor B. Griffiths' small but valuable book *Invisible barriers to Invisible Trade*, MacMillan, for Trade Policy Research Centre, London, 1975.
13 *Financial Times* Leader, 9 June 1981.
14 *Daily Telegraph* report 15 June 1981 and *Financial Times* report 18 Sept. 1981.
15 Taylor, F. 'Marketings Application to Local Authority Foreign Industrial Promotion', Paper presented at MEG Conference, 9–12 July Bristol 1979.
16 Winter, E. L. 'How to License a Service', *Columbia Journal of World Business* (Sept.–Oct. 1970) pp. 83–5.
17 *Financial Times* report 4 Oct. 1980.
18 Weinstein, A. K. 'Foreign investments by service firms: The case of Multinational Advertising Agencies', *Journal of International Business Studies*, Spring/Summer 1977.
19 *Daily Telegraph* report 17 Sept. 1981.

15. *COMPETITION POLICY, CONSUMER PROTECTION AND SERVICES MARKETING*

15.1 Introduction

Two features of government policy which affect services marketing are the measures taken to encourage competition and the measures taken to control practices which are considered to be restrictive or anti-competitive. Coupled with these are the policies employed to encourage fair trading and protect consumers. Competition policy and consumer protection are becoming issues of great importance in the service sector of the economy.

Many government departments exercise some functions with regard to competition policy and consumer protection. However the main department concerned with such matters is the Department of Trade and Industry. The Minister of State for Consumer Affairs, who is answerable to the Secretary of State of Trade and Industry, has special responsibilities for competition policy and on consumer matters. These include trading standards, fair trading, weights and measures, consumer credit and consumer safety. Significant agencies of government for whose work the Secretary of State is ultimately responsible include the Monopolies and Mergers Commission and the Office of Fair Trading. The latter is headed by the Director General of Fair Trading. This chapter gives an outline of how competition policy and consumer protection apply in services markets.

15.2 Competition Policy

Over the years the competition policies of different governments in Britain have led to the development of procedures and methods for examining and controlling monopolies and mergers, anti-competitive practices and restrictive trade practices. The current situation (1983) is that the Director General of Fair Trading administers the Fair Trading Act 1973 which regulates monopolies and mergers; the Competition Act 1980 which regulates anti-competitive practices; and the Restrictive Trade Practices Acts 1976 and 1977 which regulate restrictive trading agreements.[1] These three areas of competition policy – Monopolies and Mergers, Anti-competitive Practices and Restrictive Trade Practices – are examined in turn with specific reference to services.

15.21 Monopolies and Mergers

The Secretary of State for Trade and Industry and the Director General of Fair Trading can refer monopolies for investigation to the Monopolies and Mergers Commission. A monopoly is defined in law as a situation where at least a quarter of a particular kind of goods or service is supplied by, or to, a single person, or two or more people acting in a common manner. Local monopolies which prevent, restrict or distort competition as well as public monopolies can be referred to the Commission. Where a monopoly is found to operate against the public interest the Secretary of State for Trade has powers to make orders and to remedy and prevent the harm which may exist. Alternatively, the Director General of Fair Trading may be asked to negotiate undertakings to remedy the effects identified by the Commission. The Commission does not distinguish between goods and services.

During 1981 the Monopolies and Mergers Commission reported on a number of services. These included Roadside Advertising Services where a monopoly was found to exist and remedial measures were adopted. The Commission also found that the monopoly position enjoyed by British Posters Limited and its ten member companies operated against the public interest. The Commission recommended that the company should be broken up and not reformed. This occurred during 1982.

Proposals for a merger may be referred to the Commission by the Secretary of State for Trade and Industry if it would result in a monopoly (25% market share) or if gross assets taken over exceed £15m (formerly £5m until April 1980). If the Commission finds the merger to be against the public interest the Secretary of State can prevent it from taking place or reverse it if it has already taken place. Two recently approved mergers in the service sector have been that between British Rail Hovercraft and Hoverlloyd and that between Godfrey Davis Car Rental with Europcar (both approved during 1981).

One effect of the increased Assets criterion necessary for consideration by the Commission has been to reduce the number of mergers examined by the Office of Fair Trading. As Table 15.1 shows, in 1980, 182 mergers were examined by the office. Of these the largest number were in the Distributive Trades and the Insurance, Banking and Finance sectors. The service sector as a whole (roughly comparable to SIC orders 21 to 26 on the table) accounted for 88 out of the 182 examined or about 48% of the total.

In 1981 164 mergers were considered. The financial and distribution sectors continued to be major areas for merger and the Director General reported that an increasing number had taken place in the leisure and entertainment fields.

Table 15.1 is not an accurate reflection of all merger activity in Britain as there are special provisions relating to newspapers (like the Lonrho takeover of *The Observer*) and certain other mergers.

The Director General of Fair Trading refers in his annual report to the work of the Monopolies and Mergers Commission. The 1980 Report[2] for example referred to the investigation on UK credit card franchise services. In this case the Commission recommended that the 'no discrimination'

Table 15.1

Merger Activity (analysis by main activity, number, asset size and nationality of target companies)

SIC Order		Number	Average Assets £m	assets £m	Foreign Companies Target	Bidding Number
1	Agriculture, forestry, fishing	1	8.0	8.0	1	0
2	Mining and quarrying	4	340.2	85.1	3	1
3	Food, drink and tobacco	19	776.8	40.8	8	6
4	Coal and petroleum products	1	15.0	15.0	1	0
5	Chemical and allied industries	8	154.5	19.3	3	4
6	Metal manufacture	5	74.7	14.9	1	0
7	Mechanical engineering	11	397.9	36.2	5	3
8	Instrument engineering	1	21.0	21.0	0	0
9	Electrical engineering	9	1,393.0	154.8	4	5
10	Shipbuilding and marine	3	78.0	26.0	0	1
11	Vehicles	5	224.2	44.8	1	6
12	Metal goods NES	6	185.9	31.0	1	0
13	Textiles	3	137.1	45.7	0	1
14	Leather goods and fur	0	0.0	0.0	0	0
15	Clothing and footwear	0	0.0	0.0	0	0
16	Bricks, pottery, glass, cement	6	379.7	63.3	2	1
17	Timber, furniture	3	45.0	15.0	3	3
18	Paper, printing and publishing	4	285.2	71.3	2	0
19	Other manufacturing	1	0.7	0.7	0	0
20	Construction	4	71.5	17.9	2	1
21	Gas, electricity and water	1	510.0	510.0	1	0
22	Transport and communication	6	426.5	71.1	1	4
23	Distributive trades	21	1,092.5	52.0	5	4
24	Insurance, banking and finance	51	15,176.5	297.6	19	20
25	Professional and scientific	1	1.4	1.4	0	0
26	Miscellaneous services	8	494.3	61.8	2	0
	Total	182	22,289.3	122.5	65	60

Source: Annual Report of the Director General of Fair Trading, HMSO, London, 1981.

policy between cash and credit being pursued was against the public interest. This was reflected in garages, making an additional charge on petrol sales where a credit card was used to make a purchase. The Director also reported that previous reports from the Commission relating to services still be considered by ministers included:

(a) whether individual solicitors should have greater freedom to advertise their services as he had recommended. This took place in 1984. (Certainly in the US where advertising restrictions have been lifted, the American Bar Association has reported that the profession's new-found freedom has resulted in new clients and lower fees);

(b) that discussions were continuing on the removal of restrictions on advertising of veterinary surgeons' services and accountants' services. (In the 1981 report the Director General reported the progress made; the four main professional accountancy bodies had agreed to amend their rules to permit members to advertise their professional services in local newspapers and other local publications)[3];

(c) in respect of other services the Director General reported that as far as architects' services were concerned the Office of Fair Trading was having difficulty during 1980 in obtaining an undertaking from the professions for a more competitive fee system. (Interestingly, an internal poll during 1980 showed 28% of the profession to be against advertising by architects);

(d) the Institute of Quantity Surveyors was reported to be moving towards a more competitive fee policy. (The conservatism of the profession at this time was however reflected in the opposition to the move by the Abbey National Building Society when it began to reveal the contents of surveyor's valuations to prospective house-buyers. This practice has since been followed by other building societies.)

By the time of the 1981 report the Director General was able to report that his discussions with the professional bodies representing veterinary surgeons, architects and surveyors were concluded and advice had been submitted to the Secretary of State.

15.22 Anti-Competitive Practices

The Competition Act has been on the statute book since 1980. This abolished the Price Commission, transferring some of its powers to the Director General of Fair Trading and the Monopolies and Mergers Commission. Subject to certain exemptions the Director General is now empowered to investigate anti-competitive practices in the public or in the private sector. Such practices should have, or are intended, or likely to have, the effect or restricting, distorting or preventing competition in the production, supply or acquisition of goods or services in Britain. The Director may also investigate particular prices and charges on reference by the Secretary of State. If, as a result of enquiries, an anti-competitive practice is found then the Director General can either refer the matter to the Monopolies and Mergers Commission or accept an undertaking to remove the practice by the business under investigation. If the Monopolies and Mergers Commission finds the practice against the public interest it can recommend remedial action to the Secretary of State, who is ultimately empowered to make an order prohibiting the practice.

One novelty of the Act is that the Secretary of State may also refer to the Commission any question relating to the costs and efficiency of the services provided or the possible abuse of monopoly power by named bodies in the public sector (i.e. nationalized industries). The Commission however cannot take account of the financial obligations and objectives imposed upon such a public body by statute or ministerial direction. Nor may it consider conduct permitted by the Restrictive Trade Practices Act [*see* Section 15.23]. A recent illustration of the work of the Commission in its investigation of public bodies was the controversy raised over the hold

British Gas had over the supply of gas appliances through over 200 gas showrooms in the United Kingdom. The Commission recommended that British Gas should discontinue its retailing function but implementation has been fiercely opposed.[4]

On the working of the Competition Act 1980, the Director General of Fair Trading concluded in his report for 1980[2] that, at that time, it was too early to assess its effects. However, he did report that the number of complaints received which had justified preliminary enquiries were smaller than might have been expected. He did not however differentiate between those concerning goods and those concerning services.

15.23 Restrictive Trade Practices and Services

Restrictive Trade Practices have to be registered with the Director General of Fair Trading under the Restrictive Trade Practices Act, 1976. Basically an agreement has to be registered if two or more parties to the agreement who are engaged in business in Britain accept some limitation on their actions in matters connected with such things as:

(*a*) charges to be made for services;
(*b*) the terms or conditions of supply of such services;
(*c*) the extent to which such services are made available;
(*d*) the form or manner in which such services are to be made available;
(*f*) the persons or classes of person for whom services are to be made available.

If an agreement is not registered any restrictions are void and the parties involved are liable to legal action. Equally, registered agreements may be referred to the Restrictive Practices Court by the Director General of Fair Trading to decide, according to criteria laid down in the Act, whether the agreement is against the public interest. The Act chiefly attempts to prevent 'market sharing'.

In practice though many services are excluded from the provisions of the Act. These include:

(*a*) Professional services such as:
       legal services of barristers, advocates, and solicitors;
       medical, dental and ophthalmic services;
       veterinary services;
       nursing and midwifery services;
       architects' services;
       accounting and auditing services;
       patent agents services;
       surveyors' services;
       the services of minsters of religion;
       the services of professional engineers and technologists;
       financing terms (e.g. making a loan).
(*b*) Services relating to:
       international sea transport;
       carriage by air;

road passenger transport;
building societies;
financial control by the Treasury of the Bank of England;
banking services (in Northern Ireland);
insurance services;
unit trust schemes;
implementation of decisions of the city panel on takeovers and mergers.

In addition to the above, other exclusions to the Act may apply. These include agreements authorized by Statute, certain agricultural and marketing agreements, know-how agreements, and agreements affecting exports. The Secretary of State is also empowered to exclude agreements of 'importance to the national economy'.

These exclusions obviously cover many services within the service sector of the economy. While it can be argued in respect of certain professional services that restrictive practices can be justified because they protect the consumer (e.g. from those unqualified to practice by training and licence) the nature of many others' exemptions remains controversial. This is in spite of the fact that the professions ultimately may be scrutinized by the Monopolies and Mergers Commission (e.g. like the recent Royal Commission on Legal Services).

In addition to exclusions from the Act there is the possibility that many restrictive agreements for services are not registered. Both the Office of Fair Trading and the National Consumer Council have produced evidence of undisclosed agreements for goods and services. Non-disclosure may be due to ignorance on the part of the parties concerned. It may also be due to blatant evasion. This is particularly where the consequences of ignoring the law and subsequent prosecution under the Act are outweighed by the commercial benefits of not registering an agreement.

The Director General of Fair Trading in his annual report for 1981[2] indicated that 191 new agreements for services were entered on the register in 1981. This took the total entered since 1976 to 686. Of these 686 he reported that:

94 had been ended;
35 had all restrictions removed;
86 were the subject of representations to the Secretary of State (on 82 of which directions have been given);
5 were (now) before the courts (Aerodromes Owners Association; Society of West End Theatre(two); Association of British Travel Agents; Stock Exchange).

In addition he reported that discussions were continuing on agreements affecting a range of services. These included mortgage lending, advertising, actuarial services, commodity markets, bookmaking, freight transport and storage.

The number of agreements registered for goods during 1980 (63) and agreements terminated during 1980 (18) were similar to those for services, however the number of agreements entered in total on the register for goods (3,873) and terminated for goods (3,211) were larger. This is because Restrictive Trade Practices for goods have been in force (and therefore enumerated) since 1956. For services the starting date for enumeration was 1976.

Examples of services on which some of the most onerous restrictions have been removed in recent years are:

Bailiffs;	Local hotel associations;
Banks;	Motoring schools;
Commodity dealers;	Shipbrokers and shipowners;
Football pools promoters;	News agencies;
Goldsmiths;	Recording and film studios;
Investigators;	Wharfingers.
Local coach operators groups;	

Price restrictions have been given up but there is still work to do on the services of:

Cold storage;	Freight forwarding;
Commercial/home removals;	Road haulage.
Electrical testing;	

Also at the end of the year discussion on some 250 services agreements were under way. At that time the Director General was able to report that particular progress had been made in the banking sector.

In addition to these main exclusions the Direct General of Fair Trading has discretion in adjudicating whether certain trade practices are of 'significance' enough to call for investigation by the Restrictive Trade Practices Court. Broadly each case is considered on its merits but the discretionary element does mean that the Director General can reach agreement with the parties concerned without resort to a court hearing. The Director General's 1980 report contained a number of illustrations relating to acceptable restrictions on trade. These were in respect of such things as standard terms and conditions, joint ventures and codes of practice with a variety of service organizations.

15.3 Consumer Protection

In the United Kingdom the Fair Trading Act 1973 now provides machinery for the review of consumer affairs, for action to deal with trading practices and offenders under the law and for the development of codes of practice to raise trading standards. In respect of services the most visible consequences of consumer protection attempts are:

(*a*) Legislation;
(*b*) Consumer Protection Agencies;
(*c*) Voluntary Codes of Practice.

15.31 Legislation

There are still a number of differences in England between the law as it applies to 'goods' and as it applies to 'services'. A major problem as far as the law as it applies to services is concerned that it is still being developed and there are disagreements about interpretation. The law about services is not yet as well codified as the law about goods. It is likely that in the 1980s further laws will be introduced to regulate practices in respect of the marketing of services. Such laws will be in response to changes occurring both in Britain and in the E.E.C.

Some of the main pieces of legislation related to services marketing are outlined below.

(a) Sale of Goods Act, 1893 as amended by the Supply of Goods (Implied Terms) Act, 1973

Services are not covered by the Sale of Goods Act. But anyone offering a service – things like hairdressing, holidays, car parks – must carry it out in a careful and workmanlike way. If a job is not done properly, or loss or damage is suffered, then it may be possible to claim compensation. However, there is no legislation covering services which is equivalent to the Sale of Goods Act.

(b) Unfair Contract Terms Act, 1977

Some service firms try to escape responsibility by using 'exclusion clauses'. Until recently exclusion clauses were valid for services as long as the exclusion clause(s) were brought to the attention of consumers when a contract was entered into. Under the Unfair Contract Terms Act, 1977 liability is put on a paper footing. A trader is not allowed to restrict or limit liability, or contract out of liability, for death or personal injury which result from negligence or breach of duty.

For claims which do not involve death or personal injury, exclusion clauses are only valid if they are fair and reasonable in the circumstances. The guidelines in the Act used for the reasonableness test include:

the strength of the bargaining positions of the various parties to the contract;

whether the customer received an inducement to agree to the exclusion clause;

whether the customer knew or ought reasonably to have known of the existence of the exclusion clause;

in the case of an exclusion clause which applies when some condition is not complied with, whether it was practicable for the condition to be fulfilled.

In addition some businesses cannot exclude liability for their own breaches of contract; cannot use small print to allow them to provide a substantially different kind of service from that reasonably expected of them; nor are exclusion clauses in guarantees valid. In hiring agreements e.g. TV or car rental, the company renting the goods cannot use exclusion clauses to take away its responsibility for seeing that the goods are fit for their purpose.

The Act applies to a wide range of services including government departments, local authorities and nationalized industries. It does not however apply to insurance, the sale of houses, copyright, trade marks or shares in a company.

(c) Trade Descriptions Act, 1968

The Act makes it a criminal offence for a trader to describe inaccurately the goods he is selling or the services he is offering and he can be fined or imprisoned. A spoken false description is just as much an offence as a written one. A wide range of information is covered such as about size, quantity or strength; how, where and by whom something was made or what it is made of; what it is for and how well it will work; any standards to which it conforms; its previous history. Under this Act some kinds of false price reductions or 'markdowns' are also an offence.

In theory this Act should mean that consumers can rely upon descriptions given of services they buy. Thus if a holiday tour operator describes a hotel as 'secluded and peaceful' or as 'one kilometre from the beach' then these statements must be true. If a theatre is displaying a notice which is clearly false it can be prosecuted under this Act. However, if you book in advance to see a play with a famous actor taking the lead, you cannot claim your money back if he is unwell and not performing on the night; though the theatre should protect itself against misrepresentation on the night by announcing any change.

In practice the rules for goods and services are different. A service business is liable only if a wrong description can be proved to have been made 'knowingly or recklessly'. In addition certain kinds of service producers are excluded. Estate agents are immune from responsibility under the Act because houses are not legally either goods or services.

According to the Annual Report of the Director General of Fair Trading 1982[2] there were 125 convictions under the Act for false statements about services compared with over 1,000 convictions for false descriptions about goods – about the same order of magnitude as the previous year.

(d) Unsolicited Goods and Services Act, 1971

The main way this Act affects the general public is to make it an offence for traders to demand payment for goods or services which people have not ordered. If you receive goods which you did not ask for and you do not agree to keep them, the sender can take them back during the six months after you have received them. If you have not agreed either to keep or to send back the goods they become your property after six months. You can then use them, sell them or otherwise dispose of them as if they had been a gift.

You can, if you like, cut short the six months' period by writing to the sender giving your name and address and stating that the goods were unsolicited. If the sender then fails to collect them within 30 days they become your property. But in either case you must give the sender reasonable access to collect them. Anyone who demands payment for unsolicited goods can be fined. Corresponding legislation in Northern Ireland is the Unsolicited Goods and Services Act (Northern Ireland), 1976.

In addition it is a criminal offence for the sender of unsolicited goods or services to make any demand for payment from the recipient, unless he has reasonable cause to believe there is a right to payment. The consumer's position has been further improved by the Unsolicited Goods and Services (Invoices, etc.) Regulations, 1975 which require the notification of price to be clearly shown as not one obliging payment. Further there are penalties if senders threaten to bring legal proceedings, places, or threatens to place, the consumer's name on a black list of defaulters or invokes any other collection procedure.

(e) Negligence

In recent years the Law of Negligence has been widened and applied increasingly in services situations. That is, where there is reliance by an inexpert individual on the care, skill and advice of an expert; and where it can be proved that there was negligence – the failure to employ skill and reasonable care – liability will arise. What was originally thought to apply only to manufacturers has now been extended to many others including banks, accountants, solicitors, surveyors, local authorities and government departments, though the application of the law remains a grey area. Thus a bank manager who gives investment advice could be liable; an estate agent or insurance broker could be liable; and the Unfair Contract Terms Act, 1977 nullifies any disclaimer which may have been used in the past unless it can be proved fair and reasonable.

Solicitors have long accepted that the negligent handling of a client's affairs can oblige them to compensate the client. Every practicing solicitor has to be insured against liability of this kind. Barristers, however, are immune from liability for errors in their handling of court cases. In a recent case in which a firm of investment brokers was taken to court [Stafford *v.* Conti Commodity Services[5]] the judge expressed the view that a broker cannot be right all the time about the advice he gives. Incorrect advice, it was ruled, is not necessarily proof of negligence.

(f) Other Legislative and Quasi Legislative Controls

There are of course other forms of control to try to ensure that people who provide services are qualified and honest. These include giving a public body like the Office or Fair Trading the power to issue or withhold a licence for certain occupations as under the Consumer Credit Act, 1974; or by establishing some body to control membership as with the Solicitors Act, 1974, and the Insurance Brokers (Registration) Act, 1977.

In his 1981 report, for example, reviewing licensing under the 1974 Consumer Credit Act, the Director General identified a number of

Sectoral practices found to be unfair or illegal. These included services like double glazing, debt collection and money lending. The Director General's actions varied in each case but included receiving an undertaking to improve trading conduct, issuing a public warning about unfair methods and strong arm tactics, to withdrawing a trader's licence.

15.32 Consumer Protection Agencies

In addition to the framework of legislation relating to services there are a large number of consumer protection agencies which have been established. These agencies collect and distribute information and advice, negotiate on behalf of consumers and exert pressure to reform and improve trading standards and other standards of practice. A major difficulty faced by consumers is the sheer number of agencies with interests in consumer protection and the difficulty of finding out who does what.

It is inappropriate here to describe in detail the activities of the various consumer protection agencies that exist to work at a general level to improve consumer protection or at the specific level to obtain redress for particular grievance. The institutional framework reflects the state of development in Britain and like any institutional arrangement is subject to change and adaptation over time. An excellent guide to the agencies involved is produced by the Office of Fair Trading[6] and detailed descriptions are available in books and articles specifically devoted to the topic.[7] A number of general observations are however appropriate about the institutional framework.

(a) There is no separate system of institutions to deal with services. Certain institutions may restrict their work to goods (e.g. British Standards Institute) but this is due to their range of concern rather than the deliberate separation of goods and services by the system.

(b) There are a great number of public, semi-public, independent and voluntary organizations involved in consumer protection whether directly or indirectly. They are funded in different ways. The Consumers Association, for example, is funded by subscription while the Citizens Advice Bureaux receive a government grant and rely on voluntary help and subscriptions. Their range of interests can be wide, as with the Office of Fair Trading, or narrow, as with a local consumer group concerned with specifically local issues. Many government departments have interests in the general field of consumer protection (e.g. Ministry of Agriculture, Fisheries and Food, the Department of Health and Social Security, the Home Office) but the Office of Fair Trading, ultimately responsible to the Secretary of State for Trade and Industry, is the main official body in this field.

(c) A broad distinction can be made between institutions concerned with making policy and those concerned with implementation. Usually policy is formed at Central Government level through the influence of pressure groups, government sponsored bodies like the National Consumer Council and other independent bodies like the

Consumers Association. Generally policy is implemented at the local level through Local Authority Trading Standards or Consumer Protection Departments. In addition advice is available locally through Consumer Advice Centres, Mobile Advice Centres, Citizens Advice Bureaux, Local Consumers Groups and Law Centres.

(*d*) Inevitably there is overlap between many of the agencies involved in the institutional system of consumer protection. Also the range of possible sources of advice, information and help, is complicated by the separate Consumer Councils that exist for the nationalized industries (*see* Section 15.4) to say nothing of the international dimensions such as the effect of E.E.C. membership (*see* Section 15.5). The range is often too complex for the consumer to comprehend.

Figure 15.1 presents a much simplified outline of some of the sources of help available to a consumer who has a complaint about a particular service.

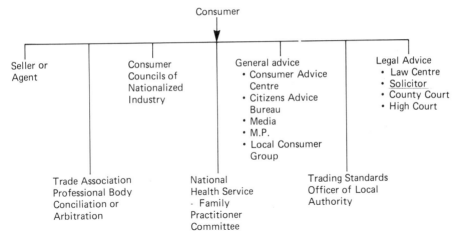

Figure 15.1 Outline of some of the agencies involved in Redress of Consumer Complaints for Services

Source: Based on Harvey, B. W. *The Law of Consumer Protection and Fair Trading*, Butterworths, London, 1978, p. 301

(*e*) Consumer protection is very much a political arena with arguments about who should be involved; whether it is necessary for the state to be involved; who should pay for services and how; whether there is an unnecessarily large number of agencies and parties involved, and so forth. Such issues are likely to be fiercely debated in the 1980s with the increasing polarization of views between politicians of left and right of the role that the state should play in economic and social life.

(*f*) Institutions for consumer protection are, in the main, characteristic of economies in an advanced stage of economic development. Economies in an advanced stage of economic development tend to be service economies. The services of consumer protection are spawned by the service economies of which they are a part.

15.33 Voluntary Codes of Practice

Certain professional and trade associations have codes of practice relating to the services they provide. For example professional bodies concerned with accounting, architecture, management consulting and market research have established codes of practice and trade associations representing such fields as package holidays, shoe repairs, car repairs, laundering and dry cleaning have also laid down codes for their members. Under the Fair Trading Act 1973 the Director General of Fair Trading has a duty: 'to encourage relevant associations to prepare . . . codes of practice for guidance in safeguarding and promoting the interests of consumers'.

These codes are designed to improve traders' standards of service and to ensure the consumer gets a fair deal. The first Director General, John Methven, placed great emphasis on the need for voluntary codes as a means of improving standards, arguing that the more effective voluntary controls there were the less would be the need for statutory control.

The advantages of codes of practice are that they do help to establish minimum acceptable standards for services, they deal with a specific trade or profession and they are probably cheaper to establish and operate than using statutory measures. On the other hand they are voluntary, they do not give an immediate solution to all consumer problems and they only apply to members of the association. Furthermore, they do not give extra rights in law, though they do usually supplement legal remedies. An additional weakness of codes of practice is that they are often drawn up by members of the profession or trade without outside help or advice. However, the Office of Fair Trading is taking an increasing role in assisting associations to draw up Codes of Practice and has been actively involved in helping to draw up some of the recent codes issued. The office also encourages the strengthening of existing provisions within codes of practice e.g. improving conciliation and arbitration of disputes under codes. Thus the revised code of practice for the Glass and Glazing Federation incorporated suggestions made by the Office of Fair Trading.

Certain conditions must apply if the code of practice operated by an association is to be effective. The association must have a respected and representative central body; it must be efficient in operating the code; and it must have the will and enthusiasm to be more than a self-protecting organization. In particular, membership of the association must be valued by those who belong to it or who aspire to belong to it, if the code of practice is to have any impact.

Codes of practice are specific to a particular profession or trade and therefore vary considerably in content. The office of Fair Trading issue explanatory leaflets dealing with codes of particular interest to consumers. The examples included below are for services dealing with car repairs and servicing, dry cleaning and laundries, package holidays abroad and hotels.[8]

Car Repairs and Servicing

Codes of practice have been produced by the Motor Agents' Association, the Society of Motor Manufacturers and Traders Limited, the Vehicle Builders and Repairers Association Limited, and the Scottish Motor Trade Association Limited, which give the following protection.

Cost

You should be given a firm quotation for the job if possible or at least an estimate in writing. In either case it must be clear whether VAT is included, and the rate of charge.

Should dismantling be necessary for the purposes of an estimate or quotation (e.g. lifting out an engine) this must be pointed out to you and the charge for this service made clear. Once any job is under way and it appears to the garage that the price quoted is likely to be exceeded by any significant amount (for example, if they come across further difficulties) the garage should ask your permission to continue.

Guarantee

Repairs must be guaranteed for a specified time or a number of miles against failure due to poor workmanship. In addition VBRA members under their code must guarantee their repair work for not less than six months or 6,000 miles' use from the date of repair. The repair guarantee will normally be extended if your vehicle is off the road due to faults or because further work has to be done as a result of previous defective work. Furthermore, the repairer should permit any unexpired period of guarantee on repairs to be transferred to a new owner of the car.

Care of the Car

The garage must take adequate care of your car and other possessions, and should tell you about any additional defects found, even if they have nothing to do with the work in hand.

Invoices

Any invoice should give you full details of work carried out, and parts used, the amount and rate of VAT, the date of repairs and the mileometer reading at that time.

If you feel that you have not been treated fairly and that the garage has not honoured the codes, you should complain to the particular motor trade association of which the garage is a member. An arbitration service is provided under the codes, under which a member of the Insitute of Arbitrators will be appointed to study the papers and make a judgement of your complaint.

Package Holidays Abroad

The Association of British Travel Agents (ABTA), in consultations with the Office of Fair Trading, has drawn up codes of conduct for its members to follow, designed to protect the holidaymaker and to ensure that complaints are dealt with quickly and fairly. The aspects covered are these.

Cancellations

Once you are fully booked for your holiday (i.e. when you have had to pay the full balance of the cost of the holiday) the tour operator can only cancel your holiday if there really are reasons beyond his control, such as an outbreak of war or disease in the country to which you are going. Should this happen you are entitled to a speedy refund of your money (less reasonable expenses) or the offer of another holiday of at least the same standard. Should you, on the other hand, be forced to cancel, you may have to pay the full price. The holiday brochure must therefore explain the cancellation conditions and how much money you may have to forfeit.

Alterations

You must be informed without delay should the tour operator or travel agent wish to alter your holiday in any significant way. In this event you must have the choice of either accepting the change – the alternative holiday offered must not be of a lower standard – or of having your money refunded promptly.

Surcharges

You must not be asked to pay currency surcharges less than thirty days before you go on your holiday if you are already booked. Surcharges for other items (such as jet fuel) can be requested up to the point of departure if they are really necessary for reasons beyond the tour operator's control. However, in any event the brochure must explain what sort of surcharges could crop up, and why.

Overbooking

Under the code of ABTA members promise to do all they can to avoid overbooking. In some cases, however, the fault lies really with the local hotel management and not with the ABTA member. In this event, if the tour operator or travel agent finds that this has happened before you go, he must offer either another holiday of at least equal standard or refund your money promptly. Should the overbooking be discovered after you have left, the tour operator must find you somewhere else to stay and pay up a 'disturbance' compensation if the new location is not up to the same standard as the hotel originally booked.

Booking Conditions

Travel agents are not entitled to disclaim legal liability in their brochures for the misleading statements of their staff or agents, or for negligence on the part of their staff in arranging your holiday. Likewise brochures may not state that complaints will be considered only if they are made within a certain period (or conversely, will not be considered if they are made outside that period).

If you should have reason to complain about your holiday you should do so first to the representative of the tour operator at the resort. If the complaint cannot be settled at the location then you should take up the complaint when you return home. In this case you should see your travel agent who must, under the code, try to settle the complaint, or liaise between you and the tour operator. If you still receive no satisfaction, the ABTA can provide a conciliation service free of charge and you should write to ABTA at 53/54 Newman Street, London W1P 4AH. ABTA also runs an arbitration scheme which you can use if all else fails. Unlike most arbitration schemes where they can only operate with the consent of the trader, ABTA members are obliged to submit to arbitration if you require it.

Remember, however, you yourself do not have to go to arbitration and you can pursue your ordinary legal remedies by suing the travel agent or tour operator (the travel agent is not your agent, but the agent of the tour operator or airline) for breach of contract or misrepresentation. Should you have been seriously misled in any brochures, advertisements or sales material, you should report the matter to the Trading Standards Officer at your local authority, who may bring a prosecution under the Trade Descriptions Act.

Dry Cleaning and Laundries

Cleaning, laundering, dyeing and garment repairing are covered by a code of practice produced by the Association of British Launderers and Cleaners (the ABLC) whose membership encompasses over 75% of launderers and dry cleaners in England, Scotland and Wales. The code deals in particular with the following.

Disclaimer

The members of the ABLC agreed not to use disclaimers (now illegal anyway!) limiting their liability for negligence if an article is damaged. A cleaner cannot therefore rely on any condition to the effect that the article is left at the owner's risk or that the cleaner 'cannot be responsible for any damage'. If a cleaner or launderer negligently loses, destroys or damages one of your articles, you are entitled to receive fair compensation (the value of the article). If the article can be repaired the launderer or cleaner will pay the cost of repair, up to the value of the item at the time.

Fire or Burglary

ABLC members will pay compensation if your article is lost or damaged as
the result of a fire or burglary while in their care.

Faulty processing

If an article of yours is unsatisfactorily processed the launderer or dry
cleaner will process it again free of charge if you ask for this to be done.

Prices

A price list for standard items should be displayed in the shop or should be
available from a van driver in the event of a collection or delivery service.
Carpet cleaning prices will normally be expressed as a cost per square
metre or square foot.

Delicate or Valuable Items

Should you point out that an item is delicate or valuable the shop may
decide to send it away to their main office for examination, in which case
they must give you, if you so require, a quotation for the processing before
the work beings.

Delays

ABLC members will try to ensure that they keep to their indicated delivery
times. If an item has been mislaid or its treatment delayed you should be
able to get a reduction in the charges.

If you have cause for complaint, you should take the matter up first with
the particular shop. If the problem is not satisfactorily resolved (and
provided that the launderer or dry cleaner is a member), you can take the
matter up with the ABLC and make use of their Customer Advisory
Service at Lancaster Gate House, 318 Pinner Road, Harrow, Middlesex,
HA1 4HX.

The Advisory Service will ask you to submit details of your complaint in
writing, and they will try to bring about a satisfactory conclusion by
conciliation. They may arrange for a laboratory test to be carried out –
which will be free of charge. You will, however, be expected to accept the
test findings.

Hotels

In 1977 the hotel industry, in consultation with a number of Government
Departments and organizations (including the Department of Trade, and
the Office of Fair Trading) agreed voluntarily to adopt a standard Code of
Booking Practice to apply to all hotels, motels, inns, guest houses and
similar establishments with four or more bedrooms. The purpose of the
Code is to ensure that you are properly informed, before you commit

yourself, first as to the services and facilities you will be getting, and secondly as to the price you will have to pay.

Consequently, under the Code, you now have the following safeguards:

(*a*) You should be informed, in writing, before taking up your accommodation, what price you will be charged, particularly of the 'total obligatory charge'. This information should be given to you at the earliest possible opportunity when the booking is being made, and if you book in advance (by letter or telephone) the information should be confirmed in writing at the point of reception. If the hotel offers a choice of accommodation on different terms, full information should be given to you under the Code.

(*b*) The written notice given to you as to the total obligatory charge for the intended booking must be expressed either per person or per room (single, double or family) according to the hotel's practice; it must be quoted overnight/per day/weekly (or as otherwise appropriate to the booking), and must be stated to be inclusive of VAT and any service or other obligatory charge which may apply. The written notice must also indicate whether the charge includes a private bath, shower or WC, and whether the charge is for accommodation only or includes meals (and if so, which meals are included). In addition, if breakfast is not included in the total obligatory charge, the information you are given in writing must indicate whether breakfast is available, and if so the total minimum charge for continental breakfast.

(*c*) If bookings are made in advance by correspondence or telephone or accommodation is sought on arrival, you must, under the Code, be given a card giving you your room number and the information in (*b*) above. The card must also make it clear either that the charges are standard throughout the hotel, or that you can see the charges for whatever different classes of accommodation exist.

(*d*) If there is an extra charge for heating, baths or uncovered parking space, or if the facilities and services included in the hotel's advertising carry a special charge, this fact must be clearly stated at the earliest possible opportunity when you make the booking, and must be confirmed in writing at reception before you take up your accommodation.

(*e*) Details of charges for optional extras such a dogs or covered garages should be readily available.

(*f*) If accommodation is offered in unconnected premises or in a separate establishment (such as an annex) its location and any difference in comfort or amenability must be clearly stated at the time that it is offered.

(*g*) If you request it, you must be given an adequate detailed account for your charges and a receipt for payments made.

The Director General of Fair Trading reported in his 1980 Annual Report that his office has so far been involved in helping to draw up codes of practice for nineteen different types of goods and services. Preliminary discussions were taking place on site and letting arrangements for holiday caravans; he foresaw the likely completion in 1981 of a code of practice for mechanical breakdown insurance for motor vehicles though the discussions on launderettes had ended without a code being accepted. He also indicated that the Office of Fair Trading is encouraging a move towards flexible but standard procedures and systems of arbitration in the light of its experience so far. A year later in the 1981 Annual Report the Director General indicated that he was not willing to continue negotiations for a code for site and letting arrangements in view of the conditions usually applied to purchase and resale of holiday caravans and to security of tenure. He put pressure on the trade associations involved to make further proposals.

Thus the Office now takes an active role in encouraging the formation of trade associations and codes of practice. According to one report[9] marriage bureaux and dating agencies have been urged to form a trade association and improve their business methods. Failing voluntary action, the report suggests, the Office of Fair Trading would press for legislation for some form of licensing system.

15.4 The Nationalized Industries

The nationalized industries are 'public corporations' with a separate legal personality conferred by statute or charter. They fulfil a range of functions which often gives them a monopoly of the supply of goods or services. In Britain services like water, gas, electricity, postal and telecommunications services are all provided chiefly by the nationalized industries. Their very existence apparently contradicts the measures taken by various governments to encourage competition, to restrict competitive practices and thereby encourage fair trade and protect consumers. The political, economic and social arguments for and against nationalization need not be rehearsed here. However, it is worth noting that the role of the state does vary in different industries and in different countries.

The activities of the nationalized industries can be controlled to some extent through Parliament. As far as the interests of the consumer are concerned however the main representative mechanism is the appropriate consultative council or committee. These vary considerably in their structure, powers and influence. For example, there is no consumers' council dealing with the water industry. In contrast the Electricity Consultative Council is an active body which helped to sponsor a code of conduct for the industry and which included provision for using an independent arbitration scheme. Also the Post Office Users National Council was influential in securing reductions in tariff increases proposed by the Post Office during 1981.

Consumers' councils, where they exist in the nationalized industries, seem to have three main problems. First, they are only consultative bodies. Neither the boards of the nationalized industries nor the government has to take note of, or act on, their views. Secondly, they need to develop their independence and expertise if they are to be effective representatives of consumers. The annual government grant of around £2m goes only some way towards helping them assert their independence. Thirdly, there seems to be ignorance still at local level of the existence of such councils. This ignorance acts as an obstacle to their more effective operation.

15.5 The European Economic Community

As a member of the European Economic Community, Britain is affected by its competition rules which are set out in the Treaty of Rome. Article 85 of the Treaty of Rome deals with practices likely to affect trade and prevent, restrict or distort competition. Article 86 is concerned with the abuse of a dominant market position. Policy on mergers is less clear. In all cases only a limited amount of case law is available and some of the provisions of the articles have yet to be tested. However, they do only apply where trade between member states is concerned. The articles of the treaty are implemented by the Directorate General IV and fall within the scope of the European Court of Justice which acts as a court of appeal if firms are dissatisfied with the Commission's findings. In some cases the Commission will exempt certain agreements which, though they may restrict competition, are of ultimate benefit to the European Economic Community. The Office of Fair Trading has a number of liaison functions with the European Economic Community Commission and represents the United Kingdom on the Advisory Committee on Restrictive Practices and Dominant Positions. This committee is consulted on matters connected with the infringement, enforcement, exemption procedures and so forth which relate to the Community's competition rules.

Consumer protection has become an important part of the European Economic Community's work. In 1975 the Council of the Commission adopted a Consumer Protection and Information Programme covering a number of important topics such as health, safety, protection of the consumers' economic interests when purchasing goods and services, consumer education and stronger representation of consumer interests. In addition, the Environment and Consumer Protection service within the Commission received help and advice on consumer affairs from the Consumers' Consultative Committee and the European Bureau of Consumers' Unions. The views of British organizations interested in consumer affairs are represented by the European Community Group (UK). Some of the products, services and practices which have come under the scrutiny of the Commission in recent years include public transport, doorstep sales, correspondence courses, consumer credit, advertising and after-sales services and repairs.

15.6 Complaints about Services

Each year there are over half a million formally recorded complaints about goods and services in Britain. An analysis of consumer complaints by type of goods or service (for 1979–80) shown in Table 15.2 reveals that under 25% of these complaints were to do with services (123,759 in total).

Table 15.2
Consumer complaints analysed by type of goods or service

Goods	No. of complaints 1979–80	Complaints per £m spent 1979–80
Food and drink	39,672*	1.22
Footwear	26,225	14.02
Clothing and textiles	54,633	5.92
Furniture and floor coverings	55,794	18.06
Household appliances	61,158	25.88
Toilet requisites, soaps, detergents, etc	2,498	1.86
Toys, games, sports goods, etc	8,928	12.11
Solid and liquid fuels	6,439	1.19
Motor vehicles and accessories	65,009	11.61
Other consumer goods	83,199	—
Non-consumer goods	2,665	—
Land, including houses	1,491	—
Services		
Home repairs and improvements	15,315	3.93
Repairs and servicing to domestic electrical appliances (excluding radio and TV)	4,390	23,93
Repairs and servicing to motor vehicles	12,752	10.44
Other repairs and servicing	13,031	39.25
Cleaning	8,093	36.54
Public utilities and transport	13,006	0.84
Consumer credit	5,693	—
Entertainment and accommodation	12,715*	1.65
Holidays	8,060	2.90
Professional services	10,650	2.05
General services, etc	20,054	—

*Consumer complaints reported by Environmental Health Officers are included in these sectors. They are:

| Food and drink | 18,111 |
| Entertainment and accommodation | 7,482 |

Source: Annual Report of the Director General of Fair Trading, HMSO, London, 1981

Of course figures of this kind are only the tip of the iceberg as many complaints do not find their way into official figures as reproduced here from the Annual Report of the Director General of Fair Trading.[2] Two general features of the recorded data are revealing:

(a) complaints about goods substantially exceed complaints about services;

(b) the number of complaints decreased in 1979–80 compared with

1978–9, the previous year for which comparable data were available (123,759 against 150,460). Also, the number of complaints for each individual service category shown decreased except for consumer credit which increased from 5,121 to 5,693. This may be partly attributed to the implementation of the Consumer Credit Act. Equally the substantial decrease in the number of complaints about 'Repairs and Servicing to Motor Vehicles', 'Other Repairs and Servicing' and 'General Services', may be partly attributed to measures introduced in recent years to protect the consumer. These include the provision of mechanisms for complaint and redress, as set out, in Codes of Conduct. (See Table 15.3).

The National Consumer Council's[10] own Consumer Concerns Survey reveals discontent with services. Their survey conducted by Research Services Ltd between November 1979 and November 1980 contained a sample size of nearly 2,000 people. It identified three main problems in connection with consumer services:

> poor quality workmanship (e.g. with car repairs, domestic appliance servicing, plumbers, hairdressers, professional services);
> delays in carrying out work (e.g. legal profession, building trade);
> prices charged (e.g. TV set repairs, car crash repairs).

The Consumer Concerns Survey suggests that in some cases up to one-fifth of respondents were dissatisfied with some aspects of the service they received. The survey also showed that, in spite of problems with services, consumers often do not take the trouble to make a formal complaint to a trading standards department, advice agency or solicitor. It suggests that consumers may not necessarily be able to avoid problems by careful 'shopping around'. This is because either they may be limited in their choice anyway or it is often difficult to assess a contractor's reliability in advance. The National Consumer Council therefore recommend that where it is difficult for consumers to protect themselves before they make a contract they should be given the best avenues for redress after the contract is made. Their belief is that law reform is the best method of obtaining minimum standards with which all traders must comply. In their report they make detailed legislative proposals for ensuring that at the very least services are performed with reasonable care and skill, within a reasonable time and at a reasonable price.

Overall then the situation in the service sector of the economy in respect of consumer protection is complex and inadequate. The imperfection of much machinery in existence to protect the consumers' interest (whether legislative, institutional or in the form of codes of conduct) in the service sector, was amply illustrated during 1981 by various 'incidents' in the City of London. These exposed many weaknesses. The failure of investment advisers, Norton Warburg, lead to calls for controls of financial advisers by the government. The city 'watchdog' – the Council of the Securities Industry – suspended stockbrokers Halliday Simpson, an unprecedented act although they were not insolvent. There was an investigation into the

Table 15.3
Consumer Complaints by Type of Service

Services	1978–9	%	1979–80	%
	No. of complaints			
Home repairs and improvements	17,984	12	15,315	12
Repairs and servicing to domestic electrical appliances (excluding radio and TV)	6,147	4	4,390	4
Repairs and servicing to motor vehicles	17,510	12	12,732	10
Other repairs and servicing	17,459	12	13,031	10
Cleaning	10,340	7	8,093	7
Public utilities and transport	14,658	10	13,006	10
Consumer credit	5,121	3	5,693	5
Entertainment and accommodation	13,628	9	12,715	10
Holidays	9,423	6	8,060	7
Professional services	12,210	8	10,650	9
General services etc.	25,980	17	20,054	16
TOTALS	150,460	100	123,759	100

Source: Compiled from Annual Reports of Director General of Fair Trading 1979 and 1980

activities of executives in the firm of Arbuthnot Latham. There were a series of 'dawn raids' on the shares of companies, like Consolidated Gold Fields. There were 'hammerings' of firms like Norman Collins and Hedderwick Sterling. Equally the reactive measures of the Council of the Securities Industry in drawing up a much criticized set of draft rules for the management of clients' investment funds: and the belated appointment by the Government of Professor J. Gower to review existing legislation covering investment management to prevent fraud and control dealers in securities were further signs that all was not well. They revealed that the mechanisms currently available to protect customer interests – clients, investors, institutions – were far from adequate. All this in a relatively sophisticated services marketing setting.

Unfortunately, as this brief review has suggested, imperfections and anomalies in respect of competition policy and consumer protection remain. The correction of these weaknesses is likely to become a significant issue during the later 1980s for the service sector of the economy plays such an important role in economic and social life. Also as the consumer movement extends its influence, service markets represent a new frontier for its activities.

15.7 Summary

1 Services marketing policies are effected by Competition Policy, including policy on Monopolies and Mergers. Anti-competitive Practices and Restrictive Trade Practices.
2 The most visible consequences of Consumer Protection attempts in services markets are Legislation, Consumer Protection Agencies and Voluntary Codes of Practice. The framework though is complex.
3 Many complaints about services are formally recorded each year; many more do not get into official records.
4 There are many imperfections and anomalies in respect of competition policy and consumer protection in services markets. There are likely to be changes here in the next few years, partly through the consumer movements' influence.

Questions for Discussion

1 What measures exist to ensure 'fair competition' in services markets?
2 How adequate are these measures?
3 What are the arguments for and against excluding services from the effects of Restrictive Trade Practices Legislation?
4 Comment on the adequacy of the legislative framework that exists at present, to protect the consumer in services markets.
5 What Consumer Protection Agencies can be used by a consumer with a complaint against:
   (*a*) a solicitor;
   (*b*) a garage;
   (*c*) a funeral director;
   (*d*) the Post Office.
6 What are the advantages and disadvantages of voluntary codes of conduct?
7 What elements should a 'good' code of conduct contain?
8 What are the three main services about which consumers complain?
9 What kinds of things do consumers complain about?
10 How would you set about improving measures to protect consumers against abuses by service marketors?

References and Notes

1 'Britain 1981. An Official Handbook', Central Office of Information, London, 1981.
2 'Annual Report of the Director General of Fair Trading 1980', H.M.S.O., London, July 1981.
3 'Annual Report of the Director General of Fair Trading 1981', H.M.S.O., London, July 1982.
4 Report of the 'Monopolies and Mergers Commission', Gas Appliances, 1980.
5 Money Management 'Legal light on duties of Investment Brokers', Aug. 1981, p. 777.

6 'Fair Deal – a shoppers guide', prepared by the Office of Fair Trading and the Central Office of Information.
7 See, for example, 'Consumer Legislation in the United Kingdom and the Republic of Ireland', Whincup, M. H. Van Nostrand Reinhold, New York, 1980, and 'The law of Consumer Protection and Fair Trading', Harvey, B. W. Butterworths, Sevenoaks, 1978.
8 Based on 'Consumers: know your rights', J. Harries, Oyez Publications, 1981.
9 *Daily Telegraph*, 24 July 1981.
10 'Service Please', Services and the Law: a Consumer View, National Consumer Council, Oct. 1981.

16. *PRODUCTIVITY OF SERVICE ORGANIZATIONS*

16.1 Introduction

In spite of failure to agree on whether the marketing of services is different to the marketing of goods most writers on services marketing do acknowledge two things:

(*a*) We, in advanced economies, now live in a service society. The distinctive feature of the service economies is that the majority of the workforce is engaged in the service industries like restaurants, hotels, domestic services of all kinds, transportation, communication, professional services, finance, health care, education and recreation. Conversely a minority of the workforce is engaged in agriculture and in manufacturing industry (*see* Chapter 1).

(*b*) The costs of performing, maintaining and improving services in the economy have focused attention on how to improve productivity in the service sector. Marketors in particular have become interested in productivity improvement: 'One of the major concerns of marketors in the future will be to increase marketing productivity.'[1]

There have been few studies undertaken on marketing productivity. The initiative of the American Marketing Association which began a major study on marketing productivity in the mid-1970s was therefore welcome. The challenge to improve marketing productivity applies equally to goods and services marketing although this chapter considers the problems of productivity measurement and productivity improvement only in services.

16.2 Productivity in the Service Sector

A number of sources suggest that productivity in the service sector of the economy is lower than in the goods-producing sector. This is a growing problem because wages in the services sector have been going up as fast as in the goods-producing sector. Thus service organizations have been faced with rising costs but have often been unable to offset these rising labour costs with rising output. As services account for over 50% of United Kingdom employment and because cost increases have been largely passed on as price increases, lower productivity in services may have contributed to give overall prices an inflationary push.[2]

There are a number of reasons why productivity in the service sector may be lower than in the goods sector. These reasons include:

Services are more Labour Intensive

Services are generally more labour intensive and therefore to increase output requires even more labour. The goods sector is generally more capital intensive. To increase goods output more capital is needed; and it is usually easier to reduce costs per unit of output in capital-intensive organizations than labour-intensive organizations.[2] Linked with the idea that services are more labour intensive is the suggestion that there has been a slower increase in labour quality in service industries.[3] Any aggregate measure of labour quality though is very difficult to make.

Fewer Opportunities for using Labour-saving Devices

Coupled with the labour intensity of services is the point that the opportunities for using labour-saving devices in services may be fewer. There are a number of factors contributing to this including:

(*a*) slower technological changes in services and less capital investment compared with manufacturing;
(*b*) fewer opportunities for economies of scale particularly in small service organizations;
(*c*) less opportunities for labour specialization;
(*d*) some services are people dependent (e.g. counselling; consultancy).

Small Size of many Service Organizations

Many service organizations are small, employ few people and therefore may not be able to introduce machinery, encourage job specialization and obtain the benefits which flow from the division of labour. In addition it has been suggested that there has been inadequate attention to the need for good management in some services like the arts, health care and government services.[4]

There is though conflicting evidence on whether there has been a lag in productivity in the service sector. Wilson[5] shows that there have been improvements in some major service sectors, which are not necessarily reflected in growth in output per man using conventional measures (e.g. entertainment). He says that:

'where it has been possible to pinpoint productivity improvements some surprising results have been noted. The largest increases in Britain in productivity in the 1950's were in the gas, electricity, and water utilities, and in public administration and defence'.

A major difficulty in discussing whether service output has increased or decreased and whether the service sector lags behind the goods producing sector, is the problem of measuring productivity.

16.3 The Meaning of Productivity

The problem of productivity measurement is fundamental to any discussion of productivity in the service sector. Productivity is usually defined as the ratio of output of a production process to an aggregate value of inputs. As traditionally conceived the productivity concept contains two important assumptions:[6]

(*a*) that output and the factors of production are perfectly defined, homogeneous and can be measured. If these criteria can be met then it is possible to calculate the contribution of each factor of production, and changes in the input–output ratio resulting from changes in the use of factors. In addition information on the attainment of objectives and feedback on the consequences of action taken may be made and productivity trends compared.

(*b*) the utility of the output is not questioned. It is assumed that there are no side effects beyond the satisfaction engendered by consumption of the goods produced. In other words, the traditional conception of productivity isolates the production process from the social setting: it assumes closed system characteristics.

The problems of measuring productivity in the service sector, therefore, stem from the continued use of traditional measures designed for goods contexts rather than services contexts. New kinds of measures have to be devised to take account of certain important characteristics of services and their marketing which influence productivity assessments. In particular the fact that services are 'performed' and not 'produced'; that service facilities must exist before they can be used; that services cannot be stockpiled; all have an influence upon the scope for productivity improvement. Another factor that influences productivity measurement is that many service settings are open systems, subject to external influences, rather than closed systems. Also with traditional productivity measures, quality is assumed to be constant; in the service sector of course quality varies greatly. One can increase the number of patients seen by a doctor but what of the quality of subsequent health care? One can increase the number of students taught by a lecturer but what effect might this have on the quality of their education?

A further problem is that the consumer often plays a role in service production and the quality of this input affects productivity:

'Productivity in banking is affected by whether the clerk or customer makes out a deposit slip and whether it is made out correctly or not. Thus we see that productivity in many service industries is dependent in part on the knowledge, experience and motivation of the consumer.'[3]

The consumer's role in service productivity derives from the fact that:

(*a*) goods are produced whereas services are performed and the customer may be involved and present while the service is being performed;

(*b*) the place of marketing in the exchange process is different:

'Goods are produced, sold and consumed. Services are sold and then (performed) and consumed simultaneously. . . . In place of the one interface between buyer and seller of goods–marketing–there are two interactions between the buyer and the seller of services–marketing and production.'[4]

Productivity measures in services then require both quantitative and qualitative dimensions. In fact, in many services settings the qualitative dimensions of the service product (e.g. restaurants, business consultants) are fundamental in any consideration of productivity. A hypothetical positioning of major services classes according to their qualitative – quantitative mix has been proposed. It suggests that conventional productivity measures are less appropriate for the services shown on the right of Figure 16.1.

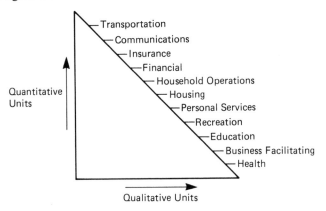

Figure 16.1 Productivity of Services: Output Measures
Source: Rathmell, J. M. *Marketing in the Service Sector*, Winthrop, Cambridge, Mass. 1974

A final difficulty in measuring productivity in services is due to the linkage of demand for certain services with the demand for the output of other firms or agencies. The productivity of a consulting engineer or of an educational institution or of a fire service rests upon the value of the service provided to other individuals and institutions in the system affected by the services provided. There are great problems involved in evaluating the contribution of a service at such a general level and social costs and benefits enter any consideration of productivity in these settings.[7]

Given these problems of measuring productivity of services it is not surprising that the evidence on productivity in the service sector at the macro level, at least, is inconclusive.

16.4 Services Productivity and Manufacturing Productivity[8]

Table 16.1 compares productivity in the services sector in the UK with that in the rest of the economy and uses change in output per worker as the common base. Though the three studies shown in Table 16.1 do not use the same definition of the services sector nevertheless services productivity apparently grew more slowly than in the rest of the economy even after some adjustment to the groupings (*see* Table 16.1).‡

Table 16.1
Percentage changes at an annual rate

	Labour* input	Output†	Output per unit of labour
(a) A. D. Smith's results 1951–66			
Services (excluding Transport and communication)	0.7	2.4	1.7
Other	Nil	2.8	2.8
Total GDP	0.3	2.6	2.3
(b) G. Briscoe's results 1948–73			
Services (including Construction, Public utilities)	1.1	2.3	1.2
Adjusted services‡	0.6	2.9	2.3
Manufacturing	0.4	3.2	2.8
Total GDP	0.6	2.7	2.1
(c) Author's calculations 1961–77			
Services	0.7	2.1	1.4
Adjusted services‡	–0.2	2.0	2.2
Manufacturing	–1.3	2.2	3.5
Total GDP	–0.3	2.3	2.6

*Smith used Census of Population data of full-time equivalent, employed and self-employed: Briscoe used DE numbers in employment: the author's calculations use Census of Population data for 1961 and Census of Employment for 1977, both full-time equivalent of employed persons. (2 part-time taken as 1 full-time equivalents) plus self-employed.
†At constant prices.
‡i.e. excluding professional and scientific, and public administration.

Source: Whiteman, J., 'The Services Sector–a poor relation?', N.E.D.O., reproduced by permission of HMSO, 1981 Discussion Paper No. 8

On the other hand comparison of the value of output per employee in the services sector with the rest of the economy shows the services sector has maintained its position compared with manufacturing. In fact it is consistently higher than in manufacturing (*see* Table 16.2). However this method of comparison contains pitfalls. Price comparisons among sectors may be affected by demand changes and by market imperfections (e.g. monopolies) and not just changes in efficiency of supply. Thus volume output changes show services performing less well; value of output changes show services performing as well.

Table 16.2
The value of output per head in UK, £, current prices, per full-time equivalent employed person

	1961	1971	1977
Total economy	1,055	2,265	5,743
Manufacturing	990	2,010	5,144
Services	1,097	2,253	5,541
'Adjusted services'*	1,169	2,494	6,216
Transport and communication	1,169	2,610	7,003
Distribution	920	1,910	4,728
Insurance, banking, etc.	2,537	3,765	8,834
Public administration	1,126	2,497	6,336
Professional, scientific, misc.	994	1,906	4,649

*excluding professional and scientific, miscellaneous and public administration.

Source: Whiteman, J. 'The Services Sector – a poor relation?', N.E.D.O., reproduced by permission of H.M.S.O., 1981 Discussion Paper No. 8

The problem of measurement is bedevilled by poor data quality and weak measurement methods. Service organizations need alternative ways of measuring productivity. Present measures tend to focus on how productive people and technology are for organizations. Service organizations need to focus on how well people are served; whether services are necessary; and how well exceptions are dealt with. Present systems of measurement with their narrow focus on measures of resources used (e.g. staff employed) or on how resources are allocated may be useful for budgetary controls over spending. In service organizations they are less relevant to the critical issue of delivery, and controlling the services organizations provide for people. In the absence of customer-satisfaction-based measures of service, organizations tend to use other surrogate measures for control purposes – measures which are often specious.

16.5 Can Productivity be Improved?

Increasing productivity, given the problems of productivity measurement mentioned earlier, remains a challenge for all kinds of service marketing organizations. Organizations with profit objectives need to improve their productivity to maintain their position in the marketplace and not outprice themselves in the markets in which they operate; non-profit organizations, depending upon donations, need to ensure the maximum value is extracted from the support that they obtain; public organizations need to improve productivity to ensure that rising deficits do not cause cutbacks in levels of service provision.[9]

Stanback[7] argues that in the private sector the marketplace acts as an arbiter and directs resources to their most economical use. Here the buyer responds to market prices; he will either accept price increases, or make adjustments in service purchases through substitution or by curtailing purchases over time. Thus maximizing productivity is of vital concern to the seller in the private sector and can be left to the individual firm. In the public sector, however, he believes the implications for failure to increase productivity are more serious. The response to rising service costs may be less sensitive, more protracted and lead to dissatisfaction with government costs. If the costs of providing services are not reduced, then the standards of services may be reduced if productivity increases are not made or the price of services may have to rise. In all services settings there is the challenge of how productivity increases may be made.

There are opposing views on the extent to which service productivity can be improved. One view is that service productivity will always lag behind productivity in the goods-producing sector and that the lower rate of improvement in productivity in services is a 'cost disease'. Wage levels tend to be set within the goods sector, where productivity can be more directly related to wages. But these levels then tend to be applied in the service sector where they are high relative to productivity and where wages tend to be a larger proportion of costs anyway. As costs increase so prices tend to increase. In the public sector, particularly in local government, higher costs may bring about a deterioration in service quality or a reduction in services or the imposition of higher taxes. In the arts, for example, the limited scope for productivity improvement means high cost operations and increasing competitive disadvantage. The problem, of course, is not limited to local government or the arts, but can apply to many services where productivity improvements lag (e.g. education, care of the elderly, park maintenance).[10]

The other point of view[1,4,9] holds that productivity improvements in the service sector are possible and a number of ways of improving service productivity are suggested.

16.51 Improving Staff

One way is through improving the knowledge, skills, attitudes and behaviour of existing and new staff involved in service delivery and performance through better systems of recruitment, training, development and motivation. Thus staff in contact with customers handling the visible elements of the service can be trained in handling queries and complaints, in product knowledge, in the operations of internal systems. Productivity bargaining schemes with considered measures of output and formulae for sharing gains can be operated to provide incentives for improved productivity. In other words staff can be encouraged to work harder and more skilfully (*see* Chapter 11).

16.52 Introducing Systems and Technology

Levitt[11] argues that what is also required is for manufacturing approaches to be taken in service industries. He suggests that a constraint to thinking about improvement in service is that too often the solution is seen as depending on improvements in the skills and attitudes of people who perform the service and attention is diverted from other possibilities. He suggests that:

> '. . . to improve the quality and efficiency of service, companies must apply the kind of technocratic thinking which in other fields has replaced high cost and erratic elegance of the artisan with the low cost, predictable munificence of the manufacturer . . .'

He uses McDonald's to illustrate how applied manufacturing thinking has been applied to a people-intensive service situation:

> 'The tissue paper used to wrap each hamburger is colour coded to denote the mix of condiments. Heated reservoirs hold prepared hamburgers for rush demand. . . . Nothing is left to chance or the employees' discretion. The entire system is engineered and executed according to a tight technological discipline that ensures fast, clean, reliable service in an atmosphere that gives the modestly paid employees a sense of pride and dignity. . . . What is important to understand about this remarkably successful organisation is not only that it has created a highly sophisticated piece of technology, but also that it has done this by applying a manufacturing style of thinking to a people-intensive service situation.'

Levitt believes that many services executives think in outdated ways. Change is possible though:

> 'Once service industry executives and creators of customer service programs begin seriously to think of themselves as actually manufacturing a product, they will begin to think like product manufacturers. They will ask what technologies and systems are employable here? How can things be designed so we can use machines instead of people, systems instead of serendipity?'

In essence the recommendation is that service organizations can reap productivity improvements if they become more systems and technology orientated. The systems approach looks at the task as a whole. It attempts to identify key operations to be undertaken, examines alternative ways of performing them, devises alternative methods, removes wasteful practices and improves co-ordination within the system as a whole. Alternative layouts, better job design and consideration of overall costs of the system are important features of the systems approach. For example productivity improvements in grocery retailing have been made possible by a systems approach to physical handling of goods, layout, job design and merchandising.

The systems approach to service can be applied in three ways: through hard technology, soft technology and hybrid technology.[12]

(a) Hard technology means substituting machinery and tools for people (e.g. automatic car washes, airport x-ray surveillance equipment, automatic car parking, automatic vending equipment, audio visual equipment, computers).

(b) Soft technology means substituting pre-planned systems for individual service operations. The systems may involve some technology, but their basic characteristic is the system itself which is designed for optimal results (e.g. fast food outlets, pre-packaged tours).

(c) Hybrid technology is where equipment is combined with planned systems to give greater order, speed and efficiency to the service process (e.g. limited service, fast repair facilities for car exhausts, tyres and brakes).

This approach to service activities can have important effects upon productivity. The systems approach, like the marketing approach, is as much about attitudes and outlook as it is about tools, techniques and hardware or engineering. But the combination of division of labour with industrialization of service can produce new solutions to old problems.

The effects of this kind of thinking when applied to services are reflected in features like:

(a) greater standardization of performance and the mass production and greater impersonalization of services (e.g. telecommunications, group travel schemes);
(b) the appraisal of jobs. Attention is focused on how improvements can be made in the ways of doing the present job, what new methods can be employed to do jobs differently, and how the jobs and tasks themselves can be changed;
(c) reconsideration of the scale of operations. Economies of operation through chain operations or franchising may be sought;
(d) specialization of effort and of markets to make labour more productive.

These features are particularly of interest in service situations where standardization is possible and appreciated by customers. One problem is that the ability to standardize tasks across a broad range of services is seriously limited. It may be because customers demand personal attention, or it may be due to the nature of the task itself which is highly ideosyncratic (e.g. professional services).

Also there may be constraints on the extent to which hard technology can be used in services. Greater proficiency in performance of some services is certainly possible through improving the technical core of the service. This may be as a substitute for labour or as a way of strengthening the personalized nature and quality of the service (e.g. tools available to garage mechanics, computers used for business purposes). The impact of technology on the improvements to existing services and the development of new services has been considerable in recent years in fields as diverse as materials handling, transportation, automatic control systems in workshops, electronic banking, timekeeping systems, and in libraries and hospitals. Many service industries have become a major target for developers and sellers of technology. Certainly the benefits of technological solutions in the manufacturing industries in improving productivity, reducing costs, eliminating mundane jobs and extending the possibilities for human capacity are good reasons for seeking technological solutions in the service industries. However even technological solutions may not always be successful in the service sector. There are limits to how far such technological solutions can apply because:

(*a*) many services are provided by organizations which are small, and labour intensive;

(*b*) they may not have the resources to consider, let alone adopt, methods of service performance and delivery which are capital intensive rather than labour intensive;

(*c*) there may be some situations where it is not always cheaper to replace labour by capital because of the relative costs of factors of production involved;

(*d*) many services – even those where there is little contact between the service provider and the customer – may still ultimately depend upon what contact there is to shape the customer's perceptions of the service product. In 'high contact' services the interaction between service provider and customer may be an even more dominant component of the customer's perceptions of the service product. Certain services may just not lend themselves entirely to technological solutions because of the nature of the problems involved;[3]

(*e*) while technology has been responsible for some dramatic improvements in productivity it also has brought associated human problems. For example: 'Work force alienation in the manufacturing sector has been caused in large part by the use of operating systems which both pace the employee and remove most of the employee's discretion in the performance of his assigned tasks';[4]

(*f*) technological solutions of course cannot be divorced from the wider settings – social, organizational, procedural – into which they are applied. Technological changes have to be carefully grafted on to existing social and institutional arrangements if they are to fit in and not to be rejected by both producers and consumers.

16.53 *Reducing Service Levels*

Productivity can also be improved by reducing the quantity of service and/or the quality of service (e.g. doctors could give less time to each patient). There are dangers in these approaches particularly where a service organization has promised to deliver a higher level of service in the past. Also competitors can differentiate their services by broadening and upgrading their service quantity and quality.

16.54 *Substituting Products for Services*

Productivity can be improved by providing a product substitute for the service (e.g. new data transfer technology has removed the need for the telegram service).

16.55 *Introducing New Services*

It is possible to design a more effective service that eliminates or reduces the need for the less effective service. For example, transatlantic travel by air has largely replaced transatlantic travel by sea; the credit card has replaced the former system for obtaining overdrafts.

16.56 Customer Interaction

It is possible to change the way in which customers interact with service providers. This is particularly possible with 'high contact' services. Using the consumer more in the production process demands greater understanding of consumer behaviour and its underlying causes (*see* Chapter 11). Ways have to be found to harness consumers or to change their behaviour through education and persuasion for the benefit of service delivery. Consumers are involved in service delivery anyway, whether actively or passively. To improve the useful, active role of the customer in service delivery may mean new managerial approaches, changed organizations or organizational structures, the employment of para professionals and perhaps a changed role for the professional service manager. He may become more of a catalyst, stimulator, orchestrator or manager directing energies toward the maximum involvement of the consumer, student, client, parent or whatever. In other words more consumer-intensive designs have to be developed to maximize the contribution of the customer to service performance and delivery.[15] Certainly the diversity of organizations within the service sector means that industrialized and bureaucratized attempts alone cannot apply in all situations where improved services productivity is sought. The very character of some services constrains against mechanization and rationalization.

Some basic problems in the marketing communications area in services have already been considered (*see* Chapter 9). Some of these problems derive from the nature of what is being sold (e.g. intangibles) and the professional or legal restrictions that may apply say on advertising certain kinds of services. But these are particular problems with particular solutions. Another dimension of the communications problem with services is that:

(*a*) there is the challenge of how to obtain and maintain the co-operation of consumers as buyers or users of the services in question;

(*b*) there is the challenge of how to obtain and maintain the co-operation and collaboration of consumers in the production process. The kind of rhetoric used is likely to vary depending upon whether the services market concerned offers wide choice (as with package holidays) or whether there is limited choice (like a social service provided to a citizen as a right). In the case of the former service great reliance is placed upon persuasive messages and appeals intended to encourage purchase and to sell the benefits of the service. In the case of the latter no such persuasive approach may be desirable or necessary.

Interestingly, in labour markets, workers have formed protective organizations (i.e. trade unions) to look after their interests in their dealings with their employers. Customer and client organizations on the other hand are less highly developed but may become more prominent in the service sector. Of relevance to the customers interaction with many service organizations is that:

> 'the fine "details" of the bargain cannot be completely foretold in advance of assuming a membership role in a service organisation. . . . he (the consumer) may be constrained to keep his end of the bargain; yet the organisation is in an advantaged position to impose constraints and expectations upon him which where either totally absent or only vaguely suggested in the rhetoric by which the consumer was originally captured.'[15]

The potential for strengthening the institutions protecting the customer as consumer and as worker suggest that in the future greater constraints may be imposed upon the communications efforts of service organizations. Greater clarification will be sought and will emerge as far as 'who does what' and 'who has responsibility for what' in service transactions. [This has happened in recent years with package holidays (*see* Chapter 15)]. Greater attention will be devoted to ensuring that exchanges in the service sector are more 'fair' to all parties involved. This could well impose greater constraints on the promotional messages marketors may use to help sell their services.

16.57 *Reduce the Mismatch between Supply and Demand*

A significant feature of many service organizations is the mismatch that often exists between supply of the service and demand for it. A major goal in marketing services is to get greater control over supply and demand and to obtain a better balance between the two. If more people want to use an airplane than there are seats available then business may be lost to competitors; unsold seats for a theatrical performance mean revenue lost forever. Service marketors may therefore face problems of:

increasing demand (e.g. using up spare capacity);
decreasing demand (e.g. where demand is excessive);
obtaining a better balanced service supply (e.g. to meet fluctuating demand patterns).

Kotler[16] has used the term 'demarketing' to describe the strategy which an organization may actively adopt to discourage additional customers on a temporary or a permanent basis. He uses the term 'syncromarketing' to describe the strategy which an organization may actively adopt to bring supply and demand into better balance.

A number of strategies may be used by service marketors in their efforts to

manage demand;
manage supply.

These strategies which were introduced in Chapter 13 are reviewed below.[17]

Managing Demand

Some strategies which have been suggested to manage demand are:

Differential Pricing

One way to increase demand during quiet periods and to curb it during peak periods is to use differential pricing (e.g. prices based on the time, season or facilities). Higher prices may be charged to discourage use, lower prices to encourage use. Tour companies, British Telecom and British Rail are examples of service organizations using differential pricing as a regulator of demand.

Reservation and Appointment System

Better control over workflow in some service situations is possible through the use of reservation systems and appointment systems. Doctors, airlines, professional services, hotels and hairdressers are illustrations of services where such systems are common practice.

Facilities Management

Service organizations can obtain better control over demand by offering alternative product offers. Squash clubs offer a range of services (e.g. coaching, junior competitions, social activities) to make better use of facilities. Universities rent out rooms and catering services for conferences, functions and holiday use out of term time.

Sasser[17] gives several examples of how demand may be shifted like differential pricing and new service packages (e.g. breakaway weekends). Also technology may be introduced (like automatic cashing facilities) to ease demand on facilities and persuasive advertising (like encouraging early mail posting at Christmas) may also help shift demand patterns.

If attempts to influence customers to change patterns of demand are to succeed it is essential that customers understand the reasons why such attempts are made and that they have freedom in respect of their ability to alter their demand patterns. Attempting to persuade commuters to travel at off-peak times may mean that marketing efforts have to be aimed at employers to encourage them to introduce more flexible working practices and hours rather than at employees alone.

Managing Supply

Strategies that may be used for varying supply – making more available when demand is high, cutting supply back when it is not include:

Using the Consumer More

This was mentioned in the previous section. The consumer is encouraged to play a larger role in the exchange process. Customers filling in paying-in slips in banks, self-service restaurants, self-service petrol stations – all illustrate the consumer taking on an operational role in service delivery.

Using Part-time Employees

Peak demand often means having additional personnel on hand. Part-time employees and job sharing help to accomplish more flexible supply. Retailing, catering, education, telephone operation and hotels are all examples of service industries where part-time working is commonplace.

Utilizing Existing Personnel Better

Service employees can be trained to perform a variety of jobs so that peak demand in one area of the service operation (e.g. a jumbo jet unloading passengers) can be met. This requires flexibility in working practices and sensitive management of the varying supply roles required. Some professionals (e.g. doctors and dentists) may relegate some of their tasks to assistants who perform paraprofessional services. This enables the professional to concentrate on and specialize in key tasks.

Shared Facilities

Service organizations may share their facilities to make best use of expensive equipment or indeed of highly trained staff. In health care for example one hospital may specialize in certain treatments, another for certain kinds of patients. Universities share central services like computing facilities or the central services of professional staff (e.g. O & M units), priests in rural parishes may service a number of churches in their district. Thus service organizations can improve their ability to service by sharing facilities, technology and staff.

Simplification in Service Delivery

Fluctuations in supply may also be managed by actions like:

> performing only essential tasks at peak times;
> pre-preparing tasks (e.g. partially completing forms) to meet peak demands;
> training employees to be able to undertake more jobs so they can switch tasks as demand requires;
> critically examining existing procedures and processes to eliminate the unnecessary, simplify the complex and speed up performance through routinization and specialization;
> using technology for human labour to make the system more productive (e.g. automatic car washes, microprocessors).

16.6 Conclusion

This chapter has considered two key problems which face service marketors. These problems are:

(a) how to gain more accurate measures of productivity in the service sector;

(b) how to increase productivity in services.

A major problem with some of the suggestions put forward to improve productivity is they are essentially ideas which attempt to get the consumer to service the needs of the organization. In that sense they are production orientated rather than market orientated. Heaton[18] recognizes this in his consideration of productivity in service organizations where he argues that conventional measurements of productivity focus on the productivity of people for organizations. What is required are new patterns of measurement which show the productivity of service organizations in serving people. Thus while one agrees with the view of Stanton[19] that: 'the biggest problem facing service industries, as we look to their continued growth, is the need to increase productivity' as Heaton indicates our methods of productivity measurement still lag behind our need to do so, both conceptually and practically.

16.7 Summary

1 The improvement of productivity is a major concern in service organizations.
2 A constraint on productivity improvement is the problem of productivity measurement. Traditional ways of measuring productivity are not always appropriate in services (e.g. because of qualitative factors).
3 Comparisons of productivity in the service and non-service sectors of the economy are hindered by weak measurement methods and poor data quality.
4 Nevertheless many suggestions for improving productivity can be put forward including improving staff performance, introducing systems and technology, reducing service levels, substituting products for services, introducing new services, using customers more in service production, reducing the mismatch between supply and demand.

Questions for Discussion

1 Why is productivity improvement an important concern for service organizations?
2 What role does the consumer play in productivity in service organizations?
3 Suggest *six* ways in which a service organization can improve the productivity of its operations?
4 What problems are involved in productivity measurement in services?
5 Suggest methods you would use to measure the productivity of a:

fireman?
marketing lecturer?
business consultant?
final year undergraduate marketing student?

6 Why do technological methods of productivity improvement have their limitations in services?
7 Identify and describe six methods you have observed in which service industries have tried to improve productivity.

8 'Improved productivity often means that quality suffers.' Discuss.
9 How can the mismatch between supply and demand in some service industries, be reduced?
10 'Many ways suggested for improving productivity is service organizations are production orientated.' Discuss.

References and Notes

1 Nickels, W. G. *Marketing Principles*, Prentice-Hall, Englewood Cliffs, 1978.
2 Markin, R. *Marketing – Strategy and Management*, J. Wiley & Sons, New York, 1982.
3 Fuchs, V. R. *The Service Economy*, Columbia University Press, New York, 1968.
4 Rathmell, J. *Marketing in the Service Sector*, Winthrop, Cambridge, Mass. 1974.
5 Wilson, A. *The Marketing of Professional Services*, McGraw-Hill, London, 1972.
6 'Policies for Innovation in the Service Sector', OECD, Paris, 1977.
7 Stanback, T. M. *Understanding the Service Economy*, Johns Hopkins University Press, Baltimore, 1979.
8 This section is based on an excellent discussion paper by Whiteman, J. 'The Services Sector – a poor relation?', National Economic Development Office, Discussion paper No. 8, 1981.
9 Lovelock, C. H. and Young, R. F. 'Look to consumers to increase productivity', *Harvard Business Review*, May–June, 1979.
10 Baumol, W. J. 'Macroeconomics of Unbalanced Growth: The Anatomy of Urban Crisis', *American Economic Review*, June 1967, pp. 415–26.
11 Levitt, T. 'Production line approach to service', *Harvard Business Review*, Sept.–Oct., 1972, pp. 41–52.
12 Levitt, T. 'The Industrialisation of Service', *Harvard Business Review*, Sept.–Oct. 1976, pp. 63–74.
13 Chase, R. B. 'Where does the consumer fit into a service organisation?' *Harvard Business Review*, Nov.–Dec. 1978, pp. 137–42.
14 Sasser, W. E. and Arbeit, S. P. 'Selling jobs in the service sector', *Business Horizons*, Vol. 19, June 1976, pp. 61–5.
15 Gersuny, C. and Rosengren, W. R. *The Service Society*, Schenkman, Cambridge, Mass. 1973.
16 Kotler, P. 'The major tasks of Marketing Management', *Journal of Marketing*, Oct. 1973, p. 47.
17 This section is based on Sasser, W. E. 'Match supply and Demand in Service Industries', *Harvard Business Review*, Nov.–Dec. 1976, pp. 133–40.
18 Heaton, H. *Productivity in Service Organisations*, McGraw-Hill, New York, 1977.
19 Stanton, W. *Fundamentals of Marketing*, McGraw-Hill, New York, 1981.

PART 4
The Future for Services

17. *THE FUTURE FOR SERVICES*

17.1 Introduction

In Chapter 1 the factors which have influenced the growth of the service sector of the economy were identified. The point was made that it is misleading to suggest that the United Kingdom has become a 'post-industrial' society where consumer services dominate. What seems to have happened is that growth has occurred in intermediate, goods-related services and in publicly-provided services. It has been growth in demand for these kinds of services which seems to have caused the increase in employment in the service sector of the economy.

The objectives of this chapter are to:

(*a*) consider what is likely to happen to the service sector in the future;
(*b*) identify some priorities for those marketing services.

17.2 The Future of the Services Sector

As far as the United Kingdom is concerned the possible trends in demand for services have been examined by Whiteman.[1] He uses a framework proposed by Katouzian[2] which puts services into three categories.

Old Services

These are services which in the past came from a less equitable distribution of income, the monopoly position of buyers and lack of alternative employment. They include services like public transport, cinemas, laundries, shoe repairs and domestic service. There is a tendency for these services to be substituted by durable consumer goods and by new services.

New Services

These are services which have experienced a shift in demand with the advent of mass consumption. Consumption of these services seems to be a function of per capita income and the growth of leisure time. Examples include health and education. In the United Kingdom many of these services have been provided by the Government.

Complementary Services

These are services directly connected with the rise of industry, the growth of intermediate markets, the growing unification of domestic and international markets, the growth of bureaucracy and increased urbanization. Examples are scientific, professional and business services.

According to Whiteman,[1] there are these likely trends in the service sector for the different kinds of services.

Old Services

Demand will continue to fall (e.g. public transport, laundries). However because these services have a fairly small share in service consumption and output they will have little influence upon services as a whole.

New Services

Demand will be fairly close to the trend of output and income in the economy overall (e.g. health, education, tourism). Private consumer demand for leisure and recreation-related services may tend to increase faster than personal income if the economy is growing. The resources devoted to new services that are publicly provided (e.g. health and education) will be influenced by political decisions. The complexion of the government in office will clearly influence what share of resources will be devoted to public services, although this decision in turn will be influenced by factors like the general health of the economy and general demographic trends (e.g. the increasing numbers of old people).

Complementary Services

Demand for these services will be influenced by the health of the sectors which use them. If the fortunes of the manufacturing sector improve then intermediate services will grow (e.g. computing, finance, research). If on the other hand manufacturing continues to stagnate then intermediate services will suffer too. Generally they have grown faster than manufacturing in the past but it is unlikely that under stagnant conditions in the 1980s they could continue to enjoy such exceptional growth.

As far as internationally traded services are concerned (e.g. tourism, financial services) their growth is less constrained by what happens in the United Kingdom economy and more by what is happening in the world economy. Such services could continue to develop but would be particularly influenced by two factors:

(a) Competition
This is already intense in fields like financial services and shipping (*see* Chapter 14).
(b) Exchange Rates
An overvalued £ makes United Kingdom services relatively less attractive in competitive world services markets.

Overall Whiteman concludes:[1]

'the broad trends in demand for services may continue as in the past. Government policies will influence the level of provision of public services, and the balance between internationally traded and non-traded services may shift slightly as a result of the impact of

North Sea oil. Overall a continuing increase in the share of services in output seems probable, if the economy is growing.'

Table 17.1
Future Influences on Services

	Direct influence of government on demand or supply?	Likely general trend of demand in relation to income	Impact of North Sea oil on demand	Significant direct impact of techno- logical change?	Possible overall trend of output
	1	*2*	*3*	*4*	*5*
Transport	No	–	=	No	–
Communications	Yes	+	+	Yes	+
Distributive trades	No	–	+	?	=
Insurance, banking and finance	No	+	–	Yes	+
Professional and scientific services	Yes	=	=	?	=
Miscellaneous services	No	–	+	No	=
Public administra- tion and defence	Yes	=	=	Yes	=

Key: + means expansion faster than economy as a whole
– means expansion slower than economy as a whole
= means expansion at similar rate to that of the economy

Source: Whiteman, J. 'The Services Sector – a poor relation', Discussion Paper, No. 8, N.E.D.O., reproduced by permission of HMSO, 1981

Various influences upon United Kingdom Services up to 1990 are summarized in Table 17.1. Column 1 indicates where the government can have a significant impact upon provision, but it does not take account of factors like tax or other regulations which could influence demand and supply for some services (e.g. private transport). Columns 2 and 3 refer to effective demand and do not indicate whether people would like more or less public services. Column 4 refers to the impact of technological change on the service sector. Column 5 refers to the possible overall impact of the factors identified.

In his projections Whiteman ignores the effects of any stimulation resulting from new products and services made possible by new technologies. Given these assumptions he believes that the more dynamic subsections of the service sector will be insurance, banking, finance and communications; transport and miscellaneous services (e.g. cinemas) will tend to lag behind the economy as a whole; while professional and scientific services and public administration and defence will move in line with total output and income.

17.3 Influences on the Development of the Service Sector

Section 17.2 above presents one view of what is likely to happen to the service sector over the next decade. Some factors which might influence these developments are considered in this section. In particular five factors are considered which have an effect upon any assumptions made about the service sector. These factors are:

(a) limitations on growth in service industries;
(b) attitudes towards services and the service sector;
(c) technological innovation;
(d) service quality;
(e) the 'black' economy.

They illustrate influences to which any projections about the future of services must be subject.

17.31 Limitations on Growth in Service Industries

The overall conclusion from the previous section that services will continue to be important in the economy and that growth is likely in some sub-sectors is reasonable. Even in times of economic decline and stagnation there is evidence to suggest that demand for services is less sensitive to economic fluctuations. But any optimistic forecasts should take account of possible limitations on growth in the service sector. Stanton[3] identifies two forces which could limit their growth. These are external forces and internal forces.

External Forces
Some constraints on growth include:

customers can perform services themselves. The degree of essentiality of service purchases varies (e.g. people can eat at home instead of eating in restaurants);

manufactured goods will be produced which replace service roles (e.g. TV replaces cinemas, DIY tools replace the services of skilled labour, like carpenters, easy-care fabrics replace cleaning and laundry services);

manufactured goods will be produced which require less service attention (e.g. cars with longer service intervals, equipment with throwaway replaceable parts).

Internal Forces
Some internal constraints on growth include:

the small size of the average service firm;

the shortage of people with certain special skills (e.g. doctors);

the limited competition in some service sub-sectors (e.g. rail transport, local authority services);

little emphasis on research and development in many service fields;

the general failure to recognize the importance of marketing in some service businesses.

17.32 Attitudes towards Services and the Service Sector

There is a need for a change in attitude towards services and the service sector of the economy, particularly by Government. It was suggested in Chapter 2 (Section 2.2) that services are still not regarded as valid forms of wealth; that services are treated still as 'unproductive'. This narrow view of the unimportance of services is reflected in a number of ways. Four examples are:

(a) The manufacturing sector in the United Kingdom is accorded higher status than the service sector: 'It is probably a consequence of services' lower status that the quantity and quality of data on the sector is poor – which itself has discouraged research.'[1]

(b) The basic measurement problems of defining the quantity and quality of services remain unresolved. More attention needs to be devoted to the measurement of productivity in the service sector (*see* Chapter 16). As recent work has identified, this remains a fundamental and difficult problem and hampers any attempted objective discussion of the service economy.[4]

(c) Emphasis upon manufacturing only, at the expense of services – and particularly through cut backs in public services – perpetuates the myth of services as invalid forms of wealth. In a modern advanced economy there are close links between manufacturing and services. All sectors can be productive:

> 'Modern economic theory has come to the conclusion that there is no point in the distinction between productive and unproductive activities. If the product of an activity is wanted by the individuals who are consuming it, then that activity must be productive. This criterion applies both to products that are bought and sold (either physical goods or services) and to products that are allocated through the State (again, either physical goods or services).'[5]

A reflection of the relative unimportance of services is that many government support schemes in development areas have often excluded service industries despite their employment potential.[6]

(d) Finally there appears to be a prejudice against service industries particularly among the male United Kingdom workforce. According to Cannon[6] this is reflected in reluctance to seek employment in service industries and the negative attitudes towards service on the part of some service industry employees. Many service organizations are complacent about the level and the quality of service that they give. There are many unrecorded complaints about services not included in the official figures shown earlier in Chapter 15 (Section 15.6).

17.33 Technological Innovation

Technological innovations will influence employment and output in the service sector. New technologies are already used in a wide variety of service organizations (e.g. airlines, hotels and banking). It is expected that technological innovations will increase in the future. Generally technology gives the ability to service organizations to handle larger volumes of service, to offer a wider range of services, to provide quicker and more accurate services and to permit more efficient management.

For example the technology already exists to permit the 'paperless' office.[7] Documents can be transmitted and received in electronic form, direct speech interpretation could mean the replacement of typists, large volumes of data can be collected, stored, processed and transmitted automatically. Service industries are adopting and experimenting with much new technology. Banks have installed cash dispensers and use electronic cheque clearing: the distributive trades are experimenting with electronic price coding and stock control systems; telephone exchanges are going electronic; the postal service uses mechanized sorting. Larger service organizations in particular have generally adopted a more systematic policy towards innovation. But even smaller services like solicitors are adopting microprocessor-based equipment for routine needs. Many possibilities exist in the future for adoption of new technology.

However the impact of new technology is contradictory. It is unreasonable to assume that the main effect of the adoption of new technology will be less jobs. First the introduction of new technology usually means the reorganization of work, new administrative organizations and changed physical layout. These changes are often resisted and slow down the pace at which technology is adopted. Secondly there are legal barriers to the introduction of new technology (e.g. the importance of signed documents). Thirdly reduced costs of service encourage even more use. Fourthly new products and services are themselves made possible by the new technologies.

In theory the use of technology like microprocessors and other advances in information technology should make it possible for job relocation. Modern methods of information collection, dissemination and control allow separation of different job functions from any central control (e.g. satellite computer networks). This affords the opportunity to take jobs to areas of high unemployment; technology enables the spatial transfer of jobs in accordance with social needs.[8]

17.34 Service Quality

One effect of the growth of services has been greater variation in quality between different kinds of services. If services grow in the future a particular challenge to managers in service operations is to improve and maintain high standards of service. The use of systems approaches to service delivery and mechanization and technology where appropriate can be instruments to accomplish this end. The danger with the application of systems thinking and technology to services is that it may do what it did for goods production (i.e. produce better quality goods); but increases in quality have been achieved at a price. Very often that price is the alienation of the workforce in the production system. In service industries there could be alienation of the customer too. Some implications of applying operational management approaches to services could be the growing impersonalization of services; what Regan[9] called the 'massification of taste'. The substitution of equipment for personalized attention encourages a reduction in the 'extrinsic values of a service'. (In an example of a study course 'intrinsic' qualities of the service would be the basic exposure to the course; the 'extrinsic' qualities would be all the extra curricular activities and qualities associated with college life.) Most decreases in the value of services Regan suggests are attributable to disatisfactions with extrinsic qualities (e.g. queuing time, procedural steps required to obtain service, less personal service attendants, systems which lead to conformity in presentation and conformity in taste).

The use of systems and technology then offer opportunities for routinization and more efficient service; their use also may lead to the impersonalization of service.

17.35 The 'Black' Economy

An increasingly recognized feature of the United Kingdom economy in recent years is the so-called 'informal' or 'black' economy. This refers to a number of activities.[10] These include:

(a) 'moonlighting' or casual employment for cash;
(b) 'fringe benefits', usually associated with employment like 'expense accounts' and petty pilfering;
(c) 'household activities' like do-it-yourself and voluntary work;
(d) 'immoral and criminal activities' like theft or prostitution.

Current estimates of the size of the black economy range from $7\frac{1}{2}\%$ to 15% of total output. Of interest, in this context, is that much activity in the 'black economy' consists of service operations.

Some factors which have contributed to the rise of the black economy include:

(a) more do-it-yourself activity;
(b) lower costs of consumer durables relative to services;
(c) growth of home ownership providing an expanding market for domestic services;
(d) increasing taxation (personal and business);
(e) increasing regulation in business;
(f) high levels of unemployment;
(g) higher levels of social security payment providing a base for informal activities.

The 'informal' or 'black' economy is likely to remain an important, unofficial area of the service sector if high levels of unemployment continue in the United Kingdom in the 1980s.

17.4 Priorities for those Interested in Marketing Services

In recent years the marketing of services has received renewed attention from practitioners and academics. Practitioners have found that some of the suggested ideas and approaches which were developed for marketing

tangible items fitted uneasily and uncomfortably into their pattern of
needs. Academics, seeking new fields in which to develop marketing ideas,
have given increasing attention to non-goods sectors like non-profit
organizations, causes, people, place marketing and services. There is now
common agreement that the broad principles of marketing are applicable
to all of these areas; there is less common agreement about how readily
broad marketing principles are of value in specific services contexts.
Nevertheless marketing ideas and practices are being more widely used
and are likely to be more intensively used in the future. Professional
service organizations, for example, like lawyers, accountants and opticians
are beginning to adopt a more market-orientated approach to their
businesses. They no longer equate marketing with selling. The central issue
facing many professional service organizations is not whether to practice
marketing but how they can do so, more effectively.[11]

Service organizations that are market-orientated face a number of
interesting challenges in the future. How they respond to these challenges
will influence their success or failure. Their ability to respond to future
challenges will be influenced by the priority they give to making
improvements in service marketing practices. To achieve improved
marketing practices some priorities are suggested:

(a) Service marketors should not expend too much time and effort
     focusing on defining services. As Lewis[12] suggests: 'there is enough
     scope for arguing the finer points of such definitions to delight a
     medieval theologian'. Much of the recent academic writing on
     marketing services has focused unproductively on definitional
     aspects of services marketing. In doing so writers have exhibited all
     the classic symptoms of product orientation, the very antithesis of
     marketing. It is sterile to focus on how services may be defined from
     the performers' or producers' point of view. What matters is
     whether customers perceive differences between services and if so
     what criteria they use in making their evaluations.

     A further reflection of the narrowness of some thinking and
     writing in the services marketing area is the attention devoted by
     some researchers to 'cosmetic' aspects of marketing like using
     'internal' marketing, using advertising as a way of reaching
     employees as well as customers, keeping customers sold through
     restating benefits, and after-sale service and attention. What is
     disappointing about some of these ideas is not that they are being
     presented; but that they are being presented as though they are new
     and of particular relevance to service marketing.[13] They are not.
     Market-orientated organizations have always and will always
     implement such ideas whatever they are marketing. There is a
     danger that in thinking too much about service marketing it will be
     forgotten what marketing is about. Marketing is essentially action
     orientated. As Wilmshurst[14] writes:

         'There is a grave danger inherent in the writing of books about marketing, and
         indeed in the whole idea of marketing as a course of study, that by analysing each
         aspect of it and trying to understand the mechanics and thought processes behind

it we begin to believe that marketing is the fact-finding, the analysis, the careful weighing of one alternative against another. It is not. To study all these processes may be an aid to successful marketing, just as the study of strategy may help a successful general, but marketing, like war, is about activity. It is doing, not merely thinking.'

Another feature of the renewed interest in the marketing of services has been a too ready willingness to make generalizations about marketing in all service situations based upon evidence drawn from particular service situations. (It is hoped that such over-generalizations have been avoided here!) Services is an area to which generalizations should be applied cautiously. The sheer size of the service sector and the problems of defining what is a service anyway (*see* Chapters 1 and 2), demand that caution be exercised in making generalizations about service marketing. Many more rigorous, empirical studies of marketing practice in a variety of service situations are required to support any generalizations made.

(*b*) In terms of actions some key aspects of services marketing where attention is needed are these.

People

The key to services is not that they are provided *by* people (they may be performed by equipment) but that they are provided *for* people. Service organizations must obtain greater understanding of why customers behave the way they do, how they make their choices, what role intangibility plays in these choices.

Process

There are opportunities in service performance and marketing to reduce the barriers that exist between the operations side of an organization and the marketing side of an organization. Service performance and delivery are difficult to separate. Service marketors should encourage and develop closer relationships with their operational management colleagues.

Physical Evidence

Physical evidence and atmosphere have always been important in marketing. There is a need for a better understanding of how this element of the marketing mix influences customer choice, satisfaction and response to service organizations.

Finally according to one source the future success and well-being of service marketing organizations will largely be a function of their understanding and reaction to the following propositions:

(*a*) there are greater opportunities for growth and expansion in the future in the area of services than of goods;
(*b*) mass production, industrial design and systems engineering are being increasingly implemented and adapted to service businesses;

(c) use of mass production and systems engineering increases productivity but leads to increased depersonalization of service
marketing;

(d) the whole range of strategic marketing activities are relevant for
service marketing and their use will tend to satisfy the growing
demand for diversity in service market offerings.[15]

17.5 Summary

1 There is likely to be a continuing increase in the share of services in output
and the more dynamic sectors are likely to be insurance, banking, finance
and communications.
2 A number of factors will influence the development of the service sector
like attitudes of government towards services, technological innovation,
improvements in service quality and the development of the black
economy.
3 The focus for service marketing activity must be the customer. Particular
attention needs to be given to people, process and physical evidence in
service marketing.

Questions for Discussion

1 What will happen to the service sector of the United Kingdom economy
in the future?
2 What new kinds of services do you think will emerge over the next ten
years?
3 What factors influence assumptions one can make about the growth of
the service economy?
4 What factors may limit the growth of services? What factors may
encourage the growth of services?
5 How does technology influence service growth?
6 Does quality of service necessarily have to decline as service output
grows?
7 How can services be prevented from becoming impersonalized?
8 Suggest reasons for the emergence of the 'black' economy.
9 Identify five research priorities for marketors of services.
10 Is service marketing different from goods marketing?

References and Notes

1 Whiteman, J. 'The Services Sector – a poor relation?' A review of its
role performance and prospects in the U.K. Discussion Paper No. 8,
National Economic Development Office, 1981.
2 Katouzian, M. A. 'The development of the service sector: a new
approach', Oxford Economic Papers, 1970.
3 Stanton, W. J. *Fundamentals of Marketing*, McGraw-Hill, New York,
1981.
4 Bodoff, J., Leveson, I. and Wattell, H., 'The effect of innovation on
productivity in the service industries'. Report prepared for National
Science Foundation, Aug. 1975, York College, U.S.A.

5 Green, F., Baugh, P. and Hadjimatheon, G. 'The myth of the industrial money-spinners', *The Times Higher Education Supplement*, 4 Sept. 1981, p. 11.
6 Cannon, T. *Basic Marketing: Principles and Practice*, Holt, Rinehart & Winston, New York, 1980.
7 Sleigh, J., Boatwritht, B., Irwin, P. and Stanyon, R. 'The manpower implications of micro-electronic technology', H.M.S.O., London, 1979.
8 Gershuny, J. I. *After Industrial Society? The emerging self-service economy*, Macmillan, London, 1978.
9 Regan, W. J. 'The Service Revolution', *Journal of Marketing*, July 1963, Vol. 27, No. 3, pp. 57–62.
10 Central Statistical Office, 'Economic Trends', Feb. 1980.
11 Wilson, A. *The Marketing of Professional Services*, McGraw-Hill, London, 1972.
12 Lewis, R. *The New Service Society*, Longman, Harlow, 1973.
13 Upah, G. D., Berry, L. L. and Shostack, G. Lynn 'Emerging themes and directions for services marketing'. Summary of the AMA Service Marketing Conference, Florida, Nov. 1982.
14 Wilmshurst, J. *The Fundamentals and Practice of Marketing*, Heinemann, London, 2nd edn 1984.
15 Markin, R. *Marketing – Strategy and Management*, J. Wiley and Sons, New York, 1982.

AUTHOR INDEX

INDEX